# HUMAN RESOURCE MANAGEMENT

# HUMAN RESOURCE MANAGEMENT
## A CONCISE INTRODUCTION

**Edited by**

*RONAN CARBERY*

*and*

*CHRISTINE CROSS*

First published 2013 by
PALGRAVE MACMILLAN

Palgrave Macmillan in the UK is an imprint of Macmillan Publishers Limited,
registered in England, company number 785998, of Houndmills, Basingstoke,
Hampshire RG21 6XS.

Palgrave Macmillan in the US is a division of St Martin's Press LLC,
175 Fifth Avenue, New York, NY 10010.

Palgrave Macmillan is the global academic imprint of the above companies
and has companies and representatives throughout the world.

Palgrave® and Macmillan® are registered trademarks in the United States,
the United Kingdom, Europe and other countries.

ISBN: 978–1–137–00939–5

This book is printed on paper suitable for recycling and made from fully
managed and sustained forest sources. Logging, pulping and manufacturing
processes are expected to conform to the environmental regulations of the
country of origin.

A catalogue record for this book is available from the British Library.

A catalog record for this book is available from the Library of Congress.

Typeset by Aardvark Editorial Limited, Metfield, Suffolk

# SHORT CONTENTS

# CONTENTS

# LIST OF FIGURES

# LIST OF TABLES

# ABOUT THE EDITORS

**Dr Ronan Carbery** (Dip. Hotel Management, B.Comm, PhD) is Lecturer in HRM at the Department of Personnel and Employment Relations, Kemmy Business School, University of Limerick, Ireland. Ronan is associate editor of the *European Journal of Training and Development*. His research interests include career development, workplace learning, and participation in learning and development activities. He is a Chartered Member of CIPD Ireland and a member of the University Forum for Human Resource Development and the Academy of Human Resource Development. Ronan has published articles in the *Journal of Managerial Psychology, Human Resource Development Review*, the *Journal of European Industrial Training, Thunderbird International Business Review* and *The Learning Organisation*, and has undertaken studies and surveys for the CIPD, the Garda Representative Association and the Programme for University-Industry Interface.

**Dr Christine Cross** (B.Comm, MBS, PhD) lectures in Organizational Behaviour and Human Resource Management at the Kemmy Business School, University of Limerick. Prior to this, she worked for a number of multinational organizations in both management and HRM roles. This experience has led to a wide range of research, consultancy and publication interests, covering areas such as the workforce experiences of immigrants, training and development in call centres, and investigating the glass ceiling. Christine is also a co-director of the Age in the Workplace Research Network at the Kemmy Business School. This network focuses on researching multiple issues associated with age in the workplace.

# ABOUT THE CONTRIBUTORS

**Dr Claire Armstrong** (B.Comm, PhD) is Lecturer in HRM and Organizational Behaviour at Dublin City University and an Associate Lecturer in Research Methods at the Open University. Prior to this, she held posts at the University of Limerick and Limerick Institute of Technology. She also held a visiting faculty appointment with the Work Psychology Department at Aston University. Claire's main areas of expertise are in HRM, organizational behaviour, research methods and healthcare management. She has published extensively on these topics in academic journals, including *Human Resource Management*, *The International Journal for Human Resource Management* and the *International Journal for Quality in Health Care*. She has also published several practitioner-oriented reports on topics such as high performance work systems, training and development benchmarks and teamworking in healthcare teams. She is a reviewer for a number of HRM, organizational behaviour and healthcare management journals.

**Dr Marian Crowley-Henry** (BBS & German, MSc, PhD) is Lecturer in Human Resource Management and International Management at the National University of Ireland, Maynooth. Her research interests are in international HRM, migration, careers and identity. She supervises PhD students researching in these areas. Marian has published in international peer-reviewed journals such as *Career Development International*, the *Journal of Management Development*, the *Journal of Organizational Change Management* and *International Studies of Management and Organization*, and presented papers at international conferences of the European Group for Organizational Studies and the Academy of Management. Prior to academia, Marian performed various functions at the Europe, Middle East and African headquarters of multinational organizations in Germany and France.

**Dr Colette Darcy** (BBS, MBS, PhD) is Vice Dean for Postgraduate Studies and Research in the School of Business and Senior Lecturer in HRM at the National College of Ireland. She is a former Government of Ireland Scholar and was awarded the European Foundation for Management Development/Emerald Outstanding Doctoral Thesis Award for her research examining employee fairness perceptions and claiming behaviour. Her research interests extend to organizational justice, work–life balance and claiming behaviour. She has published in a number of academic journals, including the *European Journal of Industrial Training*, which awarded her the Outstanding Paper Award Winner at the Literati Network Awards for Excellence 2008.

**Thomas N. Garavan** (BBS, MBS, Ed.D.) is a professor at the Kemmy Business School, University of Limerick, where he specializes in the research and teaching of human resource development, leadership development and vocational training and education. He has authored or co-authored 14 books and over 100 refereed journal papers and book chapters. Thomas is currently editor-in-chief of the *European Journal of Training and Development* and associate editor of *Human Resource Development International*. He is a member of the editorial board of *Human Resource Development Review*, *Advances in Developing Human Resources*, the *Human Resource Management Journal* and *Human Resource Development Quarterly*.

**Dr Jonathan Lavelle** (BA, MBS, PhD) is a Research Scholar at the Department of Personnel and Employment Relations, Kemmy Business School, University of Limerick. He is a former postdoctoral fellow, Government of Ireland Scholar and current Marie Curie Fellow. His main research interests are in the field of international and comparative employment relations, with a particular interest in employment relations in multinational companies. He is currently involved in a number of international collaborative research projects. Jonathan has presented papers at several leading international conferences and has published in leading international journals, such as the *Industrial and Labor Relations Review, Human Relations, Human Resource Management,* the *Human Resource Management Journal,* and the *Journal of World Business,* as well as co-authoring a book and a number of book chapters.

**Dr Alma McCarthy** (Dip. Training & Education, BBS with French, MCIPD, PhD) is Director of the Executive MBA Programme and Lecturer in Human Resource Management at the National University of Ireland, Galway. Her research interests include performance management, employee training and development, work–life balance, and multi-rater feedback systems. Alma's publications include HRM books and chapters as well as a number of articles in journals, such as *The International Journal of Human Resource Management,* the *European Management Journal, Personnel Review, Advances in Developing Human Resources,* and the *Journal of Managerial Psychology.* She is a Chartered Member of the CIPD and the American Academy of Management, and chair of the Irish Academy of Management.

**Dr Colm McLaughlin** (BA, M.Comm, PhD) is Lecturer in the School of Business at University College Dublin, where he teaches Industrial Relations, HRM and Business in Society. He is also a Research Associate of the Centre for Business Research at the University of Cambridge. Prior to this, Colm was an ESRC Research Fellow at the University of Cambridge and Lecturer in Management and Employment Relations at the University of Auckland. He has also held management positions in local government and the hospitality sector. His research interests include labour market protections and low-paid work, gender equality, the relationship between labour market institutions and economic performance, and comparative industrial relations.

**Dr Gerry McMahon** (B.Comm, MBS, FCIPD, MIITD, PhD) is Lecturer in Human Resource Management at the Faculty of Business, at the Dublin Institute of Technology. He is the lead presenter on a number of practitioner-oriented programmes run by the CIPD and managing director of the training and advisory company Productive Personnel Ltd. An expert in the area of people management, Gerry has extensive experience working as a presenter/lecturer in the field of HRM and industrial relations across a host of public and private sector, third-level educational and academic institutions. He also works as a consultant, trainer, practitioner, investigator, facilitator, mediator and arbitrator on behalf of a wide range of government departments, public sector enterprises, semi-state entities, blue-chip companies, professional institutes, trade unions, employer and community/voluntary/religious organizations. Gerry has also had a vast range of books and articles published across a host of reputable media.

**Dr Juliette McMahon** (BBS with French, MCIPD, FIITD, PhD) is Lecturer and Course Director in Human Resource Management and Employment Relations at the Kemmy Business School, University of Limerick. Her areas of interest in teaching and research are employment legislation, performance management, HRM and employment relations in small firms, social exclusion, wellbeing at work, and workplace bullying. Juliette is a Chartered Member of the CIPD and a Fellow of the Irish Institute of Training and Development. She has extensive consultancy experience in the areas of performance management and employment legislation, and has participated in a European-level project on work and social inclusion.

**Maureen Maloney** (BSW, MBA, Dip. Economic Science, M.Economic Science) is the Programme Director of the Masters in Industrial Relations and Human Resource Management, and Management Lecturer at the National University of Ireland, Galway. Her research interests include pensions, reward systems, and organizational communication. Her work has strengthened the connection between the management discipline and the Western Region of the CIPD. Maureen has presented papers on pension research to the CIPD and the Irish Association of Pension Funds and has worked on a variety of EU-funded projects, including the Adapt project as a trainer for the Services Industrial Professional and Technical Union to develop business partnership groups in Irish-based organizations.

**Dr Michelle O'Sullivan** (Dip. Employment Law, BA, PhD) is Lecturer in Industrial Relations at the University of Limerick. Her primary expertise is the regulation of low-paid work and she has contributed to public policy in the area. She has published widely on employment relations in non-union companies, employee representation, employment law, and workplace bullying. She is currently co-editing a book on union recognition in Ireland and is part of research teams on projects on precarious work and bullying in nursing. She is a member of the executive committees of the Irish Academy of Management and the Irish Association for Industrial Relations. She previously worked as a trade union official in the health sector and has also worked with a range of private sector companies on employment relations issues such as redundancy.

# FOREWORD

One of the most gratifying features of current and recently published textbooks on the world of work and employment is the degree to which they can draw on both the evolving body of prescriptive knowledge in the field and the growing body of empirical research. Not so long ago things were very different. When I first studied personnel management as a student during the 1970s, the main textbooks available drew little on research. The US and UK books that were widely used then and for a good many years afterwards were invariably dull and poorly written, and teachers and learners in countries other than those in which texts were written and published had to transpose their content to make them relevant to other countries' experiences. Few cases were used to illustrate the nature and practice of personnel or industrial relations in different organizations and to enliven the narrative. This world has receded and current texts draw systematically on the burgeoning research literature on human resource management (HRM) and on associated debates concerning trends and developments.

A second change over recent decades that has had a major bearing on learning in the field of HRM is that the field itself has become so much more vibrant and sophisticated as an area of management knowledge and specialization. Although we might dispute the practical meaning of the much uttered phrase 'our people are our greatest asset', there can be little doubt that people-related concerns now loom larger in business, and the past three decades have involved a sea change in the sophistication of HRM theory and practice – once little more than sound good sense and broadly progressive values, allied to a collection of essentially administrative techniques. As more organizations become knowledge dependent or knowledge intensive, this trend seems set to continue and now nobody who works in an organization where they must, in some way, engage with or manage other people can function credibly without some knowledge of modern HRM theory and practice.

These developments converge in this textbook, edited and written by a group of experienced teachers and scholars. The book covers all the major areas of HRM in a light and vibrant style that should prove attractive to learners, while often drawing on relevant international research and cases to illustrate and assess the practical application of theory and techniques. This interweaving of key concepts and prescriptive knowledge with research and illustrative cases represents the best possible combination of learning resources. I welcome and commend the book as a major learning resource and a significant addition to the literature.

**William K Roche**
Professor of Industrial Relations and Human Resources
School of Business, University College Dublin

# PREFACE AND EDITORS' ACKNOWLEDGEMENTS

Our search for an introductory human resource management (HRM) textbook to use with students on our own courses has led to us editing and writing one ourselves. This book has been written primarily with 1st and 2nd year undergraduate students in mind who are taking HRM modules for the first time. While many of these students may not go on to specialize in HRM, the concepts discussed are relevant to any business student and, indeed, anyone in employment.

Many existing HRM textbooks are drawn from UK and US-based academics and so have a dominant UK/US focus. All the contributors to this book are Irish and work in Irish institutions. We therefore draw on a number of Irish examples, but situate these in an international context. Each chapter also has a broad balance of examples from the UK, Europe and the USA.

We have written this book in easy to understand language and have presented the material in such a way so as to highlight the practicality of the issues involved in work and employment. There is a strong emphasis on skills and career development throughout each of the 14 chapters, with key features such as up-to-date news pieces (HRM in the News), Active Case Studies, discussion activities (Consider this …), highlighted key terms with on-page definitions, and video interviews with experienced HR professionals (Spotlight on Skills). The book's companion website provides extra resources, including videos, multiple choice questions and more skills development guidance.

We would like to acknowledge the help we received with writing this text. Ursula Gavin, Amy Grant and Alice Ferns at Palgrave Macmillan provided tremendous assistance and support from the initial proposal stage to the design and layout of the final text. Maggie Lythgoe's attention to detail as copy-editor improved the book significantly. In addition to the contributors to the textbook, we would like to thank our colleagues at the University of Limerick who provided us with support along the way – Patrick Gunnigle, Michelle Hammond, Noreen Heraty, Sarah MacCurtain, Deirdre O'Shea, Jill Pearson and Tom Turner. We are grateful for the time the participants in the Spotlight on Skills video features so readily gave us and for their excellent insights into industry practice.

We are also grateful to the members of our review panel for their detailed and constructive feedback at different stages of the project:

- Magda Bezuidenhout, University of South Africa, South Africa
- Edel Conway, Dublin City University, Ireland
- Scott Hurrell, University of Stirling, UK
- Geoff Plimmer, Victoria University of Wellington, New Zealand
- Rea Prouska, Middlesex University, UK
- Fiona Robson, Northumbria University, UK
- Henrik B. Sørensen, Aarhus University, Denmark
- Russell Wordsworth, University of Canterbury, New Zealand

Finally, we would like to thank our families: Michelle and Julie Carbery; and Dave, Oisín and Luíseach Cross.

**Ronan Carbery and Christine Cross**
January 2013

# MAPPING THE TEXT TO CIPD STANDARDS

The CIPD HR Profession Standards capture what HR people do and deliver across every aspect and specialism of the profession. They identify ten professional areas and the underpinning skills, behaviour and knowledge that HR professionals need to be most successful. The map below shows which chapters will enable students to achieve these core standards.

For a detailed description of each standard, please see www.cipd.co.uk/cipd-hr-profession/hr-profession-map/. To access this document, you need to be a CIPD member or, as a non-member, register free on the website. For a more in-depth mapping of standards and their various subsections against chapters, visit www.palgrave.com/business/carbery.

| CIPD Standard | | Chapter(s) |
|---|---|---|
| **1** | **Insights, strategy and solutions** | |
| 1.1 | Building a picture | 1 |
| 1.2 | Developing actionable insight | 1 |
| 1.3 | Delivering situational HR solutions that stick | 1 |
| 1.4 | Building capacity and capability | 1 |
| 1.5 | Working with agility | 1 |
| 1.6 | Business knowledge | 1 |
| 1.7 | Contextual knowledge | 1, 14 |
| 1.8 | Organisation knowledge | 1 |
| 1.9 | HR professional knowledge | 1 |
| **2** | **Leading HR** | |
| 2.1 | Personal leadership | 1, 10, 13 |
| 2.2 | Leading others | 7 |
| 2.3 | Leading issues: HR function design and service delivery | 1 |
| 2.4 | Leading issues: HR resource planning and development | 9 |
| 2.5 | Leading issues: delivering value and performance in HR teams | 7, 8 |
| 2.6 | Leading issues: managing HR budgets and finances | 1 |
| 2.7 | Leadership | 6 |
| 2.8 | HR service delivery models | 1 |
| 2.9 | Commissioning services | 1 |
| 2.10 | Resource management | 2 |
| 2.11 | Performance management | 7 |
| 2.12 | Financial management | 2 |
| **3** | **Organisation design** | |
| 3.1 | Set the context for design | 6 |

$\rightarrow$

| CIPD Standard | | Chapter(s) |
|---|---|---|
| 3.2 | Assess current organisation design | 1 |
| 3.3 | Design organisation model | 1 |
| 3.4 | Identify key organisation processes | 6 |
| 3.5 | Define measures and governance | 1 |
| 3.6 | Implement and evaluate design | 1 |
| 3.7 | Situational organisation design | 1 |
| 3.8 | Organisation design tools | 1 |
| 3.9 | Design blockers and challenges | 1 |
| 3.10 | Job evaluation methodology | 8 |
| **4** | **Organisation development** | |
| 4.1 | OD strategy, planning and business case development | 1, 9 |
| 4.2 | Organisation capability assessment | 1 |
| 4.3 | Culture assessment and development | 1 |
| 4.4 | Organisation development intervention and execution | 1 |
| 4.5 | Change communications | 1 |
| 4.6 | OD methodology | 1 |
| 4.7 | Project and programme management | 1 |
| 4.8 | Cultural differences | 6 |
| 4.9 | Culture change | 1 |
| 4.10 | Change management | 1 |
| 4.11 | Change communications | 1 |
| **5** | **Resourcing and talent planning** | |
| 5.1 | Workforce planning | 2 |
| 5.2 | Resourcing | 2 |
| 5.3 | Talent identification and succession | 2, 7 |
| 5.4 | Assessment and selection | 3 |
| 5.5 | Induction | 4 |
| 5.6 | Exit | 4, 12 |
| 5.7 | Legal framework | 12 |
| 5.8 | Resourcing | 3 |
| 5.9 | Recruitment | 2 |
| 5.10 | Talent and succession | 2 |
| 5.11 | Assessment | 3 |
| 5.12 | Induction | 4 |
| **6** | **Learning and talent development** | |
| 6.1 | Capability and skills assessment | 9 |
| 6.2 | Organisation capability strategy, planning and business case development | 7, 9 |
| 6.3 | Design L&D solutions | 7, 9 |
| 6.4 | Deliver L&D solutions | 9, 10, 11 |
| 6.5 | Leadership development | 9 |
| 6.6 | Talent management | 7, 10 |

| CIPD Standard | | Chapter(s) |
|---|---|---|
| 6.7 | Capability assessment | 9 |
| 6.8 | Learning styles | 9 |
| 6.9 | Blended learning solutions | 9 |
| 6.10 | Supplier management | 9 |
| 6.11 | Facilitation | 9 |
| 6.12 | Diversity | 6 |
| 6.13 | Measure and evaluate interventions | 9 |
| **7** | **Performance and reward** | |
| 7.1 | Develop performance and reward strategy | 7, 8 |
| 7.2 | Performance and reward policy | 7, 8 |
| 7.3 | Developing a performance culture | 7 |
| 7.4 | Performance and reward interventions | 7, 8 |
| 7.5 | International, expatriate and executive reward | 13 |
| 7.6 | Attracting and motivating through performance and reward | 7 |
| 7.7 | International remuneration | 13 |
| 7.8 | Benchmarking | 8 |
| 7.9 | Financial understanding | 8 |
| 7.10 | Communications | 8 |
| 7.11 | Cultural understanding | 7 |
| **8** | **Employee engagement** | |
| 8.1 | Engagement drivers and developing strategy | 5, 14 |
| 8.2 | Measuring levels of engagement | 2, 5 |
| 8.3 | Employee engagement interventions | 9 |
| 8.4 | Employer brand | 2 |
| 8.5 | Workplace behaviour | 11 |
| 8.6 | Diversity of needs | 6 |
| 8.7 | Internal communications | 1 |
| **9** | **Employee relations** | |
| 9.1 | Employee relations strategy, policy and practice | 12 |
| 9.2 | Policy, advice and guidance | 6, 12 |
| 9.3 | Complex casework | 12 |
| 9.4 | Collective negotiation and consultation | 12 |
| 9.5 | Health and well-being | 11 |
| 9.6 | Employment law | 12 |
| 9.7 | Employee relations | 12 |
| 9.8 | Communications | 12 |
| 9.9 | Supplier management | 12 |
| **10** | **Service delivery and information** | |
| 10.1 | Service delivery models and execution | 1 |
| 10.2 | Service management and metrics | 1, 4 |
| 10.3 | Business process redesign and continuous improvement | 1, 12 |

# TOUR OF THE BOOK

## Learning Outcomes

A set of learning outcomes are identified at the start of each chapter. After you have studied the chapter, completed the activities and answered the review questions, you should be able to achieve each of the stated objectives.

## Key Terms

Each chapter contains an on-page explanation of a number of important words, phrases and concepts that you need to know in order to understand HRM, its theoretical basis and its related areas.

## Making Links

To allow you to see the interconnected nature of the topics in the field of HRM, ideas that link to concepts in other chapters are identified.

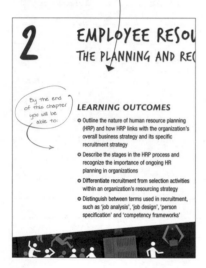

**2  EMPLOYEE RESOU**
**THE PLANNING AND REC**

By the end of this chapter you will be able to:

### LEARNING OUTCOMES

- Outline the nature of human resource planning (HRP) and how HRP links with the organization's overall business strategy and its specific recruitment strategy
- Describe the stages in the HRP process and recognize the importance of ongoing HR planning in organizations
- Differentiate recruitment from selection activities within an organization's resourcing strategy
- Distinguish between terms used in recruitment, such as 'job analysis', 'job design', 'person specification' and 'competency frameworks'

---

people employed in
the skills the
to be competitive.
re not available
ation may decide
loyees to develop
ruit people with
s. The organization
w many people
ill be required for
ents. For instance,
termines to use
coordinating its
ensure that sufficient numbers of
the particular technology, and may
embers or recruit new employees
ed in the use of that particular
, if an organization decides to
er service focus, it must determine
ing staff up to the required customer
eeds to recruit new employees who
er service skills. In today's
anning is increasingly looking at
and practices, such as recruitment,
ns of the organization.
nt to which organizations can
the future is contentious, since the
ur which can render plans useless.
nt of the global economic recession

**Human resource planning (HRP)** – the ongoing consideration of staffing requirements – now and in the future – with regards to the specific jobs and skills that are and will be required in the organization. It results in the development of specific HR strategies to achieve organization-specific staffing requirements

**Recruitment** – a process whereby the organization sources or attracts people to apply for a position in the organization

its customer se
on customer se
differentiator t
organization's
should reflect t
of people with
technology, or
qualified custo

Other pract
staff in custom
also need to be
organization's
instance, if an o
strengthen its technology knowle
customer service, this needs to be
plans, where existing staff are train
technology, or customer service r
▶ Chapter 9 ◀. The strategic focus
measured during performance ap
training has been completed, emp
working with the technology or in
assessed. In aligning the focus on
customer service with the organiza
management ▶ Chapter 7 ◀, empl
encouraged to be competent with
customer service, and the strategi
of new technology or superior cus
instilled in the mindset of the emp
show how different HRM strategie

---

However, informal recruitment suggests a lack of consideration towards developing a diverse workforce, because it often brings in recruits who are similar in background and experience to the employees already in the organization.

organi
use of
suitab
used b
For
may h
narrow
This is
indust
where
to find
supply
search
contac
lookin
file, an
but th
indivi
of em
the cli

### CONSIDER THIS ...

What are the advantages and disadvantages of the different formal methods of recruitment (print, radio, TV, online advertising and recruitment agencies)? Have you experienced any of these formal recruitment methods in your search for a job? Shortlist three or four criteria that could be used by organizations in determining which formal method(s) to choose.

## Consider This ...

This feature is designed to stimulate your thinking about a specific issue, idea or perspective related to the chapter topic.

---

### Working Abroad Expo in Ireland

Unprecedented numbers queued for hours to attend the Working Abroad Expo recruitment fairs in Dublin and Cork (Ireland) in March 2012. Thousands of visitors attended the fairs, along with their partners and children, in search of advice and, more importantly, jobs overseas.

Given the employment problems in Ireland, with over 440,000 people unemployed in a population of approximately 4 million, the Working Abroad Expo job fairs were considered by many as a rare sign of optimism that their skills and qualifications were still required globally, even if this was not the case in Ireland at present. Many wishing to attend the events had to be turned away, with advance tickets sold out.

In the Dublin Expo, the organizers charged €10 admission in an attempt to control the vast numbers of people attending, and

sectors, including farming, construction and healthcare across skills, including carp fitters, machine operators, mechanics and electricians multinational exhibited, inc Primark, PayP eBay and He Packard.

Participant advised to br their CVs with them to give directly to potential/prospe employers at the Expo. The exhibitors were looking to specific job vacancies and conducted interviews on th at the event. Statistics give suggest that over 2,000 inte were held at the Dublin eve alone, with over 250 job off made by the prospective employers/agencies attendi exhibiting at that event.

According to the organiza feedback from the exhibitor that they were impressed w people they met at the even

**HRM IN THE NEWS**

## HRM in the News

Each chapter contains an example of coverage of its main topic in the media. The aim here is to highlight how you can apply the constructs and concepts in the chapter to the management of people in the real world of the workplace. A set of questions accompanies each feature to assist with this application to a practical situation.

## Building Your Skills

This feature asks you to place yourself in the position of a line manager and to think about what you would do in the situation that has been presented to you.

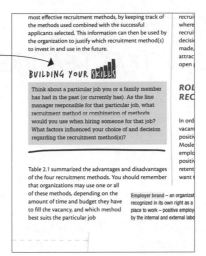

## Active Case Study

These short case studies provide the opportunity for you to link the material covered in the chapter to a real-life situation. Companies featured include large MNCs such as Apple and Volvo. Questions are posed at the end of the case studies, which can be answered either in class, or as part of an assignment.

## Chapter Review Questions

These questions can be used as class exercises or for self-testing and evaluating your knowledge and understanding about the chapter topic.

## Useful Websites

An abundance of websites exist on topics related to HRM. At the end of each chapter we have identified those we believe you will find most useful in furthering your knowledge and understanding of the discipline.

## Companion Website

The book's companion website at www.palgrave.com/business/carbery offers a number of resources for both lecturers and students, including PowerPoint slides, solutions to the Active Case Study questions, multiple choice questions, an Irish appendix to Chapter 12, Managing the Employment Relationship, a searchable glossary and much more.

## Further Reading

There are numerous textbooks on HRM and other topics that are also covered in this textbook. The aim here is to highlight a few specific texts we believe are the most useful and relevant to the ideas introduced in this chapter.

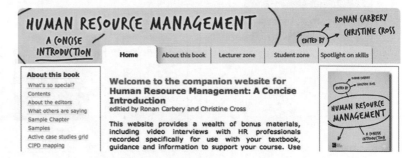

# SPOTLIGHT ON SKILLS: VIDEO AND TEXT FEATURES

## Video interviews with HR practitioners on the companion website at www.palgrave.com/business/carbery

This innovative feature encourages you to develop your skills in people management by outlining a particular workplace scenario in relation to the chapter content and asking you to consider specific questions and undertake a variety of activities in relation to it. This gives you the opportunity to identify and diagnose real-world HR problems and develop possible solutions to overcome them. Each of these features is accompanied by a link to a video interview with an experienced HR professional on the book's companion website. The skills-related questions posed in the text feature are addressed by the practitioner in the video in order to provide you with guidance. To maximize this resource, you should first attempt to answer the questions in the book and then watch the video.

### SPOTLIGHT ON SKILLS

1 You are aware that a positive employer brand provides an added incentive to candidates to apply for a position in an organization. Prepare a short report for your manager, outlining the reasons, in order of priority, why the organization should focus on developing a positive employer brand. Suggest how your organization could improve its employer brand in practice.

2 You are working for a medium-sized organization in the manufacturing sector, which relies on a full-time permanent workforce. Set out the business case for introducing the flexible firm model. What challenges do you anticipate with implementing the flexible firm model? Outline the advantages and disadvantages of this model to the organization and to existing and new employees.

To help you answer the questions above, visit www.palgrave.com/business/carbery and watch the video of Olga Donnelly talking about recruitment.

Spotlight on Skills features appear at the beginning of Chapters 2–13 of the textbook. They set up scenarios typical in the real world of business, then ask you to answer questions and undertake tasks and activities in relation to them.

These are followed by a link to the companion website, where you can watch a video interview with an experienced HR practitioner based at a multinational organization, such as Google, AOL or Kerry Group, outlining how they would approach the problem or issue at hand.

Chapter 4:
Gretta Nash-Cadden, Brown Thomas Group

Chapter 5:
Áine Hynes, St John Solicitors

Chapter 6:
Karen Burns, Sun Life Financial

Chapter 7:
Eamonn Collins, Quality and Qualifications Ireland

Chapter 8:
Miriam Cushen, Kerry Group

Chapter 9:
Judi Kinnane, pharmaceutical company

Chapter 10:
Anthony Brennan, CityJet (Air France)

Chapter 11:
Phillip Thornton, University of Limerick

Chapter 12:
Sinead Mullins, IBEC (Irish Business Employers' Confederation)

Chapter 13:
Claire Campion, Google

Chapter 14:
Karen Burns, Sun Life Financial

**Chapter 5:**
Áine Hynes, St John Solicitors

**Chapter 6:**
Karen Burns, Sun Life Financial

**Chapter 7:**
Eamonn Collins, Quality and Qualifications

**Chapter 8:**
Miriam Cushen, Kerry Group

**Chapter 9:**
Judi Kinnane, pharmaceutical company

# THE INTERVIEWEES

There are 12 Spotlight on Skills features in the book, which each link to videos online. Here is a list of the practitioners and the chapters in which you can find them.

### Chapters 2 and 3

Olga Donnelly has over 13 years' recruitment and selection experience, across financial services and the digital and online media sector. She currently holds the position of Staffing Manager at Google's European headquarters in Dublin, overseeing its talent acquisition across Europe, the Middle East and Africa. She recently led Google's creation of a two-year developmental programme for graduate hiring, offering a new approach to learning to equip new hires with the business, analytical and leadership skills needed to be successful at Google. Olga graduated with a Bachelor of Commerce degree from the National University of Ireland, Galway, specializing in Human Resources.

### Chapter 4

Gretta Nash Cadden has over nine years' generalist experience in managing a full spectrum of HR programmes, services and functions. Gretta's experience spans the hospitality and retail sectors. Her HR career began with Marriott International Hotels and she is currently employed as an HR and Training Manager within the Brown Thomas Group, a chain of large, luxury department stores in Ireland. Gretta has a proven track record in recruitment, learning and development, change management, organization development, conflict resolution and performance management. She holds an honours degree in HRM from Dublin Institute of Technology and an MBS in HR Strategy from Dublin City University.

### Chapter 5

Áine Hynes is a partner in St John Solicitors and her experience in employment law dates back to 1998 when she first acted for the Health and Safety Executive in defending employment-related claims. She has acted in all employment forums, from Rights Commissioner hearings to complex employment-related stress and bullying personal injuries claims. She is interested in equality law and represents clients regularly before the Equality Tribunal. She is a regular lecturer and tutor at the Law Society of Ireland and is involved in the Department of Jobs, Enterprise and Innovation workshops and discussions seeking to simplify employment law, thus reducing the resulting administrative burden felt by business. Áine is a member of the Litigation Committee of the Law Society of Ireland and a Council Member of the Dublin Solicitors Bar Association.

### Chapter 6

Karen Burns is the General Manager for Sun Life Financial in Ireland and Assistant Vice President of HR for Sun Life's Shared Services Division based in Ireland, Bermuda and the USA. Having started her career with Dunnes Stores, a leading Irish retailer, as an HR Manager, Karen then moved to AOL Europe, initially as HR Manager before being appointed as the Director of HR for its Waterford, Dublin and Bristol offices. A Bachelor of Commerce graduate of University College Cork, Karen also holds a Higher Diploma in Employee Relations from the National College of Ireland and an MBS in HRM from the University of Limerick.

### Chapter 7

Eamonn Collins is Corporate Business Manager at Quality and Qualifications Ireland, with responsibility for HR and finance. He has over 20 years' experience of HR in the public sector including the Department of Social and Family Affairs, as HR Manager for the Refugee Legal Service and the National Qualifications Authority of Ireland, and as Training Manager at the Legal Aid Board. He has significant experience of reviewing, implementing and advising other public bodies on performance management. His education qualifications include a degree in Law, a Postgraduate Diploma in Public Management and a Masters in HR from the Institute of Public Administration.

### Chapter 8

Miriam Cushen is an experienced business professional with strong HR experience, including generalist and functional expertise such as reward, recruitment, HR systems, HR data management and organization design. Her HR and business experience is with successful global businesses such as Kerry Group, a leading organization in the global food industry, and Diageo, who house brands such as Guinness and

Smirnoff, where she has been responsible for the design, implementation and embedding of strategic HR programmes in dynamic and changing environments including Ireland, the UK, Africa, Continental Europe and the USA. Miriam currently holds the role of Kerry Group Benefits Manager, where she has global responsibility for strategy, policy and implementation plans relating to Kerry Group's benefit offering. She has a Bachelor in Commerce from National University of Ireland, Galway, a BSc in HR from Dublin Institute of Technology and an Advanced Diploma from the Charted Institute of Management Accountants.

### Chapter 9

Judi Kinnane has more than 18 years' experience in the areas of talent management, particularly talent acquisition and development. She has a breadth and depth of experience in complex multinational Fortune 500 companies. Having led significant sourcing and development strategies during turbulent times, she is energetic and passionate about maximizing individual, team and organizational potential. She specializes in an evidence-based approach to HRD and HRM. Having held interim management positions and HR consultancy roles in the past, she is focused on delivering results and improving processes. She is currently leading a recruitment and staffing function for Ireland and the UK for a world-leading pharmaceutical company.

### Chapter 10

Anthony Brennan has held senior positions as Head of HR and Director of Human Resources across international, UK and Irish organizations, including Forte Hotels UK, Thorn/EMI Music UK, Merchants Group, Concern Worldwide and, more recently, CityJet, a subsidiary of Air France. Anthony's areas of expertise include HR strategy, organizational and management development, resource planning, employee engagement, and reward and benefits.

### Chapter 11

Philip Thornton is Head of the Health and Safety Unit at the University of Limerick and lectures on the Higher Diploma in Safety, Health and Welfare at Work. He has over 30 years' technical and scientific experience in both multinational and public sector organizations. He is Chair of the Mid-West District of the National Irish Safety Organisation and a member of Limerick local authority's Road Safety Together Committee. Philip has worked with Asahi Synthetic Fibres Ltd and Baxter SA. He has a degree in Industrial Biochemistry and an MSc in Health and Safety Management. He is a chartered member of the Institution of Occupational Safety and Health and contributed *to The Irish Health and Safety Handbook* (2nd edn) (Garavan, 2002).

### Chapter 12

Sinead Mullins is Human Resource and Industrial Relations Executive with the Irish Business Employers' Confederation (IBEC). With over seven years' experience in the field, Sinead has represented and advised clients in several industries, including manufacturing, financial services and hospitality sectors. In her role with IBEC, she has represented employers at the Employment Appeals Tribunal, Equality Tribunal, Rights Commissioner and Labour Court. She has also represented Ireland at the International Labour Organization and was an employer nominee on the Catering Joint Labour Committee. Sinead has a BBS in Economics and Finance from the University of Limerick, a BA in Law from Dublin Institute of Technology, and is currently studying for her Masters in Human Resource Management at the University of Limerick.

### Chapter 13

Claire Campion currently works as an HR Business Partner at Google Ireland. In the past 12 years, Claire has worked as an HR business partner in a broad range of industries, including hospitality, TV and broadcasting, and the online/tech industry. Her background is diverse and includes experience in the UK and Ireland, predominately working for large multinationals, such as Viacom International Media Networks, BSkyB and InterContinental Hotels. Her areas of HR experience include recruitment, change management, international HR, and employee engagement. Claire has an International Diploma in Hotel Management and Business Studies from Shannon College of Hotel Management and an MA in Human Resources from London Metropolitan University. She is an active member of the Chartered Institute of Personnel and Development.

# ACTIVE CASE STUDIES GRID

| Chapter | Title | Industry and location | Focus |
|---------|-------|----------------------|-------|
| 2 | Recruitment Strategy at ValuOutlets | Food retail sector in the UK and Ireland | Recruitment: external recruitment agencies; use of flexible workforce; choice of recruitment methods; job analysis; job advertisement |
| 3 | MsTAR | Web-based technology firm in Wellington, New Zealand | Choice of selection methods; preparation of selection interview questions; employment legislation in recruitment and selection |
| 4 | The Exit Interview and Employee Retention | Computer gaming in the Netherlands | Reasons for employee turnover; strategies to tackle employee turnover; using information to improve employee retention |
| 5 | Dromlona Whiskey | Whiskey production and distribution in Ireland, France and China | Designing procedures and developing policies and practices to comply with equality legislation; creating links between community and organization to promote diversity |
| 6 | Volvo Cars | Automobile manufacture in Sweden | Matching diversity management to business objectives; drivers for diversity management; senior management support for diversity management |
| 7 | Performance Appraisal at the Cool Call Centre Ltd | Inbound and outbound call centre in New York, USA | Creating a performance management system specific to an organization |
| 8 | Employee Bonus Schemes | Adventure and leisure in Galway, Ireland | Evaluating an employee bonus scheme in detail; identifying costs of failure of a bonus scheme |
| 9 | Upskilling your Training Team | Financial services organization in Denmark | Creating a learning and development consultant or business partner role in the organization |
| 10 | Apple Computers | Computer manufacture and call centre in Cork, Ireland, with outsourcing in Southeast Asia and Eastern Europe | Impact of changing business context on individual careers; the role of HR during a radical change in an organization |
| 11 | Health and Safety in an Irish Police Station | Police station in rural Ireland | Identifying attitudes towards safety at work |
| 12 | Firefighting on the Job | Apps development and software company in Ireland | Key principles in grievance and disciplinary procedures; preparation for an employment rights hearing |
| 13 | IrishCo Acquires French Company | Manufacturing in Ireland and France | Preparation of pre-departure training programme for the different types of employees; design of a repatriation programme |

# SKILLS DEVELOPMENT

Employability is a key concern for all graduates. In your career, regardless of whether or not this is within the HR field, there are particular skill sets that are central for your career progression. Importantly, employers are particularly interested in not just your disciplinary knowledge, but also the abilities and attributes that have been linked to employability. These include communications skills, creativity and collaboration. Many of these skills can be initially developed during your time at university. Here, we identify three such key skills and some of the ways you can begin to develop them while studying.

## PRESENTATION SKILLS

Regardless of the industry sector or size of organization you will work in, you will need to have the ability to present your ideas clearly and succinctly. This will often happen in a setting where you use a software program such as PowerPoint to provide an overview of the context and the key points. Increasingly, job vacancies also require you to make an oral presentation as part of the selection process. During your time at university, you will probably be asked to make a presentation as part of a module. In order to communicate your ideas and arguments cogently, we suggest that you think about your presentation as involving a number of stages, which we outline below. We identify the main points you should consider, which will enable you to develop this important skill, either through your coursework or after university in your work life.

### Planning your presentation

These points should be considered prior to giving your presentation:

- *Core message:* Be clear about what your core message is and repeat this at different stages during the presentation in order to increase its impact. Is it to inform? To sell your idea? To defend a position? To present a new idea? Whatever the answer, keep asking yourself this in different ways. What is the objective I want to achieve? What will I accept as evidence that my presentation has succeeded? What do I want the audience to think or feel at the end of the presentation?
- *Audience:* Analyse your audience. What are their expectations of your presentation? Do they expect to be informed? Persuaded? Have their existing ideas challenged? What do they already know? The key to a successful presentation is to know what your audience expects and ensure that you meet or exceed that expectation.
- *Timing:* Ensure you know how much time you have for your presentation. Be careful not to run over an allocated time slot as this will detract from its effectiveness.
- *Appearance:* Think about what you look like. What should you wear? This may seem a little strange to include here, but confidence is an important element in an effective presentation. You need to be comfortable and appropriately dressed to project the 'right' message.

### Handling nerves

Many people find handling their nerves the most difficult part of making a presentation. Here are a few pointers to help overcome these nerves:

- *Be well prepared and organized:* Most people will feel nervous before a presentation. Knowing what you are going to say will reduce your level of nervousness. The first two minutes of any presentation are the most crucial. If you feel confident and clear about what you are going to say in the early stage of the presentation, this will help alleviate your nerves for the remainder. Once you have passed the first two minutes and have started to believe that the presentation is going well, you can then be more confident that it will be a success.

- *Don't read directly from your notes – use visual aids:* This means that the words and/or images you select should act as your 'prompt'. Try not to look down at the hard copy notes in your hand as they will just provide a false sense of security. If you lose your place in the notes, or have learned them off by heart and then accidentally mix them up, your level of effectiveness in the eyes of the audience will be diminished.
- *Rehearse in advance:* Trial runs are an excellent method of preparation and allow you to establish how long your presentation will take. This also develops your self-confidence, which will help to reduce your nervousness.
- *Pay attention to your 'mannerisms':* Ask a friend or family member to highlight any repeated unconscious behaviours you might have, such as running your hands through your hair, shaking the change in your pocket, swaying from side to side or speaking too quickly. These are distracting for the audience, so awareness of these should help you to work to overcome them.
- *Practise deep breathing:* Do this before you get to where your presentation is taking place. This will help reduce the overall feeling of nervousness.
- *Arrive early:* This gives you plenty of time to check the equipment and ensure that, if you are using a software program, your presentation is working.
- *Think positively:* This means you are more likely to feel and behave positively.

## Structuring your presentation

The golden rule is simple:

- Tell them what you are going to tell them (introduction)
- Tell them (main body)
- Tell them what you've told them (conclusion).

### The introduction
- The introduction should comprise approximately 10 per cent of your presentation. It should provide a map for the audience of what is going to come. Introduce the topic and yourself (if necessary).

- Start with an attention-grabbing hook – make a bold claim, present a striking fact/statistic, ask a question, use a quotation. If you have a suitable quote, surprising information, or a visual aid – use it to grab the audience's attention.

### Delivery and body language
- Speak clearly and audibly throughout. Vary the tone of your voice as this will hold the audience's interest in your message.
- Don't speak too quickly as your message can get lost due to the audience not being able to follow it.
- Project your voice out towards the audience. Do not speak down to your shoes.
- Face the audience, not the screen behind you or your laptop. Speak directly to the audience and make eye contact with people in the room. This demonstrates that you are paying attention to them and encourages them to pay attention to you.
- Show enthusiasm for the topic/issue/idea, as enthusiasm is contagious.
- Regard the presentation as an opportunity to shine.

### The conclusion
- Remind the audience of what you set out to do at the start. This means stressing the main message or aim of your presentation.
- Briefly repeat the main points you made.
- End on an interesting note, as this will assist people in remembering your presentation.
- Thank the audience for listening and invite questions.

## TIME MANAGEMENT SKILLS

People who effectively manage their time are the highest achievers in all walks of life, from business, to sport, to public service. Yet they have only the same number of hours in a day as the rest of us. This is why time management is believed to be a critical skill for success. Many students and employees spend their days in a frenzy of activity, but achieve very little because they are not concentrating on the right things. Mobile phones, laptops and email mean we are contactable 24 hours a day and technology has made us accessible no matter where we are, whether it's in the Outer Hebrides or on the Amazon. But is it necessarily the best use of our time to constantly be in touch? Here we provide some tips and techniques to help you become more effective at managing your most valuable resource – your time.

## Your study space

Your workspace has a significant impact on your productivity and mental wellbeing. While some people are happy to work surrounded by paper and teacups, other people prefer to work at a clutter-free desk. In reality, the brain can only concentrate fully on one thing at a time. The more 'stuff' on your desk, the more you will be distracted by it and want to pick it up. Cluttered desks are *not* conducive to clear thinking. You should:

- Clear your desk of *everything* not related to what you are specifically working on/studying at that particular moment; otherwise your attention is constantly being drawn to other issues and tasks.
- Resist the temptation to leave your mobile phone on your desk.
- Always leave your desk tidy and empty when have finished for the day, so the next day you will feel less overwhelmed by all that has to be done.

## Work efficiently

Handle each piece of paper or each email only *once*. The principle behind this is that it forces you to make a decision immediately about every piece of paper or email you have to deal with. Avoid reading something and then thinking 'I'll deal with that later'. The rules are:

- Do it straightaway, or
- Decide to postpone it until later but clearly indicate that it still needs to be done so you don't forget about it.

## Managing phone calls/texts

The phone seems to have taken over our lives. We are now no longer able to go anywhere without a mobile phone. How much time do you spend on your phone at university or work? How much of that time is necessary? Talking/texting on the phone can be time-consuming and unproductive. If you spend six minutes an hour on the phone, that equates to 10 per cent of your day. Therefore:

- Don't reply to each text as soon as you receive it.
- During a break, deal with all your outgoing calls/texts together, rather than interrupting your study each

time you want to make a call/send a text. This makes much more efficient use of your time.
- Set your phone to voicemail to help manage your time. People can leave messages and then you can answer them all when you have a break.

## Managing your online communications

Email, Facebook, Twitter and other social media platforms have become the standard way of communicating at university and work. The biggest problem with this is that they consume large portions of your day, and yet help you achieve relatively little. Email inboxes can be overwhelming. Email is also the lazy option – especially when you want to avoid making a decision. To deal with these problems and also manage your time better:

- Check your email/Facebook/Twitter pages just three or four times during the day – in the morning, at lunchtime and in the afternoon. If something is really urgent someone will contact you on your phone. Web apps such as Anti-Social for Macs and Cold Turkey for Windows are free productivity programs that you can use to temporarily block yourself off from popular social media sites, addictive websites and games, if needs be.
- Make a phone call to reply to an email or a text. We spend vast amounts of time composing and replying to emails and texts when one phone call would have dealt with the issue much more quickly.
- Set up email messages with auto-preview as this will allow you to see if the message needs to be opened and actioned straightaway.
- Delete an email once you have read and replied to it, or move it to a personal folder.

# PERSUASION AND INFLUENCING SKILLS

Learning how to influence and persuade people to do something they would otherwise not have done is an important life skill. Influencing is essentially getting your own way, unobtrusively. Managers do it most of the time. People are usually not aware that every human interaction involves a complex process of persuasion and influence, and being unaware, they are usually the ones being persuaded to help others rather than the ones who are doing the persuading. The key points to consider in developing this skill are:

- Know what you want. If you are not clear about what you want, it will be difficult for you to persuade others around to your way of thinking.
- Look for points of mutual agreement and build on these.
- Build rapport and make a connection with the person you are trying to influence.
- Ask questions. The type of question is important. You need to use a mixture of questions to get the response you are looking for, for example:
  - Find out what the other person is hoping to get out of the interaction, for example: 'What do you want to get out of this discussion?' 'What do you want to achieve from this discussion?'
  - Probe to find out why they don't agree with you, for example: 'What is the reason why you can't do that?' 'What is stopping you from agreeing with me?'
  - Ask hypothetical questions, as this allows you to gather information without the person actually committing to anything, for example: 'What would happen if you agreed with me?' 'What would happen if we went ahead and did it?'
  - Find out what they need you to give them in order for them to agree with you, for example: 'What do you need to get in order for us to agree?' 'What do I need to give you to get you to agree?'
  - Ask challenging questions to test the person's resolve/ position. Search for specifics, for example: 'Why don't you agree with this proposal?' 'What specific reason do you have for not wanting to do this?'

- Listen actively. This includes being able to paraphrase what the other person has said.
- Use positive body and verbal language. This creates the right atmosphere and is more conducive to agreement. For example:
  - Don't use 'flowery language'. Using too many adjectives and adverbs will lose the listener.
  - Use strong not weak words. For example, which of these two sentences would persuade you? 'I think you might like this new product we have.' 'You're really going to like this new product we are offering.' 'Think' in the first sentence is a weak word. Here is another example: 'I was wondering if you might want to go for a drink with me at the weekend?' A stronger question would be: 'Would you like to go for a drink this weekend?'
  - Focus on using the active not the passive voice. An example of the passive voice would be: 'An account was opened by Mr Smith' versus the active 'Mr Smith opened an account'.
- Stress the benefits to them of agreeing with you.
- Work towards a decision. Use all the techniques above to keep building towards their agreement.

These are just some of the key issues involved in developing the skills of presentation, time management, persuasion and influence. These skills are part of the new focus colleges and universities are placing on graduate employability and, as such, are skills you can and should aim to develop during your time as a third-level student.

# PUBLISHER'S ACKNOWLEDGEMENTS

The editors, contributors and publisher are grateful to the following for permission to reproduce copyright material:

Elsevier for Figure 10.1, Super's life span model, from Super, D. (1980) 'A life-span, life-space approach to career development', *Journal of Vocational Behaviour*, **16**: 282–98. Copyright © 1980, Elsevier.

Gerry McMahon and Patrick Gunningle for Table 7.1, The objectives of performance management systems, and Table 7.2, Characteristics of successful performance management systems, in *Performance Appraisal: How to Get It Right*, Dublin: Productive Personnel Ltd/Institute of Personnel Management.

John Wiley and Sons for Figure 1.2, The Michigan model of HRM, in Fombrun, C.J., Tichy, N.M. and Devanna, M.A. (1984) *Strategic Human Resource Management*. Copyright © 1984. Reproduced with permission of John Wiley & Sons, Inc. Also for Figure 1.3, The Guest model of HRM, in Guest, D.E. (1987) 'Human resource management and industrial relations', *Journal of Management Studies*, **14**(5): 503–21. Copyright © 2007, John Wiley and Sons.

Palgrave Macmillan for Figure 13.2, U-shaped curve of cross-cultural adjustment, in Black, J.S. and Mendenhall, M.E. (1991) 'The U-curve adjustment hypothesis revisited: a review and theoretical framework', *Journal of International Business Studies*, **22**(2): 225–47. Reproduced with permission of Palgrave Macmillan.

The publisher is also grateful to iStockphoto and Fotolia for supplying some of the images in the book, and to Cassiah Joski-Jethi for editing the Spotlight on Skills video interviews on the companion website.

# ABBREVIATIONS

| | |
|---|---|
| Acas | Advisory, Conciliation and Arbitration Service |
| CIPD | Chartered Institute of Personnel and Development |
| CSR | corporate social responsibility |
| ETI | Ethical Trading Initiative |
| EU | European Union |
| HCN | host country national |
| HR | human resources |
| HRD | human resource development |
| HRM | human resource management |
| HRP | human resource planning |
| IHRM | international human resource management |
| IT | information technology |
| L&D | learning and development |
| MBO | management by objectives |
| MNC | multinational company |
| NER | non-union employee representation |
| NGO | nongovernmental organization |
| OECD | Organisation for Economic Co-operation and Development |
| PCN | parent country national |
| PRP | performance-related pay |
| ROI | return on investment |
| SHRD | strategic human resource development |
| SHRM | strategic human resource management |
| TCN | third country national |

# 1

# INTRODUCING HUMAN RESOURCE MANAGEMENT

**Christine Cross and Ronan Carbery**

By the end of this chapter you will be able to:

## LEARNING OUTCOMES

- Define the term 'human resource management' (HRM)
- Describe the main activities of the HRM function
- Outline the historical development of HRM
- Be able to engage with the 'personnel' or 'HRM' debate

- Recognize what the term 'strategic HRM' (SHRM) means
- Describe the key models and theoretical underpinning in the study of HRM
- Contextualize HRM within the macro- and micro-environment

© DOC RABE MEDIA/FOTOLIA

*This chapter discusses ...*

# INTRODUCTION

Here, at the start of this book, it is worth identifying that the term 'human resource management' (HRM) is most often used to describe the activities involved in managing the employment relationship. Thus, if you are an employer, a manager or an employee, the issues dealt with in this book are going to be relevant to your working life. HRM is essentially about managing people in a way that both maximizes and rewards the contribution each person makes to the organization. In order to accomplish this aim, organizations choose from a range of policies and practices that can assist in achieving this objective. By this we mean policies and practices such as:

- how to recruit and select employees
- how to pay and reward them
- what terms and conditions they work under
- what training and development opportunities the organization should pay for
- how to deal with employees who break organizational rules
- how to ensure that everyone in the organization is treated equally.

These are just a few of the questions that face those charged with the management of employees and each of these is dealt with in this book. The choice of which policies or practices, however, is not as straightforward as it first seems. Do you think McDonald's uses the same HRM policies and practices as your local convenience shop, or the same ones you would use if you were starting up your own company? Why do you think there may be a difference? In this chapter, we set out some of the issues involved in making these choices.

Given that the focus of this book is pitched at an introductory level to HRM, it would be impossible to provide a detailed description of every single issue involved in the choices we are talking about. Instead, we concentrate on identifying some of the key concepts and encourage you to read more about these in order to further your understanding of them. Here, we first explain what we mean by the term 'the employment relationship', as it is in this context that HRM operates. We then identify what the term HRM means, and where it originated. This leads us to a problematic issue in the study of HRM, that of the name – should we refer to it as HRM or stick with the more traditional term of 'personnel management' (PM)? We identify the key HRM activities and outline the evolution of HRM roles in organizations. We then outline the key models involved in the study of HRM and consider the concept of 'strategic HRM'. Finally, the importance of the environmental context within which these choices occur is identified. At the end of this chapter, you should be able to understand why HRM is such an important area of study for you as future managers.

# THE NATURE OF THE EMPLOYMENT RELATIONSHIP

Before we look at the history of HRM and consider its theoretical basis, it is important to understand the nature of the employment relationship that exists between employers and employees. We need to consider how this relationship is conceptualized, experienced and regulated. All employment relationships have to be regulated in some form or another so that each side understands its obligations. For example, rules need to be set down regarding rates of pay, working hours, holiday entitlements and working conditions. Traditionally, organizations negotiated these matters with **trade unions**. This was because the employment relationship was usually characterized by an imbalance of power between a powerful employer and a relatively powerless employee. To counteract this imbalance, employees group together to form or join trade unions, to exert greater power over the employment relationship and therefore have greater influence over their working conditions and so on than would otherwise be the case. The main reason employees join trade unions is to express solidarity, to have collective protection, and to improve their terms and conditions of employment. Most analyses of the employment relationship focus on the concept of **industrial relations** or employment relations ▶ **Chapter 12** ◀. Arising from a belief in the 1960s and 70s that management did not share the same goals as employees, employees referred to themselves as 'us' and managers as 'them', highlighting a division between two sides with conflicting interests (Clegg, 1979). Traditionally, most HR managers were essentially industrial relations

**Trade unions** – an organized group of employees who represent employees' interest in maintaining or improving the conditions of their employment

**Industrial relations** – areas of the employment relationship where employers deal with employee representatives rather than individual employees

managers, where their main responsibility was to negotiate and interact with trade unions.

However, a decline in trade union membership and the perceived significance of trade unions in managing the employment relationship has meant that managers, acting on behalf of employers, now have a significant amount of control over this relationship. Organizations increasingly seek to take greater control over the employment relationship by refusing to deal with trade unions and deal at an individual level with each employee – hence the phrase 'the open door policy'. Without trade unions, however, there will generally be less opposition to changes in working conditions and terms and conditions of employment. In order for this approach to be effective, it is important that employees are seen as assets that can be developed and nurtured, rather than resources to be exploited, and that a partnership exists between management and employees. This necessitates that organizations offer a range of HRM practices targeted at developing a committed and cooperative workforce. The rationale for using specific HRM techniques is based on the belief that if employees believe they are being 'looked after' and their interests considered, there is no need for trade union representation (McLoughlin and Gourlay, 1994).

Regardless of whether or not you eventually work in an HR-type job or pursue a career in HR, how the employment relationship is managed will affect almost every position in an organization. It would be a challenge to look at any media outlet on any given day, and *not* find some aspect of the employment relationship being discussed. Employment relations disputes, strikes, pay talks, forced layoffs and legislation covering the employment relationship all receive considerable media attention on a regular basis. Chapter 12 provides more detailed information on the key aspects of managing the employment relationship.

## WHAT IS HUMAN RESOURCE MANAGEMENT?

Since the beginning of modern management theory, the terms used to describe HRM have included 'personnel', 'industrial relations', 'employee relations' and 'human resource management'. Those who work in the area of HRM are familiar with the debate that has been present for decades over the actual title that is given to the activities undertaken in the field. This may seem unimportant to you, but most colleges and third-level institutions use the term 'Human Resource Management' to label your courses. You will, however, still find some colleges and third-level institutions where your course is located in an academic department called the Department of Personnel Management. Also, the professional body for those who work in the area of HRM is called the Chartered Institute of *Personnel* and Development (CIPD). You may also know someone who works in an organization and has the job title of 'personnel manager'. However, you are more likely to find many more people working in roles titled 'human resource (HR) manager', situated within an HR department in the organization. Indeed, most of the textbooks in this area, like the one you are currently reading, are titled 'Human Resource Management'. If you analyse the term 'human *resource* management', you can see the focus is on people (humans) as a resource, similar to plant, machinery or capital. Do you believe this is the right title for the management of people at work? Which title do you think should be used? Interestingly, and just to confuse the issue further, many multinational corporations (MNCs) use the term 'people managers', rather than either human resource or personnel managers. Here, the focus of the title is on the management of people and the ways in which they are managed to achieve organizational goals. This would appear to more closely reflect the actual role played by those involved in the management of people at work.

From an academic perspective, despite the widespread use of the title HRM, it is a subject without an agreed definition (Brewster, 2007). In this book we refer to **human resource management** in a broad sense, in order to highlight the importance placed on empowering employees to assist the organization in the achievement of its strategic objectives. In this perspective, people are viewed as an asset rather than a cost, and a source of competitive advantage (Pfeffer, 1994). Unlike other resources such as land or capital, it is difficult for competitors to duplicate people and so by protecting, nurturing and developing employees over time, organizations can ensure that their workforce will be a source of ongoing competitive advantage. By using a definition such as this, we are taking the approach that the 'human' resources of the organization should be managed as carefully as other valuable resources.

**Human resource management** – the strategic and integrated approach taken by an organization to the management of its most valued assets, namely its people

CONSIDER THIS...

The BBC has a 'People Director', Google has a 'Director for HR and Staffing', the Royal Navy in the UK has 'Personnel Logisticians' and AEG Europe recently advertised a position for a 'Human Solutions Director'. Why do you think there are so many different titles for what is essentially the same job? What title do you suggest?

## The impact of HRM on organizational performance

The advent of the global financial crisis has highlighted the need for organizations to focus on ways of improving competitiveness, while keeping costs as low as possible. Given that employee salaries and related costs are often the single most significant element of the expenditure involved in operating any business, most employers believe it is important for organizations to maximize the return on their investment in their employees. For most organizations, effectiveness is measured in different ways:

- the achievement and maintenance of sustainable competitive advantage
- organizational survival
- the development and maintenance of corporate reputation.

The HR function has a key role to play in the achievement of all these goals. It is, however, outside the scope of this chapter to discuss *how* HRM policies and practices have a positive impact on overall organizational performance, and particularly on organizational profitability and shareholder value (see, for example, Guest, 2011 for a discussion). But, it is important to make you aware of the prominence of this question in the field of HRM and to identify the difficulties involved in answering this question.

Many leading academics hold the view that HRM positively improves organizational performance (see, for example, Huselid, 1995; Huselid and Becker, 1995; Guest, 1997; Purcell et al., 2003). However, the difficulty occurs when you try to identify which specific policies or practices are responsible: How can you measure and quantify the improvements? What aspects of organizational performance are important? This is because it is difficult to isolate specific issues that may have positively impacted on aspects of performance,

given the integrated nature of work and the different industries and organizational contexts. One of the 'holy grail' issues for many HRM researchers is to clearly establish what we intrinsically know, that is, that HRM can cause positive changes in organizational-level performance. (For a detailed discussion of the Bath Model of People and Performance, which identified 11 HRM practices that contribute to organizational performance, see Purcell et al., 2003.) Notwithstanding this, many empirical research studies have been published that demonstrate the existence of this link between HRM practices and some measures of organizational performance (see, for example, Huselid, 1995; MacDuffie, 1995; Delery and Doty, 1996; Guthrie, 2000; Combs et al., 2006; Tregaskis et al., 2012).

Despite the difficulties involved in this measurement effort, this has become one of the most critical aspects of HRM. Measurement is needed in order to judge the effectiveness of a policy or practice and to provide credibility for the endeavour. Both internal and external evaluations need to be conducted, where the focus is, respectively, on the costs and benefits of a practice and the overall contribution to organizational performance. The CIPD commissioned work by John Purcell and colleagues in Bath to investigate which aspects of HRM had a positive impact on organizational performance (Purcell et al., 2003). This three-year study of 12 companies found that it was the actual implementation of the HR policies, rather than their existence or number, which was the vital ingredient in linking people management to business performance. The role of the line manager was found to be key to this success and this is discussed later in this chapter. As Boxall and Purcell (2003) suggest, by employing better people in an organization with better processes, HR advantage can be achieved.

## EVOLUTION OF HUMAN RESOURCE MANAGEMENT AS AN ORGANIZATIONAL FUNCTION

To gain a better understanding of where the difficulty arises with the use of the term HRM, it is useful to briefly trace the development of the HRM function. During the Industrial Revolution in England in the late nineteenth century, the working conditions of men, women and children were dreadful. There were, however, some enlightened employers, often Quakers, who wanted to improve the working conditions of their employees. In the 1890s, companies started providing workplace and family amenities for workers such as lunch rooms, medical care, company magazines and housing. The impetus was good business, humanitarian concern and religious principles. This led to the creation of stand-alone employment offices, employing an industrial welfare officer who dealt solely with employment issues. The changes during this period to working conditions were driven not only by a welfare agenda, but also by a drive to improve productivity. Regardless of this, the industrial welfare movement represented a shift in the way management viewed employees and resulted in the creation of some of the benefits now taken for granted at work today, such as sick pay and pensions.

The next phase in the development of HRM concerned F.W. Taylor's scientific management movement in the early part of the twentieth century. His work focused on developing a systematic approach to the design of jobs and employment and pay systems. Taylorists were concerned with achieving 'one best way' of working and aimed to increase productivity through greater efficiency in production practices, selection and training practices and, interestingly, incentivized pay for workers (a recognition of the link between pay and performance). Allied to these were the tight control of workers; thus these practices often met with resistance from workers and their union representatives. This led to a significant increase in trade union membership, with a quarter of UK employees holding trade union membership by 1914. In the USA, trade union membership doubled between 1896 and 1900 and again between 1900 and 1904. With the emergence of the production line and large factories in the 1920s, positions such as 'labour manager' and 'employment manager' emerged and their roles were to deal with issues such as absences, recruitment and queries over bonuses (CIPD, 2012a). Their work involved the centralization and standardization of certain employment-related functions, such as hiring, payroll and record keeping.

Around the time of the Second World War, the work of Elton Mayo and his colleagues on the Hawthorne experiments in Illinois in the USA highlighted new areas of concern for employers. These led to an emphasis on personal development, a better understanding of groupwork, and the importance of working conditions as a means of motivating employees, all areas that are covered by the work undertaken by today's HR function. The 1960s and 70s saw the introduction of a large body of legislation, both in Europe and the USA, which provided rights for employees around dismissals, equal pay, pension rights, and health and safety. This development created additional work for the personnel officer, as they were charged with understanding and applying these pieces of legislation. During this time, there was also an increased emphasis on industrial relations and the personnel office was heavily involved in workplace bargaining with the trade union and shop stewards, increasing the profile of the officer in the organization. This resulted in a rise in both the status and professionalism of the personnel function (Gunnigle et al., 2011).

A number of important developments took place in the 1980s and 90s, which effectively strengthened the role of the HR function. The recession of the 1980s and the resultant high unemployment levels were coupled with significant competition in the marketplace, especially from Japan, leading to a focus on productivity and 'excellence', seen to be associated with leading-edge companies. Allied to this was a decline in traditional manufacturing industries and a significant growth in the service sector. At the same time, shifting demographics, the move towards a 24/7 society, and changing workforce values led to employers and employees seeking nonstandard hours of work. Rapid technological developments, including the advent of smartphones and mobile broadband, allowed large numbers of employees to work away from their office desks and to be on call for many hours outside the normal 9–5 working day. The combination of all these developments necessitated new HR policies and practices to effectively manage these changes and a corresponding rise in the position of the profession to the same level as other functions in the organizations, such as marketing and finance (see Figure 1.1 below).

We can see from the above how the role of the original personnel officer has grown and developed over time and has expanded to the situation today where HR departments employ many people with responsibility for specialized areas in HR (the specific activities of the HR function are detailed in a later section). It is essentially the context in which people are managed that has changed and continues to change, and this has led to a repositioning of the role and importance of the management of people in organizational life. We now need to examine how the term 'human resource management' evolved from the phrase 'personnel officer' and what the term means today.

## Development of the use of the term HRM

The issue of the term 'HRM' is in many ways central to the move away from a traditional approach associated with the early administrative work undertaken by those involved in the welfare of workers. The term first appeared in the mid-1960s in the USA and is attributed to the economist E. Wight Bakke, who gave a lecture entitled 'The Human Resources Function' (1958). He said: 'the function is related to the understanding, maintenance, development, effective employment and integration of potential in the resource "people" that I shall simply call the human resource function' (pp. 5–6). It is interesting that this description is similar to many of the current definitions of the term HRM we find in a lot of today's textbooks.

From the 1960s to 1980s, personnel management and human resource management largely coexisted as terms and were used interchangeably. Then, in the 1980s, there was a move to differentiate traditional PM from HRM. This distinction grew in momentum and you can find many writers who focused on distinguishing HRM from PM and trying to identify the key differences. This led to two schools of thought, one where HRM and PM were different labels for the same subject and the other where HRM represented a new model and philosophy of people management. The first concept is often referred to as a 'relabelling' or 'repackaging' of PM, where HRM is simply PM with a new title (Gunnigle and Flood, 1990; Lawton and Rose, 1994; Legge, 1995). The second concept was proposed by Michael Beer and his colleagues at Harvard in *Managing Human Assets* (Beer et al., 1984: 293) and represented a new HRM paradigm, where HRM represents the then emerging view that people are an asset and not a cost, and the HR function must be fully aware of and involved in all strategic and business decisions.

Storey (1989) identified four features of HRM, which he believed differentiated HRM from traditional PM:

1 HRM is explicitly linked with corporate strategy.
2 HRM focuses on commitment rather than compliance of employees (see Walton, 1985 for a full discussion of this issue).
3 Employee commitment is obtained through an integrated approach to HR policies in the areas of rewards, selection, training and appraisal.
4 HRM is not just the domain of specialists in the HR function, rather HRM is owned by line managers as a means of fostering integration.

Storey (1992) later added to this work by identifying 27 'points of difference' between HRM and PM. In this work, he identified HRM as a proactive, strategic management activity in comparison with PM's representation as relatively passive and reactive.

Since the 1980s, writers have built on these differences and have identified the distinctive features of HRM in order to clearly identify it as a new philosophy regarding the management of people in organizations. HRM can therefore be described as more than simply an alternative approach to traditional PM. It is worth noting that when comparing HRM and PM, more similarities than differences occur; however, concepts such as 'strategic integration', 'culture management', 'commitment', 'investing in human capital', together with a unitary philosophy are viewed as essential parts of the HRM model.

There are a number of major characteristics normally associated with HRM and these include:

● *A strategic approach to the management of people*: a key feature of HRM is the linkage between HRM strategy and business strategy. Here, HR are included in the creation of business strategy and therefore workforce strategies are designed to support business strategy (this is explained in more detail later in the chapter).
● *Line managers work in partnership with HR*: as Storey (1995: 7) highlights: 'if human resources really are so critical for business managers then HRM is too important to be left to operational personnel specialists' (see the following section for discussion of the role of line managers). 'Devolvement to the line' is a common phrase in HRM and identifies the delegation of certain HR practices, for example selection interviews and performance reviews, to those who are involved in managing employees in their day-to-day work.
● *HR policies and practices that are integrated and consistent with the organizational culture*: 'vertical integration' refers to the matching of HRM policies and practices with business strategy and is also referred to as 'external alignment', while 'horizontal integration' involves strong consistency and interconnection between HRM policies and practices internally in order to achieve effective performance. This is also known as 'internal alignment' or 'internal fit'.
● *Unitarist frame of reference*: unitarism as a perspective views the employment relationship as one where both managers and employees have a common purpose and the organization is integrated and harmonious, acting as 'one big happy family' ▶ Chapter 11 ◀.
● *A 'soft' HRM approach*: a distinction has been made in the literature between 'hard' and 'soft' HRM approaches. A 'hard' approach is one in which

employees are a resource like any other and should be managed as such, while a 'soft' approach is based on the HR school of thought and involves treating employees as valued assets and a *source* of competitive advantage, rather than simply *using* people as another resource (Storey, 1989).

HRM is therefore not simply a set of individual practices, rather it must be viewed as a system, where the elements are integrated and mutually reinforcing in order to produce an effective outcome at an organizational level (Kepes and Delery, 2007).

> **Devolved** – the process of moving decision-making downwards, from HR to line managers
>
> **Line managers** – managers who have employees directly reporting to them and who have a higher level of responsibility than those employees

## WHO IS RESPONSIBLE FOR HRM IN THE ORGANIZATION?

If, after college or university, you decide to start up your own company, are you likely to have a HR function from the beginning? The answer is probably no. You will make all the decisions yourself about who to hire, what to pay them and how to dismiss them if needs be. So, for many startups and small businesses, the owner makes all those decisions. Given the significant amount of legislation covering employment law, many owners use consultants to advise them on specific HR-related issues, or they outsource the main HR functions ▶ **Chapter 2** ◀. This allows them to reduce costs while still ensuring specialist expertise, although it is external to the company. The outsource provider can manage all or part of the HR function, including pay and benefits, administration and the creation of new organization-specific HR policies and practices.

Many organizations do, however, have a designated HR 'person' or department. Interestingly, many employees believe that every aspect of HRM should be the responsibility of those who work in that function, in the same way as those who work in finance are responsible for all aspects of financial preparation and reporting. But, the key to understanding who is responsible for HRM in an organization is that simply having a range of HRM policies and practices does not automatically mean that high levels of organizational performance will follow (Purcell et al., 2003). It is the implementation and interpretation of these that actually matter. Therefore, the supervisor, team leader or line manager has a crucial role in bringing these

policies to life (Purcell et al., 2003). For many years, textbooks have identified that the various day-to-day HR activities, once the sole remit of the HR department, needed to be **devolved** to **line managers** in order to allow for faster decision-making that is more in tune with business needs. The rationale is that the line manager is the person who works most closely with the employee. The types of activities normally devolved to line managers include employee selection, discipline and performance management. In this role HR provide support and guidance to line managers in these activities; this also allows HR to move towards aligning the people management agenda with the strategic goals of the organization. This move towards a partnership approach between HR and the line manager is viewed as central to achieving successful outcomes for the employee and the organization. This approach requires that line managers are equipped with the appropriate skills, knowledge and attitudes to effectively manage and develop their staff. It should be noted, however, that this approach can create tensions between line managers and HR practitioners, as line managers often believe they are already busy enough with the technical aspects of their role.

It is the overall vision, values and managerial ideology of the owner that have a critical influence on the way HRM operates in an organization. In a larger organization, it is still the managing director or senior management team who create the environment for the operation of people management policies. The status, role and profile of the HR function are influenced by the strength of the belief of senior management in the added value that HRM can contribute to the organization. One interesting example of how a leader's vision and philosophy can impact on the function and operation of the HR department can be found in Jack Welch's approach. He was the chairman and CEO of General Electric (GE) from 1981 to 2001. His unique perspective on the management of people included that every year he would fire the bottom performing 10 per cent of his employees. He also dismantled the nine-layer management hierarchy and fostered a more informal organizational culture. During his tenure as head of the organization, GE's revenues increased by almost $100 billion. It is clear that his method had a positive effect on organizational performance, however unconventional it may have seemed.

**CONSIDER THIS...**

We talked about devolving day-to-day HRM activities to line managers. If you are the finance manager in your organization, are you a line manager? If you are the HR manager in your organization, are you still a line manager? If you are the finance manager, what types of people management activities would you expect to be part of your job and what would you expect to be the responsibility of the HR function?

## KEY HUMAN RESOURCE MANAGEMENT ACTIVITIES

Before we examine the specific activities of the HRM function, we need to identify the role of the HRM function and where the HRM function is located within the organization. As it is a key organizational function, in the same way that finance or marketing are, you will see it is positioned at the same level in the organizational chart (see Figure 1.1). The key role of the HRM function is to enable the organization to achieve its strategic objectives and to positively impact organizational effectiveness by dealing effectively with all aspects of the employment relationship. As the organizational chart in Figure 1.1 highlights, the HRM function is involved in enabling growth, productivity and profitability, through the creation of an HRM strategy, in line with the overall business strategy. HRM strategies are plans that address and solve fundamental strategic issues related to the management of HR in an organization. HRM strategy is used to create a set of HRM policies designed to achieve the organization's strategic goals. These policies are then translated into specific HRM practices, again aimed at meeting the strategic goals. For example, the organization will need to have a set of policies dealing with recruitment and selection, which identify how the processes will operate. Specific practices, such as the availability of a relocation allowance for new employees or the payment of expenses associated with attending selection interviews, are then formulated.

As noted earlier, the size of the organization has an impact on how the HRM function is configured. In a large

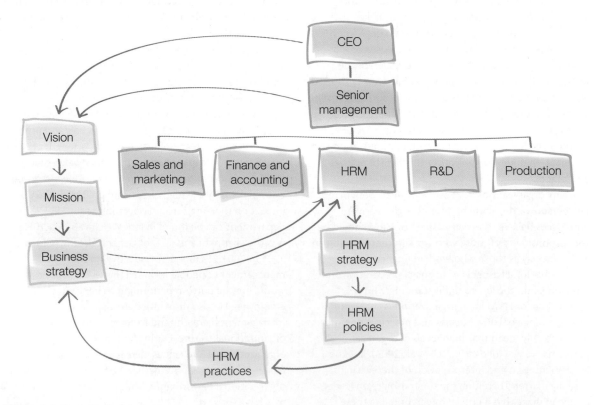

**Figure 1.1 Organizational chart**

organization, such as an MNC, the function may be led by an HR director, who has a seat on the board of directors, where they have access to and the support of the senior management team. This situation provides a real opportunity for the integration of HR strategy and business strategy. However, even within large organizations the configuration of the function may differ. Some may organize around specialist roles, where there are separate HR specialist roles, for example talent management, employment relations and compensation and benefits. Other organizations may work with generalist roles, where an HR generalist works with a specific group of employees, for example production operators, and handles all the issues related to that group. There is also a distinction in some organizations in relation to the level that the HR professional works at, that is, at strategic, administrative or executive level.

A more recent development in terms of the organization of the HR function is the creation of a shared services approach, where all the routine 'transactional' HRM services are provided centrally to all aspects of the business. These include recruitment administration, compensation and benefits administration, answering employee queries related to HR policies, and providing advice to managers on employee issues such as discipline and absenteeism. The benefit for the organization is that this reduces the number of HRM employees working at an operational level and allows them to focus on taking a more strategic approach.

It is worth noting here that there is an inherent conflict in the role played by the HR function, where the question is often expressed as: Am I representing the best interests of the employee, or the best interests of the organization? Is the role of HR to act as organizational guardians or as employee champions? This is an issue many HR professionals struggle with and there is no simple answer. A CIPD (2010a) report deals with the changing nature of the role played by HR and identifies how the HR function can grow and develop in the second decade of this new century.

Regardless of the ways in which we categorize the activities of the HR function, a standard set of activities can be identified (see Table 1.1). It is important to realize that the type, scope and number of activities engaged in will depend on factors such as the size of the organization, the industry sector and the type of employees (see later in the chapter for a discussion of the factors impacting the choice of activities).

**Table 1.1** Main activities of the HRM function

| Organization level | Employee resourcing | Inducting, developing and retaining employees | Managing the employment relationship | Exiting employees | Employee and organization welfare |
|---|---|---|---|---|---|
| Strategy formulation and development | Human resource planning | Induction | Managing disciplinary issues | Managing poor performers | Health and safety |
| | Recruitment | Performance management | Grievance handling | Dismissal | Employee wellbeing |
| | Selection | Motivating employees | Managing redundancy | Employee turnover | Counselling |
| | Providing contracts | Managing rewards | Negotiation | Employment legislation | Organization climate |
| | Managing expatriation | Learning and development | Managing employee relations | | Corporate social responsibility and ethics |
| | | Career development | Providing fair and equal treatment of employees | | Employee assistance programmes |
| | | Talent management | Managing diversity | | |
| | | | Conflict resolution | | |

## Evolution of human resource management roles

The work of David Ulrich has been influential in the identification of the roles HR practitioners play in an organization. Because organizations differ in terms of size, structure, industry and business operation, their HR function will be configured differently. However, to bring some continuity to the roles that HR professionals should play in an organization, Ulrich (1998) developed the following categorization. He suggested that HR professionals should take on a proactive role in the organization and adopt what he termed a 'strategic business partnership approach' to clarify their roles. In order to do this he proposed four requirements of the HR function: to be a strategic partner; a change agent; an employee champion; and an administrative expert. The simplicity and strength of this 'call to arms' for HR practitioners became popular in the USA and the UK, to the extent that the term 'HR business partner' has become increasingly popular as a way for HR professionals to describe themselves. Ulrich and Brockbank (2005) updated these roles for twenty-first-century HR to reflect changing roles in organizations. The change agent role was incorporated into the strategic partner role, a new role of team leader was proposed, and the employee champion and administrative expert roles were redefined:

1 *Strategic partner:* HR professionals should be strategy formulators, strategy implementers and strategy facilitators.
2 *Employee advocate:* HR should focus on meeting the current needs of employees.
3 *Human capital developer:* HR should also focus on meeting the future needs of employees in terms of their learning and development.
4 *Functional expert:* HR professionals should increase the administrative efficiency of the HR function by designing effective HR policies and practices.
5 *Leader:* Being an effective HR leader requires mastering the previous four roles and working in collaboration with other business functions to set standards for strategic thinking and corporate governance.

Ulrich and Brockbank (2005: 24) also highlight that 'HR professionals aspire to add value. But it's not always easy for the provider of a service to see what contribution they are making.' By mastering the five roles identified above, HR practitioners can conceivably enhance the credibility of the HR function. The role of HR as a strategic business partner has become more prevalent in the literature and in practice. Its hallmark is a close working relationship between HR professionals and the business units and involves building partnerships with key organizational leaders. This allows strategic business partners to identify and support strategic projects and focus on long-term business strategies and organizational needs (Gaines Robinson and Robinson, 2005). Interestingly, however, while HR practitioners view strategic partnership as the most important aspect of their roles, Murphy (2010) found that only 15 per cent of HR time is spent on strategic activities.

### CONSIDER THIS…

A reactive approach to HR in an economic downturn usually means that the budget for HR is the first thing to be cut, yet smart business thinking suggests that in recessionary times, firms should, at the very least, maintain activities designed to improve organizational products or processes. How do you think approaches to HR differ in a recession?

## THEORETICAL BASIS OF HRM

Having discussed the history of HRM and the various characteristics associated with it, we must reflect on its theoretical foundations. A number of broad models are seen as particularly influential in understanding the basis of HRM in organizations. These models, which originated in the USA, essentially legitimized HRM as an activity and significantly enhanced its status as an important organizational function. This is based on the belief that HR practices and techniques could not only help organizations meet competitive demands and facilitate organizational restructuring in the wake of economic pressures, but also that HRM could operate in a strategic capacity and enable organizations to achieve greater productivity and performance. We will look at three models in turn.

The 'matching model of HRM' (Fombrun et al., 1984) proposed that an important source of competitive advantage lay in the alignment of HR strategy, employee management activities and corporate strategy. This model is also known as the 'Michigan model of HRM', as it was developed by academics at Michigan Business School, or the 'contingency approach'. It introduced the concept of strategic HRM, where HRM policies are a fundamental consideration in the development of strategic organizational goals and objectives. The model emphasizes the importance of matching the HR strategy to the corporate strategy and having a consistent set of HR practices and techniques that are integrated with each other and the goals of the organization. The model is presented in Figure 1.2 and highlights five key areas for the development of HR practices and techniques:

1 The selection of the most suitable individuals to meet the needs of the business
2 Managing performance to achieve corporate objectives
3 Appraising performance and providing feedback
4 Providing rewards for appropriate performance that achieve specific goals
5 Developing employees to meet the needs of the business.

This model is based on two forms of fit – external fit and internal fit. External fit is sometimes referred to as 'vertical integration' and relates to the need for HR strategy to match the requirements of the organization's business strategy. In internal fit, or 'horizontal integration', HR policies and practices should be complementary and consistent. By this we mean that these policies should reinforce each other to create a coherent approach to the management of employees. Criticisms of this model include the one-way nature of the HR and business strategy relationship, and the nonrecognition of employee interests and behaviour choice. Despite these criticisms, this model forms the basis of the 'best fit' approach to HRM, discussed later in the chapter.

A second dominant model was developed by Beer and his colleagues (Beer et al., 1984) at Harvard University. The 'Harvard model' or map recognizes the influence that various stakeholders have on the development of HR policies (Beer et al., 1984). Stakeholders have a financial interest in the organization and include shareholders, employee groups and the government. Each group has different interests and the model assumes that these interests are legitimate and so HR policies should reflect these interests and be as closely aligned as possible to the business strategy. The model suggested that the effective implementation of HR policies had a number of long-term consequences, one of which was organizational effectiveness. These long-term consequences arise out of the outcomes of specific HRM policy choices which, in turn, are influenced by stakeholder interests and situational factors. Situational factors include aspects of the economic climate, the state of the labour market, the characteristics of the workforce, trade union membership, and legislation. The choice of HRM policies is dependent on reward systems, HR flows, systems of work, and the reward management system. The results or outcomes of these policies will manifest themselves in the level of commitment and competence of employees, the degree of congruence between management and employee interests, and cost-effectiveness.

The main contribution of this model was to highlight the potential benefits of adopting a soft approach to

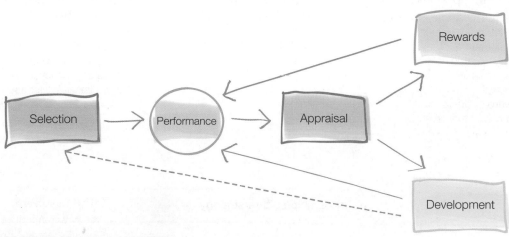

**Figure 1.2** The Michigan model of HRM

*Source:* Fombrun et al., 1984. *Strategic Human Resource Management* by Charles J. Fombrun, Noel M. Tichy and Mary Anne Devanna. Copyright © 1984. Reproduced with permission of John Wiley & Sons, Inc.

HRM. In the UK, David Guest (1989) built on this model to develop a theory of HRM, now known as the 'Guest model', founded on four key policy propositions that, if followed, will combine to increase organizational effectiveness:

1 *Strategic integration:* HR policies must be aligned to the needs of the business strategy, and the various aspects of HRM must be consistent and mutually supportive.
2 *High commitment:* commitment is sought, in that employees are expected to identify closely with the interests of the organization and behave accordingly.
3 *Flexibility:* this involves the ability and willingness of employees to demonstrate flexibility and adaptability to change as business demands change.
4 *High quality:* the quality of management and staff is important in achieving high performance.

Guest believed that these outcomes could be best achieved through appropriate HRM policy choices in the areas of:

● organizational and job design
● change management
● recruitment and selection
● appraisal, training and development
● HR flows through, up and out of the organization
● reward and communication systems.

Management leadership, organizational culture and business strategy influence HRM policies and outcomes and organizational outcomes. Figure 1.3 presents the Guest model.

Ultimately, these models identified the importance of aligning HRM policies with business strategy and gave rise to the strategic HRM approach.

# STRATEGIC HUMAN RESOURCE MANAGEMENT

Given the issues associated with defining HRM, it should not be surprising that there is also a debate around the definition of strategic human resource management (SHRM). It is beyond the scope of this chapter to engage with this debate or to include a detailed description of all the aspects of SHRM, so we will just identify the concept and some of the related issues here (students should see Barney, 1991 for a discussion of the resource-based view of the firm, which is not included here). The developments in the field of HRM identified earlier in this chapter emphasize the contribution HRM can make towards business success and emphasize HRM as an essential component of business strategy (Lengnick-Hall and Lengnick-Hall, 1988; Schuler and Jackson, 2007). The term 'strategic human resource management' has emerged as a direct result of these developments. The

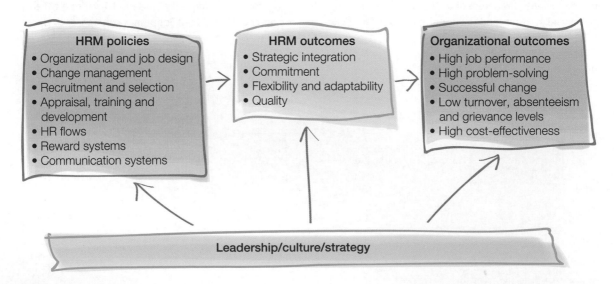

**Figure 1.3** Guest model of HRM
*Source:* Adapted from Guest, 1987. Copyright © 2007, John Wiley and Sons

integration between HRM and business strategy is believed to contribute to the effective management of HR, an improvement in organizational performance, and the success of a particular business (see Holbeche, 1999). It can also help organizations achieve competitive advantage by creating unique HRM systems that cannot be imitated by others (Barney, 1991). When we use the term strategic human resource management, we are referring to the linkage between HRM policies and practices and the strategic objectives of the organization. The emergence of SHRM has identified that the way in which people are managed could be one of, if not *the* most crucial factor in terms of organizational competitiveness (Salaman et al., 2005).

In differentiating between SHRM and HRM, we see that SHRM takes a macro-level approach within the context of organizational performance, whereas HRM operates at the micro-level. The problem alluded to above relates to the differences, if any, between SHRM and HR strategy. In other words, is SHRM a process or an outcome? (See Bamberger and Meshoulam (2000) for a detailed discussion of this issue.) Once again, we are dealing with the question of how we choose which HRM policies and practices will assist in attaining optimal organizational performance. In SHRM, there are three different perspectives as to how SHRM can contribute to organizational success and each are briefly outlined below.

> **Strategic human resource management** – the linkage between HRM policies and practices and the strategic objectives of the organization in creating organizational competitive advantage

## Contingency approach

The contingency approach is the belief that organizational context provides the direction as to which HR policies and practices should be chosen. It has its basis in the Fombrun et al. (1984) matching model discussed earlier. Proponents of this view believe there is no universal answer to the choice of HRM policies and practices; the choice is contingent on the context of the organization and its business strategy. So, each organization can choose a different set of policies and practices, depending on their organization-specific context and strategy. External fit is the key issue (Fombrum et al., 1984; Schuler and Jackson, 1987; Lengnick-Hall and Lengnick-Hall, 1988; Guest, 1997). The adoption of a contingency HRM strategy is associated with optimized organizational performance, where the effectiveness of individual HR practices is contingent on firm-specific strategy (for a more detailed discussion, see

Katou and Budhwar, 2007). A number of influential models have been proposed that aim to identify which mix of HR practices is appropriate in given organizational situations (Miles and Snow, 1978; Schuler and Jackson, 1987; Sisson and Storey, 2000). For example, the work of Schuler and Jackson (1987) suggests that different competitive strategies (Porter, 1985) imply the need for different employee behaviours and thus different sets of HR practices. The most effective way to manage people will therefore depend on issues specific to the organization, such as industry sector, organizational size and economic conditions (see below for more detail on the impact of organizational context on HRM choices). This approach is also referred to as the 'best fit' approach.

## Universalism approach

The universalism approach focuses on the existence of one set of HRM 'best practices' aimed at creating and enhancing high levels of employee commitment and performance; these will result in superior levels of organizational performance, regardless of the context in which the organization operates and the competitive strategy of the firm. Pfeffer's (1998) work was influential in this approach. He identified a set of HRM practices, which result in higher performance. His initial work identified thirteen practices, which he later reduced to seven:

- recruiting the right people
- high wages clearly linked to organizational performance
- employment security
- information sharing
- investment in training and skill development
- self-managed teams and decentralized decision-making
- reduced status differentials.

He identified this high performance system as 'profits through people'. These HR practices are also referred to as 'high involvement' (for example, Guthrie, 2001) and 'high commitment' (Arthur, 1994). A significant amount of research has focused on testing the existence of these practices and many studies have indicated a positive relationship between the adoption of a high performance work system and firm-level performance

## Ryanair's Approach to HRM

Ryanair, a low-cost airline carrier, is ubiquitous in the media almost as much for its approach to managing employees as for its business performance. The low-cost model, which has provided the foundation for its success in terms of business growth, has also been adopted in the way in which the organization views its employees. Michael O'Leary, Ryanair's chief executive, is well known for his anti-union stance. The organization has attempted in the past to dissuade its pilots from joining the pilots' union Balpa. There have been accusations of pensions being frozen and cabin crew staff are usually employed on short-term contracts, through agencies rather than the airline itself, with pay and other benefits, for example holiday entitlement, that are low by industry standards.

Ryanair employees, who already have to buy their own uniform, have to charge their mobile phones before they leave for work to save the firm a few pence per employee, as the company does not believe that using a mobile phone charger at work is acceptable. Newly employed cabin crew earn £900–£1,100 (€1,100–€1,400) a month after tax, slightly above the minimum wage in Ireland. Ryanair offers 'great promotional opportunities with the potential to … earn in excess of £25,000/€30,000 gross per annum after just one year'. Given the anti-union stance on the part of the organization, there is little scope for negotiation here. Nonetheless, the HR director suggests: 'Our wages have to be high enough to attract people. There are no salary scales that you see in legacy airlines, so we don't automatically pay someone who has been here for 25 years more than someone who has been here for two years – and we make no apologies for that.' Even so, new recruits often have to pay up to £2,700 for their training when they join Ryanair.

When O'Leary suggested in 2010 that he was looking for permission from aviation authorities to let Ryanair use just one pilot rather than two on short-haul flights as 'the computer does most of the flying now', a Ryanair pilot wrote a letter in the *Financial Times* outlining his own tongue-in-cheek idea to cut costs: replacing O'Leary with a 'probationary cabin crew member currently earning about €13,200 net a year'. The pilot was then transferred from Provence in France to Lithuania and subsequently resigned.

Unsurprisingly, using the internet at Ryanair's head office is strongly discouraged. This may in part be due to the proliferation of Ryanair websites across the internet, which allow staff to write anonymously about their grievances with the company. While these websites have been dismissed as an 'irrelevance' by the airline's HR director, the level of anger and contempt expressed by staff online has concerned the company so much that it has sought high court injunctions to uncover the identities of employees posting messages on one such site.

In an unprecedented concern for working conditions at Ryanair, the International Transport Workers' Federation urged air travellers to reflect on Ryanair's view of its employees before booking flights with the airline. A source at one pilots' association said:

Essentially, when you look at Ryanair you've got to forget about conventional business models and think about the nature of what a 'cost' is. You've got to stop thinking about employees as people who have rights – they're a resource which flows through the organization and when you're done with them, you get rid of them.

### Questions

1 What type of approach do you believe Ryanair is taking to the management of people in its organization? What specifically is Ryanair doing to cause you to identify that approach?
2 Given that Ryanair is one of the most profitable airlines in the world, do its business results justify its approach to HRM?
3 Identify the possible cost implications to Ryanair of adopting a 'best practice' approach to HRM.

### Sources

Clark, A. (2005) Ryanair's latest cut on costs: staff banned from charging phones, *The Guardian*, 23 April, www.guardian.co.uk/business/2005/apr/23/theairlineindustry. transportintheuk.

Clark, P. (2010) Pilot who crossed O'Leary resigns, *Financial Times*, 6 December, www.ft.com/intl/cms/s/0/8954e9c8-0169-11e0-9b29-00144feab49a.html#axzz1xsLk19o0.

Pope, C. (2012) Comply with me, *The Irish Times*, 28 January, www.irishtimes.com/newspaper/magazine/2012/0128/1224310781008.html.

Ryanair Careers, www.ryanair.com/en/careers/job.

outcomes such as productivity and innovation (for example Appelbaum et al., 2000; Datta et al., 2005; CIPD, 2006; Guthrie et al., 2011).

## Configurational approach

The main criticism identified with the universalism and contingency approaches is their simplistic perspectives on the complex relationship between HRM and organizational strategy. This has led to the development of a third perspective on SHRM. In the configurational or 'bundling' approach, 'the distinction between best practice and contingency models begins to blur' (Becker and Gerhart 1996: 788). Here, the view is that effective combinations or arrangements of HR practices will work by supporting and complementing each other (Huselid and Becker, 1995; Delery and Doty, 1996). MacDuffie (1995) highlights that implicit in the idea of a bundle is that HR practices within a bundle are internally consistent and interrelated.

## IMPACT OF ENVIRONMENT ON HRM CHOICES

Several times we have referred to the choices an organization makes about how it configures its HR function, the roles HR practitioners play, the HR policies it chooses, and the HR practices adopted. These choices all take place in an environmental context, which, according to contingency theory, exerts considerable influence on these choices. At its simplest, the environment is anything outside an organization that can affect an organization's present or future activities. Thus, the environment is context dependent and unique to each organization. Organizations have one of two choices about how they manage their relationships with their environment. The first is reactive, where they wait for changes in the environment and then react to them. This is sometimes termed 'firefighting'. Or, they can predict changes in the environment and plan their responses before these changes happen. Here they are being proactive. This context is normally identified as comprising the internal organizational environment and the external organizational environment and both are discussed below.

### Internal organizational environment

Organizations are effectively all distinctive. Even those that produce similar products for similar market segments are essentially different. This distinctiveness is created by many different factors, including:

- *the size and structure of the organization:* for example small organizations employing small numbers of people tend to have less formal procedures and policies and flatter hierarchical structures than larger organizations
- *the sector the organization operates in:* depending on whether it is a private, public or voluntary body, its approach to HRM may differ
- *organizational life cycle:* the length of time the organization has been operating
- *workforce characteristics:* education, background, demographics and aspirations – knowledge workers, production operatives, customer service personnel
- *financial health of the organization*
- *established 'custom and practice':* in unionized organizations, many practices are well established and are difficult to change
- *organizational culture:* 'the way we do things around here'
- *values and ideology of senior management:* deeply held beliefs and values about the way people should be managed affect issues such as communications, reward systems, management style and equality.

Thus, the internal (micro-) environment has a significant impact on the choices made in relation to HR policies and practices. In conjunction with this, the external (macro-) environment in which the organization operates also has a significant impact on the choices made.

### External environment

An examination of the external environment reveals a number of key factors that need to be considered. These factors are often classified as PESTLE, or more recently STEEPLE – social, technological, economic, environmental, political, legal and ethical. A STEEPLE analysis is a useful tool for understanding the big picture in which the organization operates. It is particularly useful for understanding the risks associated with market growth or decline:

- *Sociocultural trends:* one of the most pressing issues facing countries relates to the changing age profile of the populations across Europe and the USA. The population is ageing at a significant rate and this has caused governments across Europe to increase the pension entitlement age, to sustain labour markets and pension systems. This brings new challenges for both employees and employers as employment legislation ensures that people are not discriminated against in the workplace on the grounds of age. Additionally, we now have a multigenerational workforce, with baby boomers (mid-1940s to early 1960s), generation X (early 1960s to early 1980s) and generation Y (early 1980s to late 1990s). The millennials (2000+) are soon to enter the workforce. Other sociocultural issues include religion, health consciousness and attitudes to careers.
- *Technological changes:* rapid advances in technology have resulted in new ways of working (computerization) and have also created new industry sectors (call centres). New technology can affect how work is organized and managed, and who is recruited to do this work. It can also result in significant changes being required of the workforce. These can mean upskilling and associated training, or can result in people being replaced by technology, resulting in redundancies. The advent of smartphones and mobile broadband have also created a requirement for new HR policies regarding employee wellbeing as a result of being available to work long beyond the normal working day.
- *Economic context:* the impact of the state of the global and national economy on organizations has never been more obvious than during the global financial crisis. Unemployment rates, personal tax rates, global competition, and the demand for goods and services are just a few examples of how the economic environment impacts directly on the management of people in the workplace. For example, when governments increase the personal income tax rate to generate additional government revenue, this directly affects the disposable income available to each consumer. This, in turn, affects the demand for goods and services, which can lead to a reduction in revenue for organizations and ultimately result in closure of the organization and an increase in the number of people unemployed. The rise in competition in the marketplace and the resultant pressure on labour costs have led many organizations to cease trading, or to move production abroad.
- *Environmental concerns:* these include ecological and environmental aspects such as weather, climate and global warming, which may affect particular industries such as tourism, farming and insurance. Growing awareness of the potential impacts of climate change affects how companies operate and the products they offer, for example the car industry and the move to electric cars.
- *Political environment:* government intervention, or lack of it, is often the issue when discussing the political environment. Deregulation of markets, national-level wage bargaining, union recognition, low corporate tax rates, and government investment in infrastructure projects are all examples of how the political environment can impact on organizational choices regarding people management. In the Irish context, centralized wage agreements negotiated by successive governments from the 1970s resulted in a long period of stability, with few working days lost due to industrial conflict.
- *Legal regulatory framework:* a wealth of legislation and regulation exists, which directly impacts on employment at work. The areas covered are wide-ranging and include issues such as grounds for dismissal, terms and conditions of employment, issues related to safety at work, and the requirement for organizations to allow employees leave entitlements. Some legal issues may originate from national governments but others, for example European Union laws or global accounting regulations, may come from the European Parliament or other international bodies such as the International Accounting Standards Board. The differences that arise due to different national interpretations can be problematic for organizations operating in more than one country. One example of the significant financial implications of employment legislation can be seen in a well-publicized case against Walmart in the USA. In 2010, Walmart settled a lawsuit brought by the US Equal Employment Opportunity Commission, paying $11.7 million in back wages and compensatory damages to women who were denied jobs because of their gender. The recent emphasis on the environment and sustainability has also highlighted environmental concerns as an issue for many organizations.
- *Ethical:* there has been an increasing awareness on the part of organizations, consumers and investors about the impact of ethics on many facets of organizational life. Well-known corporate scandals include the Enron scandal in 2001, which eventually led to the bankruptcy of Enron, an American energy company

based in Houston, Texas, and the dissolution of Arthur Andersen, one of the five largest audit and accountancy partnerships in the world ▶ **Chapter 14** ◀. Personal scandals, which affect individual reputations, have resulted in senior executives having to resign. For example, John Browne, the former chief of oil giant BP, resigned in 2007 after he admitted lying to a judge while trying to prevent a British newspaper from exposing details about his personal life. Ethical consumerism and 'socially responsible investment' have created new markets. Allied to this is the focus on the working conditions of those who create the goods we purchase; for example, Nike, Apple and Primark have all come under scrutiny for outsourcing work to companies whose goods are manufactured in sweatshops or using child labour.

Thus, the internal and external environment in which organizations operate have a significant impact on the choices organizations can make in relation to the management of employees.

Do you believe HRM increases organizational performance? Or do high-performing organizations adopt more sophisticated HRM practices?

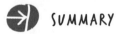 **SUMMARY**

In this chapter we have seen that the term 'human resource management' has increasingly replaced 'personnel management' as the description of choice for the management of people in most organizations. By considering the major characteristics of HRM and looking at who is responsible for HRM, we see where the HRM function should fit into the organizational structure. By understanding the link between business strategy and HRM, we can see how HRM adds value to an organization. The most important thing to recognize is the link between HRM and organizational performance and the extent to which HRM can shape the strategic objectives of the business. Having discussed HRM policies, practices and strategies in general terms, the rest of the book looks at specific aspects of the HR function, beginning with employee resourcing in Chapter 2.

 **CHAPTER REVIEW QUESTIONS**

1 Explain how HRM can contribute to improved organizational performance.
2 Legge (1995) has identified HRM as effectively being 'old wine in a new bottle'. Do you agree with this perspective?
3 Identify five key HRM activities. Describe how each of these would operate in an organization in the manufacturing sector.
4 Explain how devolving HRM practices to line managers has an impact on the role of the HR function.
5 Identify the key characteristics of HRM.
6 Do you believe that there is one set of HR practices that can be used by an organization, regardless of the context the organization operates in?
7 Explain how the seven practices identified by Pfeffer in the best practice approach to HRM can positively impact on organizational performance.
8 Explain the term 'strategic human resource management'.
9 Describe three ways in which the global economic crisis has impacted on the management of people at work.
10 Explain how the projected change in the demographic profile of your country will impact on the HRM strategy in organizations in the retail sector.

 **FURTHER READING**

Beardwell, J. and Claydon, T. (2010) *Human Resource Management: A Contemporary Approach*, 6th edn, Harlow: Financial Times/Prentice Hall.

Boxall, P. and Purcell, J. (2011) *Strategy and Human Resource Management*, 3rd edn, Basingstoke: Palgrave Macmillan.

Cheatle, K. (2001) *Mastering Human Resource Management*, Basingstoke: Palgrave Macmillan.

Sutherland, J. and Canwell, D. (2004) *Key Concepts in Human Resource Management*, Basingstoke: Palgrave Macmillan.

Torrington, D., Hall, L., Taylor, S. and Atkinson, C. (2011) *Human Resource Management*, 8th edn, Harlow: Financial Times/Prentice Hall.

**USEFUL WEBSITES**

**www.cipd.co.uk**
The Chartered Institute of Personnel and Development website is an excellent starting point for anyone interested in HRM. CIPD is based in the UK and Ireland and is the world's largest chartered HR and development professional body.

**www.shrm.org**
The Society for HRM is a US-based association that promotes the role of HR as a profession and provides education, certification and networking to its members.

**www.hrdiv.org**
The HR Division of the Academy of Management (www. aomonline.org) looks at how organizations can improve performance through effective management of their human resources. The British Academy of Management (www.bam.ac.uk) also has an HRM Special Interest Group.

 For extra resources including videos and further skills development guidance go to: www.palgrave. com/business/carbery

# 2 EMPLOYEE RESOURCING:
## THE PLANNING AND RECRUITMENT PHASE

### Marian Crowley-Henry

*By the end of this chapter you will be able to:*

## LEARNING OUTCOMES

- Outline the nature of human resource planning (HRP) and how HRP links with the organization's overall business strategy and its specific recruitment strategy

- Describe the stages in the HRP process and recognize the importance of ongoing HR planning in organizations

- Differentiate recruitment from selection activities within an organization's resourcing strategy

- Distinguish between terms used in recruitment, such as 'job analysis', 'job design', 'person specification' and 'competency frameworks'

- Explain the advantages and disadvantages of different recruitment methods

- Describe ways of generating an 'applicant pool' and attracting candidates

- Identify what a flexible workforce is and how organizations use it

- Explain key legislation in relation to recruitment and the flexible workforce

© ROCCOMONTOYA/ISTOCKPHOTO

*This chapter discusses ...*

# INTRODUCTION

Over recent years, in the context of the global financial crisis and economic recession, the demand for and supply of labour have changed. The labour market has moved from being described as 'tight' to being described as 'loose'. A tight labour market is a seller's or jobseeker's market, where organizations find it more difficult to source employees due to high overall national employment levels. On the other hand, a loose labour market is a buyer's or employer's market, where organizations have a large pool of potential and available employees to hire for positions, since jobs are scarce, with jobseekers competing with many others for the same position.

A loose labour market, with high unemployment rates, has significant effects on the recruitment of staff, which include:

- a significant number of people applying for each vacant position
- wages can be reduced
- many of the people applying for scarce vacant positions are overqualified.

With this context in mind, in this chapter we look at human resource planning (HRP) in organizations and how an organization's human resource plans link in with its overall business strategy and corresponding recruitment strategy. First, we look at the key concepts of the chapter, namely HRP, recruitment and labour flexibility. Next, you will learn more about the different stages in the HRP process. Then we focus on the recruitment aspect. We go on to look at flexible work practices and the different types of labour/workforce flexibility. Finally, we consider legislation in the area of recruitment and flexibility of which you should be aware.

# AN OVERVIEW

As Chapter 1 has underlined, people in organizations fundamentally influence business performance and impact on an organization's competitiveness. It is argued that people create the competitive difference, since other resources, such as technology, finance and raw materials, may be copied, but it is impossible to copy human beings (Pfeffer, 1994, 1995; Gratton, 2000). This makes the HRM function in organizations very important. Although

## SPOTLIGHT ON SKILLS

1  You are aware that a positive employer brand provides an added incentive to candidates to apply for a position in an organization. Prepare a short report for your manager, outlining the reasons, in order of priority, why the organization should focus on developing a positive employer brand. Suggest how your organization could improve its employer brand in practice.

2  You are working for a medium-sized organization in the manufacturing sector, which relies on a full-time permanent workforce. Set out the business case for introducing the flexible firm model. What challenges do you anticipate with implementing the flexible firm model? Outline the advantages and disadvantages of this model to the organization and to existing and new employees.

To help you answer the questions above, visit www.palgrave.com/business/carbery and watch the video of Olga Donnelly talking about recruitment.

many of the traditional HR practices, such as recruitment, selection and performance management, are being devolved and managed to a large extent by line managers (Whittaker and Marchington, 2003), HR professionals are essential resources in an organization, as they hold specialist knowledge on the effective management of human resources.

It is fundamental that organizations consider and develop strategies concerning their present and future staffing requirements, with regards to the specific jobs and skills that are and will be required in their organizations. This is called human resource planning (HRP). Effective HRP is essential in order to avoid skills and/or staff shortages (or surpluses) in the organization.

It ensures that the people employed in the organization have the skills the organization needs to be competitive. If the relevant skills are not available in-house, the organization may decide to train existing employees to develop those skills, or to recruit people with those necessary skills. The organization needs to consider how many people with different skills will be required for its different departments. For instance, if the organization determines to use more technology in coordinating its activities, it needs to ensure that sufficient numbers of staff are familiar with the particular technology, and may train existing staff members or recruit new employees who are already skilled in the use of that particular technology. Likewise, if an organization decides to strengthen its customer service focus, it must determine if it can train its existing staff up to the required customer service level, or if it needs to recruit new employees who already have customer service skills. In today's organizations, HR planning is increasingly looking at aligning HR policies and practices, such as recruitment, with the strategic aims of the organization.

However, the extent to which organizations can adequately plan for the future is contentious, since the unexpected may occur which can render plans useless. For instance, the extent of the global economic recession that started in 2007/08 was a shock for many organizations, forcing them to readjust their plans, with many having to postpone or downsize their expansion plans. Therefore, while planning is essential for organizations to prepare for the future, there must be flexibility inherent in the plans, should environmental conditions change that force the organization to reconsider its plans. Many organizations have contingency, or 'what if' backup plans that consider a variety of scenarios that may present themselves over time. However, organizations cannot spend all their time planning for all eventualities, but must make do with the most probable scenarios.

The **recruitment** process commences with HRP. Recruitment needs should be determined in line with the organization's current and proposed future business strategy focus in mind. In other words, the demand and supply of people with relevant skills in particular areas across the organization should match the organization's strategic intent. In keeping with the examples above, if an organization plans to use more technology, or strengthen

> **Human resource planning (HRP)** – the ongoing consideration of staffing requirements – now and in the future – with regards to the specific jobs and skills that are and will be required in the organization. It results in the development of specific HR strategies to achieve organization-specific staffing requirements
>
> **Recruitment** – a process whereby the organization sources or attracts people to apply for a position in the organization

its customer service offering and focus on customer service as a primary differentiator to competitors, the organization's recruitment strategy should reflect this, in the recruitment of people with experience of that technology, or the recruitment of qualified customer service staff.

Other practices, such as training staff in customer service innovations, also need to be aligned with the organization's overall strategy. For instance, if an organization plans to strengthen its technology knowledge, or focus on customer service, this needs to be reflected in its training plans, where existing staff are trained in the new technology, or customer service respectively ▶ **Chapter 9** ◀. The strategic focus should also be measured during performance appraisals so that once the training has been completed, employee performance in working with the technology or in customer service is assessed. In aligning the focus on new technology or customer service with the organization's performance management ▶ **Chapter 7** ◀, employees would be encouraged to be competent with the technology or in customer service, and the strategic importance of the use of new technology or superior customer service would be instilled in the mindset of the employees. These examples show how different HRM strategies – recruitment, training and performance management – need to be aligned with the organization's overall strategy.

In determining the organization's recruitment needs, the strategic options available, such as having a flexible workforce, also need to be considered. The organization may decide to recruit people on a full-time permanent basis, or on a part-time or temporary basis. With a loose labour market, organizations may opt for more part-time or temporary staff, while in a tighter labour market, the organization may be more inclined to offer permanent employment contracts in order to entice people to join the organization. For instance, during the global economic recession (2008–12), the public sector in many EU countries experienced employment control restrictions, limiting the recruitment of permanent staff. Such externalities, sometimes beyond the organization's control as in the case of the public sector hiring embargo (a freeze on hiring permanent employees in the public sector), influence the types of workers who are recruited (full time, permanent, temporary, fixed-term contract, or part time). We will be looking at labour flexibility and flexible work practices later on in the chapter. Thus, the macro-context, exemplified in the example regarding the public sector hiring embargo, also needs to be considered in HRP.

We will return to and elaborate on the concepts of HRP, recruitment and labour flexibility later. Next, we examine the HRP process in more detail.

# HUMAN RESOURCE PLANNING

You have learned that HRP is the continual analysis of staffing requirements, now and in the future, to ensure that the correct number of employees with the required skills are employed. HRP results in the development of specific HR strategies to achieve organization-specific staffing requirements. There are five key stages in the HRP process (Figure 2.1), which are described in detail below. These require HR planner(s) to:

1 analyse the current situation
2 forecast future staffing demand/supply
3 develop plans aligning current situation with future needs
4 implement plans
5 control, review and adjust plans (if needed).

As Figure 2.1 depicts, these five stages form a continuous process. This means that HRP is a cyclical process, with organizations engaging in HRP on an ongoing basis. We will look at each of these stages in more detail next.

## 1 Analyse the current situation

The first phase in HRP is to analyse the current situation with regards to the human resources in the organization.

This includes taking stock of the organization's existing employees and their details, such as name, length of service, organizational role, skill set, qualifications, training received, and performance reviews. This information, normally found in existing HR records, is of strategic relevance, in that it provides the organization with a wealth of data regarding the existing competencies and future potential of current employees. It informs the organization about the particular skills, educational qualifications and experience of the current workforce, which gives the organization an idea of where those employees could be deployed, that is, in which department(s) or area(s) they could work, in the future. In assessing the current situation concerning staffing, a job analysis is often undertaken. This is discussed in more detail later in the chapter.

## 2 Forecast future staffing demand/supply

Forecasting future staffing demand/supply is necessary, in that it forces HR planners to consider the future strategic orientation of the organization, and to identify the skills that will be required to fulfil that strategic direction, in what numbers, compared to the existing skills in the organization. From the organization's perspective, forecasting future *demand* for labour combines elements of subjective judgement (from the organization's management) and quantitative modelling, while forecasting future *supply* of labour involves an analysis of the internal and external labour markets. The internal labour market encompasses all those currently working for the organization. In analysing the internal labour market, factors such as retirement, staff turnover and promotion within the organization are considered. A clear outlook on these aspects should pinpoint potential areas where there could be skill shortages in the organization at

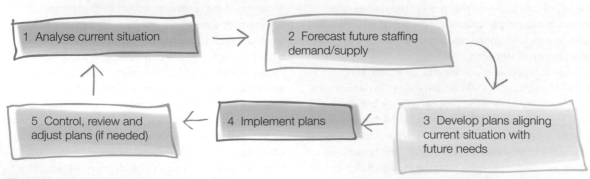

**Figure 2.1** Stages in the HRP process

a future point in time. With regards to the external labour market, the outlook for labour force participation rates – the number of working age people available in a country or region and unemployment trends – can be considered. This helps organizations plan where they could be able to access new recruits in the future.

As you can imagine, this forecasting phase is difficult in practice, as there is always a risk involved in forecasting demand and supply: we cannot be 100 per cent sure what the future holds. The global financial crisis and economic downturn is one example of the challenge forecasting presents in reality. Had organizations globally forecast the financial crisis and economic downturn and planned accordingly, the mass closures and layoffs encountered by many organizations may not have materialized, or not to the same extent.

## 3 Develop plans aligning current situation with future needs

The third phase in HRP involves the development of plans to balance existing staff numbers and abilities with future requirements. This results in the formulation of plans concerning the types of people who may need to be recruited for particular jobs over time. The previous two stages involved identifying how HR needs are determined. This stage seeks to clearly lay out where skill shortages may be and how they need to be addressed in the organization's recruitment strategies, as well as showing where surpluses in skills may come about in the future.

In this context, eventualities are planned for with strategies such as the training (upskilling), redeployment or downsizing of existing staff that may be in the skills' surpluses area, succession planning to replace staff retiring or moving to other areas, and retention strategies to attempt to retain key skills in the organization where skills shortages exist. It is in this phase that the organization also considers its strategic approach to a flexible workforce, with regards to recruiting for full-time, part-time or temporary positions in the organization.

**Resourcing** – a process where people are identified and deployed to undertake work within an organization

## 4 Implement plans

The fourth stage is the implementation stage, where the plans decided in stage 3 are put into action. These plans might concern recruitment, training or reorganization.

For the purposes of this chapter and the focus on recruitment, it is in this phase that the recruitment activities are implemented; for instance, when the job advertisement is created and advertised.

## 5 Control, review and adjust plans (if needed)

The final stage is where the implemented plans are reviewed and reconsidered with regards to their success, for instance in recruiting for particular positions in the organization. It is important to monitor how plans have worked out, to capture learning from previous activities. In this stage, it may be necessary to adjust the formulated plans or to reprioritize plans depending on how the plans are being fulfilled. For instance, if plans to recruit graduates for a particular department in the organization do not prove fruitful, the organization may be forced to reconsider these plans and potentially open the recruitment up to non-graduates or retrain existing employees.

Thus, the five stages are linked in the HRP process. Each stage is equally important in its own right. You can see the necessity for the HRP process to be aligned with the organization's overall strategy, so that the right jobs and people are hired and are in the right place, at the right time. Next, we take a closer look at what is involved in the recruitment process.

## RECRUITMENT

Hiring people for deployment to positions within the organization is a fundamental HRM practice. Resourcing consists of two discrete components: recruitment and selection ▶ **Chapter 3** ◀. In this chapter we focus on the recruitment aspect, from HRP to specific recruitment methods. In Chapter 3 you will learn more about the selection aspect of resourcing, where the focus is on finding the most suitable person for the job in question from a pool of candidates.

Recruitment includes searching for and obtaining job candidates in sufficient numbers and quality, so that they feed the selection process. Once the pool of candidates has been collected, it is over to the selection process to filter these candidates further, shortlisting them until agreement is reached on which candidate(s) should be offered the position(s). The selection process is where the organization evaluates and decides who to employ for specific jobs/positions within the organization. It is important to note that recruitment and selection are discrete practices, and both need to operate effectively if the organization is to make optimal staffing decisions. The Consider This … feature below explains why.

## CONSIDER THIS …

An organization may have an excellent system for evaluating and selecting candidates, but if the pool of candidates that come through the recruitment process is insufficient or of a low standard/quality, the resultant choice of candidate will not be optimum. Similarly, an organization may have an excellent recruitment system that results in a pool of highly skilled and competent candidates for an open position in the organization. However, if the selection process fails to undertake, for instance, due diligence in checking references and academic qualifications, the resultant choice of candidate will not be optimum. Therefore, while recruitment and selection are discrete practices within an organization, they are linked and depend on each other to ensure the best person is hired for the job in question.

HR professionals often work in cooperation with line managers in the relevant department(s) that are looking to employ someone new, in order to determine the most appropriate method of recruitment and selection. The aim is to attract the right numbers and types of candidates to apply for the vacant position. Line managers work with HR professionals in specifying the details regarding the position available and the type of skills and competencies required by the particular department to fulfil that position. The input from line managers in the recruitment and selection process is essential, since line managers know and understand the tasks involved in the role. Equally, they need to investigate if the new recruit will fit in with the rest of the team as regards their skills and experience. Line managers are also involved in the selection process, where they usually form part of the interview panel and ask job-specific technical questions.

For example, for an engineering position, where the HR manager may not have the technical knowledge regarding the specific skills required for the job, the engineering manager would play a key role in formulating the job description and person specification, as well as ultimately selecting the candidate for the position.

## THE RECRUITMENT PROCESS

The recruitment process begins with a job analysis. Different jobs have different tasks associated with them, and conducting a job analysis allows you to gain detailed information about particular jobs, which is then used for recruitment, selection, performance management, reward management/compensation and training purposes in the organization. For instance, a job analysis for a teacher could identify tasks such as class preparation, communication with pupils and parents, attending relevant training activities to update skills, setting tests and marking work. It could also identify the need for the teacher to be qualified from an accredited institution and competent in the respective subject, to perhaps have previous teaching experience, to be a good presenter and communicator, to be an impartial marker and so on. This detailed information from the job analysis provides the basis for determining the recruitment and selection criteria, as well as the performance management, rewarding and training of the recruit. For instance, in our teacher example, they will be appraised in line with how well they fulfil the tasks required for the position. Depending on the experience and ability of the individual, their rewards and compensation will be determined accordingly ▶ **Chapter 8** ◀. The training needs of the teacher will also be determined from the job analysis, where it will be identified if there are particular areas where the teacher should receive training and development in order to improve job performance ▶ **Chapter 9** ◀.

When the organization knows what each job entails with regard to the tasks and skills required to complete that particular job, then the organization can plan how to staff that job accordingly. For instance, the organization could decide to train existing staff members to do the job, redeploy existing staff members from other departments where they are currently doing similar jobs, or recruit someone new to do the job. The decision

**Job analysis** – the process used to gather detailed information about the various tasks and responsibilities involved in a position. Through this process, the knowledge, skills, abilities, attitudes and behaviours associated with successful performance in the role are also identified

depends on the skills available in the organization, the timing – if there is time to train someone in the organization to do the job or if there is a need for someone with the relevant skills to do the job as soon as possible – and the strategic relevance of the post – if the job is considered as core and long term, or if it is deemed more temporary in nature.

You could consider the job analysis to be like an audit of a job, detailing the different tasks the job entails as well as the particular skills and competencies needed to do that job. A job analysis results in both a **job description** and a **person specification**. In other words, after conducting a job analysis, you are in a position to write a detailed job description and person specification for the role, which form the basis for the job advert.

The job description is a detailed inventory of what a particular job entails. In the earlier example, this would include listing the duties a teacher would be required to fulfil, such as preparing classes and class plans, organizing parent–teacher meetings, setting and marking assessments and so on. The person specification addresses the kind of person the organization needs to do that particular job. In our teacher example, this would include details such as the educational qualifications

**Job description** – the detailed breakdown of the purpose and various tasks and responsibilities involved in a particular job

**Person specification** – specifies the type of person needed to do a particular job. It essentially translates the job description into human terms

and/or number of years' experience a candidate should have in order to be able to perform the job. The person specification, therefore, lays out the qualifications, knowledge, skills, personal attributes and experience required of an individual in order to match the particular job, some of which may be essential and others more desirable.

Many organizations search for the ideal candidate when they are writing the person specification, but it is important to differentiate between qualities that are essential for the role and those that are desirable. Focusing on too many 'nice to have' qualities is likely to limit the number of people who apply for a role. For instance, a person specification criterion for a particular position may be that it is essential to have an honours degree in HRM. In other words, anyone without an HRM honours degree would only be considered if the number of applicants in total was disappointingly low, but the organization needed to fill the position immediately, that is, is unable to wait for more qualified candidates to apply. The person specification should be developed from and accurately match the job description. Here, we provide an example of a job description and a person specification.

**Job Description:** Student Union Senior Receptionist

**Post title:** Senior Receptionist
**Department:** Student Union Centre
**Responsible to:** Student Union General Manager

**Purpose of the position**
- To provide and coordinate high-quality reception service.
- To provide general administrative support to Student Union officers.

**Principal duties and responsibilities**
- Organize reception duty on a rota basis and deal with general queries from students and the general public both in person, by telephone and via email.
- Direct the Union's customers to appropriate services in the SU.
- Maintain good presentation of reception and front of house.
- Deal with incoming and outgoing post, ensuring it is correctly franked and despatched.
- Sell and record ID card and SU ticket sales.
- Assist with the dissemination of information to students about Union services, events and activities.
- Work with Union departments to maintain a wide range of up-to-date, relevant information such as leaflets, booklets, posters and forms.
- Deal with poster stamping, flyer passes and any other general administrative tasks associated with counter duty.
- Use the public address system for messages to members and staff.
- Coordinate the booking of the Student Union facilities for meetings for internal and external customers.

→

**Other duties and responsibilities**
- Open and close the Reception area as and when required.
- Work in a way that reflects the values of the organization as demonstrated in the SU Constitution, policies and strategic plan.
- Carry out duties with due regard to the SU Equal Opportunities Policy at all times.
- Act in accordance with the personnel policies and procedures as approved by the Staff Committee of the Union including Health and Safety Procedures and Staff Protocol Agreement.
- Act always in accordance with the financial regulations of the Union as outlined in the Constitution and detailed in the Financial Procedures Manual.
- Undertake such other duties as may reasonably be expected, given the incumbent's qualifications, experience and grade.
- Contribute to the positive image of the Union with students, university and community.
- Attend meetings and provide reports as and when required by the Union.
- Carry out the above duties at other sites of the university as necessary.

**Person Specification:** Student Union Senior Receptionist

| | Essential (E) or desirable (D) requirements |
|---|---|
| Qualifications that demonstrate proven numeracy, (English) literacy and keyboard skills | D |
| IT, typing or word processing qualifications | D |
| Experience of office activity, which must include receptionists' duties as well as clerical work | E |
| **Skills, Knowledge and Ability** | |
| Ability to represent the Students' Union to staff and external contacts in a professional manner | E |
| Ability to handle difficult situations with tact, discretion and assertiveness | E |
| Ability to handle and accurately account for cash and resources | E |
| Ability to communicate, both in writing and orally, at all levels | E |
| Ability to undertake basic research tasks | D |
| **Personal Attributes and Attitudes** | |
| Has a strong customer focus | E |
| Ability to work flexible hours | E |
| Trustworthy, reliable, approachable and flexible, with good attention to detail and demonstrable integrity | E |
| Ability to remain calm under pressure | E |
| Demonstrates a positive approach to best practice and exceeding customer expectations | E |
| Excellent customer care skills | E |

# BUILDING YOUR SKILLS

Think about a job you are considering applying for after your studies and imagine that you are the line manager with responsibility for managing you, the new recruit. What would you list as essential and desirable in the job description and person specification for that particular position? Justify why you have listed certain tasks in the job description and certain skills/experience in the person specification.

As well as, or instead of, the person specification criteria, many organizations formulate competency-based criteria to filter candidates for particular jobs ▸ **Chapter 3** ◂. The Chartered Institute of Personnel and Development (CIPD, 2012b) defines competencies as: 'the behaviours that individuals must have, or must acquire, to perform effectively at work – that is, the ... focus [is] on the personal attributes or inputs of the individual'. Competency frameworks are developed for different positions in the organization. Competencies can include soft skills such as communication skills, presentation skills, leadership skills and collaborative skills (teamwork). Whether certain competencies are desirable or essential will depend on the particular job; hence the importance of conducting a job analysis. For instance, if we return to the teacher example, the essential competencies for a Montessori teacher may differ from those for a secondary school teacher. Competencies such as flexibility and use of own initiative may be prioritized more for Montessori and junior school teachers, whereas the competencies for secondary school teachers, who are following a prescribed curriculum leading to state examinations, may include more of a focus on communication skills. The detailed inventory of the position and all it entails results in being able to establish the job description, person specification and the competencies, both essential and desirable, for that position. These are also often included in job adverts.

Review the job advertisement section of a national newspaper. Note how many adverts include person specification details, competency frameworks or both. Are similar person specification criteria used for similar positions? Or across positions? What about competencies? Why do you think this is the case?

We now have all the information we need to begin recruiting for the position. Once a position has been identified as being vacant, the organization must decide on the method(s) to use in recruiting for that position. Different authors suggest different methods of recruitment. However, we can identify four broad methods: internal, external, online and overseas/international, each of which are discussed below. You should note that the organization can use one or more (even all) of these methods in any one recruitment process. The choice depends on the amount of time and financial resources the organization has at its disposal for the purpose of recruitment. These four methods can also be collapsed into two main methods: internal and external recruitment, with online applicable to both and overseas/international applicable to external recruitment only.

## Internal recruitment

**Internal recruitment** is a recruitment method where an open job position is advertised internally within the organization and current employees can apply for the position. This is also called the 'make' approach to recruitment, since it involves hiring someone to a new role from within the same organization.

There are many advantages of internal recruitment. It is cost-effective since the job vacancy advert can be posted on the intranet site (a form of e-recruitment), asking interested candidates to apply directly, rather than taking out expensive print media space. Internal recruitment advocates staff development and internal mobility in the organization. Existing employees gain the opportunity to move vertically to more senior positions through promotions, or laterally to enable employees to experience different roles in different departments. This opportunity to move internally can motivate existing staff to work towards achieving other positions in the organization. Loyal and hard-working employees are therefore rewarded. Internal recruitment is also advantageous for the organization in that the 'new recruit' is actually an existing employee, who is already familiar with the organizational culture, products and processes. This increases the probability of staff retention in the organization, with existing employees motivated by their potential to move to other positions in the organization. It also reduces the probability of early staff turnover of 'new recruits', since the recruits are from the internal labour market and are already familiar with and comfortable in the organization.

However, there are some disadvantages of internal recruitment. The primary disadvantage is that it limits the pool of applicants to those already employed within the organization. These employees may not have the skills and competencies required to perform the job to the highest standard. It also means that an existing employee, deployed through internal recruitment to another position, leaves a skills gap in the position they vacate, which may be more difficult to fill. Another key issue is that it can actually restrict innovation and diversity of mindset in the organization. This is because you are hiring people who are familiar with the organization and indoctrinated in its culture, and so are potentially unable to present novel approaches to performing in the position. The cost of training or upskilling an existing employee to fill a vacancy is a further disadvantage to choosing internal recruitment. While internal employees may feel motivated and empowered to apply for a new position in the organization via internal recruitment, these same employees may feel demotivated if their application is unsuccessful. This could cause a reduction in job satisfaction and ultimately a reduction in organizational productivity.

**Internal recruitment** – a vacancy is advertised to potential candidates from within the existing employee base in the organization

## Working Abroad Expo in Ireland

Unprecedented numbers queued for hours to attend the Working Abroad Expo recruitment fairs in Dublin and Cork (Ireland) in March 2012. Thousands of visitors attended the fairs, along with their partners and children, in search of advice and, more importantly, jobs overseas.

Given the employment problems in Ireland, with over 440,000 people unemployed in a population of approximately 4 million, the Working Abroad Expo job fairs were considered by many as a rare sign of optimism that their skills and qualifications were still required globally, even if this was not the case in Ireland at present. Many wishing to attend the events had to be turned away, with advance tickets sold out.

In the Dublin Expo, the organizers charged €10 admission in an attempt to control the vast numbers of people attending, and to filter attendees to only those really interested in work overseas. Nonetheless, given the large attendance numbers, the event was described in some quarters as being more an emigration expo than a jobs expo. SGMC, the organizers, said it was the company's biggest ever event. Over 80 exhibitors from around the world, such as Canada, Dubai, Australia and New Zealand, as well as from other European countries, had stands. They were capitalizing on the recent impact of the global economic crisis in Ireland by marketing the job vacancies in their respective companies/countries. Advice and jobs were on offer to those interested in emigrating, and living and working in the various countries. Companies were recruiting for positions across

sectors, including farming, mining, construction and healthcare; and across skills, including carpenters, fitters, machine operators, welders, mechanics and electricians. Large multinationals also exhibited, including Primark, PayPal, eBay and Hewlett-Packard.

Participants were advised to bring their CVs with them to give directly to potential/prospective employers at the Expo. The exhibitors were looking to fill specific job vacancies and conducted interviews on the day at the event. Statistics given suggest that over 2,000 interviews were held at the Dublin event alone, with over 250 job offers made by the prospective employers/agencies attending/exhibiting at that event.

According to the organizers, feedback from the exhibitors was that they were impressed with the people they met at the events and how they were able to recruit for specific positions in their organizations/countries and fill the vacancies/skills gaps in their organizations/countries. However, the lack of foreign language proficiency emerged as a stumbling block for the general Irish attendees seeking jobs. While Scandinavian exhibitors stressed that there were plenty of jobs available in their countries, the lack of attendees with the language competency required to work in those countries rendered many unsuitable for positions on offer there, or for any of the organizations requiring a specific competency/proficiency in an international language. Nevertheless, for the hundreds of attendees leaving the Working Abroad Expo with job offers, it was clearly well worth the queuing.

### Questions

1 What method(s) of recruitment can you identify in the case study?
2 What advantages to this approach can you identify? What disadvantages to this approach can you identify?

### Sources

Baker, N. (2012) Careers fair 'more like an emigration expo', *Irish Examiner*, 3 March, www.irishexaminer.com/ireland/careers-fair-more-like-an-emigration-expo-185873.html.

Independent.ie reporters (2012) Up to 3,000 job seekers queue for working Abroad Expo in Cork, *Irish Independent*, 7 March, www.independent.ie/national-news/up-to-3000-job-seekers-queue-for-working-abroad-expo-in-cork-3042828.html.

Newstalk (2012a) Cork Work Abroad Expo extends hours until 9pm today, Newstalk.ie, 7 March, www.newstalk.ie/2012/news/cork-work-abroad-expo-extends-hours-until-9pm-today/.

Newstalk (2012b) Over 12,000 attend Dublin Working Abroad Expo, Newstalk.ie, 5 March, www.newstalk.ie/2012/news/over-12000-attend-dublin-working-abroad-expo/.

O'Brien, T. (2012) Fianna Fáil talks of its hopes for Ireland but nearby jobseekers look for a way out, *The Irish Times*, 5 March, www.irishtimes.com/newspaper/ireland/2012/0305/1224312795424.html.

O'Halloran, G. (2012) Thousands attend Working Abroad Expo in Cork City, *The Irish Times*, 8 March, www.irishtimes.com/newspaper/finance/2012/0308/1224313004039.html.

Riegel, R. (2012) 'There is no future here: we want a better life for our children', *Irish Independent*, 8 March, www.independent.ie/national-news/there-is-no-future-here-we-want-a-better-life-for-our-children-3043822.html.

Internal recruitment is considered good practice, as it allows internal candidates the opportunity for lateral and vertical movement through the organization ▶ **Chapter 10** ◀. In general, however, it is often the case that organizations use a combination of internal and external methods, as this is likely to produce the best possible candidates. We look at external recruitment in more detail next.

## External recruitment

The second method of recruitment is external recruitment, also known as the 'buy' approach to recruitment. External and internal recruitment mirror each other in terms of advantages or disadvantages. The positive elements of one approach are the drawbacks of the other, and vice versa. External recruitment reaches a wider target audience, directly attracting potential candidates with the required person specification or competencies needed for the job. The training costs should therefore be reduced as the external recruit should already have the qualifications and skills required for the position. The external recruit should bring fresh blood, new skills and new ideas to the organization, which should improve organizational performance. This approach is also in keeping with promoting diversity in the organization. External recruitment can, if conducted well, improve the image of the organization in the wider community, as it presents the organization in a positive light by bringing employment to the local community.

There are a number of disadvantages, however, which involve the costs associated with external recruitment. There are the costs of placing job adverts in a variety of media outlets, such as newspapers or trade magazines. Another expensive method involves the use of recruitment consultancies to attract candidates. Other costs include those of acculturating the external recruit to the organization's distinctive culture, products and processes. While every attempt will have been made to select the right candidate, the external recruit is, to all intents and purposes, unknown by the organization and may turn out to be unsuitable for the position and/or the organization. Recruiting externally can also demotivate existing employees who had applied for and hoped to get the new position. This demotivation and dissatisfaction can ultimately lead to problems with employee retention and increase employee turnover ▶ **Chapter 4** ◀.

**External recruitment** – a vacancy is advertised to potential candidates outside the existing employee base in the organization

Many organizations employ a less expensive form of external recruitment by using what are termed 'internal employee referrals' when seeking to fill a vacancy. Employee referral schemes work by inviting existing employees to recommend someone from outside the organization for the vacant position. This is a cost-effective means of external recruitment as there are no external advertising costs involved. The internal employee receives monetary compensation for their recommendation if the proposed candidate proves successful and remains in the organization for at least a minimum period of time (often six months). Additionally, the organization is more confident that the new recruit is suitable as the internal employee has recommended that person based on their prior experience of working with that person. The employee who made the recommendation will have a vested interest in ensuring their proposed candidate fits the organization, as the success or failure of that recruit could ultimately affect the employee's monetary compensation for the recommendation and their reputation for reliability. It could also be expected that the proposed candidate will fit in with the organization's culture or way of doing business, as people usually associate with others of the same beliefs/values and so are more likely to recommend someone who will fit the organization.

Let us consider the following scenario. You have worked for the previous two summers as a promotions assistant in a marketing promotions and events management company. While doing this job, you frequently meet employees from different marketing companies, sometimes to work on the same event for a client. If a vacancy for a promotions executive arises in one of those other companies, an internal employee may recommend you as a potential candidate for the position. The internal employee is confident of your abilities, having seen your work in the past. You may be more interested in the position since you know that internal employee and have found out from them about the company and what it is like to work for it.

However, quality employee referrals may not be possible across all organizations. Smaller organizations, with fewer employees to begin with, may not have the social network capacity to recommend people for a vacant position. In tight labour markets, where skills shortages exist, many organizations make use of employees' social networks in order to attract talent. The IT and telecommunications industries have widely used and continue to use the employee referral scheme to attract talented specialists to their organizations, in a win–win–win deal for the organization, the successful referral and the employee who made the referral.

## Formal and informal methods

Both formal and informal methods are used when recruiting. Formal methods are those where the vacancy is officially advertised through a variety of media. Informal methods are those where candidates find out informally about a potential vacancy and apply for it. For instance, with external recruitment, the candidate can be made aware of the vacancy through word of mouth, employee referrals, or informal social media channels such as Facebook or LinkedIn. Candidates may also send spontaneous (unsolicited) applications. Formal methods, on the other hand, include advertising the position through different media (print, radio, TV, corporate website, recruitment-specific websites, social media) and/or via employment/recruitment agencies. It would be usual for organizations to use a variety of such methods in their recruitment campaign in order to attract a wide pool of applicants from different sources.

Interestingly, research suggests that informal recruits often perform better than formal recruits (Barber, 1998). This could be because informal recruits take a more proactive approach to seeking to fill the vacancy because they are interested in the position and/or the organization. Formal recruits, on the other hand, wait until there is a position officially advertised before applying. They are more reactive, in that they react to the specific job advert before making their application. However, informal recruitment suggests a lack of consideration towards developing a diverse workforce, because it often brings in recruits who are similar in background and experience to the employees already in the organization.

CONSIDER THIS ...

What are the advantages and disadvantages of the different formal methods of recruitment (print, radio, TV, online advertising and recruitment agencies)? Have you experienced any of these formal recruitment methods in your search for a job? Shortlist three or four criteria that could be used by organizations in determining which formal method(s) to choose.

## Graduate recruitment

Graduate recruitment programmes take place when organizations visit the campuses of universities and other third-level institutions in order to attract graduates to apply to and join their organizations. In this way, the organizations go directly to the source for their recruitment purposes. It is categorized under external recruitment as it is effectively seeking to recruit someone from outside the organization. Alternatively, graduate recruitment fairs take place in a neutral venue where several employing organizations exhibit and present their business to graduates who may become recruits in the future.

Graduate recruitment is advantageous for an organization in that it allows that organization to cost-effectively target qualified graduates to apply for open positions in the organization. By going directly to graduates in a certain discipline, such as business or IT, organizations seeking to fill positions in those areas have saved time, money and effort in seeking quality candidates for specific roles where such disciplines are essential. Graduate recruitment is also advantageous for the potential recruits/graduates as it allows them to familiarize themselves with different companies and the types of jobs on offer.

## Recruitment consultancies

Some organizations avail themselves of recruitment consultancies, which manage the recruitment process for them. The outsourcing of recruitment to specialist agencies frees up HR resources in the organization and allows them to focus on other matters. For small organizations that may not have an HR department, the use of recruitment consultancies may be the most suitable approach. However, recruitment consultants are used by both large and small organizations.

For specialized positions, recruitment consultancies may have a database of potential candidates on file, which narrows the recruitment search – thereby saving time. This is particularly true in the IT and pharmaceutical industries or for accountancy and legal professionals, where the skills required are specific and possibly difficult to find. For senior-level recruits or where skills are in short supply, some recruitment consultancies offer an executive search or 'headhunting' facility, whereby they directly contact individuals with the skills a client organization is looking for. They do not have that individual's details on file, and the individual is not necessarily looking for a job, but the headhunter attempts to entice the skilled individual – with offers of better compensation and terms of employment – to at least apply for the open position in the client organization.

Government agencies also provide a recruitment service, but these tend to be for lower level jobs. Such agencies have a comprehensive database of jobseekers and their skills/experience. They can then serve as the mediator between organizations seeking someone to work for them and the jobseeker. These public agencies offer back to work schemes to promote the employment of jobseekers.

## E-recruitment

The third method of recruitment is e-recruitment. This method can be used alongside both internal and external recruitment, to create the most comprehensive recruitment process. Basically, e-recruitment is the use of the internet to aid in the attraction of candidates to apply for vacancies in the organization. Job adverts can be placed on the organization's intranet page (internal recruitment) or webpage (external recruitment), with details of the job description and person specification, and timelines for receipt of applications. The vacancy could also be posted on recruitment websites or through commercial online e-recruitment bodies that act as consultants and place the relevant job vacancy notice on different online websites for their clients for a fee.

The main advantage of e-recruitment is the size of the target market that can be reached, at a relatively low cost when compared to other external recruitment methods such as print advertisements. The speed of response also tends to be much faster through e-recruitment. CV filtering software is available that can help in reducing the numbers of initial applicants to a manageable list for selection purposes. Quite often, applicants need to complete an online application form with standardized questions and information requests. The software can then filter the applications using specific keywords based on different criteria, depending on the requirements of the client hiring organization. This can save time in filtering down candidates that apply for the position to those most suitable for the position.

The main disadvantage with e-recruitment, however, is the sheer number of potential applicants that result from an online job advert, which can then be difficult to filter and shortlist. Given the openness of e-recruitment, it can attract large numbers of underqualified candidates. There are also issues with security and data protection when applying for positions advertised online. Organizations

**E-recruitment** – a vacancy is advertised to potential candidates via the internet. It can target internal and/or external recruits

**International recruitment** – a vacancy is advertised to potential candidates who are currently residing overseas

cannot be sure that the information provided online by candidates is completely honest, but can only take that information at face value. This can result in a poor quality shortlist of candidates. Nonetheless, the growth of e-recruitment has been phenomenal, and is not expected to abate in the near future.

## Overseas/international recruitment

The fourth and final recruitment method to be considered in the search for potential candidates is overseas or international recruitment. This method of recruitment is used particularly where the vacant position requires skills and/or competencies that are not readily available in the national context, so organizations resort to overseas recruitment in order to widen the pool of potential applicants.

The main advantage of overseas recruitment is that it increases the probability of finding the specific candidates required for the position. For instance, in the IT sector, organizations may look to India with its large number of IT graduates for IT skills that may be in scarce supply among graduates in their own country. Organizations could attend graduate recruitment fairs in India in order to find candidates with the IT skills required. Earlier, HRM in the News presented an example of overseas recruitment with international organizations attending the Working Abroad Expo in Ireland in 2012 in order to attract educated and experienced applications for a variety of positions outside Ireland. International recruitment is often used for senior executive positions, where the best person for the job is sought, regardless of nationality. You can also see this in the international football arena, where managers of the national team can be recruited from different countries, provided their track record is positive.

However, the costs associated with overseas recruitment can be very high. If the candidates are shortlisted, the organization will have to cover transport costs for interviews and relocation. There may also be an issue with immigration laws and work visas, which the HR department would need to work through and adhere to.

Table 2.1 summarizes the main advantages and disadvantages of these four recruitment methods. Organizations should keep track of the recruitment method(s) they use and their respective effectiveness in attracting a pool of quality applicants for the relevant

**Table 2.1** Recruitment methods

| Recruitment method | Advantages | Disadvantages |
| --- | --- | --- |
| **Internal recruitment** | Cost-effective<br>Form of staff development<br>Motivational tool<br>Increases probability of retention | Limits pool of applicants<br>Not suitable where skill shortages<br>Can restrict innovation and diversity<br>Training costs may be high<br>Morale issues for unsuccessful internal applicants |
| **External recruitment** | Widens the pool of applicants<br>Reduces training costs<br>Advocates diversity<br>Improves employer brand | Expensive to advertise externally<br>Candidates unknown to organization<br>Demotivating for internal employees |
| **E-recruitment** | Cheap<br>Access to large quantity of applications and applicants<br>Speed of response | Too many applicants<br>Security and data protection issues<br>Cumbersome to filter |
| **Overseas recruitment** | Access to larger quantity of candidates<br>Access to skill shortages<br>Access to best candidates internationally | Costly<br>Cultural ramifications of hiring non-nationals<br>Increased administration work |

positions. On application forms and/or new employee records, it could be recorded where/how the individual initially found out about the position. This information allows the HR manager/department to evaluate their most effective recruitment methods, by keeping track of the methods used combined with the successful applicants selected. This information can then be used by the organization to justify which recruitment method(s) to invest in and use in the future.

# BUILDING YOUR SKILLS

Think about a particular job you or a family member has had in the past (or currently has). As the line manager responsible for that particular job, what recruitment method or combination of methods would you use when hiring someone for that job? What factors influenced your choice of and decision regarding the recruitment method(s)?

Table 2.1 summarized the advantages and disadvantages of the four recruitment methods. You should remember that organizations may use one or all of these methods, depending on the amount of time and budget they have to fill the vacancy, and which method best suits the particular job

**Employer brand** – an organization is recognized in its own right as a desirable place to work – positive employer brand – by the internal and external labour market

description and person specification for the vacant position. This will vary considerably between recruiting someone for a low-level production line job, where employee referrals may be used and prioritized, to recruiting a new football manager for the national team, where internal, external, e-recruitment and overseas recruitment methods may all be used. Once the decision regarding the recruitment method has been made, the organization must decide how it is going to attract candidates to submit their applications for the open position.

# ROLE OF EMPLOYER BRAND IN RECRUITMENT

In order to attract the most suitable candidates for a vacant position, it is helpful for an organization to have a positive **employer brand** (Knox and Freeman, 2006; Mosley, 2007), which refers to their reputation as an employer. Being considered 'employer of choice' is positive for organizations, as it increases labour retention and attracts strong, talented applicants who want to work in such a positive environment. Recently, a variety of awards have gained prominence in this area such as the Great Place to Work Awards. Organizations such as Google or Microsoft would be considered as having positive employer brands. They have positive images as employers, offering competitive financial and nonfinancial rewards as well as structured internal career paths. Organizations with positive employer brands are considered 'good/great places to work'. Having a positive employer brand can often be seen in the amount of unsolicited applications an organization receives from people wanting to join that organization.

In tight labour markets, where there is a shortage of skilled applicants, it is particularly useful for organizations to have a positive employer brand so that they can better entice candidates to apply to join their organization. Informal methods of recruitment, such as spontaneous applications, often arise where organizations have a positive employer brand, as candidates are keen to join such organizations. The recruitment costs may fall as a result of having a database of potential recruits through unsolicited applications.

## THE JOB ADVERT

As discussed earlier, the job description and person specification are the raw materials used in drafting the job adverts. Once the recruitment method is determined and the type of approach(es) to be used agreed upon, the job advert must be shared with the potential candidates. The job advert will include the relevant information concerning the position, such as:

- name of organization
- job title
- duties
- essential skills/competencies required
- desirable skills/competencies
- the application details (if the candidate needs to send a CV, cover letter, or if they need to complete an online application form)

**Job advert based on job description and person specification**

# Senior HR Administrator
**Reference code:** XX-OO-11-22-33
**Location:** London
**Salary:** £20k to £30k p.a.
**Job type:** 2-year fixed-term contract
**Education level:** Degree in HRM
**Contact:** A. White
**The client:** Our client is a leading multinational and is currently looking for a HR Administrator for a 2-year fixed-term contract role.

**Job responsibilities**
- Operation and maintenance of interview schedule
- Screening CVs for vacancies
- Updating employee HR system including setting up new employees
- Management and filing of interview notes in line with legislation
- Taking minutes at internal meetings
- Provide administration assistance to the managing director
- Preparing and coordinating group meetings
- Coordinating social events and company initiatives
- Administering monthly expenses

**Skills and experience required**
- Degree in Human Resource Management, minimum 2(1) award
- 1–3 years' experience in an HR environment
- Ability to deal with sensitive/confidential issues
- Excellent written and verbal communication skills
- Strong attention to detail
- Ability to prioritize workload in a fast-paced environment
- Excellent working knowledge of Microsoft Office Suite, particularly Excel, PowerPoint and Word
- Prior experience working with an Applicant Tracking System

- the closing date for applications
- the address/contact details where the application should be sent.

It is important that the job advert is placed in the most suitable medium. For instance, if you are looking for a legal expert, you would advertise in legal/law magazines and websites.

The job advert should be drafted using AIDA criteria – attention, interest, desire and action. In other words, the job advert should gain the attention of potential candidates. It should then rouse their interest in finding out more and reading through the details of the job advert. The job advert should instil desire in the potential candidate to want to fill that vacancy. This leads to action – the candidate applies for the position.

CONSIDER THIS ...

Review some job adverts in the recruitment section of a local or national newspaper. What common information do they include in the job advert? Compare them using AIDA criteria from your perspective.

Now we move on to the flexible workforce and flexible working practices, and look at the type of employment contracts organizations can offer new recruits.

## THE FLEXIBLE WORKFORCE

A strategic decision that an organization makes with regards to its recruitment strategy includes considering a **flexible workforce**. When sourcing people to take up positions in the organization, and after having conducted the research required as part of HRP, the organization may decide that it needs to employ someone on a temporary/fixed-term contract basis, a part-time basis, or a permanent long-term contract as required. In recessionary times, where

**Flexible workforce** – a workforce that an organization can quickly and easily adjust in order to meet its changing labour needs

**Core workers** – workers whose skills and competencies are considered 'core' to the effective operation of the organization, whom the organization will seek to recruit and employ on a full-time permanent basis

**Peripheral workers** – workers whose skills and competencies are considered 'peripheral' or nonessential to the effective operation of the organization, and so the organization will seek to recruit and employ them on a part-time, fixed-term contract or outsourced basis

there is a loose labour market and much market uncertainty, organizations may decide to hire more temporary or part-time staff. In so doing, the organization's obligations in terms of redundancy payments would be less should the organization need to cancel that job in the short term. This reduces the risk for employers. When deciding on the degree to which the organization will have a flexible workforce, it will determine the necessity for a core and peripheral workforce, and the types and degree of workforce flexibility required. Atkinson (1984) is credited with the flexible firm model, which consists of two categories of workers – core and peripheral – each category demonstrating its own particular type of labour flexibility, as explained below.

### Core and peripheral workforce

**Core workers** are in the primary labour market. Their skills and competencies are believed to be central to the success and strategic development of the organization, as they often possess firm-specific skills and knowledge. They are typically paid a regular salary, benefits, receive training and development, have defined career paths with promotion opportunities and are involved in a performance management system. In return for their job security (permanence), they are considered most committed to the organization. Recently, due to intensive cost-cutting on behalf of organizations, there has been a shift away from the employment of core, full-time, permanent workers towards the employment of peripheral workers.

**Peripheral workers** are viewed as a method of keeping labour costs low in an organization. However, their skills and competencies are often needed on an ad hoc basis, such as to meet increasing demand at peak times, for example a retailer during the lead-up to Christmas, or for a specific short-term reason, such as installing a new IT system. Peripheral workers include temporary, part-time, fixed-term contract, outsourced and self-employed workers. They are part of the secondary labour market, where their employment is not secure or stable, but depends on market conditions. Peripheral workers lack firm-specific knowledge, have less job security and less opportunity for internal career advancement in the organization. There is often a high turnover of peripheral workers, particularly in a tight labour market ▸ **Chapter 3** ◂.

The main advantage of a peripheral workforce for organizations is cost-effectiveness: the organization only employs and pays workers when they are required. This has become even more popular since the global economic crisis. One of the advantages for peripheral workers themselves is that this form of employment allows them to work on a short-term, fixed-term or part-time basis, and combine their work with other activities, such as childcare or studying. For instance, many students have part-time jobs while they are at university and/or take on temporary/fixed-term work over the summer vacation period. This allows students to gain valuable work experience and helps them pay for their education.

**Functional flexibility** – the ability to develop skills in line with demand

**Numerical flexibility** – the ability to increase or decrease the number of people working in the organization

**Temporal flexibility** – the ability to adjust the hours/times people work in an organization

**Financial flexibility** – the ability for organizations to adapt their wage costs depending on the ratio of core and peripheral workers employed

during busy periods and then reduced when no longer needed. People employed for numerical flexibility could be on short-term temporary contracts. Peripheral employees also provide temporal flexibility, in that their working hours can be adjusted, for example part-time or job-sharing positions. There is also an element of financial flexibility associated with the peripheral workforce. Organizations can more quickly and easily adjust the number of peripheral workers (numerical flexibility) and/or hours that peripheral workers work (temporal flexibility) in order to reduce (or increase) the respective wage costs (financial flexibility).

The use and size of the flexible workforce depend on a number of macro-level environmental conditions, such as legislation, levels of national employment (or unemployment), education and marketplace competition; as well as micro-level conditions, such as the size of the organization, the sector in which it operates, and the stage within the life cycle ▸ **Chapter 1** ◂.

## Labour flexibility

The need for flexibility across organizations has grown. Flexibility includes labour flexibility, the flexibility of technology, organizations and systems (Procter and Ackroyd, 2009: 495). It concerns the degree to which there is the ability to be adaptable depending on different circumstances, places and periods of time. Organizations that succeed in being flexible have a competitive advantage over those that are not, since flexible organizations can quickly adjust to changes in the environment.

With regards to labour flexibility, it is the organization's point of view that is normally considered. According to Atkinson's (1984) model, there are three types of labour flexibility: functional, numerical and temporal flexibility. Core employees provide **functional flexibility**. This means that organizations invest in training and developing their core employees so that they can meet changing demands for different skills or competencies. They are numerically stable, in that their number does not vary, but remains constant.

On the other hand, peripheral employees provide **numerical flexibility**, as the organization can increase or decrease the numbers employed depending on demand, over time. For instance, staff numbers are increased

**CONSIDER THIS ...**

Think of a part-time or fixed-term contract job that you or a friend or a family member has had. Compare that peripheral job with a core job in the same organization. What (if any) are the main differences? Do these substantiate the flexible firm model? If so, how? If no, why not?

## Criticisms of the flexible firm model

The flexible firm model, while conceptually well accepted, has a number of critics who see it as a means for the organization to control the workforce, offering security to core workers in return for functional flexibility, at the expense of peripheral workers having their hours and numbers increased and decreased in line with the organization's needs. The peripheral workforce is also considered the 'atypical' workforce, which suggests the different status of positions held by core and peripheral workers, with the core workers prioritized with regards to initiatives such as training and development and/or promotions. It is argued that the flexible firm model breeds conflict between the different types of workers in an organization. The result is that one of these sets of workers' needs are prioritized over the other.

On the other hand, it has also been argued that functional flexibility leads to the intensification of work, with core workers expected to be functionally flexible and carry out different roles as part of their privileged position in the organization. Core workers can then be used on an ad hoc basis to cover skills shortages, such as holiday cover or sick leave cover, while continuing to do their primary jobs, and without receiving any additional compensation for this. This can lead to motivational problems and health and safety issues, with core workers potentially more stressed due to more demands on their skills.

The flexible firm model is also criticized for failing to address contemporary practices in HRM, where the gap between core and peripheral workers seems to be narrowing in practice. For instance, in periods of economic downturn, the number of core employees in an organization can be reduced in similar proportions to the peripheral employees, through downsizing and redundancy activities. The suggestion that core workers are more committed to their organization than peripheral workers is also contentious, in an era where individualism and boundaryless careers suggest the increased mobility of workers across the broad employment categories of core and peripheral ▶ Chapter 10 ◀. In other words, the differences between core and peripheral workers seem to be diluted nowadays, where job security cannot be assured for any worker, core or peripheral. Today, job security is more aligned with market demand rather than residing in the core or peripheral workforce.

## Flexible work practices

Flexible working practices refer to an organization's working arrangements in terms of working time, pattern and location of work and include practices such as teleworking, which enables employees to work remotely without having to be present in an office. Other flexible working initiatives include flexitime, where employees can choose when they start and end work, within broad time parameters. For instance, a family in which both parents work may avail themselves of

Flexible working practices – a range of initiatives where the organization provides more flexible work schedules to employees, to adequately staff positions when, where and how required

flexitime so the father starts later and takes the children to school, while the mother finishes earlier to pick the children up from school. Job-sharing is a similar initiative where two employees share a particular job, with each of them potentially working alternate weeks or parts of weeks. Thanks to technology advances, which enable employees to access information remotely, from outside the office, more and more organizations are implementing flexible working practices, which enable their employees to balance their work and personal lives to a greater extent. There are also cost advantages for organizations, in that they may not need to provide office space for employees who work from home (telework).

These initiatives are promoted by organizations as part of a positive employer brand. Existing and potential employees often value flexible working practices as much as the other elements that make up the complete pay and benefits package ▶ Chapter 8 ◀. In this sense, the organization offers potential and existing employees a choice of flexible working conditions, such as job-sharing or working part time (often associated with women returning to work after maternity leave), teleworking (working from home, thereby reducing time spent commuting, or enabling parents to continue to work if they need to look after a sick child on an ad hoc basis), or flexitime (staggering the start times and finishing times in the office, provided the employee still works the required agreed average hours a week). Many employees enjoy the flexibility that this provides. For example, a programmer working for Nokia HQ in Finland can work remotely from their home in Mauritius on a daily basis, with only brief monthly trips to Nokia HQ required. In this example, the programmer is able to combine work with their personal pursuits (for example surfing in Mauritius).

Offering flexible working practices to existing and potential employees has met with primarily positive responses from employees, who see it as a way to balance work and personal life, as well as an opportunity to take control of when and where they work, provided the work gets done to the employer's satisfaction. Others, however, consider that flexible working practices have had a negative outcome for employees, with employees being constantly 'on call' through mobile and other technologies and, in effect, working longer hours as a result. There is a clear distinction between the benefits for employees of flexible working practices, which enable and facilitate work–life balance (through temporal flexibility and IT), and labour flexibility initiatives on behalf of organizations that seek to promote functional, numerical and temporal flexibility for the organization's advantage.

When undertaking recruitment, organizations need to determine the degree of a flexible workforce they wish to adopt, recognizing the associated advantages and disadvantages. Also, having a positive employer brand can assist in attracting a higher number of quality candidates. Offering flexible working practices is one means of developing a positive employer brand, since these are generally viewed favourably by employees.

We now turn our attention to key elements in employment legislation with which you should be familiar in regard to the recruitment function and the employment of flexible workers.

## RECRUITMENT, FLEXIBILITY AND EMPLOYMENT LEGISLATION

Here, we consider some key elements in the employment legislation that are relevant in the recruitment stage, most notably the equality legislation. Since we also considered labour flexibility in this chapter, we include information on relevant legislation concerning part-time, fixed-term and agency employees as well.

When drafting job adverts and the terms and conditions of employment, the organization must abide by existing legislation. Of most significance is the equality legislation. All member states of the EU must adhere to anti-discrimination law and equal opportunities legislation ▶ **Chapter 5** ◀. The Equal Treatment Framework Directive (2000/78/EC) required the governments of all EU member states to draft anti-discrimination laws. EU anti-discrimination law ensures that potential applicants are not discriminated against on grounds of age, sex, sexual orientation, race/ethnicity/national origin, religion and disability. Specific to the Republic of Ireland in its Employment Equality Acts (1998–2008) is the protection against discrimination for members of an ethnic group known as the 'travelling community'. Employers must adhere to the anti-discrimination legislation relevant to their respective countries in order to protect employees/ potential employees against discrimination on the specific grounds listed above.

With regards to the flexible workforce, legislation also calls for equality of treatment across the different categories of workers (part-time, fixed-term and temporary agency employees). The EU Part-Time

Workers Directive (1997/81/EC) and the EU Fixed-Term Work Directive (1999/70/EC) ensure that part-time and fixed-term workers are treated comparably (pro rata) to full-time staff on permanent contracts. The EU Temporary Agency Work Directive (2008/104/EC) came into effect in December 2011. Although it was proposed in 2002, the British, German, Danish and Irish governments blocked its enactment until 2008. This calls for people employed in organizations through employment agencies to receive the same/equal treatment (equal pay and conditions) as employees of the organization doing the same work. These EU Directives stress the need for equal treatment of workers regardless of any physical differences or workforce categorization (core, periphery). For more details on EU legislation of relevance to recruitment and flexibility, refer to the EU legislation website, given below.

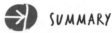 **SUMMARY**

This chapter focused on human resource planning and the recruitment aspect of HRM. We examined how HRP needs to be aligned with the organization's strategy so that the organization will have the right quantity and quality of employees it requires to operate a successful business, now and into the future. We set out the stages in HRP, describing important terms and concepts such as job analysis, job description, person specification and competency framework. We then moved our attention to recruitment, distinguishing recruitment from selection. We focused on the four recruitment methods, both formal and informal methods, open to organizations in attracting a pool of candidates to apply for a particular position, and the advantages and disadvantages of each method. We noted that more than one method of recruitment is often used by organizations, to attract the largest number of quality applicants possible. We also highlighted the relevance of a positive employer brand in attracting quality candidates. One of the important aspects in recruitment is the flexible firm model, which has both benefits and limitations. Finally, we identified the role that legislation plays in regards to recruitment (equality legislation) and flexible workers (part-time, fixed-term (temporary) and agency (contract) workers).

This chapter covered the recruitment part of the resourcing function. As you recall from earlier in the chapter, resourcing consists of recruitment and selection stages. Chapter 3 focuses on selection.

## Recruitment Strategy at ValuOutlets

Ann Yates is the HR manager at ValuOutlets, a firm in the food retailing sector in the UK and Ireland. Following five years in HR in the hotel sector, Ann joined ValuOutlets a month ago, after achieving a first class honours Masters degree in HRM. She is enjoying the challenging role at ValuOutlets so far. While she is relatively new, her position is quite senior and she is the person responsible for HRM for the entire organization in the north of Ireland, with total staff numbers (full time, part time and fixed term) currently just over 50. Her predecessor left the organization to take up a role in another organization.

While ValuOutlets is a relatively small organization, its strategic plan is to roll out more stores across the UK and Ireland. The organization is expanding and the senior management team wants to open a new retail outlet/store in a growing town in the north of Ireland. Ann Yates is tasked with determining the recruitment strategy and ultimately recruiting for this retail outlet. She calls together the small HR team (three others work in the HR department with her) to discuss the project and brainstorm how best to approach the recruitment strategy for the new store. She needs to present the proposed strategy to the senior management team at the end of the week. It will be her first presentation so she feels extra pressure in ensuring her proposed strategy is agreed on and signed off by the senior managers. She needs to decide if she will engage an external recruitment agency to take over the project completely, which could prove costly, or if she will handle it in-house.

There is a graduate student placement programme in operation at ValuOutlets, and this year the student placement is in Ann's HR department. She decides to dedicate that student to work on the recruitment strategy with her, allowing the other three members in the team to concentrate on their normal tasks. Together with the student, Ann considers how many permanent, fixed-term and part-time staff members she will need to employ for the store. She must also determine the positions that need filling, from store manager, assistant store manager, to customer service and sales assistants.

Due to the heavy workload in the department and scarce resources, Ann decides to engage an external recruitment agency to manage the filtering of candidates for the open positions, resulting in the agency providing a shortlist of candidates, which must then go through the selection process. However, Ann must determine the recruitment methods and job advert to be used in recruiting for the store. Ann, with the student's help, pulls together her research and work into a presentation for the senior managers.

1 Weigh up the pros and cons of using an external agency to handle recruitment for the new store.
2 What do the student and Ann need to prepare in order to have a detailed overview of the positions required?
3 What factors do they need to consider in order to decide on the types of flexibility in worker categories they need for the various positions?
4 What recruitment method(s) could/should she choose, and why?
5 For the store manager job on offer, undertake a job analysis (job description, person specification, competency framework) feeding into the development of the job advert.
6 Given the growth plans of ValuOutlets, what other HR strategy reports should Ann consider preparing for the senior management team?

© BRAND X PICTURES

## CHAPTER REVIEW QUESTIONS

1 Why is it important for organizations to engage in HRP?
2 Describe how HRP is influenced by the organization's business strategy and recruitment strategy.
3 Differentiate between a job analysis, job design, person specification and competency frameworks.
4 Undertake a job analysis (job description and person specification) of any job of your choice. How well does the person specification match the job description? Can you see how the job description and person specification form the basis of a job advert? What other information may be required in a job advert?
5 Describe and differentiate between the four methods of recruitment identified in the chapter, presenting the advantages and disadvantages of each.
6 When should an organization employ the services of a recruitment agency?
7 Describe ways of generating an 'applicant pool' and attracting candidates.
8 What are the advantages and disadvantages of flexible working practices for organizations and for employees?
9 Under which conditions would you advise an organization to implement numerical, functional and temporal flexibility?
10 Outline the key equality legislation concerning the recruitment of core and peripheral workers in an organization.

 ## FURTHER READING

Gunnigle, P., Heraty, N. and Morley, M. (2011) *Human Resource Management in Ireland: An Introduction*, 4th edn, Dublin: Gill & Macmillan.
Maund, L. (2001) *An Introduction to Human Resource Management*, Basingstoke: Palgrave – now Palgrave Macmillan.

Noe, R., Hollenbeck, J., Gerhart, B. and Wright, P. (2009) *Fundamentals of Human Resource Management*, 3rd edn, New York: McGraw-Hill.
Taylor, S. (2010) *Resourcing and Talent Management*, 5th edn, London: CIPD.

 ## USEFUL WEBSITES

http://europa.eu/legislation_summaries/index_en.htm
The Summaries of EU legislation website provides a database of EU employment legislation directives. Click on the relevant subject area.

www.ft.com/home/europe
Keep up to date with business matters through the *Financial Times*.

http://hr.com
HR.com has an online community and provides interesting fact files, surveys and case studies within the HRM domain.

www.irishtimes.com/jobsboard/
The recruitment page of the *Irish Times* website has numerous examples of job descriptions and person specifications.

www.monster.co.uk/
www.monster.ie
Monster's website is full of interesting links and articles on selection methods, such as telephone interviews, as well as an excellent example of an e-recruitment site.

www.peoplemanagement.co.uk
People Management provides daily updates in the latest happenings in HR. Note that it is UK specific.

 For extra resources including videos and further skills development guidance go to: www.palgrave.com/business/carbery

# 3 EMPLOYEE RESOURCING: THE SELECTION PHASE

Christine Cross

*By the end of this chapter you will be able to:*

## LEARNING OUTCOMES

- Identify how the shortlisting process forms a fundamental part of the employee selection decision
- Explain how a shortlisting matrix operates
- Outline the issues involved in choosing a selection method(s) for each hiring decision
- Discuss the range of employee selection methods available and outline how they operate
- Describe the limitations associated with using the interview as a selection tool
- Outline how employment legislation affects the employee selection process
- Identify the key stages involved after the final selection decision is made

© IMAGE SOURCE

*This chapter discusses ...*

# INTRODUCTION

The selection decision is arguably one of the most important issues for any employer, regardless of organization size. Selecting the right employee during the process is critical, as not doing so can be costly for employers for a number of reasons. First, the selection process itself is expensive, as it includes the time costs of those involved in the various selection methods. Second, an employee's ability to perform has an impact on overall organizational productivity and profitability levels. Finally, a wealth of legislation safeguards an employee's employment rights, making it difficult for an employer to dismiss an employee after a certain time has passed. So, it is vital for an employer to ensure that the selection process identifies the most suitable employee. The purpose of this chapter is to explain how the selection process operates in order to achieve this aim. There are three stages to the selection process – the shortlisting stage, making the selection decision, and the post-offer stage – which are outlined in this chapter. It is worth noting here that despite the availability of sophisticated selection techniques, which have been acknowledged as having higher levels of ability to predict job performance, for example online screening, psychometric testing and assessment centres, organizations continue to rely on variations of the interview (CIPD, 2010b). Thus, there is an emphasis in this chapter on the different types of interviews available to employers. We begin by outlining the importance of taking a strategic approach to the selection decision and then move on to examine the main features of the three phases of the selection process.

# STRATEGIC SELECTION AND COMPETENCIES

It is important to understand that the selection decision should not be made in isolation. Chapter 1 identified the broader context of managing people in organizations and highlighted the strategic nature of HRM. In order to achieve the competitive advantage that can accrue from having a superior workforce, **selection** has been identified as one of the key elements of the 'best practice' approach ▶ **Chapter 1** ◀. This concept is rooted in the philosophy that people are an organization's most valued asset and a key source of

> **Selection** – a process used to find the candidate who most closely matches the specific requirements of a vacant position

## SPOTLIGHT ON SKILLS

You have decided to set up an online business and need to hire a person to work with you. Their role is to create a social media-based marketing campaign for your product. Identify some of the key criteria for this vacant position:

- Will it be a part-time or a full-time position?
- How will you recruit for this position?
- How will you screen the initial applicants?
- What selection methods will you use?
- What are the costs involved in these selection methods?
- What questions will you ask the candidates?

To help you answer the questions above, visit www.palgrave.com/business/carbery and watch the video of Olga Donnelly talking about the selection process.

strategic competitive advantage (Bartlett and Ghoshal, 2002). The identification and development of potential is a critical element in the success of an organization. In taking this approach, competencies become an important element in the identification of new hires. Competencies can be defined as the behavioural characteristics of an individual that are causally related to their effective performance in a role (Boyatzis, 1982) ▶ **Chapter 2** ◀. Competencies are often compared with knowledge, skills and abilities. They are, however, different, in that while they both indicate an ability to perform in a role, competencies are broader than knowledge, skills and abilities. Competencies are normally worded in a way that identifies specific behavioural aspects of the role. They are often developed by organizations to represent a set of factors that can assist in achieving success at an organizational level, rather than just in one role. Using a competency-based approach to selection allows the development of more objective selection criteria, which are focused less on applicants' qualifications and more on their ability to perform in the role. Additionally, competencies can form the basis of the questions asked at interview, providing a consistent, objective approach to the selection decision. We examine competency-based interviewing in more detail later in the chapter.

Recently, the two-way nature of the selection decision has become even more important, where candidates' impressions of the organizational context and culture become as important a determinant of their decision to accept a job offer as their concern with the job itself. This is particularly true in a tight labour market and employer branding plays a crucial role in this situation ▶ Chapter 2 ◀. As the CIPD (2011) notes in its survey on resourcing and talent planning, despite high unemployment over the past two years, 52 per cent of respondents believe that competition for talent is even greater, as the pool of available talent to hire has fallen sharply. Thus, communication between the candidate and the organization plays a pivotal role in creating a positive relationship between both parties. The overall objective of the selection process is that when the most suitable candidate is offered the position, they accept the job and do not turn it down to accept a better offer elsewhere. The recruitment and selection behaviour of those in charge of this process are crucial elements in a successful selection process. It is important to ensure that candidates know in advance what to expect from the selection process; for example, the type of assessment they are going to undergo, the length of time it will take, and when they will be notified of the success or otherwise of their application.

### Application forms and CVs

Those involved in making a selection decision must first ask candidates to supply their personal and work-related information, and must decide whether to use application forms or curriculum vitae (CV). Application forms are designed by the organization and are normally used to gather specific information on prospective candidates, either electronically or on paper. The information is required in a standard format, which allows for the same job-related information to be gathered from all candidates, which is difficult when allowing applications

**CONSIDER THIS …**

What is the cost of hiring the wrong person for the job? This is a question those involved in selection don't consider often enough. Employment legislation has made it difficult to let an employee go once the probationary period has passed. If an employee is hired at €45,000 per year, and stays with the organization for 20 years, that is over €1 million for that person's employment in your organization, after bonuses, pension contributions, sick pay and other company benefits are included. Additionally, if the person is a poor performer, there are myriad indirect costs, such as poor customer service, additional training costs and productivity-related costs. This highlights the importance of hiring the right person, the first time.

by CV. Information normally required includes educational qualifications and work history. The use of application forms also speeds up the shortlisting process as it simplifies the process. Recently, employers have also included sections where they ask candidates to answer competency-based questions. For more senior roles, however, it is more common for CVs to be required. One factor to be considered in the decision is the need to ensure that questions on an application form do not breach any areas of the employment equality legislation (see end of chapter for more detail).

## SHORTLISTING STAGE

In Chapter 2, we established how to generate interest in a vacant position and produce (hopefully) a large group of applications for the position. It is unlikely that all applicants will have the necessary skills, abilities, education, experience or competencies required, so we need to reduce the number of applicants and identify those who most closely match the specific requirements of the vacant position. The time, effort and money required to engage all those who have applied for the position in the full selection process is prohibitive. For senior positions or job vacancies that have a large response, this stage may be preceded by an initial longlisting stage to identify those applicants who meet the essential criteria.

The aim of the shortlisting stage is, therefore, to reduce the number of applicants and narrow the field by a process of elimination. This process is known as shortlisting. Shortlisting takes place once the advertised closing date has passed and is based on the submitted applications, which are measured against the requirements specified in the selection criteria. A shortlisting matrix is used to evaluate each candidate against these criteria. Using a shortlisting matrix is an efficient method of identifying the candidates who will take part in the next stage of the selection process.

> **Shortlisting** – a sifting process where those candidates who most closely match the predetermined job-specific requirements are separated out from all other applicants

> **Shortlisting matrix** – a scoring mechanism for placing the candidates who have applied for the position in a ranking order, based on their suitability for the role

The selection criteria used in this matrix are drawn from the job requirements and person specification and should have already been identified prior to the position being advertised. These criteria define the particular skills, knowledge, attributes, qualifications and experience a person needs to successfully carry out the role. Well-designed selection criteria:

- provide a consistent standard that applicants can be assessed against
- represent the key requirements of the position
- improve the quality of applications.

The criteria are normally divided into two sections, essential criteria (E) and desirable criteria (D), drawn from those predetermined by the job description and the person specification. Table 3.1 presents an example of a shortlisting matrix with the criteria identified in both categories – essential and desirable.

One method of scoring candidates involves the weighting of certain criteria, where particular criteria (normally essential criteria) are viewed as more important than others. For example, if you were recruiting for a chartered management accountant, you might apply a double weighting to the requirement to have the CIMA (Chartered Institute of Management Accountants) qualification, as this may be the most important aspect of the role. Or, for a sales role, experience may be twice as important as a sales qualification, so you would weight sales experiences by two. Alternatively, you can decide not to apply a weighting to any of the criteria, so that no more importance will be given to one essential criterion than another. In terms of scoring, the scoring system includes a '0' for no evidence of the criteria or qualification. You can then use a four-point scale to score different levels of evidence of a criterion (see Table 3.1). It is recommended that if a candidate gets a '0' for any of the essential criterion, they should not be shortlisted as they do not meet the essential requirements of the post.

The outcome of using this matrix is to create two groups of applicants – those who are suitable and those who are unsuitable. The decision as to who is suitable or unsuitable will be based on a cutoff score, which you will need to decide in advance of beginning the scoring process. Candidates who score above the cutoff mark will be called to the next stage of the selection process and those who do not will be rejected. In Table 3.1, only applicants 1 and 2 would be called to the next stage of the selection process, as applicant 3 has not met the essential criteria and has the lowest score. In countries such as the UK, Ireland and the USA, employment legislation highlights the need for a rigorous approach to the shortlisting stage, as those who are not shortlisted can use the discrimination legislation as the basis of a

**Table 3.1 Example of shortlisting matrix completed three ways for each candidate**

| Applicant number | 1 | 1 | 1 | 2 | 2 | 2 | 3 | 3 | 3 |
|---|---|---|---|---|---|---|---|---|---|
| Criteria (E) | P | 5 | X 2 = 10 | P | 5 | X 2 = 10 | x | 0 | X 2 = 0 |
| Criteria (E) | x | 0 | X 2 = 0 | P | 3 | X 2 = 6 | x | 0 | X 2 = 0 |
| Criteria (D) | P | 3 | 3 | P | 3 | 3 | P | 5 | 5 |
| Criteria (D) | P | 3 | 3 | P | 3 | 3 | P | 3 | 3 |
| Total | P | 11 | 16 | P | 14 | 22 | x | 8 | 8 |

*Key:* x = no evidence; P = evidence present; E = essential; D = desirable; X 2 = weighting of 2

*Scoring:* 0 = no evidence; 1 = little evidence; 3 = moderate evidence; 5 = strong evidence; cutoff score: 15

claim for unfair non-selection. In general, using a shortlisting matrix affords those involved in the selection phase some protection against such claims. The completed matrix should be kept with the other selection documents, such as the interviewer's notes, in order to meet the freedom of information requirements in many countries. The shortlisting matrix can also be used at the interview stage to score each candidate's answers based on the criteria used during shortlisting.

In many larger organizations, and in the public sector, panel interviews are normal practice in the selection of candidates. Where a panel interview (see later section for more detail) is being used, all members of the panel should be involved in the shortlisting process. Panel members are typically drawn from a number of organizational functions, internally and externally. A typical panel might comprise:

1 an HR person
2 a technical specialist
3 a line manager
4 a person from another internal function that may work with the role
5 a person external to the hiring organization
6 a chairperson who manages the proceedings.

Each person who is shortlisting does so independently of the others and then their information is communicated to the person charged with collating all the scores. The panel then meet to agree on the candidates to be called to interview. The shortlisting matrix should be used to document the panel's considerations of each applicant and it should clearly identify which applicants meet each of the criteria, and why they were shortlisted. This matrix will also show the date of the shortlisting panel's meeting, the job title of the vacant post, and the names and signatures of those involved in making the shortlisting decision.

The shortlisting matrix can be used in conjunction with a **ranking matrix**.

**Ranking matrix** – a document that lists those candidates who scored highest in the shortlisting, from highest to lowest

## Online screening

For many organizations, the volume of applications that need to be screened means that it is too labour intensive to undertake this process manually. This is particularly true where potential applicants can apply online through the organization's website. We saw in Chapter 2 that online recruitment has grown in popularity in recent years. The graduate recruitment market has adopted the

**CONSIDER THIS...**

The costs associated with making the wrong selection decision can be surprising. You are responsible for hiring a new full-time sales assistant for a well-known retail chain, who will earn 20k per annum. They decide to leave after they have worked with you for six months. How much do you think the cost of replacing that employee will be?

1 less than €1k?
2 between €1k and €4k?
3 between €4k and €8k?
4 over €8k?

Why have you chosen that amount?

use of online screening for some time. These positions are often ones that have broad selection criteria and generate a large volume of applications. In these cases, online screening tools provide a significant advantage in reducing the time and associated labour costs.

A software package, which identifies specific keywords on submitted CVs and application forms, based on the selection criteria, can be used to screen initial applications. Those applications that contain the keywords are accepted and those which do not are rejected by the system. This is a useful way to reduce the number of applicants; however, it may eliminate suitable candidates who actually meet the criteria but have not used the specific words searched for by the software package. As part of the online screening process, organizations can use online ability tests and personality questionnaires as an initial method of screening applications. (These types of psychometric tests are dealt with in more detail later in the chapter.)

There are, however, difficulties with these tests being taken online. There is the possibility that the person taking the online test is not the person who is actually applying for the position. Also, there are 'experienced' applicants who learn how to 'work' the system in order to produce the 'right' answers.

## MAKING THE SELECTION DECISION

Once the number of applicants has been reduced to a manageable number, there are a wide range of selection

# BUILDING YOUR SKILLS

methods an employer can use to decide on the most suitable candidate. The overall aim of the selection process is to predict an applicant's job performance capability specifically related to the vacant role. This prediction element is seen to be particularly problematic and so more than one method is often used to assist in the decision-making process. Additionally, person–organization fit and person–job fit are viewed as critical elements in the selection decision for many organizations. **Person–organization fit** refers to the extent to which a person and an organization share similar characteristics and/or meet each other's needs (Kristof, 1996). **Person–job fit** is the degree to which there is a match between the abilities of the person and the demands of the job, or the desires of a person and the attributes of the job (Edwards, 1991). Research has shown that where this fit occurs, employees are more satisfied

> **Person–organization fit** – the values, interests and behaviours of the individual match the organizational culture
>
> **Person–job fit** – the enthusiasm, knowledge, skills, abilities and motivations of the individual match those required by the job

with their jobs and this is related to higher levels of productivity (Caldwell and O'Reilly, 1990). Conversely, poor job fit is associated with job dissatisfaction, higher levels of job-related stress, and intentions to leave the organization (Lovelace and Rosen, 1996). 'Fit' is viewed by many as an important criterion in the selection decision. Yet, it is difficult to objectively search for these types of 'fit' among applicants. This is often where employers resort to using their 'gut feeling' when making a selection decision, not something recommended in taking a strategic approach to selection.

When choosing the selection methods most suitable for a vacant position, different organizational positions require different types of selection methods. The selection methods chosen will depend on the particular skills, attributes, knowledge, or competencies required for the position. The decision as to which selection method to use is impacted by a number of factors:

● *the ability of the method to predict suitability for the position:* this can depend on the predictive validity of the method.

● *the appropriateness of the method for the seniority and level of the position:* for example, a retail sales assistant role is likely to require different methods than those used for the chief financial officer (CFO) of a multinational corporation.

● *the specific selection criteria:* for example, if technical competence is required, certain methods are more suitable.

● *the time and effort required to use the technique:* if a vacancy needs to be filled quickly, some methods are more suitable than others, for example telephone interviewing is quicker than arranging face-to-face interviews. The risk factor of making a poor selection decision needs to be considered here. In the example above, time factors should not affect the selection method choice for the CFO position.

● *the skills and abilities of those involved in the selection decision:* where psychometric tests are being used, those administering the tests must be appropriately trained and qualified.

● *costs of each method:* budget restrictions may create a situation where costs dictate that certain methods such as assessment centres are too expensive.

● *equality issues:* given the volume of employment protection, does the chosen technique directly or indirectly discriminate against any of the groups identified?

**CONSIDER THIS...**

Do you think being in a job you really enjoy and working with colleagues you get along with would affect your job performance?

Put yourself in a situation where you cannot find anything in common with the people you work with on a daily basis. How will this affect your performance at work?

Now picture yourself working on the reception desk in a busy solicitors practice and answer the two questions above again. Are your answers any different this time?

## RANGE OF EMPLOYEE SELECTION METHODS

As mentioned above, there are a range of methods available to assist with making the selection decision. Normally, more than one method is used in the selection process in order to improve the validity of the process. These include application forms, interviews, psychometric tests, assessment centres, work sample tests and graphology, each of which are described below. A recent study in the UK highlighted that CVs, references, structured interviews and application forms are the most common selection methods with clear similarities in the use of different selection methods in organizations of different sizes (Zibarras and Woods, 2010). They also found that public sector and voluntary organizations use formalized techniques, such as application forms rather than CVs, and structured rather than unstructured interviews.

First, we need to identify the importance of validity in the choice of selection methods. **Validity** looks at how closely a selection method measures what it is supposed to measure and how successful it is in doing this (Kline, 1998). Here, we are interested in the evidence that supports the conclusions that are made based on the scores of the selection measure and in what is termed 'predictive validity', which is the extent to which the method used can predict successful performance in the role. If predictive validity scores are high, the method is identified as a good predictor. The closer the score is to

**Validity** – the extent to which a selection method measures what it purports to measure and how well it does this

**Reliability** – a method is identified as reliable if it consistently measures what it sets out to measure

1.0, the better the predictive validity. Research by Smith and Smith (2005) has identified that certain methods have a higher predictive validity than other methods. **Reliability** is also important when deciding which selection method to use. A method is identified as reliable if it consistently measures what it sets out to measure (Arvey, 1979). The key issue here is: Do we get the same results when we measure the same thing twice?

The selection method chosen should have high validity and high reliability. According to Smith and Smith's research (2005), the highest predictive validity scores are for the combined use of intelligence tests and structured interview at 0.63, with intelligence tests and work samples scoring 0.60. Work sample tests scored 0.54, and structured interviews and intelligence tests each scored 0.51. The methods at the lower end of the scoring are personality tests (0.40), assessment centres (0.37), references (0.26) and finally, at the bottom, graphology at 0.02.

### Structured and unstructured interviews

Reviews of the selection interview process (see, for example, Dipboye, 2005) have indicated that a structured interview noticeably improves its validity. While it may seem strange for a selection interview to be conducted in an unstructured fashion, this is the case more often than you might think. Unstructured interviews are essentially an informal chat between the interviewer and the prospective candidate and have as much predictive validity as tossing a coin in the air. They involve an interview where different questions may be asked of different applicants. On the other hand, structured interviews can provide an important and valid means of selecting an employee. The interview is structured to ensure that interview questions are based strictly on job-related criteria and these same questions are asked of all candidates and answers are rated (Arnold et al., 2010). The most common forms of structured interview are the competency-based interview and the situational-based interview. It is also important to ensure that no discriminatory questions are asked during the interview process. (This is dealt with later in the chapter.)

#### Selection interviews

Selection interviews normally involve an organizational representative meeting the candidates face to face. These

## Employee Selection at Google

Imagine having such a strong brand that you receive over a million job applications annually. What would you do? Review every 200th application? Only consider those that have the best qualifications? Google faces this situation every year. So how does Google effectively tackle this enormous 'problem'? Google has attempted to integrate a highly scientific methodology into the employee selection process. Recognizing the impossibility of trying to review over a million applicants annually, Google focuses heavily on academic achievements and also seeks out employees who have certain personality or behavioural characteristics that are favourable to success in an open job position. Rather than search for one particular skill set, Google asks that potential employees be 'smart'. It doesn't look for people with particular skills, it looks for people who have excelled. Job applicants fill out an elaborate online survey that explores their attitudes, behaviour, personality and biographical details going back to secondary/high school. The questions range from the age when applicants first got excited about computers, to whether they have ever tutored or established a not-for-profit organization. The

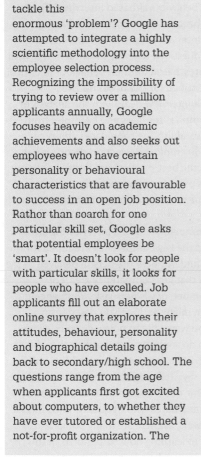

answers are fed into a series of formulas created by Google's mathematicians that calculate a score – from 0 to 100 – which is intended to predict how well a person will fit into its chaotic and competitive culture. Laszlo Bock, Google's vice president for people operations, said: 'As we get bigger, we find it harder and harder to find enough people. With traditional hiring methods, we were worried we will overlook some of the best candidates.'

Notorious for its time and intellectual demands, Google's recruitment process is based largely on a series of interviews with a number of different interviewers. It often takes two months to consider candidates, submitting them to a dozen interviews. Through a range of interview topics from programming questions to general logic puzzles to personality checks, Google expects to be able to size up how skilled and intelligent a person is. The interview process is described as 'intense' by people who are interviewed. Interviewers try to avoid 'trick questions', but they do aim to ask 'unusual' questions that are not geared towards any particular skills or experiences in an effort to measure how well a candidate does on something they haven't worked on before.

### Questions

1 Interestingly, most academic research suggests that the factors Google have put the most weight on – grades and interviews – are not a particularly reliable way of hiring good people. Given this, why do you think Google uses this approach to selecting employees? Find two academic articles that provide evidence for your argument.

2 If you were being interviewed by Google, how would you prepare for the interview?

### Sources

Chanesman, N. (2010) The Google approach to employee selection, Recruitment Extra, 14 September, http://sites.thomsonreuters.com.au/recruitment-extra/2010/09/14/the-google-approach-to-employee-selection/.

Hansel, S. (2007) Google answer to filling jobs is an algorithm, *The New York Times*, 3 January, www.nytimes.com/2007/01/03/technology/03google.html?scp=3&sq=google%20recruitment%20selection&st=Search.

Tay, L. (2006) Google's recruitment process revealed, Computerworld, 16 November, www.computerworld.com.au/article/166548/google_recruitment_process_revealed/#closeme.

remain the most popular method of selection despite their accepted shortcomings. Research over the past 50 years into the effectiveness of the selection interview highlights that they are not particularly successful in predicting future job performance. They have a relatively poor reputation as being overly subjective, prone to interviewer bias and thus unreliable predictors of future performance (Compton et al., 2009). Nevertheless, interviews have been the most popular form of selection

for many years and are used in almost every organization for selecting employees at all levels. There are a number of types of selection interview:

● *Telephone interviews:* the interview is conducted by phone. These are relatively popular, particularly for screening purposes, and are useful in that they remove the 'appearance' bias, an accusation often made of face-to-face interviews.

- *Video interviews:* a form of interviewing where technology is used to conduct the interview. This can be in 'real time', where the interview takes place at a prearranged time and place much like a standard interview, but the interviewer and interviewee can be in two different locations, even two different countries. This is viewed as being a cost-effective method of conducting a selection interview. These video interviews can also take the form of asynchronous interviews, where the candidate records the interview at a day and time that suits them. Their video is then viewed at a date and time that suits the interviewer(s), again allowing the interviewee to be anywhere in the world. The candidate is normally asked to answer a series of preprepared questions during the recording.

- *One-to-one interviews:* the candidate is interviewed by just one person (usually HR) in a face-to-face setting. This has been the standard format for interviews for many years; however, the objectivity of one person making the selection decision has been called into question and this has given rise to the panel interview.

- *Panel interviews:* the candidate is interviewed by more than one person. Panel interviews normally include a representative from HR and the technical manager. However, there can be as many as seven or eight panel members depending on the sector and the position in question. More senior positions will usually have more panel members. The roles and contributions of the various panel members need to be managed and this is normally done by a panel chairperson. Once a favourite of public sector organizations, there has been a move towards the use of panel interviewing in many sectors to improve objectivity in the selection decision.

According to the CIPD (2012c), different countries take different approaches to which interview type they use. In the UK, it is increasingly common to have a structured interview, and panel interviews are also used, while in the USA, almost all interviews follow a structured process, where all applicants are asked exactly the same questions. In France, they use a more informal, unstructured approach, while in northern Europe, it is common for the HR manager to be one of the interviewers, but this is less likely in other countries in the world.

Next, we describe two forms of structured interview in more detail, which focus on using objective factors to predict job performance, rather than subjective 'gut

feeling' interview approaches; the first is a competency-based interview and the second is a situational-based interview.

## Competency-based interviews

Competency-based interviews are conducted by using a series of structured questions designed to gather information on specific behaviours or competencies that have been identified in the job analysis phase

> **Competency-based interviews** – these interviews are structured around job-specific competencies, with candidates asked questions based on critical incidents in the role

▶ **Chapter 2** ◀. The competency-based interview is sometimes referred to as a 'behavioural event interview' or a 'behavioural-based interview'. This is because the competency-based interview uses behavioural-based questions to assist the interviewer with assessing candidates, based on their behaviour in critical competencies identified for the position. The behavioural-based interview deals with the analysis of past events and emphasizes facts and examples from real situations to establish the candidate's ability to perform the role. In employee selection theory, it has been argued that the best predictor of future behaviour or performance is present or past behaviour or performance of the same type (Wernimont and Campbell, 1968).

Questions in competency-based interviewing are structured around the key competencies required for the role; you want to find out how the person behaved in the past in relation to that key competency area. For example, if the competency is persuasion/influencing skill, your question might be: 'Can you describe an occasion when you were able to persuade your fellow team members to do something that at first they didn't really want to do?' If the competency is problem-solving ability, you might say: 'Tell me about a problem you have solved recently.' One of the problems with this type of interview is that candidates who frequently encounter it learn to 'fake' answers, as there are many books and websites devoted to learning how to 'perform' in this interview setting. They will have worked on these questions in advance, often delivering answers they believe the interviewer wants to hear.

## Situational-based interview

A situational-based interview takes a similar critical incident approach but works on the premise that the interviewer wants to establish what the candidate *would do* if presented with a situation. Questions here focus on the future. The candidate is provided with a typical situation and asked how they would respond to it. For example: 'What would you do if your manager presented you with two conflicting deadlines?' These interviews are particularly common in graduate interviewing where the individual is unlikely to have past experience of particular situations. The answers to these questions reveal how the candidate might handle the situation; however, this is only indicative and should be recognized as such.

### Stress interview

Stress interviews are less common than those described above. They are based on finding out how the candidate reacts to a stressful situation. A false stressful situation may be created by the interviewer to test the candidate's reaction. Or, questions can focus on handling work overload, dealing with multiple projects and deadlines, and handling conflict situations.

## Psychometric testing

Psychometric testing is the term most often used to encompass all forms of psychological assessment. Psychometric literally means 'mental measurement'. There has been a rise in use of these tests recently as the search for more sophisticated selection methods continues. Candidates complete 'pen and paper' tests that are used to measure individual differences in areas such as aptitude, ability, attainment and intelligence (Edenborough, 1999). These are a quantifiable measurement of candidates' cognitive ability and indicate if they have the skills, or the potential to learn new skills, required to perform successfully in a particular role. The premise here is that those who do well in the tests will perform well on the job. Most tests are designed and developed by occupational psychologists. These tests must also be administered and scored by persons qualified in the tests being used. Types of tests include the following:

● *General intelligence tests:* these measure the ability to think about ideas, analyse situations and solve problems. Various types of intelligence test are used
● *Attainment tests:* these measure levels of knowledge and skills
● *Cognitive ability tests:* these include
  – *verbal comprehension:* the ability to understand and use both written and spoken language
  – *numerical ability:* the speed and accuracy with which a candidate can solve arithmetic problems
  – *reasoning ability:* the ability to invent solutions to diverse problems.

## Personality profiling

Personality profiling is based on the fact that personality is viewed by many organizations as an important determinant of behaviour at work. Personality tests are often used as employers search for predictors of success in a role. These personality tests are usually based on the trait-factor analytic model of personality (Arnold et al., 2010). Commonly used profiles include the Myers-Briggs Type Indicator, Eysenck Personality Questionnaire, The Big Five and the Sixteen Personality Factor Questionnaire. The Big Five is based on the five factor model of personality, which proposes that differences in an individual's personality can be measured in terms of openness, conscientiousness, extraversion, agreeableness and neuroticism. The CIPD has cautioned against the use of personality profiles as the sole basis of making the selection decision and suggests they are used in combination with other selection methods (Pilbeam and Corbridge, 2006). The debate around the use of personality tests centres on a few key issues, namely, the extent to which personality is measurable and remains stable over time and across situations, and the extent to which a questionnaire can provide enough suitable information on which to base a selection decision.

## Assessment centres

Assessment centres were first used in the Second World War to select officers for the army and the Royal Navy. In an assessment centre, a range of techniques are used to assess candidates on multiple competencies. This is undertaken by a group of assessors who identify the most suitable candidates by using a series of exercises and tests that take place over one or two days (see Table 3.2). The techniques used include work sample tests, leaderless group discussions, psychometric tests, in-tray simulations and one-to-one interviews. These centres are used particularly in graduate recruitment. An assessment centre is not actually a place, but describes the process, which normally last for one or two full days. Typically, the same competencies are assessed multiple times during the course of the centre. At the end of the assessment centre, the assessors come to an agreed cumulative rating for each individual based on the observations and test scores. Despite their high level of predictive validity, there is one key disadvantage of using assessment centres, which is that they are expensive to operate. The University of Melbourne has an open access video link to a video of an assessment centre, available at http://vimeo.com/9815762.

**Table 3.2 Example of an assessment centre day**

| Time | Activity |
|------|----------|
| 9.00 | Introductions |
| 10.00 | Personality and psychometric tests |
| 11.00 | Coffee break |
| 11.30 | Leaderless group exercise |
| 12.30 | Lunch |
| 1.30 | Role-play exercises |
| 2.30 | Individual interviews |
| 3.30 | In-tray exercise |
| 4.15 | Tea and departure of candidates |
| 4.45 | Assessors begin discussion of candidates |

## Work sample tests

Work sample tests are used to test applicants by asking them to complete tasks similar to those involved in the actual job. This can involve working in the role for a short time, often for one day. They are based on the premise that the best predictor of future behaviour is observed behaviour and they have a high predictive validity. These tests are common in the service sectors where an assessment of the candidate's work ability is based around customer service provision and where the outcome of their interaction can be measured immediately. One example of a work sample test is found in a lecturing role. Many universities include a presentation as part of the selection process, as both presenting and lecturing involve similar skills and abilities.

## Graphology

Graphology is the study and analysis of a person's handwriting, which is believed to reveal a behavioural profile of the individual. It is regularly used by organizations in Europe, particularly France, where three-quarters of small companies use it in the selection decision. Employers in Belgium and Germany also use graphology (Taylor, 2005). However, popularity should not be confused with validity, as it has zero predictive validity score.

Using more than one selection method is advisable as this increases the amount of job-related information available on which to base the selection decision. As noted above, selection methods vary in their reliability, as a predictor of performance in the job, and in their ease and costs to administer. It is becoming more common for

particular positions to involve psychometric testing and selection interviews, for example graduate entry positions and public sector positions.

## PROBLEMS WITH THE SELECTION INTERVIEW

There are a number of negative issues associated with selection interviewing and these relate mainly to perceptual distortion, subjectivity and lack of interviewing skill on the part of the interviewer:

- *Confirmatory bias:* interviewers are often accused of making their mind up about a candidate within the first 30 seconds of the person entering the room. They then focus on asking questions to confirm their initial impression, either positive or negative. This is referred to as 'confirmatory bias' (Snyder and Swann, 1978) or the 'first impression error'. A related issue is the effect the perceived attractiveness of the candidate has on the interviewer. Research has highlighted that, in general, more attractive people are identified by interviewers as having more favourable traits (Marlowe et al., 1996).
- *Horns or halo effect:* a perceptual error, where one single characteristic of the individual creates an overly positive or negative impression of the interviewee and this then carries unbalanced weight in the selection decision. For example, if the person was being interviewed for a customer-facing role and had tattoos on their neck and hands, this might be viewed by the interviewer as a negative characteristic and may have an unduly negative effect on the selection decision. This is the 'horns' or negative effect, while the 'halo' effect is the opposite.
- *Stereotypes:* stereotypes are qualities seen to be associated with particular groups or categories of people. When an interviewer stereotypes the interviewee, this can negatively affect the outcome of the decision for the candidate. For example, people who are overweight may be thought of as lazy, or blonds may be viewed as less intelligent than brunettes. The interviewer may alternatively hold a stereotyped image of the 'right' candidate and judge all candidates against this image.
- *Contrast error:* the interviewer compares and contrasts one interviewee with other candidates in a way that artificially inflates or deflates the evaluation of the

candidate. Contrast error has the effect of distorting the decision-making process, as each candidate should be judged independently.

- *Projection error*: the interviewer rates candidates with characteristics, experiences or preferences similar to themselves more favourably than other candidates. The reverse is also true.
- *Excessive talking*: some interviewers have a tendency to dominate the interview by talking too much, so not allowing the interviewee the opportunity to make their case. The 80/20 rule is viewed as most appropriate, where the interviewer talks for only 20 per cent of the time.
- *Lack of interviewing skill*: many interviewers receive little or no training in interview skills. There is a belief among some interviewers that interviewing is a natural skill and one that cannot be taught and so experience is the key to a successful interview. Thus, because they have been interviewing for years, they think they know how to interview.

Despite these issues, it is unusual for an organization to hire a candidate without having conducted an interview, and thus their popularity is unlikely to diminish as there is no other method that allows the prospective employer such flexibility in meeting the candidates in advance of offering the position. This is because the interview is useful for determining if the applicant has the requisite communication and interpersonal skills necessary for the job; it is a flexible method of gathering important information, allowing the interviewer to ask questions that may reveal additional information which can be used in making the selection decision.

## EMPLOYMENT LEGISLATION AND THE SELECTION PROCESS

The selection process is expected to operate within a framework of fairness and consistency, which removes discrimination and ensures equality of opportunity ▶ Chapter 5 ◀. In the UK and Ireland, this is provided by a number of pieces of legislation, which also cover the recruitment process ▶ Chapter 2 ◀. Discrimination means treating one person less favourably than another under specific grounds, either directly or indirectly. Europe and the USA take a similar approach to protecting individuals affected by the selection process.

### BUILDING YOUR SKILLS

Think back to a recent interview you have attended. If you were being interviewed, how did you feel immediately after the interview? Were you able to tell the interviewer exactly how good you were at certain aspects of the job? Or did you feel that they really didn't give you a chance to shine? This is a common problem for interviewees. The interviewer's role is to ensure that they allow the interviewee the opportunity to explain how well they can fit into the role. Otherwise, it's a wasted opportunity for both sides.

As a line manager, what would you do to ensure that you give each interviewee the same chance to 'sell' themselves? What do you believe are the key issues involved in making the selection decision? What are the most difficult aspects of making the selection decision? How can you ensure that you act in an objective way when making a selection decision?

Discrimination law in Europe is covered by the Equal Treatment Framework Directive (2000/78/EC), which applies to all EU member states. Despite some differences in the specifics of the interpretation of the Directive, the same broad principles apply to all countries. The USA's discrimination legislation is similar to Europe. For example, an employer cannot intentionally discriminate on the grounds of age, race, colour, sex, national origin, or disability under Title VII of the Civil Rights Act 1964, the Americans with Disabilities Act 1990 and the Age Discrimination in Employment Act 1967.

Case law has created a framework for the procedure and operation of all elements of the selection process, which protects those involved in the employment selection process. One example can be found in a case taken by the US Equal Employment Opportunity Commission – *EEOC* v. *Dial Corp.* (2006) – where the finding in favour of the EEOC was that strength tests must be job related and consistent with business necessity to ensure they do not disproportionately exclude women. An award of $3.3 million was made to 52 rejected applicants, highlighting the seriousness of ensuring compliance with equality legislation. The seven-minute test in question, which formed part of the selection process, required applicants to carry 35lb (15.8kg) weights back and forth, lifting them up specific distances in the air. More than 95 per cent of men passed the tests but fewer than 40 per cent of female applicants passed. In Ireland, under the Employment Equality Acts 1998–2011, it is also unlawful to discriminate on the grounds of gender, marital status, family status, sexual orientation, age, disability, religion, race, and, specific to Ireland, membership of the travelling community, in any area of employment, including the selection of candidates.

Earlier, we discussed the issue of asking for and supplying references in relation to prospective or potential employees. Employment legislation has begun to develop in relation to this issue. In the UK, a woman who received a 'damaging' reference, because she had previously taken tribunal proceedings against the employer, successfully sued the employer when the reference resulted in the job offer being withdrawn. The ruling by the employment appeals tribunal was that the giving of the reference by the former employer was an act of unlawful discrimination by way of victimization – *Bullimore* v. *Pothecary Witham Weld Solicitors* [2011] IRLR 18.

Data protection and freedom of information have become important areas in relation to the retention of material generated by the selection process. In the UK, the Data Protection Act 1998 applies to personal information used in the selection stage. There are eight data protection principles covered in the Act and it is the responsibility of the person managing the selection process in the organization to comply with these principles. In Ireland under the Data Protection Acts 1988 and 2003 and the Freedom of Information Acts 1997 and 2003, persons are allowed access to their own data held respectively by government departments, agencies and other designated bodies in receipt of government funding, and all legal entities in the state. Therefore, candidates who have been unsuccessful in the selection process are entitled to know what information is kept about them and to see that data. This covers the shortlisting matrix, any scoring of them in their performance on psychometric tests and, most importantly of all for many organizations, notes made by interviewers during an interview. Thus, it is of the upmost importance that all interviewers are trained and understand how to take accurate and objective notes during the selection phase to ensure no discrimination takes place.

## MAKING THE FINAL SELECTION DECISION

Once all the information is gathered from each of the selection methods used, the selector(s) needs to make a final decision on who is to be offered the position. This means that all the information from each stage of the process must be utilized. There is often a tendency to use the most recent selection method only, which is normally the interview; however, decisions need to be made in advance of the start of the selection process on how to weight the selection methods and how to score candidates where a conflict exists between data gathered from two methods. For example, if a candidate performs well in psychometric testing but poorly in the interview, each element needs to have a weighting to allow for accurate scoring of the candidate overall. The shortlisting matrix is a useful method of recording information from each selection method, as it has identified the key job-related criteria. Once the selection decision is made, the next stage involves taking references, checking qualifications and contacting the candidates.

### References

References are most often sought once the position is about to be offered to a candidate. References ask a previous employer to provide information about their current/previous employee and to verify the information provided by the candidate (Gatewood et al., 2011). Prospective employers may search for information on areas including length of employment, brief details of responsibilities, job position and title, overall performance, absenteeism, timekeeping and the reason for leaving. If the role involves dealing with children or vulnerable adults, other, more rigorous checks such as police background checks are often part of the pre-employment check. The majority of organizations ask the candidate to provide the name of a referee, who they then contact, once they are in a position to make a job offer. The majority of organizations use the reference in their selection decision-making process. If the candidate has not been previously employed, the organization is likely to ask for personal references. Information required in a reference should be based solely on fact, or should be capable of independent confirmation. There has been a move recently towards the use of verbal references, where organizations have become reluctant to provide information on job performance in a written format. This is no doubt driven by Data Protection and Freedom of Information Acts in many countries.

## Post-offer stage

It is important to note that contacting all candidates is of paramount importance, particularly for positive employer branding. This means ensuring that unsuccessful candidates are contacted in a swift manner. It can be damaging for an employer brand if candidates who attended for tests or interviews are not contacted again by the organization to advise them they were unsuccessful. Some organizations offer feedback to the unsuccessful candidates. For the successful candidate, they should be offered the position and the details of the appointment should be agreed. They are normally given a period of time within which to accept the offer and agree

on a start date. Their acceptance of the offer in writing is normally completed by their signing of the employment contract. They should be informed of how the induction process operates before joining the organization

▶ Chapter 4 ◀.

One area often forgotten about in the selection process is monitoring the success or otherwise of the selection process. It needs to be monitored to ensure the validity of the selection decision. An analysis of the candidates and their performance in the various stages of the process provides feedback about how successful various methods are in making the overall selection decision. More importantly, data should continue to be collected in order to assess the performance of the selected candidates once employed. Information from performance reviews and internal documents can be compared to performance in selection methods such as psychometric tests. This allows an evaluation of the relationship between selection methods used, selectors and successful role performance.

---

## MsTAR

© PHOTODISC/GETTY IMAGES

ACTIVE CASE STUDY

You are working in the HR department of MsTAR, a web-based technology firm in Wellington, New Zealand. You have been asked by the HR manager to identify the most suitable recruitment and selection methods to fill the vacant position of HR senior generalist. You have been given one month in which to fill this new role. You have been given the job advert, which has already been created for this role.

### HR Senior Generalist

The web is shifting from a vast encyclopedia of information to a social environment that reflects our real identities and the relationships and information we care about. MsTAR is at the forefront of that change. This is a high-profile role in a dynamic and technical environment at the leading edge of web technology. We're looking for a dynamic HR Senior Generalist and committed team player who gets excited by big questions and hard problems. Willingness to 'go the extra mile' is essential. This position is located in our offices in Wellington, New Zealand.

#### Role/responsibilities
- Provide advice and support to both employees and senior management.
- Influence and challenge key managers within the business while providing value-added HR services.
- Ensure consistent standards of service are maintained while creating a working environment that supports the organizational values.

- Develop and implement HR policies and procedures that reflect best practice and meet legal requirements.
- Ensure compliance with all employment legislation and advise managers and employees on the interpretation and application of current employment law, terms and conditions, and personnel policies and procedures including, but not limited to, equal opportunities, redundancy, paternity pay and maternity rights.

→

- Handle and document disciplinary, legal, grievance and all employee relations issues.
- Coordinate performance management, annual review processes, and identifying skill and competency gaps.
- Coordinate with the learning and development team on training and development activities including development centres.
- Review the new hire orientation procedures and processes.

**Requirements**

- Must have a third-level qualification plus 3–5 years of relevant experience in a growth environment (preferably in a technology, media or high-tech organization) with a minimum of 2 years at HR Generalist level.
- Excellent knowledge of employment legislation in New Zealand.

- Must have strong communication skills and the ability to work independently, prioritize workload and manage tight deadlines.
- Evidence of effectiveness at managing internal customer relationships.
- Strong HRIS experience.
- Ability to work to deadlines and adapt to and manage changing conditions, with the ability to generate innovative and pragmatic solutions.
- Strong competency in operational and strategic planning and management.

**Salary and benefits**

The salary for this position will be commensurate with company pay scale grading bands, individual experience and qualifications, and is negotiable. An attractive benefits package is awarded and includes performance bonuses in line with performance reviews.

1 Write a short report for the HR manger outlining which selection methods are most appropriate for this position, clearly indicating the reasons for your choices.

2 Explain how you would ensure that you adhere to the employment legislation in each selection method you outlined above.

3 Prepare a list of questions that can be used to interview the applicants. Indicate the types of questions they are and why each is useful in the selection interview.

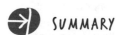 SUMMARY

This chapter has covered some of the key issues involved in making the decision about who is the most suitable candidate for a vacant position. The critical role played by the initial shortlisting process cannot be overemphasized. By ensuring that the initial shortlisting criteria are specific to the role and then utilizing these same criteria in all stages of the selection process, the chance of selecting the most suitable candidate from the applicants is greatly increased. The choice of selection method depends on many factors and the predictive validity of each method should be a factor in choosing the selection method(s). Using more than one method has the effect of increasing the ability to predict successful performance in the role. Ensuring compliance with employment legislation is important in safeguarding against the possibility of a rejected candidate taking a case for discrimination.

 CHAPTER REVIEW QUESTIONS

1 Why should an organization view selection as a two-way process?
2 Undertake some independent research to find out why organizations use different approaches to the selection process. Search the internet for examples of selection practices used by organizations. Identify the ways in which they differ and explain why they use different selection processes.
3 Identify the reasons why validity and reliability are important concepts in selection.
4 Equality and ethical behaviour should form the basis of any selection process. Explain this statement with reference to at least two additional academic sources.
5 Explain how using a competency-based interview as part of the selection process can benefit the organization and the candidate being interviewed.
6 Explain why the face-to-face interview is likely to continue to be the key aspect of a selection process.

7 Evaluate the usefulness of assessment centres for small and medium-sized enterprises.

8 'Psychometric testing should be included as part of all selection processes.' Discuss this statement, illustrating your answer with examples from the workplace.

9 Employment equality legislation varies from country to country. The underlying principles of equality and fairness are, however, safeguarded in all the legislation. The legislation in your country will dictate what you can and cannot ask a candidate during a selection interview. Prepare a list of questions that you cannot ask at an employment interview and explain why each of these are inappropriate.

 **FURTHER READING**

Armstrong, M. (2009) *Armstrong's Handbook of Human Resource Management Practice*, 11th edn, London: Kogan Page.

Leatherbarrow, C., Fletcher, J. and Currie, D. (2010) *Introduction to Human Resource Management: A Guide to HR in Practice*, London: CIPD.

Torrington, D., Hall, L. and Taylor, S. (2011) *Human Resource Management*, 8th edn, Harlow: Financial Times/Prentice Hall.

 **USEFUL WEBSITES**

www.hrzone.co.uk
HRZone is an HR community, providing discussion and analysis on employment law, employee engagement, HR strategy and employee issues.

www.personneltoday.com
Read HR news and read about HR jobs on Personnel Today. Find expert opinion, news and HR blogs – for the HR professional.

www.uniformguidelines.com
A free resource for the HR community, Uniform Guidelines on Employee Selection Procedures is a US website providing information on all selection procedures used to make employment decisions, including interviews, review of experience or education from application forms, work samples, physical requirements, and evaluations of performance.

 For extra resources including videos and further skills development guidance go to: www.palgrave.com/business/carbery

# 4 EMPLOYEE INDUCTION, TURNOVER AND RETENTION

**Colette Darcy**

By the end of this chapter you will be able to:

## LEARNING OUTCOMES

- Explain the links between employee induction, turnover and retention and how a strategic approach to their management can increase the overall competitiveness and success of the organization

- Explain what employee induction is and why organizations invest in these programmes from a strategic perspective

- Understand the term 'onboarding'

- Discuss the impact of employee turnover on an organization

- Identify specific practices to analyse employee turnover

- Identify what employee retention is and why it is important from a strategic perspective

© PHOTODISC

This chapter discusses ...

# INTRODUCTION

The focus of this chapter is on employee induction, turnover and retention. Within any organization you will find a flow of employees into and out of the organization. People leave jobs, new employees start. Companies are forced to downsize and let people go in bad times and can find themselves expanding rapidly and employing more and more staff in good times. Managers are tasked with identifying high-performing employees who they want to keep and putting in place strategies to retain them. At the same time, managers must monitor the performance of underperformers, with the view to potentially letting go those who fail to improve. This flow of employees into and out of organizations is complex and can often be viewed as something that 'happens to' an organization rather than something it actively has some control over. The HR function traditionally tracked the movement of employees, in terms of keeping figures, for example, in relation to turnover or exit interview transcripts. However, it was not considered a core strategic part of the HR function. The recent rise in prominence of the idea of people as a source of competitive advantage, combined with the high costs associated with recruiting new staff and inducting them into the organization, has caused the HR function to revisit these areas ▶ Chapter 1 ◀. Employee induction, turnover and retention have become the focus of renewed interest as HR recognizes the potential important contribution that all three areas can make to the overall strategic success of the business. Importantly, HR has also recognized the role it has to play educating senior members of the organization in terms of how all three areas are interlinked and how a strategic approach to their management can increase the potential overall competitiveness and success of an organization.

It is against this backdrop that we begin our analysis of employee induction, turnover and retention. Unlike other HR textbooks, this chapter adopts a different approach. Rather than focus on the practice of HR and a 'how to' approach, this chapter will focus on helping you to make the link between initiatives aimed at employee induction, turnover and retention and how they contribute to the strategic success of the organization.

**Tangible benefits** – benefits that can be measured and reported on

## SPOTLIGHT ON SKILLS

To manage retention effectively, HR professionals need to think about retention:

1  before employees are hired
2  while they are working for the organization
3  after they have committed to leave/have left the organization.

For each of the three key stages, think about the specific initiatives you would seek to implement in your organization to address the issue of retention. For each initiative identified, map out how it will work to increase retention rates.

To help you consider the issues above, visit www.palgrave.com/business/carbery and watch the video of Gretta Nash Cadden talking about retention policies.

# THE ROLE OF HR IN INDUCTION, TURNOVER AND RETENTION

HR professionals are tasked with understanding the business context or rationale for the introduction of any HR initiative. They must understand the real, **tangible benefits** that such an initiative will bring to the organization. What does the proposed initiative hope to achieve? How will achieving it help the organization increase its competitive advantage over its rivals? What is the link between this initiative and organizational aims and objectives? Are the links clear to all stakeholders in the organization? HR must constantly think about the organizational benefits of undertaking a new initiative or programme. As a strategic partner to the business, HR must understand the business and be able to demonstrate how its work contributes to the organization's competitiveness and ultimate success.

## CONSIDER THIS ...

If you want to borrow money from the bank for a new business idea, you must put together a detailed business plan. In this plan, the bank would expect to see details of the new business venture, what you hope to achieve, the gap you've spotted in the market, who else is doing something similar and how your idea is different. It would also expect to see details of how you intend to repay the money – essentially, it will want to see how your idea will make enough money to allow you to pay back what you owe. It is not so different internally within organizations. With limited resources available, organizations are less willing to spend money on initiatives that have no clear focus or are vague regarding the bottom line contribution they will make to the business. If the marketing department requests €1 million to spend on a new ad campaign, you can be sure that the senior management team will be looking for assurances regarding the market research it has done, the agency it is planning to use, the actual ad to be used and so on. The senior management team would also closely monitor the success of the campaign in terms of revenue growth or brand recognition. It is no different for the HR department. Why would any organization give its HR department money to spend without some clear indication of what the initiative is trying to achieve and how it will make a contribution to the business?

How would you go about building a business case for the investment in an HR initiative such as an induction programme? What steps would you take to convince the senior management team that such an investment was worthwhile?

## INDUCTION

### What is induction?

Induction as a term is often confused with 'orientation', which is a specific course or training event that new starters attend. The terms are often used

interchangeably; however, to do so is to misunderstand the importance of the induction process.

The importance of induction and settling new starters into an organization, while gaining more attention these days in the literature, is not a new idea. As far back as 1955, Hill and Trist, in connection with the UK's Tavistock Institute, conducted a number of studies on labour turnover and found that employees are more likely to leave during the early stages of employment, but the longer they remain in employment, the lower the likelihood of them quitting.

Hill and Trist (1955: 276) proposed the survival curve, which outlined three distinct phases that employees go through on joining a new organization, each with varying degrees of risk in terms of the likelihood of employees leaving the organization. The first phase they labelled the *induction crisis*, which occurs within weeks of a new starter joining the organization and carries with it the highest likelihood of an employee leaving the organization. Researchers have explored the many different reasons for this induction crisis. For example, it can come as a real shock for employees to realize that in some cases the job they applied for is not quite what they thought. The job may have been oversold at interview by the employer or the new starter simply thought it would be different from the reality. This notion of unmet expectations is common but could be easily avoided with care and attention at the interview and selection stage. Employers should provide realistic job roles and responsibilities and ensure that they answer candidates' questions as accurately as possible ▸Chapter 3◂.

The literature also points to the idea of organizational fit, which may lead to increased numbers of leavers within the first few weeks of employment ▸Chapter 3◂. Employees join an organization and bring with them a particular approach or attitude towards work. Where a clash exists between the values or attitude of the new employee and the organization, this can often lead to feelings of unease and doubt. A classic example of poor organizational fit is that of an employee who comes from a bureaucratic organization and joins one that is considered very flat, where employees are empowered and expected to make decisions and take responsibilities for their own actions without the involvement of their line manager. The change in approach to work can be unnerving for the employee and the transition too difficult to bridge, resulting in the employee leaving the organization. They are unable to make the adjustment or settle into the value system of the new organization.

# BUILDING YOUR SKILLS

You are charged with recruiting new team members for a young, dynamic IT company. How would you go about establishing if a candidate for the role would be a good organizational fit?

---

Interestingly, employees can sometimes find themselves in a position they have applied for and been appointed to, but which is simply beyond their ability. They thought they would be able to rise to the challenge, but the reality is somewhat different. The thrill of seeking a new role and additional responsibilities can often come crashing down as the reality of the situation sinks in. There is nothing worse than being in a role where you know you are unable to perform the duties required of you. The stress of being in such a situation can have a serious medical impact on the individual. Again, this realization can come within the first few weeks of beginning work in a new organization, leading to high levels of turnover in a short period.

The *differential transit phase* reflects the period when the employee begins to settle into their new work environment and starts to feel more comfortable in their new role. As this settling process continues, the risk of an employee leaving the organization tends to decrease. This phase typically occurs within the first few months of employment. The organization's ability to quickly get a new employee to this phase could be viewed as a potential measure of the effectiveness of the induction programme.

The final stage, *settled connection*, is suggestive of those employees who become properly socialized into the organization and, in the words of Hill and Trist (1955), are essentially 'quasi-permanent'. The quicker an employer can move employees to this settled connection phase, the better, in terms of ensuring that they have productive staff members contributing to the competitive success of the organization.

**Induction** – the whole process whereby new employees in an organization adjust to their new roles and responsibilities within a new working environment

**New starter** – an employee who is relatively new to or has just joined the organization

**Survival curve** – a model stating that new starters in an organization are more at risk of leaving in the first six weeks of commencing a new job. The likelihood of leaving decreases as the length of employment increases

**Organizational fit** – the 'fit' or alignment of the personal values/work ethic of the employee with those of the organization's culture and values

**Informational approach** – this approach to induction focuses on supplying new starters with basic information regarding the working of procedures within the organization

## Traditional approach to employee induction

HR professionals are often criticized for their lack of strategic awareness. There can often be a perception within organizations that HR is predominately an administrative function. The role of HR in developing and rolling out employee induction programmes can often add to this perception if handled in a traditional administrative manner.

The informational approach to induction would have included:

- a formal welcome from the new starter's supervisor and introduction to team members
- possibly a general tour of the premises
- an overview, if the new starter was lucky, which might have included information on organization-wide trends, key strategies being pursued, key clients and so on
- some sort of presentation on centralized administrative arrangements – expense claims, rules covering absence, discipline, holidays, computer and telephone usage and so on.

After that, the new starter would be free to find their own way in the new world in which they found themselves.

This administrative, informational approach was seen as an opportunity to supply a new starter with standard information regarding the organization and certain core expectations in terms of general employee behaviour. The involvement of line managers in the development or roll out of the induction programme was usually quite limited and often a source of irritation to them. Line managers tended to be critical of its effectiveness and often questioned its overall purpose. This type of induction programme was often supplemented with the distribution of a weighty and comprehensive employee handbook. As most of us know as employees, no one ever reads the employee handbook until a problem arises. The reality is that most new starters put the employee handbook in their desk drawer where it remains until the day they leave.

In any job you have had, have you ever read the employee handbook? What purpose does an employee handbook serve if it is not read by the majority of employees? Why do organizations spend money on these handbooks? What are the implications of not having an employee handbook?

As an HR professional, how would you go about making the employee handbook more relevant? What media would you use and how would you promote and ensure that employees were familiar with the content of the employee handbook?

This approach to inducting a new employee placed the onus on new starters to seek out and obtain any information they needed in order to be productive in their jobs. It was a case of learning by asking. The difficulty of this approach was that the answer often depended on who was asked and it may not always have been clear to new starters who the best person was to answer their query. The new starters themselves may be reluctant to admit they don't know something and instead of seeking help may opt to remain silent and therefore unproductive. It takes a brave person who has just started in a new position in a company to stand up and admit they don't know how to do something they have been asked to do, or even how to go about starting it. It is asking a lot of new starters to make them responsible for seeking out the information they need in order to get the job done, especially if an organization fails to provide direction on who they should approach for help.

With this type of approach to induction, the main risks associated with not offering an induction programme were considered to be limited to the direct replacement costs of replacing a new starter and undertaking a new recruitment drive. There was very little, if any, consideration given to the broader strategic issues such as ensuring that employees were productive as quickly as possible or that they settled into the organizational culture, which are the potential benefits of a more robust induction programme. The limited scope of the traditional induction programme and the absence of a clear business case as to its importance meant that

**Human capital pool** – the collection of employee skill that exists within a firm at any given time

**Onboarding** – the mechanism through which new employees acquire the necessary knowledge, skills and behaviours to become effective organizational members and insiders

there was a general lack of interest in it from both a line management and new starter perspective.

## A *new perspective on employee induction*

New starters should be a source of new focus, new energies and possibly new creativity. The flow of individual employees into and out of the human capital pool can bring fresh thinking and new skills and knowledge to an organization. The ability of organizations to quickly tap into this new perspective is fundamental to success. A new employee in a company needs to hit the ground running. Whether it is a small startup or a large multinational organization, the need to get new hires productive as soon as possible is critical. In the initial stages, while they are still acclimatizing to the new environment of the organization, they are a drain on resources without making a contribution. Not only are they a drain but they often take up valuable time of more experienced staff who are trying to help them navigate their new terrain. It is a steep learning curve for any new starter – on average the time for new hires to achieve full productivity ranges from 8 weeks for clerical jobs to 20 weeks for professionals to more than 26 weeks for executives (Rollag et al., 2005). In the fast-paced competitive environment that organizations now operate in, it is imperative that new starters become productive employees as soon as possible.

## Onboarding

Onboarding refers to the mechanism through which new employees acquire the necessary knowledge, skills and behaviours to become effective organizational members and insiders (Bauer and Erdogan, 2011). Onboarding is sometimes referred to as 'organizational socialization'. It is different to induction in terms of its focus. Onboarding is not concerned so much with ensuring that new starters understand, and are familiar with, the company's policies and procedures, but rather with getting new starters to feel like they belong and are a part of their new organization as quickly as possible.

Research has shown that a failure to socialize new starters can have a substantial negative impact on an organization (Cooper-Thomas and Anderson, 2006).

These include new starters often showing high levels of unmet expectations, leading to poor attitudes and negative behaviour that, in turn, often result in high levels of turnover (Wanous and Colella, 1989). The recruitment of a new employee is a costly undertaking. The ability of organizations to correctly select employees who are likely to share the organization's values and to socialize them into the organizational culture are key to capitalizing on the investment and ensuring a high calibre of human capital. Onboarding is seen as key to ensuring that new recruits quickly settle into their new role and begin to make a meaningful contribution as soon as possible. The ability of organizations to transform new starters into productive employees is essential (Rollag et al., 2005). A clear linkage between the recruitment drive, the induction process and the organizational culture, that is, its values, norms and politics, is required to ensure that employees are clear in terms of what an organization's values are and how best to achieve them.

> **Relational approach** – this approach to induction focuses on helping new starters rapidly establish a broad network of relationships with co-workers from whom they can access the information they need to be productive members of the team

On joining an organization, new starters quickly get a sense of what is acceptable and unacceptable behaviour within that specific organizational context. First impressions count. The first impressions of an organization for a new starter count in terms of their perception of the organization and their decision to commit or leave, but also, importantly, in terms of their work ethic and the effort they are prepared to put into their role. New starters quickly see what rate others work at and work to this standard. If this standard is high, the new starter will often maintain this level of effort. Unfortunately, if this standard is low, it can often have a permanent negative effect. Take, for example, a new starter who joins an organization and, on the first day, is eager to please and completes all their tasks within the first half of the day. The new starter approaches their supervisor seeking additional tasks but is told to slow down 'as you are making the rest of us look bad'. So, the new starter, keen to settle in and be accepted, adjusts their work rate to fit in with the information they have received. Conversely, the new starter may find that the pace of work is intense and there are high expectations around delivery of completed tasks. Everyone is responsible for the completion of their own work and this requires the use of initiative and determination to see the task through to completion. Observing their fellow colleagues for a few days, it becomes clear that employees who are not prepared to work at this high level will not survive long in the organization – this sends out a clear message to the new starter regarding expectations of acceptable and unacceptable behaviour and attitudes to work.

## What does work in terms of induction?

Those organizations that are most successful at quickly getting new starters up to speed tend to be those that adapt a relational approach to induction (Rollag et al., 2005). This approach is based on assisting new employees to quickly build relationships with co-workers so that they can access the information they need in order to perform their role.

Not only does this approach have the benefit of ensuring that new starters have clear guidance on who to approach with any difficulties they encounter, it also ensures that a new starter quickly feels part of the organization and socialized into its ways.

Most organizations realize the importance of getting new starters connected quickly to their co-workers; however, they fail to put in place appropriate strategies to make this happen. There is a belief among many managers that if you hire the right person, they will automatically fit right into the organization's way of doing things and work things out for themselves. 'Good employees' don't need hand-holding. They can quickly work things out for themselves and adapt to the new situation, making the necessary connections themselves to become productive. Interestingly, the higher up the organization a new starter is, the more truth is placed in this misconception.

In terms of induction, successful companies are those that strike a balance between information delivery and relationship development. New starters need meaningful information:

- Tailor the information given to new starters, such as what other departments do and how they interact with the one in which they will be working.
- Explain the roles and responsibilities of the key people they will be interacting with during the course of their work.
- Ensure that they fully appreciate the strategic goals of the organization and how their work will contribute to the achievement of these goals.

## Specific practices to enhance socialization process

While a new starter is traditionally taken to a department on their first day and introduced to everyone or their arrival is announced to a large group at a meeting, research has shown that a strategic approach to introductions is more effective than simply saying 'everyone, this is John'. Thinking about the individuals the new starter will interact with and then strategically targeting them for introductions early on in the organizational life of a new starter is likely to be much more effective.

It is not uncommon in organizations for employees to be allocated a formal mentor. The **mentoring process** tends to be focused on formal career development and advancement. The allocation of a **mentor** is not limited to new starters within an organization and, indeed, the allocation of a mentor can change over time as an

**Mentoring process** – a developmental process focused on formal career development and advancement

**Mentor** – the person charged with developing and assisting an employee to advance their career

**Mentoree** – the individual who is being mentored by a more senior individual within the organization

**Buddy approach** – an informal approach to assisting a new employee learn about the organization and how things work around or within the organization

employee's development and career advancement needs change. Mentoring schemes are traditionally formal, with specific goals in mind and are often limited to those employees deemed to have promotional potential. The mentors themselves tend to be more senior individuals within the organization, who are believed to be in a position to help, direct and advance the **mentoree**.

The **buddy approach**, on the other hand, is an informal approach to assisting new employees learn about the organization and how things are done within the new work environment in which they find themselves. While mentors tend to be more formal, buddies are someone who can be approached to ask basic questions: 'Where is the paper for the printer kept?' 'Who should I ask about getting a purchase order raised?' Buddies do not necessarily have to be more senior individuals within the firm and, in fact, are more likely to be individuals who are at a similar level in

**Table 4.1** Example induction schedule for rapid onboarding

| Stage 1: general induction – informational approach | Stage 2: onboarding – relational approach |
| --- | --- |
| **Introduction – explain** | **Orientation – visit and show** |
| Mission and strategic objectives of the business | Specific business unit/team objectives and how they relate |
| Nature and structure of the business | to the strategic goals of the organization |
| Roles of key business units within the organizational structure | Clear information on the individual contribution of the role |
| **Employment conditions – explain** | to the achievement of organizational goals and objectives |
| Job description and responsibilities | Roles and responsibilities of key people the individual will |
| Work times and meal breaks | be interacting with in order to achieve the set goals and |
| Time recording procedures | objectives |
| Leave entitlements | **Meet key people – introduce** |
| Notification of sick leave or absences | Buddy |
| **Work environment – show** | Key reports |
| Dining facilities | Members of the direct team |
| Washing and toilet facilities | Individuals outside the team within the wider organization |
| Locker and changing rooms | and outside the organization who are important |
| Telephone calls and collecting messages | relationships/contacts – may require site visits to key |
| Out of hours enquiries and emergency procedures | clients, customers or suppliers |
| **Payroll – explain** | |
| Rates of pay and allowances | |
| Pay arrangements | |
| Taxation (including completion of the required forms) | |
| Superannuation and any other deductions | |
| **Health and safety – explain** | |
| Health and safety policy and procedures | |
| Roles and responsibilities for health and safety | |
| Incident reporting procedures | |

the hierarchy of the organization to the new starter, thereby making it easier to ask for help.

Buddies are often overlooked by organizations, despite the fact that they provide excellent support to new starters and are often the most effective way of socializing new starters into an organizational environment. HR along with line managers need to adopt a proactive approach and identify buddies within each section and department who can assume the role of helping new starters acclimatize to their new environment. They are there to answer any questions, no matter how big or small, and to ensure that the new starter quickly builds a bond with their co-workers, either through formal or informal networks.

> **Organizational citizenship behaviours** – the behaviour of individual employees that is not directly or explicitly required by an organization as part of the role but which promotes the effective functioning of the organization
>
> **Employee turnover** – the number of people who leave an organization and need to be replaced in order to maintain production or service
>
> **Pull factors** – those factors beyond the control of the organization that may cause an employee to leave the organization – such as moving to a new location/country, the arrival of children, retirement and so on

Those companies that are successful at rapid onboarding, or quickly getting new starters to make a productive contribution, tend to adopt a combination approach, utilizing an informational and a relational approach (see Table 4.1). The balance between approaches depends on the level of the employee and the number of new starters in the organization. It is likely that general informational training and materials have a role to play, but in order to be truly effective, this must be supported by a conscious effort to combine this with a focused relational approach. The socialization of new starters into any organization ensures that they become productive members of the workforce more quickly and probably make a valuable contribution sooner. Not only this, but they are likely to become committed to the organization and demonstrate good **organizational citizenship behaviours** ▶ Chapter 14 ◀. Those new starters who fail to integrate quickly into their new environment are more likely to leave the organization, are slower to become fully productive members of the team, and are likely to be less committed to the organization.

### Line management involvement in induction

The failure of line managers to fully engage in the induction process is often viewed as a key problem by HR professionals. Line managers, however, often view induction as the sole responsibility of HR and from a traditional informational perspective, this was probably a reasonable assumption. This attitude can result in little initial attention being given to new starters who, it is assumed, would go through the induction process and then be in a position to begin work without further input from line managers other than specific day-to-day task allocation. Part of the role of HR is to convince line management of the value of an induction programme and how it can truly add value.

Building a business case to demonstrate the importance of the induction process is more likely to result in support from line managers. If HR can show how a well-balanced and structured induction process can enhance the human capital pool, while also ensuring that new starters begin to make a productive contribution as soon as possible, line managers will find it hard to resist. Placing less emphasis on the traditional informational aspect of induction in favour of a more relational approach is also likely to result in more hands-on line management involvement and commitment to the process.

## EMPLOYEE TURNOVER

**Employee turnover**, or 'natural wastage' as it is sometimes referred to, is the number of people who will inevitably leave the organization and will need to be replaced in order to maintain production or service (Gunnigle et al., 2011). Employees leaving to travel, spend more time at home, take on new positions in other organizations, who are dismissed, who retire – these are all examples of labour turnover within an organization. Some of these life events can be planned, such as retirement, but others such as an employee's decision to leave to go travelling can be difficult to plan for from a management perspective.

Some of these factors are beyond the control of the organization, such as moving to a new location, the arrival of children, retirement and so on. These are known as **pull factors** and there is very little an organization can do to hold on to an employee in this type of situation. Having said that, progressive employers may wish to consider being proactive about a high performer who leaves for these reasons. Being progressive simply means ensuring that the employee is aware that, should they wish to return to employment, the organization would welcome an approach. It is not a promise of a job but more a case of leaving the door open. There are also **push factors**, which organizations do have control over. Push factors are those factors that negatively impact on an employee and may be the trigger for them to think about leaving an organization. The main push factors tend to centre on dissatisfaction with work but mainly with the lack of promotional and developmental opportunities. Employee dissatisfaction is often evident but organizations fail to address it adequately until it is too late. Measures seeking to tap into employee attitudes and satisfaction with their work and environment are essential and a key part of HR's role.

> **Push factors** – those factors that negatively impact on an employee and may be the trigger to start them thinking about leaving an organization, such as dissatisfaction with their work, their boss or their promotional opportunities, a lack of developmental opportunities and so on

## The impact of the external labour market environment on turnover levels

In addition to push and pull factors, organizations can often find themselves at the mercy of the external environment. For example, in a booming economy, jobs tend to be in plentiful supply and so the level of turnover experienced by an organization may rocket. High performers may seek out opportunities or, indeed, be headhunted directly by competitors. The upward pressure this can place on salaries can be significant; that is, organizations find that they are having to pay higher and higher levels of salaries to good performers simply to hold on to them and prevent them from leaving for a competitor organization. The focus tends to move towards retention of key performers and putting in place attractive initiatives, which are focused on a healthy level of pay but with significant non-pay elements that bind the employee to the organization. Such non-pay elements might be childcare arrangements, flexible working arrangements, gym membership, parking schemes, training and educational opportunities.

Economics tells us that the boom and bust of economies is cyclical, that is, just as surely as there is a boom, a bust will follow. The time period between the boom and bust is tricky to predict but the cycle of boom and bust generally remains the same. Therefore, organizations will often have to deal with a downturn in the economy and the impact that can have on turnover. In a downturn in the economy, attention tends to focus on downsizing employees and the exiting of staff. While difficult decisions have to made in terms of who stays and who goes, organizations also need to focus on those individuals who remain. The idea of 'survivor guilt' is well documented. Staff who survive a downsizing exercise often feel guilty about their former colleagues losing their jobs, which can have a significant negative impact on productivity. Equally, in a situation where a workforce has been significantly reduced, additional pressures are shouldered by the remaining staff members; that is, less people have to do more in order to get the work done. Again, if not carefully managed, this can create bad feeling and impact on productivity and morale.

## Should an organization seek to minimize its turnover levels?

As we have seen, there are many reasons why someone might leave an organization and despite the negative connotations of the phrase 'turnover', not all turnover is necessarily bad. A certain level of turnover may be considered a good thing, and can result in positive benefits for an organization. As new employees enter an organization, they bring with them fresh ideas and perspectives. They may see things differently and ignite new discussions and debate. This idea of bringing new blood into the organization's human capital pool can assist in avoiding the complacency that sometimes arises within organizations. A danger for many organizations is the development of 'groupthink', whereby members of the organization begin to adopt similar thought processes that reinforce each other without question or scrutiny. It is hard to see things differently if, as happens in some organizations, it is the only thing you have ever known. New employees can be a breath of fresh air in terms of their ideas and energy, as well as new competencies that can add significant value to the organization. These new competencies can open up opportunities that might otherwise remain unrealized by the organization. They can also allow the organization to consider working differently to maximize its potential.

Turnover may also include those individuals who are underperforming and are forced to leave the organization after being through the performance management system, or who leave prior to being forced out when it is clear the situation is unlikely to improve. Again, this type of turnover is not necessarily a negative thing. While organizations do not want to lose their key members of staff, they do not want to have a low turnover rate if that means continuing to employ serial underperformers. Sometimes, organizations boast about their low turnover rate, but we must ask ourselves the question: Is the organization holding on to key talent it does not want to lose or is it stuck with a large proportion of underperforming staff whose performance should have been managed more actively? Low turnover rates are not necessarily a sign of a productive workforce.

It is ironic that the employees an organization wants to hold on to are often the very ones most likely to leave. If you think about it, it makes sense. High-performing employees are more likely to be sought after by others, are likely to be ambitious to advance their careers, and are more likely to seek out new opportunities. An underperforming employee, on the other hand, is unlikely to want to leave an organization where their underperformance is not being actively addressed. If they are permitted by their supervisors to continue to underperform without any repercussions, it is unlikely they will be motivated to improve their behaviour to reach acceptable levels of performance but, equally, they have no incentive to look for alternative work.

So, if low turnover rates are not necessarily a good thing and high turnover rates are not necessarily a bad thing, what is the appropriate level of turnover?

## What is an appropriate turnover level for a business?

An important issue for any organization is deciding what level of turnover is appropriate for their business model. Most organizations don't give sufficient thought to this matter. Different business models will have different costs associated with turnover. The cost of turnover will be higher, for example, where you have a limited pool of people you can recruit due to their specific qualifications or technical abilities, or if the cost of training those individuals is very high. The cost of turnover will be lower, however, if there is an unlimited supply of individuals who could do the work with little or inexpensive training. Equally, some businesses operate successfully with high turnover and their business model is, in fact, based around a high turnover rate. Below, HRM in the News provides two examples of different industries demonstrating how turnover, in this case of high-profile leavers, can have a negative impact on the business success of the organization.

## Costs of labour turnover

As we have discussed, the costs of labour turnover vary by sector and organization; however, there are some basic costs common to all, albeit to a greater or lesser degree financially. Every organization has to deal with the costs associated with dismissing an individual from the organization. There are payroll costs and the calculation of outstanding contractual obligations, such as holidays that have to be paid out as they cannot be taken and so on. While the replacement recruitment process is ongoing, there is the cost of cover for an employee if additional staff have to be drafted in, or if existing staff need to do overtime in order to take up the excess workload. Then there are the costs associated with the recruitment and selection process ▶ **Chapters 2 and 3** ◀. Everything from advertising the position, the time taken to arrive at a shortlist of candidates for interview to the interviews themselves are all costs to the organization. These costs can be considerable and are, essentially, repeat costs, as you had already spent on hiring in the first place. There are also costs associated with the underperformance of individuals who are working out their notice. Individuals who have decided to leave an organization and handed in their notice can often reduce their input while they work out their notice.

Costs tend to be industry specific but, in general, in a tight labour market, organizations can struggle to find a suitable pool of candidates to draw from. This can result in individuals moving quickly through promotional grades without necessarily having gained the equivalent in-depth experience. For example, in Ireland between 2003 and 2007, it was common for an employee to move five times within three years, with each move receiving, on average, a €5,000 per annum hike in salary. When the labour market opens up again, when more people are available to recruit, you have these anomalies in organizations of highly paid individuals who don't necessarily have the skills or competencies required of an individual operating at that level.

## What can organizations do to limit the impact of high-profile leavers?

Organizations can adopt a number of strategies to limit the potential damage of high-profile leavers. At a very senior level, it is essential that the organization seeks to have a clear succession plan in place so as to ensure the smooth transition of power, should the leader of the

## CONSIDER THIS...

Where an individual rises above their level of competency, it is commonly referred to as the **Peter Principle**. Organizations that seek to promote individuals based on performance and achievement and continue to do so will eventually promote an individual beyond their level of ability. For example, you have a great receptionist working for you and you promote them to the role of secretary, in which they do really well. So, you decide to promote them again, this time to personal assistant. Again, they do really well in this role, so much so that you decide they have management potential and you promote them to the position of office manager. Having taken on this role, you find they are a total disaster. They have no people management skills and avoid confrontation, while appearing stubborn with their team. They struggle with the diversity of tasks confronting them and cannot cope with all the people reporting to them seeking answers. This person had been a good receptionist, secretary and PA, but could not make the transition to the next level, that of management, and thus became a victim of the Peter Principle.

organization leave. Most organizations spend a considerable amount of time assessing and then training and developing potential successors. The cost to an organization of appearing to be 'leaderless' is significant and even if a decision is taken to recruit externally, most organizations will put in place a plan to cover any temporary vacancy that may arise.

Lower down the organizational ranks, more and more organizations are seeking to encourage a team-based approach to work in order to minimize the effects of one member of the team leaving. If knowledge is shared among a group rather than concentrated in the hands of just one individual, the ability to deal with turnover of individuals becomes manageable.

**Peter Principle** – the belief that, in an organization where promotion is based on performance and achievement, an organization's members will eventually be promoted beyond their level of ability

### *Measuring turnover*

Now we turn our attention to how to measure turnover levels in an organization. We can see from the discussion above that unplanned or unforeseen turnover is often problematic. HR professionals need to be able, as far as possible, to predict and control the rate of turnover within their organization. Different measures of employee turnover are available, and you need to be clear, particularly when it comes to comparing figures across businesses or sectors, which measures are being used. As HR professionals, it is essential that there is consistency in the measures employed and that management understand what is being measured and what is not.

Two common measures of turnover are the transitional method and the central method (Pilbeam and Corbridge, 2006). The transitional method is a useful forecasting measure and compares the number of employees in a post at the start of a given period and the number that leave during that period. It does not take account of other staff who may start in different/additional roles and subsequently leave.

The central method includes employees who join in a given period and relates the total leavers to the average number of employees in that period. Comparing the results of the two analyses can provide the HR function with some indication as to whether or not employees are leaving within a short time of being recruited and from where. These are the turnover rate calculations:

Transition rate (%) =

$$\frac{\text{Leavers from the group in post at the start} \times 100}{\text{Total employees in the group at the start}}$$

Central rate (%) =

$$\frac{\text{Total leavers from the group} \times 100}{\text{Average number of employees in the group}}$$

The ability to accurately measure labour turnover is an important part of the role of HR but it is often a crude measure of what is going on more generally within an organization. Correctly identifying problems areas if they exist is essential. Any analysis of turnover should seek not only to measure the rate of turnover but also to analyse where it is happening within the organization and why. A robust analysis of turnover allows the organization to put in place policies to tackle the retention of key members of staff.

Increasingly, organizations are looking to supplement their turnover analysis with additional information to provide a more rounded picture of what is going on within their organization in relation to turnover. Many organizations conduct exit interviews with departing employees to ascertain their reasons for leaving the organization. This usually takes place during their notice

## The Impact of a High-profile Leaver

We have discussed the cost of turnover for different industries and different business models, but what about the cost to an organization of losing a high-profile leader. Two cases that recently made the headlines demonstrate this point.

HRM IN THE NEWS

### Steve Jobs: Apple

The news in January 2011 that Steve Jobs was taking a second open-ended leave of medical absence resulted in Apple's share price taking a serious drop. When Steve Jobs took his first leave of absence in 2009, Apple's share price dropped a dramatic 10 per cent before being suspended. Jobs was considered to have such an influence on Apple as an organization, and on its products, that it is often said that the DNA of the company resides with him. When Steve Jobs died of a rare form of pancreatic cancer in October 2011, Apple's share price immediately fell by 5 per cent. In March 2010, financial magazine *Barron's* had attempted to estimate Jobs' value to Apple and came up with a figure of $25 billion. Nobody can possibly know how Apple will fare without its co-founder and

chairman; however, all eyes are now on Jobs' successor Tim Cook who, for the time being at least, appears to have the support of the markets. Only time will tell what impact the loss of such a leader will have on the organization.

### Sir Terence Leahy: Tesco

Sir Terry Leahy announced his surprise retirement as chief executive of the supermarket Tesco after 14 years at the top of a business he had helped turn into one of the UK's biggest success stories. Tesco has sales of nearly £62 billion annually. However, the announcement by Leahy that he intended to retire at the age of 55 wiped more than £750 million off Tesco's market value as markets reacted to the news. Tesco's share price dropped by more than 2 per cent. Under Leahy's stewardship, Tesco now accounts for £1 in every £3 spent on groceries.

While these two cases demonstrate the impact of the loss of key leaders to organizations, the same can often be said for employees lower down the organization who play a pivotal role in the organization's success.

### Questions

1 What are the costs, both direct and indirect, to an organization of losing a high-profile leader, such as Sir Terence Leahy?
2 In the case of Apple, why did Steve Jobs' death affect Apple's share price? What do you think the long-term impact might be?
3 What can organizations do to lessen the effect of high-profile leavers?

### Sources

Akers, C., Twitter, http://online.wsj.com/article/SB10001424052748703396604576087690312543086.html.

Poulter, S. (2010) Tesco's costly goodbye: £750m shares blow as Sir Terry Leahy retires early, MailOnline, 9 June, www.dailymail.co.uk/news/article-1284852/Tesco-boss-Sir-Terry-Leahy-step-14-years-UKs-supermarket.html.

Rao, L. (2011) Steve Jobs to take 'medical leave of absence', stays on as CEO, TechCrunch, 17 January, http://techcrunch.com/2011/01/17/steve-jobs-to-take-medical-leave-of-absence-stays-on-as-ceo/.

Satarino, A., Burrows, P. and Galante, J. (2011) Apple's Jobs takes leave as weight loss said to continue; Cook takes over, Bloomberg, 18 January, www.bloomberg.com/news/2011-01-17/apple-chief-executive-jobs-granted-medical-leave-of-absence.html.

period and is conducted by a member of the HR team. The detailed collection and, crucially, analysis of this information can provide management with useful insights as to where problems are occurring, or may arise in the future, that are causing people to leave the organization. A perceived lack of training or promotional opportunities or indeed the belief that other organizations are paying higher wages are issues that often arise in exit interviews. Such information should not just be taken at face value, but should form part of a wider analysis of organizational benchmarking against competitors, or the basis of a review of internal promotions, for example.

Another useful tool in analysing turnover is cohort analysis. The idea is to analyse the level of turnover in different cohorts, or groups, of employees. These groups may be employees from various departments or grouped by gender or ethnicity. Cohort analysis can be particularly insightful in relation to an analysis of skill sets. If a company finds that it is losing a group of employees with a particular skill set, this may trigger a review of pay or promotion opportunities for that group. The development of individual staff profiles aids this process by easily identifying where turnover rates are high among a particular set of employees with a particular skill set. In undertaking a cohort analysis, the HR function may find that one department in particular is responsible for driving up the overall turnover rate for the organization. The reasons for this high level of turnover among a particular group of employees can then be examined and strategies put in place to reduce the level of turnover.

## RETENTION

As we have seen from our discussion regarding induction and turnover, it is clear that in today's dynamic business environment, companies that want to remain competitive must adopt a more strategic approach to retention. The growing importance of retention can be seen from the costs associated with unsuccessful induction and the subsequent high turnover rates within an organization. The costs are considerable, particularly in relation to the turnover of high performers. These include the direct costs, which might include the cost of finding, selecting and training a replacement, as well as the indirect costs, which include lost productivity, reduced morale, diminished company reputation and loss of key knowledge to a rival firm. Increasingly, organizations are placing more and more emphasis on adopting a strategic approach to the management of turnover. A key tool to reducing undesirable turnover is the ability to hold on to high performers by developing a focused, strategic approach to retention. Garger (1999: 273) advocates a three-part strategy to the development of a strategic approach to retention.

> **Retention** – a strategic approach adopted by organizations to keep productive employees from seeking alternative employment

### Recruitment and selection

An effective retention strategy begins at the earliest stage of the recruitment and selection process. A company seeking to fill a position within their organization must look beyond the skills required to perform the role effectively, and ensure that the individual demonstrates a good fit with the organizational culture. In other words, in addition to having the necessary competencies to undertake the role, they must also have the right blend of attitude, traits and behaviours to match the core values of the organization. We have seen how employees who fail to successfully socialize into an organization are at greater risk of leaving. The realization that 'organizational fit' is as important as individual employee ability has resulted in organizations now considering

hiring for attitude and then looking to train new employees in terms of skills. It is often easier to provide the necessary training to a new starter with regard to specific skills than it is to change a new starter's attitude or behaviour towards their work.

In an effort to find individuals who provide a better fit with the organizational values, organizations are increasingly looking towards behavioural-based selection interviewing ▶ Chapter 3 ◀. This can provide insights as to whether an applicant not only has the appropriate experience but also demonstrates values consistent with those of the organization. Scenarios are presented to applicants who must then say how they would react in that particular situation. This type of interview allows an employer to evaluate not only the applicant's use of appropriate judgement, but also to delve into their values and work ethic. Such interviews can be conducted by incorporating behavioural-based questions designed to elicit stories from candidates about their work history, which can allow an assessment as to whether work styles and preferences match those of the organizational culture.

As we have already discussed, the importance of effective induction cannot be underestimated in terms of ensuring that new starters quickly adjust to their new surroundings and become productive members of the team as soon as possible. The longer a new starter takes to acclimatize to a new work environment, the more damaging the loss in terms of productivity for the organization.

### Training and career management

We have seen earlier in this chapter that workers leave organizations for a variety of reasons. Many employees now look to the companies they work for to provide them with growth and learning opportunities. In particular, high performers often perceive development as a benefit they are entitled to and expect employer-provided opportunities to upgrade and develop their personal skill set. In fast-paced, competitive environments, the ability to stay current in terms of your skills is considered vitally important to most employees. This, however, presents organizations with a difficult challenge. Should they invest in their staff to make them more marketable to their competitors? Should they invest in employees only for them to leave the organization once they have received their training and move on to progress their careers elsewhere? This is a difficult balance between expenditure on training and understandable concerns regarding loss of employees once trained. What we do know, however, is that investing in employees' training and promotional activities generally has a positive impact on retention (Garger, 1999). Ironically, when organizations provide opportunities for employees to become more marketable by acquiring new skills, job satisfaction and commitment generally increase, as does retention.

# BUILDING YOUR SKILLS

Organizations have a real concern about paying for training employees as this makes them more employable to competitors. The result may be that they leave before the company realizes a return on their investment. If you are the line manager in an organization, what measures would you suggest to help safeguard the organization's investment? What are the pros and cons of each of the suggestions you have proposed?

Progressive organizations work cooperatively with employees to develop learning opportunities, which not only address the organization's skills gaps but also satisfy employees' professional and personal interests. Development efforts are more successful when they are the responsibility of line managers and the employee concerned, while being integrated within the company culture. Companies that use development effectively as a retention tool recognize that people learn in different ways, and offer a variety of learning programmes and growth opportunities.

## Motivation and compensation

The traditional methods that companies use to motivate and compensate their employees do not always produce optimal results in relation to productivity and retention. Financial incentives such as cash, stocks and shares, which were once the critical components of a retention strategy, have proved less effective in recent years ▸ **Chapter 8** ◂. This is because in today's marketplace, there are too many companies willing and able to match their competitors'

financial offerings. Financial packages, such as bonuses, stock options and hefty salaries, can easily be duplicated. This, added to the recent financial turmoil, has resulted in many financial incentives, especially stock options, being rendered relatively worthless.

An organization may find that a more effective retention strategy involves nonfinancial rewards that promote feelings of achievement, ownership and involvement. Many employees also seek more open communication, more meaningful work and a better work–life balance. We know that organizations where employees feel they are valued have higher levels of employee commitment and hence higher retention levels.

Employee attitude surveys can help an organization determine the rewards that are most sought by its employees. It is likely, however, that employees do not all place equal value on the rewards offered by the organization ▸ **Chapter 8** ◂. In fact, different employees will probably value different things, depending on the stage of their career and where they are in their life cycle. For example, a younger member of staff who likes to travel may value additional leave as a method of reward, so they could travel on their holidays for an extended period. On the other hand, an older worker may value additional contributions towards their pension. A young parent may value flexible working arrangements, while an older worker may value the opportunity to reduce their working week as they approach retirement.

Given that all employees do not place the same value on the rewards on offer, either financial or nonfinancial, the key to success is that organizations know what it is their staff value and target specific groups if necessary. This may involve offering employees the option to choose from a limited selection of reward choices, ranging from additional leave to extra pension contributions. This idea of tailoring benefits to suit the needs of individual employees is known as **flexible benefits**. Offering all employees the same set of rewards is likely to please some but not all employees. Employers and HR also need to educate employees as to the value of the packages they receive. Employees often don't fully understand the benefits offered nor the value of these benefits to them – disability benefit, death in service, pension, maternity pay and so on. Organizations need to ensure that they communicate effectively with their staff regarding the uniqueness of the package on offer and why the company is a great place to work and why they should stay working there.

**Employee attitude surveys** – research carried out to assess the feelings of a target group of employees towards various aspects of their work, their team and their organization

**Flexible benefits** – from a defined set of available benefits, employees select the benefits that best meet their needs

## The Exit Interview and Employee Retention

You have recently been appointed as the director of HR for a medium-sized Dutch computer gaming organization. The company has seen rapid expansion over the past three years in particular and prides itself on being innovative and reactive in the fast-changing market. It has been successful since its foundation and there is no reason to think that this success will not continue into the future. That said, one of the key concerns of the senior management team has been the relatively high level of turnover within the organization. The loss of key individuals to competitor organizations has been of most concern. Senior management are at a loss to understand why the company is experiencing such high levels of staff turnover and while they suspect it is due to higher salaries being offered elsewhere, they have asked you to investigate.

You understand from your HR team that the organization undertakes an exit interview with each leaving member of staff. Delighted to hear this news, you ask one of your team to pull all exit interviews and to analyse and present the information contained therein. The report you receive is bland and provides no real insights into the problems that may exist within the organization. Informal chats with various members of the organization point to problems with training and development opportunities, a lack of promotional opportunities, absence of flexible working arrangements and a number of other nonfinancial issues. You are now faced with a problem. You have been told informally that problems exist but you have no real data to back this up. The current exit interviews do not hold the information you require. Tensions clearly exist with the current staff but there appears to be no mechanism to capture this information. The loss of staff is likely to continue if not increase unless you do something and quickly.

© PHOTODISC/GETTY IMAGES

1 As HR director, outline what you see as the problems facing the organization.
2 What initiatives or strategies do you propose in order to tackle the problem(s)?
3 What suggestions do you have in terms of gathering more accurate information for senior management with regard to turnover and retention?
4 How can you use the information gathered to improve overall employee retention?

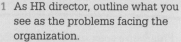 SUMMARY

We can see that induction, turnover and retention are inextricably linked. A focused and strategic approach to the management of each area, while recognizing the linkages between them, is vitally important. The process begins with good recruitment and must be followed through with appropriate induction programmes, which seek to ensure rapid socialization of new starters, while ensuring focused retention policies are in place for high performers. By ensuring all these are in place, an organization reduces its exposure to undesirable turnover effects and ensures that high-performing employees are more likely to be engaged and therefore remain productive and happy employees for the longer term.

CHAPTER REVIEW QUESTIONS

1  Why should organizations invest in providing induction programmes for the benefit of their employees? Is it money well spent?
2  What is the rationale for such a programme from a business perspective?
3  What contribution can a strategic view of employee induction, turnover and retention make to an organization's sustained competitive advantage?
4  Does it matter if an organization has high levels of employee turnover?
5  Is all employee turnover a bad thing? Discuss your answer in relation to push and pull factors as they impact on employees.
6  What is the strategic imperative for developing a focused retention strategy?
7  Does a well-financed retention strategy justify the investment required by an organization?

 FURTHER READING

Armstrong, M. (2009) *Armstrong's Handbook of Human Resource Management Practice*, 11th edn, London: Kogan Page.

Bratton, J. and Gold, J. (2007) *Human Resource Management: Theory and Practice*, 4th edn, Basingstoke: Palgrave Macmillan.

Garger, E.M. (1999) Holding on to high performers: a strategic approach to retention, *Compensation and Benefits Management*, **15**(4): 10–17.

Gunnigle, P., Heraty, N. and Morley, M. (2011) *Human Resource Management in Ireland: An Introduction*, 4th edn, Dublin: Gill & Macmillan.

Leatherbarrow, C., Fletcher, J. and Currie, D. (2010) *Introduction to Human Resource Management: A Guide to HR in Practice*, London: CIPD.

Leopold, L. and Harris, L. (2009) *The Strategic Managing of Human Resources*, 2nd edn, Harlow: Prentice Hall.

Pilbeam, S. and Corbridge, M. (2010) *People Resourcing and Talent Planning: HRM in Practice*, 4th edn, Harlow: Pearson Education.

Rollag, K., Parise, S. and Cross, R. (2005) Getting new hires up to speed quickly, *MIT Sloan Management Review*, **46**(2): 35–41.

 USEFUL WEBSITES

www.shrm.org
The SHRM Foundation has excellent resources available for students and practitioners alike. The website provides up-to-date, well-researched material across all the major HR areas. Definitely worth a visit.

www.ere.net/2009/04/06/not-all-employee-turnover-is-bad-celebrate-losing-the-losers/
A well-written, accessible article outlining why not all turnover is necessarily bad. Also some interesting commentary from those who have read it and are working in the area.

www.cipd.co.uk/podcasts/_articles/_strategiesforattractingandretainingtalent.htm
This podcast is relatively short but covers a number of issues that should be considered in relation to turnover, retention and induction.

www.cipd.co.uk/hr-resources/factsheets/employee-turnover-retention.aspx
CIPD short fact sheets are an invaluable source of information for HR practitioners, and also help students of HR to understand how the theory is applied in reality, in this case, turnover and retention.

 For extra resources including videos and further skills development guidance go to: www.palgrave.com/business/carbery

# 5

# EQUALITY IN THE WORKPLACE

Juliette McMahon

*By the end of this chapter you will be able to:*

## LEARNING OUTCOMES

- Explain the reasons why inequality exists in the labour market and in workplaces

- Understand what we mean by the 'social justice' and the 'business case' for promoting equality

- Identify the key elements of equality promotion and regulation in various countries

- Discuss the controversy relating to positive discrimination and the difference between this and positive action

- Identify key differences between equality regulation in different countries

- Explain the role of HRM in promoting equality, ensuring that the workplace is free from discrimination and dealing with complaints

- Identify and explain the key processes and procedures utilized by organizations, namely, equality and dignity at work policies

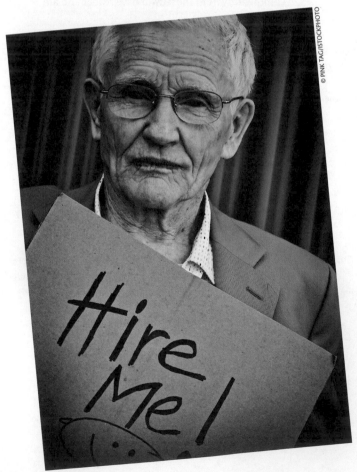

© PINK TAG/ISTOCKPHOTO

*This chapter discusses ...*

## INTRODUCTION

This chapter deals with the concept of equal treatment at work and the issue of discriminatory practices in the workplace. We look at what we mean by terms such as 'equality' and 'discrimination', examine why discrimination occurs in the first place, who is most at risk, and the key aspects of legislation that exist to counter discrimination.

What do we mean by equality and discrimination? These are terms we often utilize but rarely define; indeed, it is difficult to find accepted definitions. In broad terms, equality can be viewed as the state of being equal, particularly in relation to status, rights or opportunities; while discrimination focuses on treating a person or group differently, or unfairly, on the basis of certain traits or characteristics, such as sexuality, gender, race, religion or disability. From these definitions, we can see that equality and discrimination are broad terms encompassing far more than a person's experience or treatment at work. This is important, as research has shown that unequal treatment in the workplace often stems from discrimination in wider society (Le Grand, 2003) and can take many forms. Consider, for instance, a woman who may not be offered a job because an employer feels she may not be committed enough to the organization as she has a number of children to care for, or someone experiencing harassment or bullying in the workplace because they have a particular sexual orientation. Consider also someone who is refused a job because they use a wheelchair and the workplace cannot accommodate them, or someone with literacy problems who cannot meet the minimum requirements for many jobs. Another question is: Why is there a persistent wage gap between men and women in most countries, which cannot be explained away by skill and experience differences alone? We can relate these and other instances of workplace disadvantage to wider social issues.

In this chapter we seek to explore the issue of equality and fair treatment at work but first we need to understand a number of underpinning issues: Why is this an important consideration? Why does inequality happen and where does it stem from? What can be done to counteract it? We then examine the legal obligations of employers in this regard and discuss the measures that organizations can take to ensure equal treatment of employees and the wider community. We also briefly examine the variations across different countries in their approaches to this issue. Finally, we look at the role of HR professionals in promoting and ensuring equal treatment in the workplace.

## SPOTLIGHT ON SKILLS

1   You are approached by Marta, a Nigerian woman who works in your restaurant. She is very upset and claims that she has been racially insulted by another employee. Outline the actions and steps you would take in addressing this issue and what procedure you would follow.

2   You have been asked to give a training session to new supervisors on their obligations with respect to equality in the selection process. Outline the key issues you would address in such a training session and why you would include these.

3   You have received a complaint of discrimination from a recent unsuccessful job applicant who says in their letter that they feel your company discriminated against them in the selection process and they intend to follow through on their complaint with the relevant national agency tasked with dealing with such complaints. How would you go about preparing to deal with the anticipated claim? When considering this, think about action you would need to take within the company, documentation you may need to source from outside agencies, and external bodies in general who you may need to liaise with.

To help you answer the questions above, visit www.palgrave.com/business/carbery and watch the video of Áine Hynes providing legal advice regarding equality issues.

## WHY IS EQUALITY AN IMPORTANT ISSUE?

The ability to participate in and to progress within employment are extremely important issues for many individuals. Much research demonstrates that the ability and opportunity to gain access to employment are key factors in what we term social inclusion, and inequality in employment is indicative and reflective of inequality in the wider society. According to a European Commission report (2005a), employment is a key factor for wider social inclusion, not only because it generates income, but also because it can promote social participation and personal development and contributes to maintaining adequate living standards in old age. Moving from unemployment to employment considerably lowers the likelihood of being exposed to the risk of poverty in general. Gaining access to employment is, however, problematic for many people and it has been shown that this is not necessarily due to people 'not wanting to work', 'doing better on welfare' or being lazy. For many people, equality at work and access to work is due to deep-rooted factors in society, which will be examined below.

There are many groups of people who are disproportionately marginalized with respect to access to employment and the ability to retain employment in times of recession. Who these groups are can vary across countries, but in general research identifies women, young unskilled workers, low skilled workers in general and older workers, ethnic minorities, lone parents, and people living in identified marginalized communities as those suffering most from marginalization in terms of access to jobs, being confined to low-paid jobs, unequal treatment in the workplace and so on (Le Grand, 2003; European Commission, 2009).

The reasons for this are explored below. We can all relate to discrimination and unequal treatment caused by people's attitudes to others, but if we take the example of someone not being successful in the job market because of a lack of qualifications, is this completely the 'fault' of that person? Should they not just go and increase their qualifications to become more competitive? However, the situation for many people is not as simple as this, as you will see in the following sections.

Equality and equal treatment in the work situation cannot be viewed in isolation. Equal access to work and subsequent career success are influenced by many factors, such as a person's social background, access to education, gender, race and disability. Key questions are: Why do certain groups find themselves

**Equality** – the state of being equal, especially in status, rights or opportunities

**Discrimination** – treating a person or group differently and unfairly on the basis of certain traits or characteristics, such as sexuality, gender, race, religion or disability

**Social inclusion** – a measure of the extent to which a person or groups can participate in aspects of society to the same level as (or relative to) the average population. Key measures of social inclusion are access to work, adequate housing, education levels and access to education, healthcare and so on

disproportionately disadvantaged in the labour market? Who are these groups? What can be done to change the situation? There are three key explanations, based on existing research, discussed below.

## Human capital explanations of inequality in the workplace

Human capital explanations of a person's competiveness in the labour market are based on an analysis of the combination of qualifications, skills, competencies and relevant existing work experience a person possesses. Possessing a third-level qualification, for instance, has been identified as a key factor in human capital terms, conferring significant advantages in competing for jobs and promotion within jobs (Russell et al., 2005; Eurostat, 2006). People with a higher level of human capital would be expected to compete more successfully in the labour market than those with a lower level of human capital. For instance, if two people apply for a job and one has more relevant experience for the position and also a higher relevant qualification, we would expect that person to have a greater chance of securing the job. This seems perfectly rational and fair. However, we need to examine why some people possess less human capital than others. Some research argues that this is based on the choices people make. Using the example of women in the labour market, it has been argued by some that the difference between women's and men's experience in the labour market is because women choose to prioritize family commitments over work. Thus, women will, for instance, take maternity leave or take leave to care for children, thereby reducing their work experience relative to men (Anker, 2001; Baron and Cobb-Clark, 2010; Turner and MacMahon, 2011). Studies internationally have shown that migrant workers suffer disadvantage in their 'host' labour markets, as their qualifications may not be recognized and they find themselves working in jobs with lower status and/or pay. In some situations, even where their qualifications may be recognized, a language barrier may have a negative effect on their ability to compete in the labour market (Chiswick and Miller, 2009).

In Ireland, a particular problem has been identified with 'early school leavers'. This is a situation whereby young people leave school as soon as they are legally entitled to, but before they have the necessary qualifications to enable them to access third-level or higher education. These young people come primarily from socially disadvantaged areas and thus often face multiple levels of disadvantage in the labour market. This issue is not confined to Ireland but is also reflected in other European counties. Recent figures from EU member states identify that currently more than 14 per cent of 18–24-year-olds have left school with lower secondary education or less (Central Statistics Office, 2012; European Commission, 2012). But how much 'choice' is actually involved?

## CONSIDER THIS ...

Do you agree with the concept that if women choose to withdraw from the workplace to care for children, they are themselves responsible for possessing less human capital? Think about other groups of people who might possess less human capital than others and why this might happen.

## Inequality as a reflection of social and cultural attitudes and norms

Human capital factors cannot be considered in isolation from the social, cultural and institutional context of any labour market (Blau and Kahn, 2006). Taking gender, for instance, the human capital explanation that women may 'choose' to opt out or take breaks from the labour market because they prioritize childcare is contested by many commentators (Petrongolo, 2004; England, 2005; Tomlinson et al., 2009). The ability of women to participate in the labour market, it is argued, is affected by deeply rooted social norms that serve to limit their choices and oblige them to withdraw from the labour market. In many Western European countries, women are overwhelmingly viewed in societal terms as the primary carer and are naturally assumed to be the parent who will take time off when needed to care for children. For instance, a study of men and women in Ireland found that only 2 per cent of people surveyed who listed their primary activity as looking after home/family were male (Central Statistics Office, 2012).

Thus, this second perspective on inequality takes into account social attitudes and norms. According to this perspective, unfairness in the allocation of jobs and promotions occurs as a consequence of the way opportunity has been embedded in societal norms (Anker, 2001; Noon 2004; Price, 2004). By that, we mean that inequality is viewed as *socially constructed* rather than based on objective criteria (Gardiner, 1998). In other words, as society develops over time, we accept certain perceptions of groups in society as 'normal' and acceptable. For instance, until the 1920s, it was considered 'normal' that women did not have the opportunity to vote in Britain. Equally, racial segregation in parts of the USA earlier in the twentieth century severely restricted the ability of African Americans to gain access to 'good' jobs, which had wider implications for this societal group in terms of wealth and social standing. The reasons these accepted 'norms' develop are complex and a combination of many historical, cultural, legal and other factors. Have you ever considered why, for instance, racial segregation was considered 'normal' in South Africa and the USA, why the ethnic Roma population of Europe were not accepted as members of 'normal' society, or why it has traditionally been accepted that women are viewed as the primary carer in families and men as the main breadwinner?

Dominant or accepted beliefs in society with respect to various groups of people may then be translated into the workplace. For example, a belief that older people may not be open to learning new skills or may not be able to cope with new technology has been shown to affect access to employment and promotion within employment for older workers. In one US case in 2008, a company that was selecting people for layoff instructed managers to rate employees based on how 'flexible' and 'retrainable' they were. Of the 31 people selected for redundancy, 30 were over the age of forty. The workers subsequently won a Supreme Court case on the basis of age discrimination (*Meacham* v. *Knolls Atomic Power Lab*, No. 06-1505, 2008).

## BUILDING YOUR SKILLS

Why do you think the employees selected for redundancy in the atomic power lab case above were considered less 'retrainable' and 'flexible'? If you were a line manager in a company, what criteria could you identify that your company might use to objectively measure a person's 'retrainability' or flexibility?

## Institutional explanations of inequality

The third explanation for inequality emphasizes the effect of institutional factors on work outcomes. Institutional barriers to employment result from dominant structures, systems and rules that can act to limit access and opportunity for certain people in the workplace. For instance, a 'long-hours' culture, often used as a measure of commitment by organizations, can act as a barrier to promotion for parents with family and childcare responsibilities (Collinson and Hearn, 1994; Kirton and Greene, 2005). Generally speaking, women work shorter hours than men and are more likely to work part time (Presser et al., 2008; OECD, 2010). Irish figures (Central Statistics Office, 2012) indicate that over 41 per cent of working men work at least 40 hours a week compared to approximately 17 per cent of women in employment, and this figure is broadly replicated in other countries. In the UK, females work, on average, 31 hours a week, while males work, on average, 41 hours a week. The difference is even more marked in the Netherlands, where females work an average 24-hour week, while males work an average 35-hour week (Eurostat, 2012a).

Indeed, the accepted unwritten norm that a committed worker is one for whom temporal barriers do not exist has been shown to disadvantage women in many professions in terms of advancement and pay. It also discourages men from availing themselves of flexible work practices for fear of being overlooked for promotion or, conversely, being selected for redundancy (Hamel et al., 2006; Harrington et al., 2008). Other

> **Institutional barriers** – those barriers to employment or progression within employment posed by existing structures, systems and rules, which act to exclude certain groups of people, for example a lack of childcare facilities

institutional barriers that have been identified are the traditional ways of doing business, and making an impression on the boss by association with the 'old boys' network'. This 'boys' club' involves activities such as golf outings and sessions in the pub, which can often exclude female employees and those from non-drinking cultures. Given these institutional barriers, it might be predicted that women will subsequently be overrepresented at lower levels in organizations, underrepresented at more senior levels and also be paid less, and this is indeed borne out by statistics (Eurostat, 2012a; Central Statistics Office, 2012).

If we take people with disabilities as another example, this cohort of the workforce have often suffered from a lack of institutionalized support to enable access to education and work. Such facilities range from physical ones such as wheelchair access, to extra supports for people with disabilities such as sight loss, dyslexia and intellectual disabilities. Thus, people with disabilities may be prevented from gaining the appropriate qualifications necessary to have sufficient human capital to compete in the workplace. Consider for a moment what difficulties you would face in your current course if you suffered from one of the following: sight loss, hearing loss or were confined to a wheelchair. If people with disabilities do gain qualifications, they often face further obstacles in gaining access to employment due to a lack of suitable workplace facilities and transport to workplaces.

Table 5.1 provides a summary of some of these three explanations of inequality.

**Table 5.1** Sample of factors contributing to labour market inequality

| Human capital factors | Socially constructed factors | Institutional factors |
|---|---|---|
| Formal qualifications<br>Acquired skills<br>Work experience<br>Formal and informal training and development, e.g. workshops, on the job training, coaching, mentoring | Accepted social and cultural norms, e.g. women as carers<br>Prejudice and attitudes, e.g. racism, ageism<br>Self-perception as 'inferior', e.g. a member of a traditionally excluded ethnic group may have low expectations<br>Prevailing political ideology | Rules and legislation, e.g. prohibiting refugees working<br>Lack of relevant support, such as childcare, funded training, transport for disabled people<br>Membership of professional associations with restricted entry<br>Informal 'customs' that facilitate progression, e.g. 'old boys' network', golf club outings<br>Lack of protective legislation |

## Variations across countries

While the three perspectives give us a useful framework with which to analyse the reasons for inequality in the labour market and the workplace, it must be acknowledged that the effect of various factors affecting equality vary across countries. Significant contemporary barriers affecting female and lone-parent participation in the labour market, for instance, include the availability of childcare support. Taking Ireland as an example, there is an absence of state support for childcare in comparison to other European countries. Childcare costs in Ireland rank among the highest in Europe (Immervoll and Barber, 2005). This situation contrasts significantly with many of the Scandinavian countries, which have state-supported childcare and paid leave opportunities for parents. In Ireland, women in the 20–44 age group are most affected by this lack of childcare (Central Statistics Office, 2007, 2012). While 88 per cent of females with no children are in employment, only 58 per cent of those with preschool children are in employment.

As already stated, the three explanations of inequality should not be viewed in isolation, as they are, in fact, interrelated and interwoven. A good illustration in an Irish context is the 'marriage bar', which existed in Ireland until the 1970s. This was a legislative provision that acted to exclude married women from public and some private sector employment in Ireland. As such, it was an institutional factor, but clearly a reflection of the social consensus of the time that a woman's primary role was to care for the family and the home (Beaumont, 1999). We can also look at the stark evidence of the significant disadvantages facing young black people in Britain today. A report by the British Institute for Public Policy Research (2010) claimed that 48% of all young black people aged 16–24 living in Britain are unemployed compared with 20% of young white people. The report also claimed that jobless figures for young black people had risen by 13% compared with 8% among white people and 6% among Asians. The 2009 figures for unemployment among black men, at 18%, are also in sharp contrast to a figure of 8% for white men. Added to this, the early school leaver rate for black children is disproportionately higher than white children and over twice as many black children are permanently excluded from schools in Britain than white children

every year. Thus, young black people face human capital, institutional and, increasingly, negative attitudinal obstacles to gaining work and social inclusion.

With respect to lone parents, the number of people living as lone parents has increased in many countries and this cohort often face multiple barriers to work and social inclusion (Millar and Evans, 2003). Studies in the UK (Millar and Evans, 2003) have shown that most lone parents are women, and over half of all lone parents have neither technical nor academic qualifications. Lone parents also tend to be concentrated in more socially disadvantaged communities, thus facing multiple barriers to work inclusion, such as potential negative attitudes and lack of a third-level qualification.

## DRIVERS OF EQUALITY AND EQUAL TREATMENT AT WORKPLACE LEVEL

Most organizations exist to make a profit and provide returns for stakeholders such as shareholders. Does the concept of fostering equality 'fit' this model? For instance, if an employer has the choice between employing someone with a disability, for whom they may have to incur a cost in terms of making certain adaptations to the workplace, or employing someone without a disability, what should that employer do? This question is rooted in the debate on whether organizations are stand-alone profit-making entities, or part of a wider societal context with social obligations. These perspectives are summed up by the social justice approach to workplace equality, and the business case, both of which are outlined below.

> **Social justice approach** – the social justice case for equality holds that organizations have a moral obligation, regardless of profit, to promote, foster and practise equality in all facets of the business
>
> **Business case** – the business case for equality holds that fostering, promoting and practising equality in business is good for business and contributes to profits; and on this basis, organizations should engage with principles of equality

## The social justice case

Social justice, as the term suggests, involves viewing the issue of workplace equality within the broader context of morality and fairness. The key principle here is that organizations exist as part of a wider society/community, are embedded within that community and, as such, should behave as 'citizens' by getting involved and contributing to the development of that community. A key objective of this approach is that organizations have a duty to contribute to creating a more equitable and inclusive society. According to this perspective, the issue of whether there are any direct gains to the organization should be disregarded. Should organizations whose goal is to make profit have an obligation to participate in this model? There is no definitive answer to this question, as our feelings on this will be driven by our own ideologies and beliefs.

## The business case

In essence, the business case approach advocates that by promoting and providing an environment that supports equality, organizations can benefit economically. In other words, equality is viewed in terms of what it can deliver by way of returns to the business. For instance, having a more inclusive workforce with equal opportunities can have a positive effect on engagement and thus productivity, and can also generate a more positive image in the minds of the company's customers. Having a more diverse workforce also enables organizations to stay in touch with what appeals to a more diverse customer base, provide goods and services that meet these needs and thus be more profitable. The problem with such an approach is that if equality is contingent on its financial contribution to the organization, it can be rationally argued that in times of recession, or where it is perceived that equality policies no longer contribute to profit, these policies can validly be set aside.

Another way of approaching the business case is to look at the potential negative outcomes and costs associated with not having an inclusive organization that treats people fairly and equitably. As we will see later, if an organization is found to be treating employees unfairly, in contravention of existing equality legislation, there can be substantial costs associated with this. In 2011, a doctor working in an NHS hospital in the UK was awarded £4.5 million in an equality case where it was found she was discriminated against on grounds of gender and race following her return from maternity leave (*Michalak* v. *Mid Yorkshire Hospitals NHS Trust*, ET/1810815/2008). Thus, organizations must also think of the negative publicity and material costs they may face if a case arouses the interest of the press. Another key consideration is the effect on employees in a workplace that is perceived as treating people unfairly or in a discriminatory manner.

**Protected grounds** – those identified by national institutions as relating to areas where discrimination has or is likely to occur, such as race, sex, sexual orientation, religion, age and disability, and which are subsequently covered by equality legislation

In such organizations, research has shown that there can be negative effects on employees' wellbeing, their perceptions of the organization, engagement, turnover, absenteeism and, ultimately, productivity and profit. For instance, if we take the example of the female doctor above, the effects of the treatment she experienced must have been quite stressful and could have affected not only her wellbeing but also possibly her ability to work effectively. High levels of stress have been shown to affect employees' ability to perform effectively and cause increased absenteeism. We must also consider the effects of her treatment on fellow employees, especially other women considering having children or those of other racial origins and how this case would affect their perception of the organization.

CONSIDER THIS ...

Do you think profit-making private sector organizations should have any responsibility towards the communities in which they operate?

## National initiatives to foster equality

In many countries, it is recognized that certain groups of people are disproportionately disadvantaged in the labour market. Governments have recognized that measures need to be taken to try and 'level the playing field', that is, create quality of opportunity for people trying to access jobs and minimize any discrimination with respect to all aspects of employment. This is not just restricted to access and applying for jobs but includes promotion, access to training, freedom from bullying and harassment, selection for redundancy and unfair dismissal. Generally speaking, governments tend to promote and support equality through funded information and awareness measures and the enactment of protective legislation. In Britain, Ireland and other countries, legislation forbids discrimination on the basis of **protected grounds**. A protected ground is a trait or condition identified by legal jurisdictions that cannot be used as the basis for employment decisions. Such characteristics can include race, gender, age, family status, disability, being a member of an ethnic minority and so on. Depending on the country, governments will focus initiatives and legislation on characteristics that have been identified as being associated with social and work disadvantage.

## LEGISLATION AND EQUALITY

Governments utilize legislative measures that confer obligations on employers with respect to equal treatment of employees. This varies from country to country. Differences between countries' approaches to legislation are influenced by the prevailing political ideology, and historical, cultural and social factors. Suk (2012), for instance, highlights a key difference in legislative provision between US and European equality legislation. In the USA, mandatory maternity leave and mandatory retirement ages are considered discriminatory, while in Europe, both mandatory maternity leave and retirement ages for employees are upheld by legislation. According to Suk, these divergent approaches are underpinned by a highly individualistic US society that values individual autonomy, while the European approach is underpinned by a more collectivist approach. Having said that, if we examine the existing legal provision for equality and nondiscrimination across different countries, we find a generally accepted idea that a violation of the principle of nondiscrimination would be said to occur in the following circumstances: a person is subject to different treatment from a **comparator** and the difference in treatment does not have an objective and reasonable justification, or if there is no proportionality between the aim sought and the means employed.

Overall, the laws governing equality in Britain, the Republic of Ireland, other EU member states and the USA are similar in terms of their principles, prohibited actions and modes of redress. A key difference between the USA and the EU is that the USA draws mainly on its own civil rights legislation and has also introduced an Act prohibiting the use of genetic information to discriminate against potential employees. Interestingly though, small companies employing less than 15 people are exempt from much of the equality legislation in the USA. One of the reasons put forward for this exemption is the cost

associated with complying with the legislation. This is not the case in Ireland and other EU member states. In general terms, in the USA, the UK and other European countries, employers are not allowed to discriminate against people who fall under protected grounds, namely race, religion, disability, sex, ethnic origin, national origin, religion or belief, and age (European Union Agency for Fundamental Rights, 2011). There are also provisions for equal pay in all these jurisdictions. In general, the legislation governing equal pay is based on the concept of 'like work'; that is, a woman is entitled to the same pay as a male comparator if that woman performs work that is either exactly the same as her male comparator, has a few differences but amounts to work of equal value to the organization, or has so few differences that it makes no material difference.

Most EU member countries adopt legislation in line with Directives issued by the EU. These Directives are based on the underpinning principles of various EU treaties; most notably, the Treaty of Rome (1957) and, more recently, the EU Charter of Fundamental Rights (enacted in the Treaty of Lisbon on 1 December 2009). As a result, most EU member countries have broadly similar laws governing workplace equality, with small variations. For instance, the equality legislation in the UK protects transsexuals and those entering into civil partnerships from discrimination in employment, while this is not addressed in all other European countries. In Germany, however, there is a legal obligation on employers whereby they must set aside a certain percentage of jobs for people with a disability. This is not the case in the UK.

Victimization of people who take a case against employers under the equality legislation is outlawed in all jurisdictions. Victimization would occur where an employer or co-workers take negative action against an employee because they are pursuing an equality claim. Examples of victimization include ostracizing someone in the workplace, sacking them or demoting them. Discriminatory advertising is also prohibited. This is advertising that acts to discourage or exclude applications from people protected by equality legislation. For instance, an upper age limit on a recruitment advertisement would be considered contrary to equality legislation. Distinctions are made between **direct discrimination** and **indirect discrimination** under EU

**Comparator** – a person or group that someone making a claim of discrimination will compare themselves to, with the purpose of demonstrating that they have been treated differently/unfairly using that comparator as a standard

**Direct discrimination** – discrimination that is obviously contrary to the terms of equality legislation, such as explicitly excluding people over 50 from applying for a job

**Indirect discrimination** – this occurs when a seemingly neutral provision attached to a job acts to exclude a person or group protected under equality legislation; for example, a requirement for people to be over 2m tall for a job in a shop would effectively exclude more women than men

legislation. Direct discrimination is obvious discrimination, for example explicitly limiting access to a job to people of one gender in an advertisement. Indirect discrimination is a more subtle form of discrimination. This is said to occur where there is a seemingly neutral condition attached to a job or access to a job but it can be shown that this provision materially disadvantages a person who has rights under equality legislation. For instance, it has been held that changing a work start time from 9am back to 7am, while not an explicit contravention of equality legislation in most countries, can materially affect the ability of women (as primary carers) and parents to continue working in a job and this has been held to be indirect discrimination on the grounds of gender and family status.

Where legislation exists, there are also institutions through which employees/prospective employees can pursue complaints and cases, and receive information regarding their rights, and employers can receive information regarding obligations. The following case is an illustrative example. In 2007 in Northern Ireland, a 58-year-old man won an equality case under the Employment Equality (Age) Regulations (Northern Ireland) 2006, in which it was found he was discriminated against on the grounds of age for a job as a salesman with a timber firm. The tribunal found that he had been asked age-related questions and also pointed to the advertising of the position, which stated that the successful applicant would display 'youthful enthusiasm'. It concluded that but for his age he would probably have been successful in getting the position. The claimant subsequently said that the experience made him feel as if he had 'been flung on the scrapheap' (*McCoy* v. *James McGregor and Sons*, 00237/07IT).

### Victimization

Across the EU, employers are prohibited from victimizing people who make a complaint or take an equality case against an employer in good faith. For instance, if an employee makes a formal complaint that they feel they have been discriminated against in a promotions process and they are subsequently fired for making that complaint, they would have a clear case for victimization. To give an example. A worker attends an interview for promotion. He does not get the job but feels he has been unfairly treated due to his age. He makes a formal complaint to his employer and thereafter

**Victimizing** – an act that treats someone unfairly

his life at work is made difficult as he is given extra work that other people don't get and is constantly reprimanded by his employer in front of colleagues and eventually demoted. This could be viewed as victimization. The concept of victimization should not be overlooked by employers, as tribunals/courts can actually add significantly to a basic discrimination award on the basis of stress and trauma caused by victimization. In a decision in the UK, where £4.5 million was awarded to a female doctor on the grounds of discrimination, approximately £56,000 of this was awarded for psychological stress (*Michalak* v. *Mid Yorkshire Hospitals NHS Trust*, ET/1810815/2008).

## EXCEPTIONS TO EQUALITY LEGISLATION

There are certain exceptions allowed to equality legislation in most countries. In general, exceptions to the rule rely on the basic principles of nondiscrimination, that is, the test for justification is an objective one, which means that an employer is required to show that the treatment or provision corresponds to a real business need, and is appropriate, balanced and necessary to achieve a valid goal. In a disputed situation, if there is evidence that a person has been treated 'differently' on the basis of one of the protected characteristics, for example disability, age or gender, then the employer must show that the difference in treatment *does* have an objective and reasonable justification and/or there *is* proportionality between the aim sought and the means employed. For example, in a German case concerning the firefighting service in Frankfurt, Mr Wolf objected to being turned down for a job as a firefighter as he was over 30 years of age. The case came before the European Court of Justice who ruled against Mr Wolf. The authorities submitted that the physical nature of a firefighter's work meant that employees older than 45 had to be assigned less demanding duties. If too many older workers were recruited, the capacity of the service to carry out its activities would be reduced. The court decided that it was an 'occupational requirement' to have 'especially high physical capacities' and that the under-30 rule was 'proportionate' in trying to meet that requirement. This was an allowable discrimination under European equality law (*Wolf* v. *Stadt Frankfurt am Main* [2010] 2 CMLR 849).

## Inequalities and the Workplace

Having landed the job of your dreams, how would you feel if you found that as well as your qualifications and skills, one of the reasons you were given the job ahead of other applicants was because of a personal characteristic such as colour, disability, age or gender? Would it have any effect on how you feel about getting the job?

HRM IN THE NEWS

This was exactly the situation facing a TV presenter who was picked to co-host a UK TV show for Channel 4 called *The Science of Scams*. Kat Akingbade, who is a trained scientist, camerawoman, reporter and TV presenter with considerable experience in both TV and radio, said she was initially overjoyed at landing the job. However, this changed when she discovered that her skin colour had been a factor in the final selection process. In an interview in 2011, she said that her self-confidence was fundamentally shaken and she began to question her abilities and successes in life and to wonder if she was just fulfilling a quota. She also said that now when she saw a black person on any panel on a TV show, she found herself wondering if they were only there to fulfil a diversity quota.

This controversy occurred just as the British government introduced the Equality Act 2010, where sections 158 and 159 allow for 'positive action' by employers. This makes it legal for employers to

choose a candidate over others of equal merit, if they feel that candidate represents an underrepresented group in the workforce. Kat, however, indicated that she felt the government initiative was 'unhelpful'; in fact, she went so far as to describe the law as 'toxic' and said it makes no allowance for why underrepresentation happens in the first place. In other words, it would not address the fundamental issues that cause inequalities in society that are reflected in workplaces. She indicated that she felt such a law could make certain groups of young people feel they were entitled to special treatment and cause them to lose any drive to succeed, self-esteem, and sense of pride and accomplishment. She said: 'Employers will face the same pressure to diversify the workforce and will recruit on the basis of protected characteristics, not on merit, [and] Positive discrimination robs an individual of drive and self-motivation; it completely undermines the achievements and abilities of the hard-working and truly gifted.' She called on employers to recruit purely on merit and urged young people to strive harder to compete on the basis of their skills and talents.

The controversy surrounding this case must be considered against the backdrop of evidence that there are significant disadvantages facing young black people in Britain today

in terms of unemployment, lack of education and risk of poverty, as discussed earlier.

### Questions

1 What is the best way to tackle the fundamental inequalities facing the black community in Britain? What are your views on the idea of positive action?

2 What alternative ideas can you offer to tackle inequality in society?

3 Can you think of any measures employers can take to address the issue of inequality in the workplace?

### Sources

Cameron, D. (2010) We'll change black Britain, *The Guardian*, 17 March, www.guardian.co.uk/commentisfree/2010/mar/17/black-britain-unemployment-conservatives.

*Daily Mail* (2011) Employed because I was black: positive discrimination robs people of their drive to succeed says TV presenter, MailOnline, 3 April, www.dailymail.co.uk/news/article-1372940/Employed-I-black-Positive-discrimination-black-white-says-TV-presenter.html.

Ramesh, R. (2010) Recession leaves almost half of all young black people out of work, *The Guardian*, 22 January, www.guardian.co.uk/world/2010/jan/22/black-unemployment-recession.

Stewart, H. and Tompkins, K. (2009) One in five black men out of work and worse to come, *The Guardian*, 13 October, www.guardian.co.uk/world/2009/oct/13/black-men-unemployment-figures.

In another German case, a nurse on a temporary contract was unsuccessful in her application for a permanent job as a nurse. The respondents' justification was that a requirement of the job was that a large proportion of the work would take place in an operating

theatre and that the claimant would be exposed to substances that could be harmful to her unborn child. However, the claimant's case was upheld on the basis that the condition of pregnancy was only temporary and the job was a permanent one. The European Court of

Justice found that while it was acceptable to impose temporary limits on the work of pregnant women based on the results of risk assessments, it was disproportionate to impose a permanent ban on their access to a job on the basis of a pregnancy. Such a ban constituted discrimination (*Mahlburg* v. *Land Mecklenburg-Vorpommern* [2000] ECR 1-549).

## Equality and the carer: a gender issue?

Employees in most jurisdictions are also protected by legislation with respect to leave they may need to take in terms of caring duties. Such legislation protects employees from victimization or unfair behaviour on the part of employers that results from their obligations in this regard and entitles them to return to work after such leave. Given the discussion earlier regarding the perception and role of women as the primary carer, it follows that such legislation should serve to increase participation of women in labour markets. If the legislation achieves its goals in facilitating participation, we should also see an increase in the ability of women to increase their human capital and thus progression in the workplace. As well as protecting women from discrimination, the increase in scope of 'family friendly' legislation aims to promote equal participation of men and women in the workplace and equal sharing of family responsibilities (International Labour Organization, 2012).

## Maternity protection

In EU member countries, all women who become pregnant while in employment are entitled to maternity leave, regardless of how long they have been in employment or what their status of employment is – part time, fixed term, full time, or casual. They are also entitled to return to their employment. This contrasts with the USA where women are entitled to 12 weeks' maternity leave, but small firms are exempt from the legislation and women who have worked for less than 12 months with the same employer are not covered by the maternity legislation. Although there is a basic right to maternity leave and protection across Europe, there are significant variations regarding the length of time given for maternity leave and levels of pay. For instance, in Iceland, maternity leave entitlement is 13 weeks on 80 per cent of wage replacement, while in the Czech Republic, it is 28 weeks with full wage replacement. In France, employees are entitled to 16 weeks of maternity leave. Similarly, payment schemes for maternity leave can vary from country to country; in some countries, payment is through social welfare, while in others there may be a combination of employer and state payments. Collective agreements may also have an effect on payments. Table 5.2 gives some examples of the statutory maternity entitlements in various countries.

In most EU countries, there are also provisions in the legislation whereby a woman may take time off work

**Table 5.2** Maternity leave, international comparisons

| Country | Standard* maximum leave duration (weeks) | Eligibility for payment | Payment |
|---|---|---|---|
| Austria | 16 | None | 100% (state/SI) |
| Bulgaria | 53 | 6 months' insurance | 90% (state) |
| Denmark | 18 | 6 months' residence | 100% (employer) |
| Germany | 14 | All insured women | 100% (employer and SI) |
| Hungary | 24 | All insured women | 70% (SI) |
| Ireland | 42 (26 paid) | 39 SI contributions paid in 12 months before leave | 70% (SI) |
| New Zealand | 12 | Currently in covered employment | 50% state |
| Norway | 9, but embedded in parental leave | 6 out of preceding 10 months, either parent | 100% state |
| UK | 52 (39 paid) | Employment for 26 week continuous period ending 15 weeks before expected week of birth | 90% (employer refunded min. 92% by state) |
| US | 12 | Minimum 12 months employment and min. 1,250 hours | No |

*Notes:* SI = social insurance; * = in some countries, there may be variations for multiple births, complications and so on.
*Source:* OECD, 2011

during her pregnancy for medical and antenatal appointments and for health and safety leave where a risk assessment reveals that there are legitimate risks in the workplace to pregnant employees. Legislation also confers obligations on employers with respect to providing time off for breastfeeding mothers. There is wide variation with regard to statutory provision for paternity leave, paid or unpaid. In some European countries such as Ireland, Iceland and Czech Republic, there is no provision, although some employers do elect to give fathers some time off following the birth of a baby. There is also provision in European states for adoptive leave similar to maternity leave. Table 5.3 gives a summary of paternity leave entitlements in a number of countries.

Cases relating to pregnancy and maternity leave often relate to claims of a change in attitude to employees who inform employers of their pregnancy, or a change in treatment at work following return from maternity leave. For example, a female employee was awarded compensation by an Irish tribunal in 2011 after it determined that she had, effectively, been demoted from a senior HR position to that of a telesales employee on her return from maternity leave (*Hazel Cosgrove* v. *Kellor Services (Irl) Ltd*, UD 884/2009).

In what may seem a bizarre case in Spain in 2010, a male employee won a case at the European Court of Justice and became entitled to a breastfeeding break for his young child. On closer examination of the issue, it transpired that the right to breastfeeding breaks was extended to bottle feeding many years before and thus the father was entitled to the break (*Pedro Manuel Roca Álvarez* v. *Sesa Start España ETT SA*, C-104/09).

## BUILDING YOUR SKILLS

Protection in terms of pregnancy can be a controversial topic. Many small firms would argue that the costs to them of fulfilling obligations under the maternity legislation (leave, health and safety, breastfeeding breaks, replacing an employee) are prohibitive, and many firms, large and small, are frustrated if they employ someone, train them and are informed after a few months that the new employee is pregnant and will be taking maternity leave. Many employers cite the US model as a better and more realistic one (see below).

If you are faced with this argument in a company you are working for, what action could you, as line manager, take to try and change opinion and also to ensure equal treatment in this area?

### Parental leave

This legislation allows parents to take a period of leave to care for a young child usually of preschool age. Unlike maternity leave, it is open to both parents to take periods of parental leave. Generally speaking, parents may take

**Table 5.3** Paternity leave: international comparisons

| Country | Statutory entitlement | Payment |
| --- | --- | --- |
| Austria | None, but may be collective agreement in place | |
| Belgium | 10 days | Employer 100% for 3 days, SI 82% for remainder |
| Denmark | 2 weeks | 90% state |
| Germany | None, but may be collective agreement in place | |
| Hungary | 5 days | Social security payment |
| Ireland | None, but may be collective agreement in place | |
| Luxembourg | 2 days at child's birth | 100% employer |
| Norway | 2 weeks after birth 'daddy days' plus 10 weeks out of parental leave entitlement | 'Daddy days' – unpaid<br>10 weeks of parental leave 100% |
| UK | 1 or 2 weeks. If 2 weeks taken, must be taken together within 8 weeks of birth | £135.45 per week or 90% of earnings, whichever is less |
| USA | None | |

*Source:* OECD, 2011

blocks of leave, as in a number of weeks or months together, or they may negotiate with their employer to take leave on a basis that suits both parties. In Europe, while an employer may ask an employee to postpone or be flexible regarding such leave, they cannot refuse the leave. The entitlement to parental leave exists in the USA and Europe, although the entitlements vary widely. In the USA, the combined leave entitlement of both parents amounts to 24 weeks and small employers are exempt. Short tenure workers are not entitled to this leave. Thus, about 40 per cent of US employees cannot legally avail themselves of such leave. In Europe, there are wide variations, ranging from a maximum of 420 days of paid leave for Swedish parents to 14 weeks unpaid leave per parent in countries like the UK and the Republic of Ireland. In general, the Nordic countries tend to have the most generous leave entitlements. One of the key objectives of parental leave has been to allow women to participate to a greater degree in the labour market. So has this worked? Certainly, there is evidence that in countries with paid leave, a higher proportion of women avail themselves of leave, particularly in the Nordic states. However, take-up is low in countries with unpaid leave. In all countries, participation by fathers is lower, regardless of whether the leave is paid or unpaid (Eurofound, 2007).

**Positive discrimination** – preferential discriminatory treatment of a minority group over a majority group to try and counter disadvantage in the labour market

**Positive action** – measures undertaken with the aim of achieving full and effective equality for members of groups that are socially or economically disadvantaged

As we can see from above, the take-up of parental leave is lower for men than it is for women, regardless of whether such leave is paid or not. What do you think this reveals in terms of attitudes to male and female roles with respect to family and childcare? What effect do you think it has on equality in the workplace?

## Does the legislation work?

It is difficult to ascertain if the legislation works, as it is hard to measure the cause and effect relationship between the legislation and intended outcomes, in terms of equality and other factors, such as changing societal attitudes and greater participation in education among

some traditionally excluded groups. Some researchers would argue that, in some instances, the effect of legislation with respect to work has had a modest impact. As Elson (1999) noted, institutional arrangements designed to combat segregation and inequality often do not work, due to the countervailing force of structures, unwritten rules and norms. As discussed above, few men will avail themselves of legislatively supported flexible work practices such as parental leave, as it is perceived to militate against promotion opportunities – a perception rooted in the long-hours culture in many organizations. Certainly, with respect to equal pay, the legislation seems to have had a limited effect. Wage gaps between men and women persist across most countries. In the USA, women earn, on average, 77 cents to every dollar earned by men. In Europe, the picture is similar, with women earning about 18 per cent less than men (Smith, 2010).

## THE POSITIVE DISCRIMINATION/ POSITIVE ACTION DEBATES

A long-running, controversial debate surrounds the issue of positive discrimination. Supporters of positive discrimination hold that certain groups of people have suffered such levels of disadvantage over a protracted period of time that employers need to positively discriminate in their favour if we are ever to have equality in the workplace. This would mean that an employer could, effectively, discriminate against other applicants in order to recruit people who are disproportionately underrepresented in the workplace. In other words, employers could use discriminatory practices to ensure that the workplace population reflects the wider population, such as discriminating against people below 40 to ensure that a representative cohort of over-40-year-olds are present in a company's workforce. This practice has not been adopted by governments and is actually prohibited by current legislation.

Positive action differs from positive discrimination in that it does not seek to discriminate in favour of disadvantaged groups at the expense of others, but seeks to enhance the employability and labour market competitiveness of certain groups in particular national contexts; for example, young black males in the UK,

North African migrants in France, members of the Roma population in Europe, women in the workplace and so on.

One form of positive action would involve governments, employers and other influential bodies identifying groups of people who, whether by race, gender, age or family status, are underrepresented in the workplace and through positive action schemes creating more opportunities for these groups. Examples of this are language training programmes funded by government or organizations, advertising that actively encourages applications from underrepresented groups, and funding for various types of training to enable underrepresented groups to compete on a more equal basis. Cohen (2007) refers to this as 'positive action' as opposed to 'negative action' or 'negative inaction'. She provides an example of how the Household Cavalry in the UK sought to address a serious underrepresentation of black and Asian recruits. An outreach programme was devised, whereby current members of the Household Cavalry joined sports centres used by black and Asian young men, visits were arranged to schools and communities to meet parents and potential recruits to persuade them that the army was a good career, and black and Asian young people were invited to visit the Household Cavalry to see what it involves and the training it offers. Following these initiatives, within four years, ethnic minority recruitment had jumped from 0 per cent to about 14 per cent (Cohen, 2007). This form of positive action is generally accepted and welcomed. More controversial, however, is where positive action becomes part of the legal obligations of employers. Section 159 of the UK Equality Act 2010 introduced a provision for positive action in relation to recruitment and promotion. Section 159, which came into force in April 2011, permits but does not require an employer to take a protected characteristic into consideration when deciding who to recruit or promote, where people having the protected characteristic are at a disadvantage or are underrepresented. This positive action can be taken only where the candidates are 'as qualified as' each other. However, there has been much debate in the British media that employers may leave themselves exposed to legal claims of discrimination if they do exercise this option to favour one candidate over another because they have a protected characteristic.

**Equality policies** – a written policy that comprehensively sets out the philosophy of the company with respect to equality and clearly indicates all responsibilities, procedures, processes, training, rules and penalties in this area

**Dignity at work policies** – policies that specifically address behaviour in the workplace that would serve to undermine a person's dignity. They are usually associated with bullying and harassment and should clearly set out the company's position on bullying and harassment, responsibilities, roles, training, procedures, rules and penalties with respect to this issue

## HRM, THE WORKPLACE AND EQUALITY

Organizations have to be cognizant of the equality legislation and implement policies, procedures and practices to ensure compliance with the relevant laws. HR has an integral role to play in ensuring that all employees and prospective employees are treated fairly and treat their co-workers in a fair and equitable manner. This can be achieved through the creation and dissemination of development and awareness programmes and clear statements and policies regarding equal treatment of employees. It is also important that HR ensures that all organization members, from senior management down, are aware of the consequences of discriminatory behaviour towards employees/ prospective employees. Methods of dissemination include employee handbooks, training seminars and induction programmes for new employees. In many countries, it is also obligatory or at least advisable to make sure that handbooks and other documentation are available in various languages, especially where a sizable proportion of the workforce may normally speak a different language. For instance, in some US states, many companies would provide employees with handbooks in Spanish. Case law in various countries has established that policies should not be treated as 'window dressing', but must be acted on by organizations and they must be seen to be acting in a fair and consistent manner. The overarching policies that organizations need to have in place are equality policies and dignity at work policies. HR plays a key role in the development, dissemination and review of such policies as well as managing the performance of all organization members in this regard. HR personnel also take responsibility for dealing with complaints, investigating issues and instigating disciplinary action where necessary. A general template for an equality policy is provided in Table 5.4.

Equality policies in the workplace are supported by clear procedures indicating how an employee can process a claim. Where an existing employee feels they have suffered discrimination, the usual method for pursuing an initial claim is through a grievance

**Table 5.4 Template for equality policy**

| |
|---|
| An opening statement outlining the organization's commitment to equality in the workplace and to encouraging and valuing diversity |
| A statement reiterating that the organization values the difference and individuality of its employees |
| A statement that the organization will act to ensure the organization is free from discrimination |
| Where relevant, a statement regarding what training and development opportunities are available to employees to ensure a more equitable workplace |
| An indication of what types of discrimination will not be tolerated in the organization |
| The consequences of engaging in discriminatory behaviour, up to and including dismissal |
| Clear indications of the procedures employees can use to process complaints and where/how they can access these procedures |
| A clear indication of who they can refer complaints to in the organization, for example supervisors, employee representatives and so on |
| A statement of non-victimization |
| Information on relevant third parties to which an employee can refer a complaint in the event that it is not resolved within the organization |
| Time limits for each stage of an investigation into a complaint by an employee |

procedure; if the situation is not resolved by this method, the claim may be heard by a third party who will adjudicate. These third parties will vary across countries. In the UK, the key institution is the Advisory, Conciliation and Arbitration Service (Acas). If a complaint by an existing employee involves another employee or manager and is felt by management to be well founded, they may have to deal with the person responsible for the discriminatory behaviour through a disciplinary procedure.

One note of caution, however; if a complaint of discrimination is discovered to be well founded, the organization should, in the first instance, examine whether the organization itself is possibly culpable in terms of lack of training of employees, lack of clarity on rules and equality policy and/or the pervading culture and norms that allow discriminatory or negative behaviour to exist. For instance, if a group of employees are behaving in a racist manner towards other employees, management, as well as dealing with the perpetrators, should also look to see why this is occurring. Did the

offending employees receive training on diversity? Did their direct manager tolerate such behaviour or even behave in this way themselves? Could there have been past instances of such behaviour being tolerated, thus sending out signals to employees that such behaviour is acceptable? In summary, organizations need to be proactive in terms of promoting and maintaining equality as well as preventing discrimination.

What about people who are not employees but feel they have suffered discrimination at the selection or recruitment stage? Do they have any redress? The answer is yes. When a prospective employee feels they have suffered from discrimination in the selection process, they will usually make a complaint to the relevant national institution with the legal responsibility for assessing such complaints, such as the Equality Tribunal in the Republic of Ireland, Acas in the UK or the Equal Employment Opportunity Commission in the USA.

A dignity at work policy differs from a broad equality policy in that it deals specifically with issues of bullying or harassment in the workplace. Such a policy is designed to prevent discriminatory harassment and bullying of employees on the basis of one of the protected grounds, such as race or sexuality. As with the equality statement and policy, it is important that information on dignity at work policies is given to and read by all employees and that all employees receive necessary training and development so that the policies can be implemented. An example of this would be the development of frontline managers to deal with complaints, diversity seminars for all employees, and social events to encourage integration of all employees.

In general, a dignity at work policy will begin with a declaration statement outlining the organization's commitment to dignity at work and reiterating that all employees have the right to be treated with dignity and respect and that complaints by employees will be treated with fairness and sensitivity and in as confidential a manner as possible. The basic contents of a dignity at work policy are outlined in Table 5.5. It is important that organizations regularly monitor and update these policies to reflect changes in the organization and changes in legislation.

## The proactive organization

Organizations can also adopt a more proactive role in fostering and supporting equal treatment of employees, prospective employees and even sections of the community outside the workplace. We have already

**Table 5.5** Template for a dignity at work policy

| |
|---|
| An explanation of what constitutes harassment |
| A clear indication to employees that the policy extends to all employees including managers and to non-employees such as customers, clients, suppliers and so on |
| A statement that harassment and sexual harassment will not be tolerated and an outline of the consequences of engaging in this behaviour: disciplinary action in the case of employees and the suspension of contracts/legal action/exclusion in the case of customers/non-employees |
| Clear indications to employees as to the action they can take if they feel they have suffered harassment and how they can progress a complaint |
| A clear statement indicating that employees will not be victimized for making a complaint |
| A clear statement that invoking the policy will not affect an employee's statutory rights and information as to where and how an employee can process a case outside the organization through the relevant agencies |
| Clear time limits given for processing complaints and for every stage of an investigation |

looked at the concept of positive action and the controversy surrounding some aspects of this in terms of recruitment and selection. Other examples of less controversial positive action are often bound up in corporate social responsibility initiatives by organizations ▸ **Chapter 14** ◂. For instance, some organizations may offer work experience placements to people with intellectual disability, ex-offenders or other groups of people who might find it difficult to access employment through conventional methods. Some organizations get more involved in trying to bring about change in the wider community. An interesting example of this in the UK and Irish context is Business in the Community (BITC). Both BITC Ireland and BITC UK are affiliated to a larger pan-European organization, CSR Europe, a corporate responsibility network that incorporates 35 national partner organizations. BITC UK currently has over 850 member companies and is involved in a wide range of initiatives from training and employment schemes to research. In the Irish context, member companies are involved in schemes that aim to increase opportunity and employability for four main groups – ex-offenders and prison-based offenders, homeless people, immigrant communities and young people in schools.

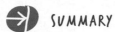 **SUMMARY**

This chapter has examined the concepts of equality and discrimination in the workplace. We find that inequality is deeply rooted in society and that certain groups of people face greater barriers than others in accessing employment and progression within employment. There are multiple reasons for this that are often interlinked, but we can identify three key explanations: human capital explanations, institutional explanations and socially constructed explanations. In recognition of the disproportionate disadvantages experienced by certain groups, countries across the world have introduced legislation in a bid to counter discrimination and level the playing field with respect to employment. Legislation varies across countries, because of people's different circumstances in these countries, political ideologies, economic issues, and social and cultural attitudes and norms. Broadly speaking, the legislative measures in various countries prohibit discrimination against defined 'grounds', which can include sex, race, disability, age and religion. There are some exceptions allowable in all counties whereby employers can discriminate on the identified grounds, but in these cases employers have to prove quite robustly that there was objective justification and there was no other option available to them.

Organizations are expected to have clear policies and procedures in place to promote equal treatment and to facilitate employees who wish to pursue complaints. The HR function plays a critical role in developing policies and procedures, communication, developing and providing relevant training and development, supporting employees and investigating and processing complaints and cases. Organizations themselves can go beyond their legal obligations in promoting equality and inclusion. They may do this from a belief that they have a moral obligation as community 'citizens' or they may recognize the business sense of engaging in positive action with respect to equality. There are enduring questions surrounding the success of measures to promote equality and minimize discrimination. For instance, pay gaps between men and women still exist, men rarely avail themselves of family friendly policies and certain groups still experience serious disadvantage in the labour market, such as young black people in Britain and lone parents in all countries. The next step for governments and organizations is how to move beyond legislative, procedural approaches to equality and find alternative approaches that work. The key question remains: Unless this is profitable for organizations, will they be interested in pursuing this agenda?

## Dromlona Whiskey

It is recognized that the HRM function in an organization plays a key role in implementing policies, procedures and practices to ensure compliance with equality legislation. However, many people would argue that organizations need to be much more proactive in 'changing the hearts and minds' of existing workers in terms of attitudes to each other, and also extending the role of the organization into promoting and fostering equality in the wider community.

© PHOTODISC

ACTIVE CASE STUDY

You have just been appointed to the role of HR manager in the Dromlona Whiskey Co., which started seven years ago employing just three people. It produces three brands of single distilled whiskey and is highly rated internationally. The company has grown exponentially and now employs 180 people in its Irish base between production, packing, distribution and administrative staff. It is expected that this will rise in the next two years by another 100 if market forecasts are accurate. There are plans to open a distribution warehouse in England, mainland Europe (probably France) and possibly China too, where the company has its fastest growing customer base. There are also plans to diversify into other drinks such as liqueurs.

The company was set up and is still managed by Brian MacBirney, an ex-army sergeant who trained as a chef while serving in the army. He took early retirement to start the company, having spotted a potential niche in the market on his many tours of duty abroad. Up to this point, he has largely managed the company himself. In the interview, he admitted that he knew very little about employment legislation but that he prided himself on having a good working relationship with most of the employees, many of whom he knew before he employed them.

You have been in the job for a month now and have made the following observations:

- Most of the 120 jobs on the shop floor and in packing and distribution are filled by men – many being ex-army – and there is definitely a 'lads' atmosphere among the employees. There are very few non-Irish or female employees and any who did join the workforce left within six months. Production operates on a two-shift system – 7.30am to 2.30pm and 2.30pm to 9.30pm.
- There are two other senior managers: finance and production (both male) and 38 various administration and professional staff employed across the company.

- There are 20 people in the sales and marketing department, ranging from the sales director to the general sales team. In spite of the proposed expansion and the growing markets abroad, only two people in sales have language skills – one French national who speaks Italian and German and one Irish person with a degree in sales and French.
- Everyone in the company works full time.

You have just come out of a meeting with Brian, where he told you he is worried about the situation on the shop floor. He needs to recruit more staff, but is aware that many of the 'lads' there might be difficult to work with, especially if he brings in more females and foreign nationals. He feels that 'lads will be lads', and so there isn't much he can do. He also mentions that he normally gets few job applications from women, but feels it might be just as well as they probably wouldn't fit in and might not be able to deal with the long hours. He mainly wants to recruit people who are young, flexible and capable of doing the work.

Brian tells you he is excited but also worried about the forthcoming expansion of the company. He wants this to be an opportunity to promote people from within, so that they can have careers and long-term prospects with the company. However, he feels that many of the shop-floor workers have very few suitable skills as they were mainly recruited as ex-army privates. Certainly, few, if any, have any language skills, but, to be honest, he is not fully aware of the skills base of his employees, as up to now he recruited people by word of mouth and personal contacts.

Brian also confided in you that as he is from a disadvantaged background, he wants to look at ways of 'giving something back' to his community in terms of job creation and encouraging early school leavers to stay at school, although he is unsure how to go about achieving this. The company is based in a small country town with very few employment prospects, a largely low-skilled community, and where the labour force comprises mainly some Polish and Eastern European immigrants working in manual jobs and unemployed miners in their fifties. There seems to be a sizable number of women in the 20–50 age group who are mainly at home looking after families. When young people leave school, they tend to remain unemployed or leave to find work in larger cities or to go to college. Recently, there

has been an increase in crime and antisocial behaviour in the community and also reports from local support agencies of an increase in older people seeking help for depression/isolation and also financial assistance.

After a discussion with Brian, you agree a number of immediate tasks:

1 Your first task is to design procedures and develop policies and practices that will protect the company in terms of compliance with equality legislation. You also need to come up with ideas to ensure that shop-floor workers 'buy into' these. Write a short report for the senior management team on what needs to be introduced and why.

2 You need to examine the existing skills base within the company and ways of attracting new talent and enhancing

career prospects within the company in a fair and equitable manner. How might you go about this?

3 Imagine the company is located in the locality where you currently work/study. Write a short report for Brian MacBirney outlining some ways in which he might be able to get the company and its employees involved in the local community, both to enhance the skills and ability of local residents to gain employment in Dromlona Whiskey and also to promote employability and social inclusion in the area in general. Make reference to other companies that might have engaged in this form of corporate social responsibility in your locality (you can check these out on the internet) and national agencies/initiatives/support groups that Brian could liaise with.

 ## CHAPTER REVIEW QUESTIONS

1 Explain the human capital, social perceptions and institutional explanations for inequality, using examples from your own experience or context to illustrate your answer.

2 Undertake some research to identify some differences in the employment equality legislation in Britain, the Republic of Ireland and the USA, and provide some explanations as to why these differences may exist

3 In some countries, small firms are exempt from some of the legislation protecting employees from unfair treatment by employers. Can you provide arguments for and against this approach?

4 A recent report in the Republic of Ireland (Central Statistics Office, 2012) showed that females are outperforming males in school and are taking up more third-level places in college. However, women are very much underrepresented in senior positions in private and public sector organizations. Can you explain why this is the case?

5 Prepare an argument addressing the following statement: 'equality legislation is working in terms of tackling inequality in the workplace'. In addressing this, you can look at one or more of the groups of people covered by the legislation in your country. To prepare your answer, examine nationally published statistics, and any published relevant research you can source.

6 'Grievance and disciplinary procedures are vitally important to employers and employees in ensuring equality in the workplace.' Explain this statement.

7 There are certain exemptions to equality legislation. Outline and explain these. Can you provide an explanation as to why these exemptions exist?

8 Women generally earn less than men. Can you justify this? Can you provide some explanations? Do you agree with this?

## FURTHER READING

Kirton, G. and Greene, A.M. (2005) *The Dynamics of Managing Diversity: A Critical Approach*, 2nd edn, Oxford: Elsevier/Butterworth-Heinemann.

Wilkinson, R. and Pickett, K. (2010) *The Spirit Level: Why Equality is Better for Everyone*, London: Penguin.

 ## USEFUL WEBSITES

### United Kingdom

www.acas.org.uk

The Advisory, Conciliation and Arbitration Service website provides useful and detailed information on statutory rights and obligations in the workplace and also provides information on relevant documentation that would be needed when processing a claim. It is also the investigating body for claims.

www.citizensadvice.org.uk

The Citizens Advice website provides information on a range of topics relevant to UK residents, plus equality information and other information on statutory issues. Will provide advice and support.

www.justice.gov.uk

The Ministry of Justice website provides information on the employment tribunal, plus necessary documentation and directions if pursuing or defending a relevant case. Click on Tribunals.

### Republic of Ireland

www.equality.ie

The Equality Authority website provides information on legislation, rights, publications on equality, and information for employers.

www.equalitytribunal.ie

The Equality Tribunal website has a database of equality cases, sample procedures, and information for employers and employees.

www.citizensinformation.ie

The Citizens Information website provides a wide range of useful information on public services and entitlements to anybody living in Ireland including information on equality legislation.

www.employmentrights.ie

The National Employment Rights Authority website provides useful and detailed information on statutory rights and obligations in the workplace as well as information on relevant documentation that would be needed when processing a claim.

www.bitc.ie

Business in the Community Ireland provides advice and guidance to leading companies on corporate responsibility. It is a network of businesses in Ireland who are proactive in developing and being actively involved in initiatives to foster inclusion and community development.

### USA

www.eeoc.gov

The Equal Employment Opportunity Commission website has information on equality issues, research, news, access to information on rights and obligations, and access to info on processing claims and cases.

 For extra resources including videos and further skills development guidance go to: www.palgrave.com/business/carbery

# 6 MANAGING DIVERSITY IN THE EMPLOYMENT RELATIONSHIP

**Claire Armstrong**

*By the end of this chapter you will be able to:*

## LEARNING OUTCOMES

- Explain what diversity and diversity management mean in an organizational context
- Discuss the factors that motivate the management of diversity in organizations
- Outline how diversity management can benefit employers and employees
- Understand the challenges and limitations associated with diversity management in organizations
- Explain how diversity management initiatives can be implemented

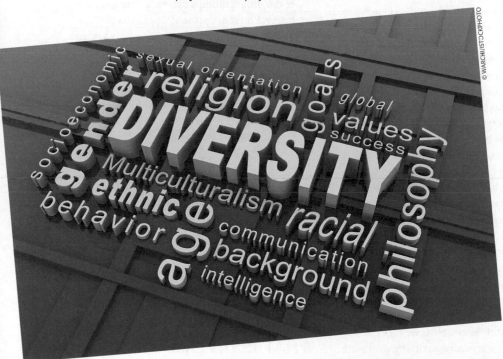

© WARCHI/ISTOCKPHOTO

*This chapter discusses ...*

## INTRODUCTION

The social and cultural map of Europe has changed beyond recognition over the past 20 years. The greater participation of women, ethnic minorities, the elderly and people with disabilities in the labour market presents companies with new sources of labour, but also challenges them to create environments that value difference and operate fairly. Taking a long-term perspective, in many European countries, an ageing population and fewer young people entering the labour market leave companies facing the prospect of labour shortages within their traditional recruitment pools, despite high unemployment rates that occur in recessionary times. It is in their interests therefore to seek to widen this pool by targeting groups that have not been represented within their workforces in the past. In addition to attracting new recruits from non-traditional backgrounds, employers also see real business benefits in having a reputation as an employer of choice ▶ Chapter 2 ◀, which allows them to attract and retain top talent from universities and elsewhere, and possibly improve their creativity, productivity and competitive edge. Other companies suggest that cultural diversity and an international focus are key attractions in the retention of staff. The increasing diversity of European citizens and residents has been matched by a similar change in customer tastes, needs and lifestyles. Thus, it is beneficial for companies to have employees who can provide appropriate services and solutions to customers from diverse backgrounds. This is particularly important for companies with international business operations, whose aims are to provide a broad cultural mix to service the needs of diverse clients and ensure that no one is discriminated against on any grounds.

This chapter is closely related to Chapter 5 in that it deals with a similar topic and it may be useful to read the two chapters together. However, the perspective taken in this chapter is somewhat different. Here, we focus on how diversity and equality are managed in the workplace. Specifically, we explore what diversity is, the differences between equality and diversity management, the factors that motivate an organization to actively engage in diversity management, the benefits of diversity management to employers and employees, the challenges of implementing diversity policies, and offer some suggestions for implementing an effective diversity management policy.

## SPOTLIGHT ON SKILLS

1  You are the diversity officer of a large public organization in your country. You have been working hard at getting it to employ more people with disabilities, so as to meet the 3 per cent target set out in your organization's policy documents. Recently, a manager of one of the organization's sections has come to you complaining about this policy. While you are aware that you could simply quote the policy to them, you would rather convince them of the benefits of a diverse workforce and encourage them to embrace the policy. How might you go about this?

2  You have been tasked by senior management with a project to work out the 'bottom line' effects of the organization's diversity management policy. You must present a plan to the organization's board explaining how you are going to do this. Prepare this plan.

To help you complete the tasks above, visit www.palgrave.com/business/carbery and watch the video of Karen Burns talking about workplace diversity.

## WHAT IS DIVERSITY?

Diversity can be defined in a variety of ways. The definitions range from focusing specifically on ethnic and cultural diversity to incorporating all the differences that make each one of us a unique individual. Diversity can be defined simply as: 'All the ways in which we differ'. This includes the obvious differences such as ethnicity, gender, age or disability, as well as more subtle differences such as education, sexual orientation, religious affiliation, work style, learning style, family status and many more. These life experiences and personal perspectives make us react and think differently, approach challenges and solve problems differently, make suggestions and decisions differently, and see different opportunities. Diversity, then, is also about diversity of thought. Workplace diversity is evident when there are increasing numbers of people with different characteristics at work together. Employees may come from different backgrounds, have different views of the world, follow different religions and speak different languages. Managing this diversity of people requires a lot of effort on behalf of the employers. However, true diversity management recognizes these differences between employees as a positive and, if managed properly, a source of significant benefit to the organization. Diversity management can be described as the systematic and planned commitment by organizations to recruit, select, retain, reward and promote a heterogeneous mix of employees.

> **Workplace diversity** – when there are increasing numbers of people with different characteristics at work together
>
> **Diversity management** – the systematic and planned commitment by organizations to recruit, select, retain, reward and promote a heterogeneous mix of employees

## Diversity in an organizational context

Like many concepts in HRM, workplace diversity is a multifaceted phenomenon, which means that there are many different aspects to it. As a result, it also has many definitions and there are many different approaches to its management. In the context of this chapter, we also like the Irish Business and Employers Confederation's (2009: 1) description of workplace diversity: 'a situation where there are increasing numbers of non-dominant employee groups or variations in the background of employees, resulting in heterogeneity in sociocultural perspectives, worldviews, lifestyles, languages and behaviours'. For organizations, managing diversity involves 'understanding that there are differences among employees and that these differences, if properly managed, are an asset to work being done more efficiently and effectively' (Bartz et al., 1990: 321). Effective diversity management is based on the understanding that every individual is a unique and complex mix of different characteristics, and workplace diversity includes, but goes far beyond, equal treatment on the basis of certain demographic and personal characteristics ▶ Chapter 6 ◀.

The idea of diversity management originated in the USA in the 1980s. At that time, increased diversity was being seen among employees – there was a shift from a predominantly white male workforce to one that included increasing numbers of women, Hispanics and African Americans. In 1987, the Hudson Institute released a report called *Workforce 2000* (Johnston and Packer, 1987), which revealed dramatic demographic shifts, and predicted that this new workplace diversity would continue to grow, leading to unprecedented changes in workforce composition. This resulted in a narrowly focused idea of diversity, being concerned only with women and minorities. Initially, diversity was seen as a threat but, later, organizations began to recognize its potential benefits. More recently, the decrease in traditional labour pools has forced companies to search more broadly for employees to hire. In order to do this effectively, they have needed to embrace diversity management for many different employee groups.

## Distinguishing between equal opportunities and diversity management

Despite having comprehensive and far-reaching equality legislation in Europe, the reality of the day-to-day experiences of employees in many European countries is that these legislative rights are not being fully translated into practice and discrimination still occurs. The idea of diversity management is that it goes beyond just complying with equal opportunities legislation and shows how diversity among the employees of an organization can result in benefits for the employees and real tangible benefits that can be measured and reported on for the organization.

The distinction between having an equal opportunities focus ▶ Chapter 5 ◀ and actively managing diversity is often poorly understood. Sometimes, people use the terms interchangeably, which adds to the confusion. At its most basic level, an organization with an equal opportunities focus would aim to treat everyone exactly the same, regardless of their differences. On the other hand, an organization that pursues a diversity management focus goes much further than this; its approach would be based on a positive attitude to difference and treating people fairly while taking account of their differences.

Generally speaking, when organizations have a focus on equality, they ensure that they do just enough to comply with legislation and, as such, it is a reactive approach. In other words, organizations are told what to do by the lawmakers and then they do it. Conversely, organizations that pursue a diversity management focus tend to be proactive; the focus comes from within the organization, but usually because it is seen as the right thing to do and can bring business benefits. We can identify some of the key issues in an equal opportunities focus:

- Uses a white, male, full-time, able-bodied heterosexual as the norm and compares all others to this norm
- Is narrowly focused towards certain groups such as women or ethnic minorities
- Is keen on removing barriers
- Is governed by law and as such is required and reactive.

We can compare this to some of the key features of a diversity management approach:

- Is internally driven based on moral arguments and organizational objectives aligned with the business case for equality
- Has no limits and participation is linked to organizational goals
- Embraces the visible and invisible differences and attributes that individuals bring to the organization
- Focuses on nurturing potential.

**Values-driven diversity management** – diversity is managed because organizations believe it is 'the right thing to do'

**Productive diversity management** – diversity is managed because of the positive effect it can have on the bottom line (profitability) of the organization

**Compliance-driven diversity management** – diversity is managed because governments and/or regulatory bodies develop legislation and regulations with which organizations are encouraged/forced to comply

## MOTIVATORS OF DIVERSITY MANAGEMENT APPROACHES

There is diversity in the motivators of diversity management. Different organizations decide to manage diversity for different reasons. Burgess et al. (2009) use a two-pronged approach, calling their approaches 'values-driven' diversity management and 'productive' diversity management. Another, more minimalist approach that is arguably more closely associated with the idea of equality than diversity is also evident (European Commission, 2005b). We have called it 'compliance' diversity management. Despite being more closely aligned with the notion of equality, it nonetheless provides companies with the initial push they need to actively engage in managing both equality and diversity.

Briefly, the three approaches are:

- **Values-driven diversity management**: Diversity is managed because organizations believe it is 'the right thing to do'. This is what drives the adoption of policies and practices to enhance diversity.
- **Productive diversity management**: Diversity is managed because of the positive effect it can have on the bottom line (profitability) of the organization. It is the belief that the organization will be more financially successful through managing diversity that drives diversity-related policies and practices.
- **Compliance-driven diversity management**: Diversity is managed because governments and/or regulatory bodies develop legislation and regulations with which organizations are encouraged/forced to comply. These are usually minimum standards that must be met. If diversity management is being driven by reasons of regulatory compliance alone, the organization will usually not go beyond the minimum standards required in its policies and practices.

We now examine the three approaches in more detail.

### Values-driven diversity management

More and more companies state that ethical reasons are the primary driver for adopting equality and diversity management practices. At its simplest, they are doing it because 'it is the right thing to do'. Such companies are aware of changes in society and social values, and their impact on how businesses operate. They know that the public has higher expectations of how companies ought to do business in relation to equal opportunities, fair trade, ethical investment, environmental impact, impact on local communities, individual human rights and other social justice issues. Employees too have changing and growing expectations of ethical behaviour in the workplace, valuing work environments that promote inclusion, respect, openness, collaboration and equity. Many companies therefore seek to achieve a positive corporate image through diversity and believe that a commitment to these issues is essential for a business to be viewed as progressive and well managed. Research has found that many companies begin to address diversity and inclusion by first considering their values. Values such as integrity, respect for community and respect for the individual are seen by many companies as crucial to business success. Some companies have been established specifically to tackle social exclusion and disadvantage. For example, Manchalan (Spain) is a manufacturing company specifically set up as a partnership between the social and industrial sector to address the economic exclusion of people with disabilities. Its success demonstrates that commercial and social objectives can be combined while making a profit, as more than 90 per cent of its employees are disabled (European Commission, 2005b). Others seek to be role models and examples to other companies and society in general in tackling prejudice and discriminatory attitudes. Examples include Danfoss (Denmark), a producer of mechanical and electronic components for several industries, which has a 'Seniority' initiative, and Pfizer, the world's largest biopharmaceutical company, which has a 'Getting Older, Thinking Younger' initiative. As their names suggest, these initiatives seek to ensure that no one is discriminated against on the grounds of age.

## Productive diversity management

Productive diversity can also be referred to as the 'business case' for diversity. Although a lot of research has been undertaken on diversity since the mid-1990s, there is mixed evidence to suggest that diversity and equality initiatives influence firm performance (Monks, 2007).

CONSIDER THIS ...

If the search for how diversity affects firm performance has failed to show any real link, why do you think organizations still seem to think there ought to be a link?

Support for the idea that there should or, at least, might be a link comes from Appelbaum et al.'s (2000) AMO theory of performance. This theory states that an employee's performance is related to their ability, motivation and the opportunity to perform well. In applying AMO theory to the context of workplace diversity, a high level of performance depends on a workforce that is:

- *Competent and able:* through nondiscriminatory recruiting and training and development practices
- *Motivated:* engaged in meaningful work combined with a sense of workplace justice
- *Has the opportunity to perform well:* employee involvement practices that provide employees with the opportunity to contribute within the firm.

So, if a diverse workforce is managed effectively, for example provided with relevant training and development and high levels of involvement, its contribution to the organization will be greater. Some of the important factors relating to productivity that are most commonly mentioned as reasons to engage in diversity management are:

- the ability to recruit from a wider selection of people and retain better workers for longer
- reduced costs linked to turnover and absenteeism
- increased organizational resilience and flexibility
- improved marketing through broader market intelligence and internationalization
- greater creativity and innovation
- improved problem-solving and decision-making
- improved community relations and an enhanced company image.

You will find more about the business case for diversity management in the section on employer benefits.

## Compliance-driven diversity management

Many guidelines currently exist to encourage workplaces to promote equality and anti-discrimination practices. These range from EU Directives and national legislation to industry-specific standards and awards. In some countries, such as the UK, France, Sweden and Australia, if companies wish to tender for public sector contracts, they must be able to show targets and quantifiable data relating to their work on diversity. This is also important for companies in order to avoid legal cases being taken against them by employees or potential employees, as well as to avoid the risk of damage to their reputation and the financial costs involved if they were to be charged with discriminating against an employee on diversity grounds. For many companies, complying with the law is a crucial reason for adopting equality and diversity policies and practices. The majority of companies, however, stress that it is not the main driver for implementation, but one of the beneficial side effects of their policies. It is also true that most companies that respond voluntarily to social changes and have proactive diversity practices want to go further than simply meeting minimum legal standards and, in fact, strive to become known for their high-quality diversity and equality management practices.

Legislation on anti-discrimination specifies the grounds on which discrimination is banned. These vary from country to country, but they typically include gender, race, disability, age, sexual orientation and religion. Diversity management programmes may focus on any of these issues but even where legislation is the main driver, it is rare to find programmes that focus on all of them.

The Republic of Ireland's workplace equality principles are founded in European legislation, such as the Treaty of Amsterdam (1997). The Irish legislation that ensures workplace equality is the Employment Equality Acts (1998–2008), which forbid discrimination against employees and those seeking employment in relation to gender, age, race, religious affiliation, disability, marital status, family status, sexual orientation, and membership of the traveller community – an indigenous ethnic Irish group ▶ Chapter 5 ◀. People cannot be treated less favourably on the basis of any of these characteristics in relation to access to employment, pay, working conditions, promotion, harassment and sexual harassment, dismissal and several other areas. For example, a person cannot be refused a job interview on the basis of their ethnicity, a disabled person cannot be paid less than an able-bodied person doing the same job, and a person cannot be dismissed from their job on the basis of being homosexual, or for taking maternity leave.

In other regions of the world, different legislation exists, but it serves the same purpose, to make workplaces more representative of the population in which they exist and so afford all an equal opportunity to participate in work. For example:

- In the USA, federal legislation such as Title VII of the Civil Rights Act 1964, the Age Discrimination in Employment Act 1967, and many state laws, which often go further than federal laws, require firms to adopt specific targets for the composition of their workforces.
- In India, the Equal Remuneration Act 1976 enforces equal pay for men and women, and the Persons with Disabilities Act 1995 sets an employment target of 3 per cent for persons with disabilities in government organizations. India has also adopted some stringent affirmative action rules in an effort to undo damage associated with the caste system. For example, 22.5 per cent of all government jobs, seats in state-sponsored educational institutions and electoral constituencies are reserved for persons who belong to specific castes and tribes, because they are considered to be at a greater disadvantage than the general population.
- Australia's principal affirmative action/equal opportunity legislation, the Equal Opportunity for Women in the Workplace Act 1999, was developed to ensure that women were not disadvantaged by virtue of their sex through biased terms, conditions and entitlements in employment. In Australia, businesses with more than 100 employees are responsible for the implementation of an equal opportunity/affirmative action programme and are required to report on current employment statistics and workplace practices to a government agency. The primary penalty for non-reporting is ineligibility for federal government contracts or specified industry assistance.
- In China, under the Employment Promotion Law 2008 and earlier legislation, discrimination on the basis of race, ethnicity, sex and religion has been prohibited since 1995. Also, discrimination against people with physical disabilities has been prohibited since 1991, against people with hepatitis B since 2007, and against people with HIV/AIDS and their family members since 2006.

Of course, employers may engage in diversity management for more than one reason – values-driven, productive or compliance-driven – and rarely act on the basis of just one motivator alone. Although many companies adopt equality policies mainly for ethical reasons, they still expect their efforts to produce business benefits, and certainly not to adversely affect productivity.

## APPROACHES TO DIVERSITY MANAGEMENT

As well as engaging in diversity management for different reasons, employers can be active, proactive or reactive in relation to how they deal with diversity. Proactive employers make forward-looking decisions to employ diverse groups for reasons of business advantage. Active employers seek to engage in best practice when faced with the issue, while reactive employers seek to comply with the provisions of the law.

## Will the Republic of Ireland ever Have a Female Prime Minister?

The Republic of Ireland's record in terms of female political representation is very poor. Only 91 women have been elected to Dáil Éireann (Ireland's lower house of parliament) since 1918. Of the total 4,744 parliamentary seats filled since the first elections in 1918, only 260 (or 5.5 per cent) have been held by women. The election of 25 women to the Irish parliament (the Oireachtas) in February 2011 represented a record high, but with just over 15 women in its lower house, Ireland falls behind the world average of 19.5 and the EU average of 24. Ireland currently lies in eighty-fifth position in a world classification table of women's political representation in parliament. The National Women's Council of Ireland has estimated that without a quota provision, it would take approximately 370 years to achieve gender balance in political representation in Ireland. Interestingly, the *Global Gender Gap Index 2011*, produced by the World Economic Forum, ranked Ireland as fifth out of 135 countries around the world. The four countries with a smaller gender gap than Ireland are Norway, Sweden, Finland and, first, Iceland, for the third year running.

The World Economic Forum ranked countries according to the size of gender disparities based on economic participation, education, health and political empowerment. Given how well Ireland is doing in this ranking, it highlights just how poorly it is doing in terms of political representation. Interestingly, in terms of women's parliamentary representation, Rwanda has become number one in the world, with 56.3 per cent of

elected members being female. Norway has had a controversial quota system for a number of years now. However, these gender quotas have been voluntarily imposed by the political parties themselves rather than by government. Over the past five years, female political representation has remained around 36–40 per cent in Norway.

In May 2011, new legislation was proposed in the Republic of Ireland, whereby political parties would have to implement a gender quota or else face a financial penalty. The planned legislation specifies that at least 30 per cent of a party's list of election candidates must be women. If not, the party's state funding will be cut by 50 per cent. Announcing the proposed legislation, Phil Hogan, minister for the environment, community and local government, suggested that the proposed legislation would 'concentrate the mind' of political parties. Enda Kenny, the Taoiseach (prime minister), said quotas cause controversy and do not, of themselves, elect candidates, but they do give a strong signal to political parties of what is expected of them. According to Tom Curran, general secretary of Fine Gael (centre-right political party and the largest in the Oireachtas), although quotas are necessary, 'there will be blood on the floor' at selection conventions. Many high-profile female politicians, including Mary O'Rourke – a former Fianna Fáil (Republican Party) politician and government minister – and Lucinda Creighton (a Fine Gael politician and a minister), have spoken out against quota

implementation. O'Rourke was especially firm in her stance against such an implementation, arguing that merit alone had resulted in her election as a representative official and she is against any policy that would 'catapult' a person into a higher position than deserved. Creighton described quotas as 'an easy solution to a difficult problem'.

### Questions

1 What do you think about having gender quotas in political life in general?
2 Gender quotas are often used to kick-start women to get elected to parliament and act as a compensation for barriers that prevent genuinely fair competition for parliamentary seats. What barriers might these be and how might they be overcome?
3 How else do you think we might encourage greater female representation in the Irish parliament without resorting to gender quotas?

### Sources

Buckley, F. (2011) Gender quotas, Blog, 25 October, www.nwci.ie/blog/2011/10/25/fiona-buckley-gender-quotas/.

Dahlerup, D. (2012) Global database of quotas for women, Quota Project, 23 May, www.quotaproject.org/aboutQuotas.cfm.

Hogan, L. (2011) Gender quotas in politics: effective policy or empty gesture?, *Sin* student newpaper, 7 November, www.sin.ie/cms/view/1374/.

*RTE News* (2012) Kenny hopes for more female Dáil candidates, 20 January, www.rte.ie/news/2012/0120/politics.html.

World Economic Forum (2011) *The Global Gender Gap Report*, Geneva: WEF.

## Proactive approach

Some companies begin as small local companies and, because of their success, grow quickly to become genuinely global businesses. In this case, they may recognize that they need to integrate people of different nationalities into the ethos, functioning and development vision of the business. This would be considered a proactive stance. Examples of companies that adopted this approach are Schneider Electric from France and NH Hoteles from Spain. Schneider Electric is a global electric engineering company, focusing on the areas of gender, ethnicity and disability in which to promote diversity. Diversity management is concentrated in three main areas: recruitment, the integration of young people into employment, and professional development. NH Hoteles is headquartered in Spain, and has nearly 400 hotels across Europe, North and South America and Africa. As a result of this cross-continent expansion, it has ended up with an extremely diverse staff profile and diverse business practices in the different continents. NH Hoteles has a flexible and open approach to rolling out diversity management, and constantly updates its programme with new policies and actions. Its diversity management activities are focused on recruitment, training and global staffing.

## Active approach

In some cases, companies make strategic business-related decisions to focus on the employment and promotion of a specific group of people. Volvo Cars in Sweden decided to focus on women's needs in automobile development. The fundamental elements that underpin Volvo's diversity management practice are zero tolerance of harassment in any form and full compliance with legislation in this area. The successful implementation of gender initiatives encouraged the company to develop a diversity management programme aimed at improving business performance. This could be described as an active approach.

## Reactive approach

Some companies begin with an approach that is reactive, whereby they realize that in order to be able to hire enough employees, they need to look outside traditional labour pools because of decreasing applicants from the usual sources. This approach was particularly evident in the Republic of Ireland between 1995 and 2007 when the economy grew at an average rate of 9.4 per cent, particularly in the hotel and restaurant sector. This growth was accompanied by an increase in the non-Irish native population. In the public sector, this approach was also sometimes evident, where employers reacted to and took advantage of the pool of new job applicants from racially and nationally diverse backgrounds, and were also conscious of the need, as public sector companies, to comply with Irish equality legislation.

# BENEFITS OF DIVERSITY MANAGEMENT

In organizations today, considerable emphasis is placed on facilitating diversity and encouraging equality, on the assumption that, if properly managed, diversity and equality management can lead to improved organizational performance (Jackson et al., 2003). In other words, some suggest that managing diversity is a sensible initiative to pursue in strategically managing HR ▶ Chapter 1 ◀.

## Employer benefits

Several studies of the effects of diversity management on organizations have shown broadly positive results. However, it appears that the ability to translate diversity management policies into improved performance is highly context specific. In other words, there is no good reason to think that what works well in one organization will work as well in another. Nonetheless, employers generally seem to be supportive of the idea of diversity management.

In 2008, the European Commission commissioned a large study from the European Business Test Panel (a group of companies representing all business sizes and sectors that the European Commission regularly consults on a range of issues), which investigated the use of diversity and equality policies and practices in European countries and the business case for such policies. The results indicated that 56 per cent of responding companies were actively engaged in promoting workplace diversity and an anti-discrimination agenda. Of those engaging with diversity management, about two-thirds of the companies suggested that diversity management policies had made a real, positive impact on their business, while about one-third claimed that they did not know (European Commission, 2008). In 2008, the CIPD published a position paper setting out its case for diversity management (Özbilgin et al., 2008). Using these sources as well as others, some key benefits reported by employers are identified:

- *Improved employee relations:* An organization that is seen to treat people fairly is more able to attract and recruit the best staff. Existing staff are impressed when their organization commits to an agenda that is seen as being fair to everyone, resulting in increased levels of staff engagement and retention. This is particularly important when traditional labour pools are unable to deliver the required skills and numbers. For example, IBM is usually in the top five of desirable employers worldwide and the most often cited reason for this is its focus on an inclusive workplace.
- *Improved innovation:* Employing a variety of types of people provides new and different ideas. Problem-solving is aided by staff with different perspectives, backgrounds and training. The more new ideas employees create, the more likely one of them will be successful. For example, Google says that in its company, diverse backgrounds lead to diverse and innovative ideas and that innovation is one of the key elements of its success.
- *More satisfied customers:* An organization that reflects the diversity of its customer base in its employee makeup is better able to support the development of new and varying product offerings to meet the needs of its diverse client base. In Sweden, Volvo made a particular effort to target woman customers. As part of this, it employed women to design cars. This was successful and not only with woman. Men also valued the useful features that women had designed into the cars. Accenture, a global management consulting, technology services and outsourcing company, asserts that diversity is essential to its ability to deliver high performance to clients and managing this diversity is critical to its success.
- *Better public image:* When organizations create a strong socially responsible image, this serves to attract customers and investors as well as employees. For example, Starbucks, the global coffee house chain, places significant emphasis on developing and maintaining its socially responsible image, whereby it specifically sources coffee from women- and minority-owned businesses, pays health insurance contributions

to its eligible employees, donates large sums of money to charity, and makes significant efforts in the areas of recycling and using greener energy sources.
- *More public sector contracts are awarded:* Public sector organizations often take account of levels of corporate social responsibility (including diversity management) when awarding contracts through a competitive tendering process. For example, diversity of the workforce is a criterion considered when public sector contracts are awarded within the EU.

Some positive findings have come from recent research, specifically in the areas of gender and racial diversity. McKinsey & Company (2011) reported that having sampled companies across Europe, Brazil, Russia, India and China in 2010, its data showed that companies with the highest share of women in their senior management teams outperformed those with no women by 41% in terms of return on equity and by 56% in terms of operating results. Other US-based research on 506 organizations in 2009 showed that organizations with greater racial diversity performed better in terms of sales revenues, number of customers and market share. For example, a one unit increase in racial diversity increased the number of customers by more than 400 and sales revenue by 9% (Herring, 2009).

As well as considering the employer benefits to be gained by engaging in diversity management, it is also important to be aware of the cost of not ensuring that well-functioning diversity management policies and practices are in place. Although most compensation paid in discrimination cases is reasonably small, sometimes it is of a size that could seriously damage the offending employer. Two landmark cases against the National Health Service (NHS) in the UK in 2011 far exceeded the normal payout sums. One case involving an 'extensive process' of sex and race discrimination against a female doctor resulted in an award of almost £4.5 million, including compensation for loss of earnings up to retirement and pension benefits. This is thought to be the largest award in a UK discrimination case ever (*Michalak* v. *Mid Yorkshire Hospitals NHS Trust*, ET/1810815/2008). In the other case, a senior NHS worker, who had been subjected to racial discrimination and unfair dismissal, was awarded almost £1 million (*Browne* v. *Central Manchester University NHS Foundation Trust*, ET/2407264/07). In the Republic of Ireland in 2012, a case was brought before an equality tribunal in which a woman complained that she had been harassed, victimized and ultimately dismissed, by her employer, because of taking maternity leave. The equality officer found in her favour on all three issues and she was awarded €315,000 (*O'Brien* v. *Persian Properties trading as O'Callaghan Hotels* [2012] IRET DEC-E2012-010). In the USA in 2000, in one of the largest payouts ever, Coca-Cola paid out over $192 million in a class action suit for racial discrimination. The case was brought by four named employees and 2,000 other employees – the total number of African Americans who had worked for Coca-Cola between 1995 and June 2000. They claimed that unfairly negative performance reviews and blocks on promotions and wage increases amounted to systematic discrimination. Clearly, the US Federal Court agreed with the complainants.

## CONSIDER THIS…

A study carried out in Ireland in 2006 (Armstrong et al., 2010) with 241 companies showed that those that actively managed diversity saw tangible business benefits, notably a more productive workforce, increased innovation and decreased voluntary employee turnover. It was estimated that increasing levels of diversity management showed an increase of sales per employee of €60,240 for a typical firm in the sample. Moreover, the fact that such organizations are more innovative is particularly important, because the future of many businesses depends on their ability to produce new products to generate future sales (for more information, see Armstrong et al., 2010).

1  Why might you expect to see benefits in terms of workforce productivity, innovation and employee turnover in companies that actively pursue diversity management policies?

2  If such financial benefits are available, why do all companies not actively engage in diversity management?

### Employee benefits

It is more difficult to list the benefits that accrue to employees. However, the benefits the organization sees are usually related to the benefits employees derive from good diversity management, such as increased job satisfaction and morale, reduced work-related stress, and an increased sense of fairness in the workplace. If you work for an employer that embraces diversity management and considers it to be more than simply meeting minimum regulatory standards, it is likely they are also concerned about treating employees fairly in general, whether in relation to diversity or other issues. As mentioned earlier, many employees want to work in organizations that engage in diversity management. This is because organizations that are employee focused enough to have good diversity management policies probably provide an all-round good place for employees to work in. If an employee believes that their employer treats them fairly, this can affect their level of commitment to and trust in the organization. In addition, some research has shown that the greater the degree to which employees perceive that their firm is providing them with a working environment where social benefits and a sense of fairness are important values, the more motivated they will be to reward their firm by doing more and/or better quality work than is strictly required of them (see, for example, Lambert, 2000).

## BUILDING YOUR SKILLS

Usually, employees are in favour of the introduction of diversity management programmes. However, imagine you are a new line manager in a 'traditional' style organization. The word that a diversity management initiative is about to be announced has made its way to the shop floor and there are grumblings about being 'inundated with women and foreigners' and fears that 'this is just a covert means of decreasing wages and conditions'.

Using the information you have learned from Chapter 5 and this chapter, prepare briefing notes for yourself in advance of a meeting you are scheduled to have with a number of staff representatives who are unhappy about the impending initiative.

## CHALLENGES AND LIMITATIONS OF DIVERSITY MANAGEMENT PROGRAMMES

A key question about diversity management initiatives is to what extent they actually work. The search for evidence to answer this question is a time-consuming and often frustrating exercise. A small number of studies show positive effects on the productivity and profitability of organizations using well-designed and well-managed diversity management programmes (Armstrong et al., 2010). However, others have reported that there was no evidence to show that diversity was inevitably good or bad for business (for example, Richard, 2000) and yet others have reported that in diverse organizations where the diversity was not effectively managed, significant problems, such as a lack of consensus and dysfunctional conflict, emerged (for example, Riordan, 2000).

## Measuring the costs and benefits of a diversity management programme

How the costs and benefits of diversity programmes are measured varies across companies. However, it is normally related to the reason for introducing the programme. Where these reasons have a strong business development element, there is usually a greater emphasis on the costs and benefits. For example, organizations may use measures such as return on investment, revenue, costs and profits. For obvious reasons, the opposite tends to be true when the drivers for diversity management are more related to legislative or ethical issues.

In general, studies that examine firm performance tend to use financial indicators such as return on investment, revenue, costs and profits, and organizations often protect such information because it is potentially commercially sensitive. However, regardless of the emphasis placed on determining costs and benefits, most companies find it difficult to identify and measure cost and benefit indicators. This is because of the fundamental difficulty of reliably measuring the benefits of any business activity and attributing changes to specific interventions. The situation in relation to monitoring ethnic diversity is further complicated by legislation in some countries. For example, in France, data protection legislation does not allow information on racial origin to be collected by companies.

Some of the most commonly mentioned potential difficulties and challenges associated with introducing and maintaining diversity management programmes are:

- *Increased training costs:* For example, a diverse workforce may require diversity awareness training to increase the understanding of diversity and to facilitate people to work productively with dissimilar others. Such training may include seminars or workshops or even comprehensive programmes. These types of training are usually given to all levels of staff within the organization and so are expensive not only in terms of paying the trainer or facilitator, but also the cost of lost productivity of staff attending the training must be considered.

- *Increased incidents of conflict:* Conflicts arise when two or more individuals differ or disagree on a particular situation. In diverse workplaces, the most common conflicts arise from feelings of superiority, ignorance or fear on either side, and can result in derogatory treatment of others. If management does not deal effectively with the situation, employee productivity tends to suffer. Ultimately, the company may suffer losses due to compensation claims.

- *Decreased productivity:* Mismanaged diversity, such as unfavourable working terms and conditions or decreased opportunities for promotion, can inhibit employee motivation, leading to lower job performance. Employees who believe they are valued members of their organization often work harder, are more involved in the organization and are more innovative in their work. However, minority group members often feel less valued than majority group members due to stereotyping and prejudice. So, if an organization ignores the existence and importance of workforce diversity, conflict can emerge and neither the organization nor its employees will realize their potential.

- *Claims of 'reverse discrimination':* Reverse discrimination is a claim by a member of the majority that a member of a minority received preferential treatment because of their minority status and not their ability or qualification. For example, if you are able-bodied and more qualified for a job than a disabled candidate, a company may choose the disabled candidate to assist in reaching their quota for employees with a disability. In many countries, reverse discrimination is considered illegal, but in the USA and India, for example, affirmative action assisting minorities is required by law. Whether or not actual reverse discrimination has taken place, if an employee feels that they have been discriminated against because of their majority status, this must be dealt with. Otherwise, it will probably result in the same negative outcomes as for mismanaged diversity.

In 2009, a group of white firefighters presented a case to the US Supreme Court (*Ricci* v. *DeStefano*). They argued that the city of New Haven, Connecticut discriminated against them in 2003 when it threw out a test that white firefighters passed at a 50 per cent greater rate than black firefighters. Because performance on the test was the basis for promotion, none of the black employees in the department would have advanced had the city accepted the results. To avoid discriminating against black firefighters, New Haven fire department discarded the test. By making that move, however, the city prevented the white firefighters eligible for promotion from advancing to captain and lieutenant rank.

The city of New Haven asserted that it had no choice but to discard the firefighting test because the exam clearly discriminated against minority applicants. In discarding the test, the city didn't seek to discriminate against whites but to give minority firefighters a test that would not have a disparate impact on them.

1  Do you think this was 'reverse' discrimination?

2  Could reverse discrimination be justified in this circumstance?

## IMPLEMENTING A DIVERSITY MANAGEMENT ACTION PLAN

Making a good beginning is the basis for any sound project that involves change, and setting up a diversity management project is no exception. It is especially important in the case of diversity management, as it is likely to be a new phenomenon to many organizations. The following action plan contains a number of activities that can be undertaken in pursuit of greater diversity management in an organization. They will not all be appropriate for every situation, but all may be relevant at some point. The steps outlined below are based on a generic change management model, but tailored to specifically introducing diversity management.

*Phase 1: achieve buy-in from senior management and establish a sense of urgency:*

- Create awareness of the 'business case', 'values-driven case' and legal reasons for diversity management and the importance of acting immediately
- Examine the market and competitive realities; for example, use a strengths, weaknesses, opportunities and threats (SWOT) analysis to examine your business as it currently is and see how effectively managing a diverse workforce might improve the situation
- Link diversity goals to strategic and business goals
- Focus on the benefits of diversity rather than accepting it as an unwanted necessity
- Start honest discussions, and give dynamic and convincing reasons to get people talking and thinking.

*Phase 2: create a vision of the desired future to direct the change effort and communicate it:*

- Develop a diversity vision, clarify how the future will be different from the past
- Set diversity goals
- Audit the current level of achievement towards the diversity vision by gathering organizational data and analysing it; for example, determine the current diversity profile of the organization and the current policies and procedures related to diversity
- Develop strategies to achieve the vision
- Allocate resources to diversity management initiatives
- Identify and discuss (potential) challenges
- Make sure as many people as possible understand and accept the diversity vision and strategy
- Use every vehicle possible to constantly communicate the diversity vision and strategy
- Ensure that senior management role model the behaviour expected of staff
- Talk often about the benefits of diversity management
- Openly and honestly address people's concerns and anxieties
- Apply diversity management in all aspects of operations – from training to performance reviews. Tie everything back to the diversity vision.

*Phase 3: implement the diversity vision, identify and overcome resistance and look for short-term wins:*

- Identify and assign the necessary resources, facilities and personnel to the prioritized activities
- Implement the activities and show people how they can become involved in them
- Look for small initiatives that you can implement without help from critics of diversity management

- When these activities are successful, publicize it
- Identify people who are resisting diversity management and help them see why it is needed. Again, use open and frank discussion
- Look at your organizational structure, job descriptions and performance and compensation systems to ensure they are in line with your vision of diversity management.

*Phase 4: evaluate and consolidate:*

- Measure performance against goals
- Assess the effectiveness of the programme's activities, costs and benefits
- Provide feedback to employees and management
- Gather information to inform future activities
- Chart and communicate success to all staff and potential recruits
- Publish good news stories.

*Phase 5: anchor diversity management in the corporate culture:*

- Talk about progress every chance you get. Tell success stories about the change process, and repeat other stories that you hear

- Include the diversity ideals and values when hiring and training new staff.

It is important to note that these steps do not necessarily happen sequentially. Clearly, step 1 is vital to carry out at the beginning, but other than this, many of the steps will necessarily happen at the same time. For example, the diversity vision must be communicated not only before but also while the diversity management initiatives are being implemented.

## BUILDING YOUR SKILLS

Take an organization of your choice that does not have a diversity management programme and, using the steps above, draw up a project plan to introduce a new diversity management programme. In this plan, include a timetable for the introduction of the initiative. At each point, explain what you will do, who you will involve, how you will do it and why.

## Volvo Cars

Volvo Cars is an automobile maker, founded in 1927 in the city of Gothenburg in Sweden. Volvo Cars was owned by Volvo AB until 1999, when it was acquired by the Ford Motor Company, and then in 2010 it was acquired by Zhejiang Geely Holding Group (known as Geely). It has large production plants in Sweden and Belgium and assembly plants in Malaysia, Thailand, South Africa and China. It sells cars in over 100 countries, with the largest markets being in the USA, Sweden and the UK.

Volvo Cars regards diversity as a concept referring to everything

that makes people different, including age, education, life experience, gender and personal values. The overall objective of its diversity policy is to increase its competitiveness and ensure profitable growth. The company aims to support an organizational culture that values and embraces individual differences, and to use this unique composition to gain a competitive advantage. The overall goal is to fulfil its business objectives by:

- improving service and customer satisfaction
- increasing sales

- increasing innovation
- recruiting and making full use of the best talents available
- strengthening the brand.

The prominence of the business motive for its diversity programme is notable compared with many other companies, where, for example, legislative concerns or HR issues are more prominent.

Volvo Cars began to look at diversity in the early 1980s, due to the introduction of equality legislation in Sweden, which stipulated that every company with more than 10 employees had to produce an equal opportunities plan. Volvo employed a full-time officer to oversee this process. This equality officer drew up 'a vision

© BRAND X PICTURES

motivation, personal values, and work style preferences.

Diversity was given serious attention in Volvo's business plan for 2008–12. Specifically, it focused on reflecting the diversity of Volvo's customers in the sales organization, both in dealerships and internally in the company. Key actions included the assessment of the current sales situation and market potential and the consequent creation of market-specific plans. Volvo also committed to targeting sometimes overlooked customer groups in its marketing efforts as well as in the sales organization.

The following lessons were learned:

- Implementing effective diversity management may call for changing power structures in an organization and this issue needs to be explicitly addressed if success is to be achieved.
- Top-level support and involvement in the programme is vital.
- There needs to be continuity in staffing in the key roles driving the diversity agenda.
- The importance of the business case to both strategic and line management cannot be overemphasized.

1 In what ways does Volvo's diversity management programme meet its business objectives?
2 What are the key drivers for Volvo's diversity management programme?

for equal opportunities', arguing that Volvo's staff profile should mirror its customer base. Another factor driving the development of diversity management in Volvo was its acquisition by the Ford Motor Company. Ford had a strong tradition of diversity and equal opportunities and this influenced Volvo Cars.

One of the key steps taken by the organization was the implementation of a diversity directive, that is, a policy document setting out Volvo's definition of diversity, responsibilities for managing and working with diversity, and a plan of action. Additionally, in 2006, Volvo Cars started an accelerated diversity management initiative, which is a focused diversity strategy for the company. It has a global diversity council led by the head of HR and comprising the line managers of the different functions in the company. It meets monthly to oversee the operation of diversity policy and practice.

The fundamental elements that underpinned Volvo's diversity management practice were zero tolerance of harassment in any form and full compliance with legislation in the area. An important aspect of Volvo's diversity policy was that it was not based on setting targets for specific groups in the workforce. The emphasis on the importance of diversity for improving the commercial position of the company highlighted the way in which Volvo saw diversity as an opportunity rather than simply an obligation.

Volvo's concept of diversity had three main themes:

1 *Demographic diversity:* embraced such population characteristics as age, cultural or ethnic origins, socioeconomic status, gender, ability and sexual orientation.
2 *Informational diversity:* covered such issues as educational background, international experience, professional experience, industry experience and so on.
3 *Values diversity:* included such concepts as lifestyle choices,

## SUMMARY

This chapter has shown that in today's diverse workplaces, the effective management of this diversity is important. Organizations engage in diversity

management for a number of reasons, such as 'it is the right thing to do', 'it makes business sense to do so' and 'we must comply with the law'. Organizations can also take a proactive, active or reactive approach to diversity management. The majority of organizations recognize that it is beneficial to manage diversity so that their businesses and their employees reap the benefits. Implementing a diversity management programme is not easy, but it is worthwhile.

## CHAPTER REVIEW QUESTIONS

1  Why has diversity management grown in importance over the past 30 years?
2  What characteristics should be taken into account when considering diversity management?
3  Distinguish between the ideas of equality and diversity management.
4  What are the motivating factors that cause organizations to engage in diversity management?
5  What is the business case for adopting a diversity management policy?
6  What are the three approaches that organizations can take to the management of diversity?
7  In what ways can employees benefit from working in an organization with a diversity management policy?
8  What are the main costs associated with operating a comprehensive diversity management programme?
9  What is reverse discrimination and is it ever right?
10  What are the key phases in implementing a diversity management action plan?

## FURTHER READING

Benschop, Y. (2001) Pride, prejudice and performance: relations between HRM, diversity and performance, *International Journal of Human Resource Management*, **12**(7): 1166–81.

Directorate-General for Employment, Social Affairs and Equal Opportunities (2008) *Continuing the Diversity Journey: Business Practices, Perspectives and Benefits*, Luxembourg: Publications Office.

French, R. (2010) *Cross-cultural Management in Work Organizations*, London: CIPD.

Klarsfeld, A. (ed.) (2010) *International Handbook on Diversity Management at Work: Country Perspectives on Diversity and Equal Treatment*, Cheltenham: Edward Elgar.

Noon, M. and Ogbonna, E. (2001) *Equality, Diversity and Disadvantage in Employment*, Basingstoke: Palgrave – now Palgrave Macmillan.

Özbilgin, M.F. and Tatli, A. (2008) *Global Diversity Management: An Evidence-Based Approach*, Basingstoke: Palgrave Macmillan.

Zanoni, P., Janssens, M., Benschop, Y. and Nkomo, S. (2010) Unpacking diversity, grasping inequality: rethinking difference through critical perspectives, *Organization*, **17**(1): 9–29.

## USEFUL WEBSITES

**www.diversityinc.com**
DiversityInc is a US-based website with information on all things diversity related. Each year it showcases the 50 best organizations based on a composite of CEO commitment to diversity management, workforce diversity and human capital, and supplier diversity.

**www.shrm.org/hrdisciplines/Diversity**
The Society for Human Resource Management has a specific diversity-related section of its website, containing a mix of academic articles and more practitioner-focused material.

**www.equality.ie**
The Equality Authority is an independent state body in the Republic of Ireland set up to ensure that all citizens in the country are treated equally and to ensure that discrimination on certain grounds does not occur.

**www.diversityatwork.net/EN/en_index.htm**
The Diversity @ Work website provides information on a wide range of policies and practices at European and national level, training via e-learning modules that provide an introductory understanding of the key issues involved in managing diversity in the workplace, and a diversity management toolkit that provides the necessary tools to design and implement diversity management policies in your workplace.

**www.quotaproject.org**
The Quota Project website is run by Drude Dahlerup of Stockholm University. It examines interesting issues around the issue of gender diversity in politics around the world.

 For extra resources including videos and further skills development guidance go to: www.palgrave.com/business/carbery

# 7 PERFORMANCE MANAGEMENT

**Gerry McMahon**

By the end of this chapter you will be able to:

## LEARNING OUTCOMES

- Describe the role and value of performance management
- Identify why performance management fails to deliver and describe the seven common pitfalls
- Explain how performance management review meetings should be conducted
- Appreciate the importance of training all staff on the theory and practice of performance management
- Critically evaluate the most common appraisal or performance management schemes
- Appreciate the importance of evaluating performance management systems
- Understand what coaching is and its relevance to the management of underperformance

© APOPS/FOTOLIA

This chapter discusses ...

# INTRODUCTION

Performance management can be described as a process by which organizations set goals, determine standards, assign and evaluate work, and distribute rewards (Varma et al., 2008). In effect, it is used to improve organizational, team and individual performance and development, including activities designed to ensure that goals are consistently being met in an effective and efficient manner. Whether it is your favourite sports team, a 'blue-chip' corporation, a community/voluntary/religious association or a government-funded operation, the management of performance, whether formally or informally, is ongoing and essential to the attainment of their goals.

For our purposes, performance management, involving the assessment and development of people at work, has emerged as one of the most important features of today's effective organizations. In an increasingly competitive work environment, organizations need to get the best out of their human resources if they are to survive and prosper. The failure of so many organizations to do this raises serious and sensitive questions about general management competence and the absence, or faulty operation, of performance management and appraisal-type systems. Thus, students of HRM should be fully aware of the practice, potential, pitfalls and prescriptions in respect of performance management and appraisal-type systems.

# THE ROLE AND VALUE OF PERFORMANCE MANAGEMENT

The term 'performance management', like many HRM innovations, is a US import that has been a major driver in the increased use of performance appraisal and management-type practices across Europe (Income Data Services, 2007). The available data indicates that 90% of UK organizations formally assess managers via a performance management system, compared with 88% in Greece and Sweden, 84% in Ireland and 81% in Germany (Brewster et al., 2007; McMahon, 2009). Indeed, it has been established that, as with many other HR measures, performance management across Europe follows the example of US companies (Barzantny and Festing, 2008). The origins of strategic performance

**SPOTLIGHT ON SKILLS**

Having just being promoted to a supervisory position, you now have to carry out performance appraisals for the first time.

1 How might an employee's perception of the performance management process differ from that of the employer?

2 What role does the HR department play in facilitating the performance of the overall organization?

3 What type of training should be provided for effective performance management?

To help you answer the questions above, visit www.palgrave.com/business/carbery and watch the video of Eamonn Collins talking about performance management.

management can be traced to the concept and practice of management by objectives (MBO), whereby an employee's objectives are derived or cascaded down from the organization's overarching goals (Raia, 1974; Price, 2004). In effect, a key feature of performance management is its integration into the organization via a system of work targets for individual employees, with objective-setting and formal appraisal at the heart of the process (Redman and Wilkinson, 2009). So, performance management is a relatively new term for an established managerial activity, that is, MBO and performance appraisal. Although the terms 'performance management' and 'performance appraisal' are frequently used interchangeably, it can be argued that performance management is more expansive than simply

**Performance management** – an ongoing activity relating to all scenarios where people meet for the purpose of attaining objectives

**Management by objectives (MBO)** – a management system in which the objectives of the organization are explicitly stated, so that management and employees understand their overall or ultimate purpose and the specific implications for their role in the organization

performance appraisal. In other words, the former tends to be associated with developments in areas such as coaching, 360-degree feedback, competency-based appraisal, performance pay and, more recently, employee engagement (Mone and London, 2009). Performance management also emphasizes the ongoing nature of the staff management process. Related to this, Torrington et al. (2008) point out that performance management is increasingly seen as the way to manage employee performance, and has incorporated the appraisal/review process.

On this theme, Armstrong (2009a: 9) suggests that performance management is a 'systematic process' for improving organizational performance, via the development of the performance of individuals and teams. In other words, within an agreed framework of planned goals, standards and competency requirements, it is a means of achieving better results, as one manages performance in a manner that focuses on future performance planning and improvement. This process entails the provision of feedback and the assessment of an employee's progress and achievements, so that action plans can be prepared.

Grund and Sliwa's (2007) review of the practice across Germany confirms that performance management or appraisal is used for a variety of purposes. The main objectives commonly associated with such systems are listed in Table 7.1. However, from a practical perspective, if the ultimate objective of all systems is to improve performance, then the essential, often unspoken, objective of all such systems is to increase employees' motivation in the desired direction arising from their interaction(s) with the manager or 'performance manager'. In this regard, it is notable that Houldsworth and Jirasinghe (2006: 56) found from their survey of 216 UK private and public sector organizations that the systems' 'main driver was perceived to be around motivation'. In fact, when forced to choose between motivation and measurement, for example the scoring or rating of employee performance, 71 per cent of respondents opted for motivation as the more dominant driver behind the performance management process in their organizations.

Performance management systems are now standard in the top organizations in the private sector and right across the public sector worldwide. Their value was underlined in a Saville and Holdsworth (1997) survey of large organizations operating in Britain, which discovered that sizable majorities agreed that such systems are 'very good/good' for reviewing past performance, setting

**Table 7.1** The objectives of performance management systems

| |
|---|
| To review employee performance with a view to learning from experience |
| To agree key objectives and explore ideas for the improvement of results achieved |
| To assist jobholders in analysing their own strengths and development needs |
| To help employees in the identification of training needs and other remedial initiatives and in the assessment and advancement of their potential and career development prospects via the provision of appropriate supports, including education, coaching, mentoring, counselling and performance improvement plans |
| To secure feedback on how effectively jobholders have been managed or supervised |
| To ensure that jobholders are fully aware of how management views their performance and contribution |
| To assist with decisions relating to pay increases or new salary levels |
| To maintain equity in the evaluation and treatment of staff, via the usage of a standard performance review and a related appeals system |
| To address the problem of substandard employee performance, and to assist with decisions in regard to staff retention. Ultimately, this may support the organization's defence against allegations of unfair dismissal or illegal discrimination |
| To maintain an updated set of personnel records for such purposes as the familiarization of new managers with the objectives, past performance and special problems or ambitions of 'inherited' staff; the validation of selection techniques and employee retention decisions |

*Source:* Adapted from McMahon and Gunnigle, 1994: 11

individual objectives, improving current performance, determining bonuses, identifying training and development needs, and motivating staff. A later survey by Armstrong and Baron (2004) found that 62% of line managers found such systems to be useful. The CIPD's (2005a) *Performance Management Survey Report* found that 75% of surveyed companies agreed that the practice motivated staff. More specifically, Campbell and Garfinkel's (1996) study concluded that firms with effective performance management processes in place outperform those without such systems on several critical measures, including profits, cash flow and stock market ratings. Bernthal et al. (2003) established that organizations with strong performance management systems are 51% more likely to outperform their competitors on financial measures and 41% more likely to outperform their competitors on nonfinancial measures, such as customer satisfaction, employee retention, and quality of products or services. A survey undertaken by the US Institute of Management and Administration (*HR Focus*, 2005) found that over half of senior managers believe that performance appraisal is strategic to their business.

The merit of the practice was also reflected in an Institute of Personnel Management (1992) survey, which found that many managers agreed that it had made a difference at individual and team level, and, in particular, found it helpful in interpreting and evaluating their organizational roles. According to Armstrong and Baron's (1998: 208) nationwide survey, 77 per cent of UK organizations regarded their systems as effective to some degree, while the review of employee and line managers'/team leaders' opinions prompted their conclusion that it can significantly enhance people management processes and was, on the whole, liked – with the phrase 'quality time' frequently recurring. Notably, their field research also found much more positive attitudes towards the practice than might be expected from the 'stereotyped views' of performance management as an inconsequential administrative and time-consuming chore.

Using the Henley and Hay Group survey of top FTSE companies and public sector respondents, Houldsworth (2003) reported that 68% of organizations rate their performance management system's effectiveness as 'excellent'. Armstrong and Baron's (2005) extensive UK review found that 75% of respondents agreed with the view that the practice motivates employees. Subsequently, Houldsworth (2007) reported that some 93% of respondents claim to have been motivated to some degree by their last review discussion, which serves to support the motivational impact finding of Armstrong and Baron's earlier surveys (1998 and 2005).

There is also a large and consistent body of research which confirms that setting targets, an integral part of the performance management process, is a powerful way of increasing motivation – and motivation is considered to be an important influence on performance (Bevan and Thompson, 1991; Torrington et al., 2008). For example, many studies indicate that effective objective-setting-type appraisals can increase employee goal achievement by as much as 30%, and an extensive review discovered that those organizations that introduced an appraisal or MBO system with a high level of senior

management commitment achieved average productivity gains of over 56%, compared with average gains of just over 6% in organizations where such commitment was lacking (Rodgers and Hunter, 1991).

What is the purpose of managing performance? Why don't organizations simply allow things to take their own course?

## PERFORMANCE MANAGEMENT PITFALLS

Performance management or appraisal-type systems have long had their detractors, however. As far back as 1957, McGregor called into question the limitations of appraisers or supervisors 'playing god' and undertaking vague personality assessments, as opposed to focusing on job performance, while, more recently, the 'total quality' guru Deming (1986) described the process as the 'third deadly disease' of management. Indeed, one might conclude that managers would drop the process entirely if they didn't have to make decisions about development needs, promotions, pay rises, terminations, transfers, and admission to training programmes. UK-based surveys have exposed widespread dissatisfaction with such systems, revealing that 68–80 per cent of organizations were unhappy with them (Bowles and Coates, 1993; Fletcher, 1993). Even in the USA, it is reported that only 3 in 10 workers consider that their system actually improves performance (Osterman, 2005).

Why, then, do so many managers and their staff have reservations about the capacity of such systems to deliver the goods? In this regard, we can identify 'seven deadly defects' commonly associated with the process.

### Managerial hostility

The reality is that senior staff and line managers who are hostile to their performance management and appraisal system do not fully understand or appreciate its purpose, and as a result don't cooperate in its proper implementation. If top management are not committed to the system and process, it is hard to see how their line managers would be. In fact, the evidence suggests that managers often have differing interpretations of such HR policies, as they are frequently ill-defined and managers themselves are inadequately prepared for their implementation (Renwick, 2003). In practice, then, it is hardly surprising that Carroll and Schneier's (1982) research found that performance appraisals rank as *the* most disliked managerial activity.

## Staff hostility

Second only to top management in ensuring the operation of a successful system is the support of the staff and, where appropriate, their representative association or union. This support is vital to the initial introduction of a successful system and its maintenance as an acceptable and useful going concern. Ideally, staff should view the system as 'theirs'; as a mechanism that is likely to benefit them and requires their active cooperation.

However, according to Armstrong and Baron's (1998: 85) study, appraisals are often 'disliked by employees and employers alike'. In the context of staff, this is hardly surprising, given that, as Price (2004: 524) notes, some managers will be 'blunt and brutal' in their approach and may not produce any improvement in employees' behaviour, but prompt 'sullen resentment and a reduction in quality of performance'. This perspective is reinforced by Marchington and Wilkinson (2005: 196), who point out that employees who are disaffected or have low levels of trust in their managers will not want to participate in the process. Those who feel themselves to be 'continuously observed' will feel that 'trust' is a hollow term. Related to this is the finding from the UK Investors in People survey that 'most staff don't trust their bosses' (Seager, 2007: 28).

## Conflicting and short-term objectives

There is a body of evidence confirming that performance management encounters difficulties when used to address a number of objectives. This defect features in the Industrial Relations Services (2001) survey of such systems, which concluded that 'appraisal' is a victim of its own expectations, in that it is expected to deliver in too many areas. In particular, this throws up the assessor/judge versus coach/counsellor role dilemma experienced by many line managers obliged to address employee development and reward agendas at periodic review meetings. The conflict in such scenarios arises because when used for reward-related decisions, for example pay and promotion, whatever developmental impetus it is intended to have is threatened. Thus, the reviewer/manager is expected to align the (practically incompatible) judge and counsellor roles at one and the same meeting. In these circumstances, the jobholder or interviewee is less likely to undertake a comprehensive self-assessment and may deny shortcomings in their performance, blame others or other factors, and/or insist that the shortcoming is of no significance – if the alleged failing threatens to affect pay increase or promotion decisions. Many reviewers will be reluctant to jeopardize their working relationship with a team member. Hence, it's little surprise that Jawahar and Williams' (1997) review of 22 studies of this process found that ratings/scores awarded by managers to their staff under such systems for administrative purposes, for example pay and promotion, were significantly higher than those obtained for research or employee development purposes.

## Inadequate interpersonal and interviewing skills

Problems associated with low-level **interpersonal skills**, human judgement and subjectivity are inherent in the performance management process and have long been associated with problematic appraisals (Maier, 1958; McGregor, 1960; Stewart, 1965). Over 40 years ago, Kay et al. (1965) concluded that appraisees often see their appraisal meeting as an occasion when they have to accept whatever their appraiser says and then it takes a long time to get over the experience. Related to this, Wingrove (2003) concluded that appraisals frequently say more about the appraiser than those appraised. According to Lawler (1994: 17), it is an 'unnatural act' for managers, and if they are not trained properly, it tends to be done rather poorly. Redman and Wilkinson (2009) agree that most managers are not naturally good at conducting performance appraisals.

> **Interpersonal skills** – skills used by a person to interact in an appropriate manner with others. In the business domain, generally refers to a manager's or employee's ability to get along with others while getting the job done. They are also described as 'people' or 'communication skills', involving techniques such as active listening, appropriate questioning, using empathy and the right tone of voice, body language and attitude fitting to the circumstances. In essence, it is about how well one communicates and behaves or carries oneself

This particular dimension featured prominently in Longenecker's (1997: 213) large-scale survey/focus group research project in the USA, where 79 per cent of respondents adjudged 'poor working relationships' to contribute to the failure of their appraisal system, while 67 per cent adjudged 'the *(related)* lack of ongoing feedback' to be a contributory factor. DeNisi et al. (2008) concur that across all cultures, interpersonal relationships play a key role in the performance management process. In respect of the periodic performance review and developmental meeting, the key question is: Was the interviewee more appropriately motivated when leaving the meeting? If the answer is 'yes', then it's a win–win process. But if the answer is 'no', it is hard to expect improved performance or real development on the interviewee's part. As a result, all parties – employee, manager, team/work group and the organization – lose out.

## Lack of interview follow-up

Reactions to the performance management system will be significantly influenced by whether agreements made in the course of the periodic review meeting(s) actually materialize. For example, the manager who promises to provide additional resources or some form of personal development option is unlikely to enhance the system's reputation (or their own) by persistently failing to deliver on their part of the agreement. Such neglect fits with the widely held belief that the appraisal process is little more than the 'routinized recording of trivialities' (Barlow, 1989: 500). Hence, reviewers and reviewees go through the motions, sign off the forms and send them to a central HR department that simply files them away, rather than utilizing the data in any meaningful way. In effect, then, parties speedily glide through the process merely to keep the 'bureaucrats' in the HR department off their back.

## Failure to evaluate or review the system

Failure to monitor or review the performance management system and make the necessary improvements are common. Complacency and comfort in a 'that's the way we've always done it around here' attitude may well prove to be the system and the organization's undoing. Many organizations exist in an environment of rapid change, where the systems that were adequate yesterday no longer serve their original purpose(s). For example, as Redman and Wilkinson (2009) point out, it would be 'clearly inappropriate' to expect those appraisal schemes operating ten years ago to be effective in many organizations today. This is an entirely valid observation, given the recent emphasis on practices such as coaching, mentoring, 360-degree feedback, competencies and so on. Performance management systems cannot be allowed to remain static and become ritualistic exercises, as they will quickly fall into disrepute and be neglected where possible. Furthermore, some problems that start out small can wreak havoc on an organization if they are not detected by a review process.

## Complex system/paperwork

Most managers already feel inundated with paperwork and many resent the further form-filling associated with their performance management system. As Torrington et al. (2008) scathingly conclude, the forms 'are not living documents' and are generally stored in the HR department's archives, as the issue of performance is neglected until the next round of performance review meetings. Redman and Wilkinson (2009) also allude to this tendency to produce overly bureaucratic systems, requiring participants to fill in large quantities of paperwork, albeit to little practical effect. The stark reality is that, in many establishments, the forms used for performance management purposes represent near 'death traps' to the all-important manager–employee relationship. In other words, they are so extensive that parties feel obliged to record all the details of the working relationship, making the paperwork resemble more of a 'lawyer's paradise' than a work-in-progress summary of the key features of an ongoing and improving work relationship.

## BUILDING YOUR SKILLS

You are working as a manager in a large manufacturing organization. One of your team members has been producing an increasing number of defective products in recent weeks. What steps would you take to provide feedback to this employee?

With reference to these deadly defects, Table 7.2 presents an extensive checklist of the key characteristics associated with successful performance management systems.

**Table 7.2** Characteristics of successful performance management systems

The system is actively supported by top management both in their practices and resource allocations

The system's objectives are clear, compatible, attainable and acceptable

There is consultation with all affected parties in the design and review processes

The system is job related and fits in with the organization's culture

Appropriately customized training programmes are provided for reviewers and reviewees, with refresher and specialized programmes available as required

The system incorporates a preparatory or self-assessment scheme

The ongoing performance management process and review meetings involve a joint approach to goal-setting and problem-solving

The goals and targets involve a quantitative and qualitative dimension

Performance is assessed inside an objective and balanced framework

The system is part of an ongoing feedback process

The system is characterized by efficiency and results rather than bureaucracy and paperwork

The system is the subject of ongoing monitoring and evaluation

*Source:* Adapted from McMahon and Gunnigle, 1994: 8

## THE PERFORMANCE MANAGEMENT REVIEW MEETING

Although it is ultimately an ongoing everyday process, performance management normally comes into sharp focus at the periodic **performance management review meeting**. It is at this meeting that the employee's past performance and development, current status, reward package and future work expectations, and development or promotion prospects are discussed and a record made thereof, to be added to the employee's file for posterity. Given that this

**Performance management review meeting** – an assessment of an employee's work and/or development, undertaken at a fixed point in time, often used to determine the degree to which stated objectives and expectations have been reached, to set down objectives for the future, and frequently bearing some relationship to promotion and/or pay rise/bonus prospects

periodic meeting is potentially the most difficult 'interview' the manager has to conduct, it is well worth considering how to make it work. In brief, this meeting should ensure that the employee's motivation level is enhanced in an appropriate manner as a result of this all-important interaction with their manager. Accordingly, the following guidelines will prove beneficial to the conduct of this crucial meeting.

### Before the meeting

The following points need to be considered before the performance management review meeting takes place:

- Reflect on the meeting's purpose by considering what you are trying to achieve. An appropriate response to this question would be: 'to increase the interviewee's motivation levels, to any extent, in the desired direction'. This is an especially important consideration in France, where it has been found that 'one very important goal in the Performance Management discussion is not to damage the personal relationship' (Barzantny and Festing, 2008: 161).
- Agree a mutually convenient time – and set aside lots of it. As Philp (1990) notes, leaving insufficient time for a proper discussion to take place is one of the most common problems associated with review meetings.
- Encourage the interviewee to prepare for the meeting. It is now common for interviewees to document and submit a self-review or assessment form to their reviewer prior to the meeting.
  - Plan a provisional interview structure. This ensures that all relevant matters will be dealt with, while allowing appropriate deviations from the 'main road' as required.
  - Agree the venue. It may even be appropriate to locate the meeting in the reviewee's office (if they have one) or to use a neutral venue.
  - Having agreed the venue, prepare the setting or layout. The manner in which a room is laid out conveys messages to people about, for example, the power relationship between the parties.
- Check the role profile or job analysis documentation, what the job entails in practice, including the required performance standards, form(s) from previous

meeting(s), objective(s) agreed at the previous meeting(s), concrete examples to support the feedback, other appropriate and substantiated views, what training/development has and/or can be provided, and potential objectives for the next period.

## During the meeting

During the performance management review meeting, bear the following points in mind:

- Establish a rapport. This entails nothing more complex than 'breaking the ice', as the reviewer tries to relax the interviewee.
- Outline the objective of the interview and the proposed agenda for the meeting.
- Take notes. A vital part of the performance review process is recalling what the reviewee said after the meeting is over. Memories are notoriously unreliable, as not only do most people forget quite quickly but they also tend to remember selectively.
- Start the interview proper by giving the appropriate positive feedback. The value of positive reinforcement for the maintenance of desired behaviour is a widely accepted fact. As Grant (2006: 47) confirms, 'research reveals that optimal functioning normally involves a 4.5:1 ratio' of positive comments to negative. This recommendation is supported by Swinburne (2001), who advises a balance of 80 per cent positive feedback to 20 per cent negative, that is, constructive criticism.
- As far as possible, get the interviewee to self-review and prescribe for themselves. The effective application of this technique is the real key to success.
- Listen as much as possible. A good reviewer can spend up to 85 per cent of the review meeting listening. By asking appropriate open, for example why? what? how?, and probing questions, inside the agreed agenda, the reviewer can direct the discussion to the most relevant issues. Clarifying and reflecting are also useful techniques for getting the interviewee to elaborate as required.
- Don't prejudge or argue over issues. By prejudging or making your mind up without looking for the other side of the story, you are in breach of the principles of natural justice. In other words, the reviewee has every right to state their case or side of the story.
- By maintaining eye contact and giving appropriate positive feedback – verbally and nonverbally – the reviewer displays an interest in the interviewee and encourages them to talk and open up.
- Take time and don't be afraid to use silence when appropriate.
- Focus on facts relating to job performance, not personality.
- Review past performance and SMART – specific, measurable, achievable, realistic and time-bound – objective(s), and set new SMART objective(s) for the coming review period.
- As with any important meeting, it is advisable to summarize the key points, including the action points, at the end. However, it may prove enlightening to encourage the interviewee to summarize first and then get them to focus on their crucial omission(s), if any.
- If it hasn't been done during the meeting, complete the form, or make appropriate arrangements with the interviewee in respect of this task. One option is for the reviewer to complete the form after the meeting. This allows them to reflect on what was agreed and to find the appropriate wording to reflect it, before passing the form to the interviewee for their approval or signature.
- The reviewer should look for feedback on themselves.
- Conclude on a positive note. If the reviewer adheres to these guidelines, they should have reason to.

## What should you do after the meeting?

The following points need to be borne in mind after the performance management review meeting:

- The reviewer and reviewee should be satisfied that the completed form is a fair and accurate reflection of the meeting. If so, the relevant form can be signed off.
- Both parties should endeavour to do what they said/agreed they would do.
- Complete the diary in regard to follow-up reviews or agreed actions, including those areas that warrant monitoring over the review period. The link with the pay review is also worthy of consideration at this stage. While performance rewards are normally given through a separate process from that of the performance review, the message at both meetings should be consistent.
- Ensure that the interviewee and other authorized parties sign and secure copies of the form or that the designated online computerized facility is utilized appropriately.

 CONSIDER THIS...

When was the last time you received feedback on an aspect of your performance or behaviour? What was your reaction? Why? What would you do differently next time?

## Feedback

Feedback is the most effective way for employees to learn more about themselves and the effect their behaviour has on other people. On receipt of such feedback, the reviewee can assess its value, the consequences of ignoring/using it, and decide what, if anything, to do as a result of it. If they are not open to it

## Performance Appraisal is not Doing the Business

If the content of two recent press reports is anything to go by, the status and merit of performance appraisal or management initiatives is now under real pressure.

Bayt.com, a Middle East job site, has revealed a trend towards inadequate and irrelevant performance appraisals in Middle Eastern workplaces. A series of polls across the Middle East reveals that despite the fact that 71% of all workers received either a quarterly, half-yearly or yearly performance appraisal, exactly half of them stated that they got no real feedback on how they were doing, while 14% stated that though they had an informal meeting with their boss, 'that was it'. The polls, undertaken across the Middle East over the 2008/09 period, found that 43% of respondents felt that appraisals served no purpose. This contrasts with the 35% of respondents who thought that their company's system was effective, while 22% believed that some changes in the process were required.

Notably, this chastening verdict was reached despite the fact that the majority believed that regular performance appraisals were important to help supervisors evaluate employee performance factually and objectively. Reflecting on the data set, Amer Zureikat,

regional manager at Bayt.com. explained that:

Performance appraisals are a hugely important element of career development and progression and can go a long way in addressing an employee's individual issues or concerns about the workplace, and can act as a tool for both employer and employee to address such issues and deal with them head-on.

In a separate survey, undertaken by HR consultants Towers Watson, only three out of ten American workers agree that their company's performance management system did what it 'says on the tin', that is, improve performance. To make matters worse, the same source reports that only two out of ten workers agree that their company helps poorly performing workers to improve. The US survey of 1,190 workers in 2004 found that nearly two-thirds of employees felt that their appraisal assessment was accurate. However, only 30% gave the system good marks for its capacity to help them to improve performance. It is also disconcerting to note that less than 40% concurred that their system established clear performance goals, generated honest feedback or capitalized on

technology to streamline the process. Having analysed the data set, Scott Cohen, Towers Watson's national director for talent management, concluded that:

The survey results clearly indicate that corporate America's performance management systems need fixing ... unfortunately, too many organizations view their performance management programs as 'organizational wallpaper'. They exist in the background and aren't expected to add value.

### Questions

1 What are the main pitfalls or problems associated with performance appraisal or management systems?
2 What are the most appropriate means of addressing these pitfalls or problems?

### Sources

Bayt.com (2009) Performance appraisals don't serve any purpose, say 43% of job seekers, latest Bayt.com online poll series finds, 27 January, www.bayt.com/en/press-release-article-3441/.

Towers Watson (2004) US workers give performance management programs a failing grade, Watson Wyatt survey finds, 19 April, www.watsonwyatt.com/render.asp?catid=1&id=13032.

and do not receive it, their scope for learning and development is significantly impaired. Having outlined the essential best practices associated with the provision of feedback above, the following guidelines pertain to the reviewee's receipt of feedback:

- Listen carefully to the feedback, rather than immediately rejecting or arguing with it. While it may be uncomfortable to hear, the reviewee is better off knowing what the other person thinks.
- Ensure accuracy in the receptivity of feedback. To protect against misinterpretations or inaccuracy, it is useful to paraphrase and comment on the relevant observation(s), rather than jumping to conclusions or becoming defensive.
- Take time to consider a response.
- Ask others, especially associates or friends who can be trusted to 'talk straight', as opposed to those who will say what they think you might like to hear.
- The reviewee can now decide whether they agree or disagree with the feedback and respond accordingly.
- Ask for feedback. Feedback is so crucial that if you are not getting it, it is entirely appropriate to ask for it. This applies to seeking feedback on all work and developmental issues of relevance or importance to the employee. Feedback is an important part of learning.

As part of the preparatory work for the review meeting, it will also be beneficial for the employee to consider the following questions:

- What is the overall objective of my work?
- Why does my job exist?
- What are my key task or result areas?
- What are the key competency requirements for my job?
- Does the job description and/or role profile accurately capture the demands of my job?
- Is the way my job is designed in need of any revision?
- What did I contribute to the team/section/department/division/organization during the year?
- Did I achieve my objectives? How?
- What were my successes or achievements? What did I learn from them?
- Did I have any difficulties in achieving my objectives or meeting the performance standards?
- What were they and what should be done to address them?
- Did the agreed training plans materialize?
- What skills did I acquire/strengthen over the review period?

- Is maximum use being made of my skill set? If not, what should be done?
- What aspects of my job gave me most satisfaction?
- What will my job and its objectives be in the coming year?
- Are these objectives prioritized and SMART?
- What can I contribute to the team/section/department/division/organization? What exactly needs to be achieved?
- How well is it being achieved?
- How could things be improved?
- What do I want to achieve for my personal development? What are my ambitions? What are my future plans? How do I want to develop my career?
- What will I do to develop it? What can my manager/the organization do?
- What support and/or training do I need?
- Are there any other issues I want to discuss?
- Do I have any suggestions to improve the way my job is done?
- Do I have any suggestions to improve the way other jobs are done?
- In what way could my performance be improved? Can I or my manager assist in this regard?

## BUILDING YOUR SKILLS

You approach your manager asking for feedback on a specified aspect of your performance or behaviour. If they agree, how would you plan your approach to the receipt of this feedback?

## *TRAINING FOR EFFECTIVE PERFORMANCE MANAGEMENT*

The provision of a professional training programme is recognized as central to the attainment of a successful performance management system (Davila and Elvira, 2008). The value of training is reflected in the fact that US and British surveys have found a correlation between successful or effective systems and the provision of management training in the area (*Personnel Today*, 1990). Furthermore, an extensive review of research in this area indicates that proper training can be highly effective in reducing the extent to which appraisers fall into the most common traps, for example arising from inadequate interviewing skills, and in bringing substantial improvements to the level of objectivity in the process (Latham and Latham, 2000).

If the appraisal process is to be seen as more than a form-filling exercise, effective training for the competent provision and receipt of feedback and the procurement of commitment to objectives and future plans is crucial. Well-resourced, designed and conducted training programmes give reviewers confidence in their ability to address issues and handle the tricky scenarios that present themselves at review meetings and in the course of standard manager–employee interactions under the performance management system. Hence, the importance of the training intervention for those managers identified by Bowles and Coates (1993) as having a good task or work orientation but poor people skills. The equally important matter of the training of reviewees is frequently overlooked (McMahon, 2009). In this regard, the value of informing staff as to the system's objectives and mechanics, their role therein, best practice in the receipt of feedback, and the case for the use of relevant assertiveness skills in their interactions with management should not be underestimated.

## The system's design/redesign

According to Redman and Wilkinson (2009: 180), performance management systems cannot simply be 'borrowed from one organization and applied in another'. Having reviewed international practices, DeNisi et al. (2008: 260) agree that it is important that organizations do not copy something that has worked somewhere else. They cite as an example the fact that visitors to India will find that the menu at McDonald's does not include its classic hamburger, instead the chain sells vegetable burgers. This 'Indianization' of the hamburger is exactly the approach prescribed in respect of performance management systems. In other words, it is not a case of 'one size fits all'. Each organization's system should be designed to cater for its unique characteristics and culture, for example the system's objectives, the organization's sector/business, employee roles/categories, the employment sector, and jurisdiction.

Too often, systems flounder due to a failure to adequately define appropriate objectives, consult and involve the affected parties in the conception, design/ redesign and implementation phases, and market the practice as a worthwhile activity. At the design/redesign

and introductory phases, care must be taken to ensure that all relevant views are elicited, helping ensure that the proposed system fits with the organization's culture. Consultation with all parties on the proposed system helps in this regard and proves invaluable in gaining acceptance of, and adherence to, the final product, while ensuring that it fits the corporate culture. All reviewers, reviewees, sections or divisions with responsibility for acting on any of the outcomes of the process, for example training or pay, should be provided with the opportunity to make an input to the design/redesign process, either en masse or via a representative sample of their cohort.

A practical option is the formation of a representative working group with terms of reference and responsibility to make specific proposals in respect of:

- *Objectives:* What should the system's objectives be?
- *Coverage:* Exactly who is to be covered by the system(s)?
- *Scheme type(s):* What performance management or appraisal scheme or combination of schemes should be used?
- *Variation by category:* Should there be different objectives and schemes for different staff categories?
- *Assessment criteria:* Exactly what will be assessed/ appraised?
- *Frequency:* How often should interviews be conducted?
- *Paperwork/format:* What documentation, that is, form(s) and explanatory booklet, should be prepared and in what format, that is, 'soft' or 'hard' copy?
- *Access:* Who should have access to what documentation?
- *Appeals:* Is there to be an appeals system?
- *Responsibility:* Who will have responsibility for follow-up actions arising from the review meetings?
- *Monitor:* Who will monitor the system to ensure that it is 'alive'?
- *Pay link:* How will the system relate to the organization's remuneration system?
- *Training:* Who will training be provided for, that is, reviewers and/or reviewees? What will the duration and content of the training be?
- *Pilot/trial:* Should the proposed system be introduced on a pilot or trial basis?
- *Title/name:* What should the system be called?
- *Reviewer(s)/reviewee(s):* Who reviews whom?
- *Legal status:* Will the system stand up to legal challenge(s)?

# PERFORMANCE MANAGEMENT SCHEMES

There is a wide range of performance management or appraisal-type schemes to choose from. The options selected will certainly influence the mechanics and success or otherwise of the whole system. Consequently, the selection decision should be taken after detailed consideration of the merits and demerits of the various schemes available (see McMahon, 2009). The most commonly used schemes are objective-setting, rating scales, self-appraisal and competency-based assessment, while 360-degree feedback systems are notable, albeit less widely applied.

The objective-setting technique entails the assessment of staff based on whether agreed goals and objectives have been met. As a performance management scheme, it is derived from the MBO system, through which the organization attempts to ensure that its overall performance is managed systematically via the linkage of organizational, divisional/departmental, team and individual employee goals. Research indicates that this is the most popular scheme, with one review of British practice reporting that 89% of their respondents measured employee performance against objectives or goals (Industrial Relations Services, 2005). Latham and Locke (1979) concluded a 14-year research programme into goal-setting as a motivational technique, after which they asserted that the level of production had increased by an average of 19%. Shortly thereafter, Locke et al. (1981: 145) concluded that the beneficial effect of goal-setting on task performance is 'one of the most robust and replicable findings in psychological literature', with 90% of studies finding positive effects arising from the process. The value of this approach was also reflected in another extensive review, which discovered that organizations introducing an appraisal cum MBO system, with a high level of senior management commitment, achieved average productivity gains of over 56%, compared with average gains of just over 6% in the case of organizations where such commitment was lacking (Rodgers and Hunter, 1991).

Rating scales take a variety of forms, although the basic model involves furnishing the reviewer with a list of job qualities or characteristics on which they then evaluate staff. It is the reviewer's job to assess the degree or level to which the employee displays these qualities.

Typical qualities or characteristics to be rated include work quantity and quality, ability to learn new duties, initiative, cooperation, judgement, and acceptance of change. There is no evidence that any single approach to the rating scale technique is superior to any other. For example, after a review of 200 studies, Landy and Farr (1983) concluded that no one approach is clearly superior to another. Chief among the criticisms of this type of scheme is 'leniency' in its application, that is, the award of high ratings (McMahon, 2009, 2012).

Self-appraisal normally requires the appraisee to complete a self-appraisal or assessment report, addressing a range of questions about their work performance and development needs. It is normally undertaken prior to the review meeting with the supervisor. Research into 'best practice' on this scheme has found that self-appraisal should be a feature of any well-designed system (Fletcher, 2004).

Competency-based appraisal is a mechanism that allows for staff to be appraised on the competencies or observable skills or abilities that are most important to job success. The key competencies associated with high performance may also be incorporated into the organization's selection, training and development systems. Although competency-based appraisal does provide some scope for comparing people, its real strength is in analysing an individual's progress and directing attention to those areas where skills can be improved. In other words, this scheme helps employees recognize their strengths and development needs and is valuable for evaluation and management development purposes. The evaluation of competencies that are central to effective job performance provides a good focus for evaluating an employee's progress on the job and directing attention to those areas where there is scope for improvement. However, it is costly to design, implement and update, and is geared more towards development, and recruitment and selection, than actual performance assessment.

A 360-degree appraisal takes a variety of forms. It is also known as 'multi-rater' or 'multisource feedback', with the feedback provided by peers, supervisors, customers, suppliers and/or other interested stakeholders. It can also entail 'upward feedback', where managers are given feedback by their direct reports. The results from 360-degree feedback are most commonly used for training and development purposes, although some use them for administrative decisions, such as pay or promotion (Toegel and Conger, 2003).

## SYSTEM EVALUATION

Performance management systems are often accorded little priority in the organization once they have been introduced. In other words, having implemented the system and (perhaps) provided the relevant training, the system is allowed to 'sink or swim'. Yet the introduction of a system may well prove to be a backward step, unless it is constantly monitored, nurtured and reviewed or redesigned. Few organizations make any formal attempt to monitor or measure the success of their systems. For example, it has been estimated that less than half of US-based organizations undertake a formal evaluation (Milkovich and Wigdor, 1991). Likewise, Armstrong and Baron's (1998) survey of British practices found that less than half of their respondents claimed to formally evaluate their systems. To exacerbate the problem, most of these used informal verbal methods, prompting the researchers to call into question the validity of the feedback. In contrast, it is recommended that a consultative review undertaken by a representative working group – charged with responsibility to review and redesign the system – is more appropriate. The three main evaluation techniques used for the purpose of assessing the operations of the performance management or appraisal system are the analysis of written reports, that is, the periodically completed forms, interviews with reviewers and reviewees, and the administration of questionnaires to these participants (see McMahon, 2009). Any combination of these can also be deployed.

## COACHING AND UNDERPERFORMANCE

Coaching is based on the premise that we all have unrealized talents and abilities. It is primarily a training and development function, where skills and knowledge are imparted. The structure, styles and methodologies of coaching are numerous, but are predominantly facilitating in style; that is, the coach mainly asks questions and challenges the individual to find answers from within themselves based on their values, preferences and unique perspective. The need for coaching can arise from formal or informal performance reviews, but can also feature as part and parcel of normal day-to-day activities across a range of work and leisure time activities, for example in sport. The surge in coaching practice has been driven by a range of organizational and societal trends, such as the globalization of business and rapidly changing and increasingly competitive marketplaces (de Geus and Senge, 1997). Research confirms that coaching is now a popular management tool, due to its capacity to deliver results (Bresser and Wilson, 2006). It is estimated that 70–80 per cent of UK employers now use coaching in their workplace (Hall, 2009). Reflecting on its growth, Cunneen (2009) points out that there are at least 10,000 external coaches at work in the USA, whereas the figure stood at 2,000 in 1996. Central to the success of the process is acceptance of the fact that 'the quality of the coaching relationship is the single most important determinant of success in coaching' (Howe, 2008).

Given workplace realities, coaching for improved performance normally arises and focuses on the employee(s) whose performance has fallen below the minimum acceptable standard for the role. As Howe (2008) highlights, based on UK evidence, coaching is used predominantly by line managers for remedial purposes (in 74–80 per cent of cases). The process is initiated by line managers and supported by the HR function, while occasionally using the expertise of the organization's employee assistance programme. In many organizations, it takes effect when the underperformance is prolonged, for example after a series of unsatisfactory quarterly reviews or an unsatisfactory annual performance review meeting. While all cases are individually assessed, the most common product in such circumstances is some form of performance improvement plan (PIP), commonly scheduled to take effect over a three-month period. The PIP process normally entails:

- Getting the employee's agreement that a performance problem exists.
- Mutually generating and discussing possible solutions.
- Evaluating and agreeing actions steps.
- Ensuring that the individual understands that improvement is their responsibility and the consequences of failure if the agreed solutions are not achieved.

Coaching – the practice of supporting an individual through the process of achieving a specific personal, professional or work-related result

In reality, the link between the performance management system and coaching most commonly materializes in underperformance-type scenarios, although it can also be applied to high-performing staff who perform short of their potential. In such settings, the GROW model has attracted much attention. Indeed, this model has been central to 'best practice' coaching for some time, recommending that answers be given to the following questions:

- *Goal(s):* What is it that the employee really wants? What are the goals for future performance?
- *Reality:* Where are they now? What is the reality in respect of current performance?
- *Options:* What could they do? What are the options for closing the gap?
- *Will:* What will they do? Is there a will to commit to a relevant action plan?

To maximize the benefits of the GROW model, it is advisable that:

1 Feedback takes place privately and as quickly as possible after the event.

2 Employees are encouraged to do the talking.
3 The relationship is based on trust. For example, in the feedback session, a partnership approach should be adopted, showing that the coach is on the employee's side, trying to help and support them. In problem performer cases, the mindset of 'we've got a problem' is preferred to 'you've got a problem'.
4 The diagnosis precedes the prescription, via active listening and trying to understand.
5 The session is guided towards action points.

Many of the skills outlined above in the Performance management review meeting section are integral to the GROW model and effective coaching practice.

---

## Performance Appraisal at the Cool Call Centre Ltd

The Cool Call Centre Ltd has been in operation for the past 15 years. It is located in New York in a large multistorey building, with 350 hourly paid employees spread over five floors. Its purpose is to receive and transmit a large volume of requests by telephone, providing product support and dealing with information inquiries from consumers. Outgoing calls for telemarketing, product services and debt collection are also made. It also operates a contact centre, where there is collective handling of letters, faxes, live chat and emails for a wide range of clients.

The company operates a performance management or appraisal system for all staff. It is primarily a rating scale system, where managers score workers on a scale of 1–10 under ten criteria: quantity of work, quality of work, attendance, expertise, telephone/communication skill, teamwork, initiative, reliability, determination and flexibility, and honesty/integrity. The assessments entail a face-to-face meeting between each staff member and their manager or team leader twice a year. Arising from this, the maximum score available per employee under the system is 200. The score attained at these meetings by each employee is the main determinant of their annual bonus payment. Naturally, all employees push for the highest score at these meetings. Some managers comply with this and some do not. Notably, the exclusive focus of these meetings tends to be the scores awarded. Frequently, the meeting descends into a negotiation process between the two parties, as the reviewer tries to reduce the scores being awarded, while the reviewee tries to increase the scores being awarded. This process is compounded by the nature of some of the criteria being assessed.

As a result, the HR department applies a 'calibration' technique, which serves to average out the scores across the company. It does this by collecting the scores awarded for each employee, calculating the company-wide average and the average for each

ACTIVE CASE STUDY

© CORBIS

→

section therein. It then adjusts the individual scores awarded for each employee in each section by the requisite amount to bring it into line with the company average. As a result, if the section's average was 180 and the company average was 150, each employee in the section would have their average reduced by 30 points. Likewise, if the section's average was 150 and the company average was 180, each employee in the section would have their average increased by 30 points. Bonus payments are then awarded based on the revised scores.

In the first couple of years of the system's operation, the scores awarded were so high that the company's board had to intervene to reduce the total bonus allocation by nearly 33 per cent. At that time, the system operated on the basis that the higher the score, the higher the overall company bonus payout. Under the current (revised) version of the system, the board decides on the total amount available annually for bonus purposes, which is then allocated on the basis of the revised scores. As a result of the various revisions, the performance management/appraisal system is held in very low regard by employees and their managers or team leaders. The feeling among managers is that there's no point in giving accurate assessments, and the higher the score they award, the better the staff–management relations. However, the scores they award seem to bear little resemblance to the eventual bonus payouts. Employees are so frustrated with the system that they sought permission to form a staff association nearly two years ago. This request was denied. Alongside this frustration, there is also a strong feeling among top management that the incidence and extent of underperformance in the company is unacceptably high.

1  In your capacity as an HR management consultant, you have been asked by the company to advise on the best way to proceed, enabling the Cool Call Centre Ltd to benefit from an acceptable and effective performance management system. What would your advice be?

 ## SUMMARY

The search for the perfect or infallible performance appraisal or management system goes on – and will continue to do so. However, given the merit associated with the practice (as noted in Table 7.1 above), there is good reason to continue this search. We detailed the range of obstacles to the effective operation of performance management in practice and how they might be overcome. The application of those characteristics associated with successful systems (Table 7.2 above) should help in this process. The key determining factor of a system's success is the capacity and preparedness of individual managers or reviewers to apply appropriate interpersonal skills, serving to build and maintain manager–employee trust levels and to translate this into a motivational work environment. In brief, the real test of the good performance management manager is whether arising from their interactions with staff – especially the periodic review meeting – employees leave more motivated than when they arrived. In acknowledgement of this reality, we offered a host of practical guidelines for reviewers and reviewees, enabling them to get the best from their periodic interactions under the performance management system. Given that the necessary skill set associated with such interactions does not come naturally to all players in the process, it is notable that there is a correlation between the provision of appropriate training and successful systems.

The priority and consequent resources that the system is accorded by the organization are also of considerable importance. In an environment of rapid change, the system should not become distorted or fall into disuse over time. The extent to which parties manage, monitor and modify it as required is also a key consideration. Even in the case of ongoing organizational stability, checks may be required to ensure that managers have not become complacent about their people or performance management duties.

Despite extensive consultation and training, and the cultivation of a supportive attitude among participants, many practical problems will continue to surface. The ability to anticipate, prepare for and deal with such problems via ongoing monitoring and evaluation constitutes a key ingredient in the attainment of a successful system. And yet, the practical reality is that effective or successful performance management entails 'informal' performance management, with ongoing feedback and discussion proceeding on a continuous basis as quite simply 'the way we do things around here'. The importance of this mindset is particularly pronounced in an uncertain or hostile economic environment, where underperformance cannot be tolerated and effective coaching and mentoring enables staff to adapt to ongoing changes and to rise to the range of challenges and opportunities now confronting them. Allied to the range of progressive HRM practices outlined in this text, performance management can make an immense contribution to this process.

 CHAPTER REVIEW QUESTIONS

1 Your HR director is unhappy with the organization's system for the management of underperformance. They believe that in the event of persistent unsatisfactory performance reviews, there should be a formal system for tackling the problem. Advise them.

2 Why should the HR manager consider redesigning or modifying their organization's performance management system?

3 What relevance has the practice of coaching to a performance management system? What are the key contributors to the art of effective coaching?

4 Your organization's performance appraisal or performance management system is currently in disrepute with management and staff. In your capacity as the HR manager, detail how you would proceed with an evaluation and redesign of the existing system.

5 You have been asked to address your organization's board/executive on 'the case for introducing performance management to our organization'. Outline the key points you will cover in support of this case.

6 You have been asked to address your organization's board/executive on 'why performance management fails'. Outline the key points you will cover in support of this case.

 FURTHER READING

Houldsworth, E. and Jirasinghe, D. (2006) *Managing and Measuring Employee Performance*, London: Kogan Page.

McMahon, G. (2009) *Successful Performance Management: Effective Strategy, Best Practice and Key Skills*, Dublin: Liffey Press.

Toegel, G. and Conger, J. (2003) 360-degree feedback: time for reinvention, *Academy of Management Learning and Education*, **2**(3): 297–311.

Varma, A., Budhwar, P. and DeNisi, A. (eds) (2008) *Performance Management Systems: A Global Perspective*, London: Routledge.

 USEFUL WEBSITES

main.opm.gov/perform/plan.asp
The website of the US Office of Personnel Management provides an extensive and comprehensive series of linkages or guides to the practice of setting performance expectations and goals for groups and individuals, to enable them to channel their efforts towards achieving organizational objectives. It includes sample measures to determine whether expectations and goals are being met. Emphasis is given to the process of involving employees in the planning, helping them understand the goals of the organization, what needs to be done, why it needs to be done, and how well it should be done.

www.tbs-sct.gc.ca/tou/pmc-dgr/intro-eng.asp
The Performance Management website of the Treasury Board of Canada Secretariat provides a comprehensive source of practical information on the key features associated with performance management, including the approach to the practice, its application to probationers, its role in dealing with underperformance and its relationship to the disciplinary process/procedure.

www.pmia.org.au/
The website of the Performance Management Institute of Australia provides an extensive range of information and tools to promote the 'World's Best Practice' in employee performance management to Australian businesses, corporations, not-for-profit and government organizations. It provides up-to-date research, news and information on the state of performance management around the world.

hrweb.berkeley.edu/performance-management/tools
The website of the Human Resources Department at the University of Berkeley, California offers visitors an impressive array of tools and resources designed to help managers and supervisors effectively engage with the performance management or evaluation process. As well as the practically oriented toolkit, it offers guidance on the planning, checking and assessing phases of the performance management cycle, together with sample forms, rating scale descriptors and an online training programme.

 For extra resources including videos and further skills development guidance go to: www.palgrave.com/business/carbery

# 8 MANAGING REWARDS

**Maureen Maloney and Alma McCarthy**

By the end of this chapter you will be able to:

## LEARNING OUTCOMES

- Outline the key aims and objectives of an organization's reward package

- Distinguish between the different elements of the reward package, that is, pay, incentives and benefits

- Explain the factors influencing an organization's pay and reward decisions and understand the advantages and disadvantages of different types of pay and reward

- List and explain the factors that affect how an organization determines the relative value of jobs

- Outline the different approaches to job evaluation

- Describe the options available to employers who implement performance-based incentive schemes

- Discuss the idea of pay as a motivator for employees

© CREATAS

This chapter discusses ...

# INTRODUCTION

A critical part of the employment relationship involves the management of rewards. Most employers operate in a competitive environment that impacts on the amount and elements they use to pay employees. However, reward management is an active process. Savvy employers manipulate the elements of their reward system to attract, motivate and retain the best possible employees.

The **reward system** refers to the combination of financial and nonfinancial elements used by an organization to compensate employees for their time, effort and commitment at work. The specific elements of the reward system depend on the organization's philosophy, strategy, ability to pay and legal responsibilities. Some organizations refer to these policies as 'compensation and benefits'. Historically, the concept of a fair day's work for a fair day's pay was a guiding principle on how employees were rewarded for the efforts they expended while at work. Although reward management is now significantly more complex, the fairness of reward policies and practices remains important.

Organizations are increasingly focused on rewarding the jobs and employees who add value to their organization. The reward system is used to attract the quality of applicants required to drive organizational performance and retain those employees who contribute to that objective. This places considerable pressure on HR departments to align pay policies to the behaviours required to execute organizational strategy. Moreover, motivating and retaining employees requires that they understand that pay policies are applied fairly and consistently. Managers may find themselves in the uncomfortable position of justifying decisions that pay one employee more than another. HR departments must therefore provide the support that assists managers in making reasoned decisions regarding payment based on employee contribution.

Reward management does not operate in isolation. Strategic organizations connect it with other HR policies, including workforce planning, recruitment, selection, training, performance management, career development and work–life balance ▶ **Chapters 7 and 10** ◀. It is the effective combination of reward policies with other HR policies that contributes to an organization's strategic advantage.

The objectives of reward management are to:

- support the organization by designing policies aligned with organizational strategies and goals

> **Reward system** – the combination of financial and nonfinancial elements used by an organization to compensate employees for their time, effort and commitment at work

## SPOTLIGHT ON SKILLS

You have been asked to assist a friend who has just started their own business selling cosmetics door to door. They are about to employ three salespeople, and want your advice on how best to pay these individuals, saying: 'I want to make sure I offer the right package so that I get the best salespeople, but I have limited resources.' To help your friend, think about the advice you would give regarding the following questions:

1  What is the best way to pay salespeople?
2  What will make salespeople work harder?
3  What benefits apart from basic pay and commission would be attractive for them?
4  How should your friend evaluate how effective their reward system is?

To help you answer the questions above, visit www.palgrave.com/business/carbery and watch the video of Miriam Cushen talking about rewards.

- attract and retain employees who add value to the organization by offering an attractive reward package
- motivate employees to perform effectively to achieve valued organizational outcomes by applying policies in a fair and consistent way
- integrate with other HR policies including career development and work–life balance
- comply with legislation.

Organizations have a range of options and choices about how to reward employees for the effort they expend and the work they do. We will now explore the different options and choices, examining their advantages and disadvantages. We then discuss the methods and information sources used by employers to determine the relative worth of jobs in their organization. Finally, the role of pay as a motivator is discussed.

## THE REWARD PACKAGE

There are many options available to organizations when rewarding employees for their performance in the workplace. The reward package refers to the financial and nonfinancial elements offered to employees in return for their labour. Because labour costs are a significant part of total costs for most organizations, reward systems are coming under greater scrutiny to ensure that they match employee expectations while also suiting the changing needs of the business.

Figure 8.1 presents the components and elements of a reward package. The organization will decide on the most appropriate elements to attract, retain and motivate the quality of employees they require. The reward package may also change within an organization, recognizing that certain categories of workers are motivated by different reward packages. For example, the sales representatives for manufacturing companies are paid differently from people who are producing the goods. First, we discuss the financial rewards outlined in Figure 8.1, then the advantages and disadvantages are described in Table 8.1, followed by a discussion of nonfinancial rewards.

**Reward package** – the financial and nonfinancial elements offered to employees in return for their labour

**Direct pay** – the part of pay received by the employee in the form of cash, cheque or direct deposit

**Performance-related pay (PRP)** – a form of direct pay linked to the performance of an individual, team or all employees when predefined objectives are achieved

### Direct pay

The largest component of the reward system is direct pay. The main element of direct pay, and the most costly part for the employer, is base pay, defined as the hourly, weekly or monthly amount paid to an employee if they conform to the terms of their contract. Later, we discuss how jobs are valued to determine their worth. Employees paid by the hour often receive overtime if they work more than the number of hours legally designated as full time. Premium pay may also be added to base pay. For example, many manufacturing organizations that operate a 24/7 schedule pay a shift premium for weekends, evenings and night shifts to recognize the hardship caused by working antisocial hours.

Performance-related pay (PRP) is another component of direct pay. It is an incentive to employees to behave in ways that will promote organizational goals. PRP is linked to the performance of an individual, team or employees throughout the organization and paid when predefined objectives are achieved. In some cases, PRP is consolidated into base pay, leading to a permanent increase of an employee's base pay. More often, PRP is variable, meaning that the payment is additional to base pay and received if, and only if, the employee achieves

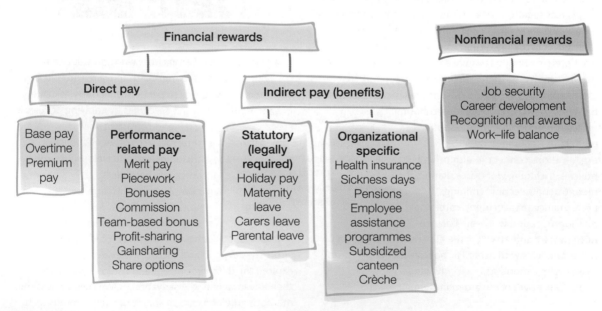

**Figure 8.1** Components and elements of the reward package

the goals and objectives established for a particular pay period. While base pay is financial recognition for past achievements, education, years of service and competence, PRP is aimed at motivating future actions.

The key objective of PRP is to allow the reward package to be responsive to the needs of the organization and its workforce. PRP is frequently used to support a performance-oriented organizational culture, and its rising popularity can be attributed to attempts to change these cultures in the direction of commercial, customer, quality or performance considerations (Armstrong, 2009b). Different forms of PRP are described below.

## Forms of performance-related pay

### Merit pay

Merit pay rewards higher performing employees with additional pay and is normally linked to a performance appraisal conducted by a supervisor or line manager. The criterion used varies. In some organizations, the payment is related to the achievement of goals and objectives established at the beginning of the appraisal period. Desired behaviours such as cooperation and leadership may also be included. Merit pay is considered to be fair if the performance appraisal system is fair. This form of individual PRP is usually consolidated into base pay.

### Piecework

Piecework is a payment given for each unit of production or 'piece' produced. It is based on a standard developed to reflect the units of output a worker can complete per period of time. While pay increases with output, most piecework schemes guarantee a base pay, particularly in jurisdictions where there is minimum wage legislation. There are special allowances for downtime due to equipment maintenance or failure. Piecework schemes are appropriate to those organizations where:

- work is repetitive and unskilled
- workers can influence the pace of production without jeopardizing quality standards
- they are easy to operate and monitor.

### Commission

Commission is usually paid to sales representatives or the sales staff in retail stores. Payments are made as a percentage of sales and are generally paid in addition to the base wage. The percentage may vary with volume, rewarding top performers at a higher rate when sales

increase beyond an agreed threshold. Commission attracts people who are mainly motivated by financial rewards and works best for employees who can work with minimal supervision.

### Bonuses

Bonuses can be paid to individuals, teams or divisions in return for the achievement of predetermined performance targets. Bonus schemes can be designed for any classification of employees. In manufacturing settings, employees are often paid for increased productivity or quality improvements. Executive directors receive bonuses for improved profits. Usually, bonuses are a form of variable pay and must be re-earned each year. It is challenging to develop bonus schemes that are affordable, understandable and motivational, promoting behaviours that lead to organizational competitive advantage. An unusual example of a bonus occurred in 2010. Car maker BMW paid its German workers a special bonus of about €1,000 to reward their commitment and performance during the economic crisis. BMW said it made this payment as the employees 'stood up for the company with stamina and commitment' (*US Today*, 2010).

### Team-based pay

Team-based pay, usually in the form of a bonus, is a payment given to members of a formally established team that is linked to their performance. For example, an R&D team may receive a bonus when a new product completes the regulatory process. The intention is to motivate team members to cooperate to enhance team performance. Team-based pay is suited to many organizations, provided that the team is clearly defined, the goals are explicitly established and performance can be measured.

### Profit-sharing schemes

Profit-sharing schemes are based on organizational performance and enable employees to share in the prosperity and success of the business. A proportion of the company's profits are paid to staff across the organization in the form of a bonus payment. This is a variable form of PRP paid out when profits exceed a threshold. In some cases, profit-sharing takes the form of shares rather than cash, where employees can buy shares in the company at preferential rates. Employees then become shareholders in their own company or a parent company. A proportion of the company's profits in any one year can be used by employees to increase their shareholding.

## Employee share ownership plans

Employee share ownership plans (ESOPs) are legally established and used by companies to distribute shares to employees. The idea behind this is simple. If employees are shareholders, their behaviour will be aligned to shareholders' interests, improving business profitability. ESOPs are a long-term incentive because employees cannot gain the full benefits from their investment for a number of years.

The European Federation of Employee Share Ownership is an international not-for-profit organization with a mission to promote employee share ownership in Europe. It believes that share ownership combined with participative management practices can lead to organizational competitive advantage. Its 2010 annual survey found that over 90 per cent of large European companies had employee ownership plans and over 50 per cent of the plans were broad based including all employees (European Federation of Employee Share Ownership, 2011). These schemes are governed by national legislation, so there are large variations in the way they operate in different European Union (EU) countries. Also, company practices differ. While some companies distribute shares relatively evenly among employees, others award a disproportionate number to top executives.

## Gainsharing schemes

Gainsharing schemes operate where companies attempt to accrue savings by changing work practices. The 'gain' is calculated using an agreed formula and 'shared' between employees and the organization. To be effective, it must be implemented with a participation structure to generate ideas. Also, the measures chosen must be under the control of employees.

## Indirect pay (benefits)

Benefits are sometimes called indirect pay because they are received by employees in forms other than cash, for example health insurance, childcare, provision of a company car. They have a financial value but this is not always transparent to employees, who use them when and if they are needed. Small companies may not provide any benefits beyond those required by law. For large companies, benefits comprise a significant percentage of total labour costs. Communicated properly, information

about benefits sends a powerful message about the organization's concern for the present and future security of their employees and can be used to develop a reputation as an 'employer of choice'. Some benefits are statutory or required by law. Chapter 12 has more information on these entitlements. Other benefits are specific to the organization.

## Statutory benefits

Both employees and employers pay into a social insurance fund. For employees, these contributions are deducted each pay period. These funds are used to provide statutory benefits to people in employment, including maternity leave and carers leave. Employers 'hold' the job of employees availing themselves of these benefits who are entitled to a social welfare payment. Parental leave is designed to allow the parents of young children to take unpaid leave. The terms of parental leave must be agreed with the employer. In the case of injury or layoffs, people who paid social insurance are entitled to disability or redundancy benefits. By law, employers are also required to pay employees for a minimum number of holidays. Employers may 'top up' statutory entitlements. They may increase the number of paid holidays or pay additional salaries to women on maternity leave.

## Organization-specific benefits

The list of organization-specific benefits is long and growing. Not only is there an array of choices, the way in which benefits are managed differs significantly between organizations. For example, some organizations choose a small number of benefits and fully pay for them. Other employers offer flexible benefit plans. Employees are allowed to divide an amount of money, usually a percentage of their salary, on a limited menu of benefits. While providing choice to employees, flexible benefit plans help employers to limit their contribution to benefits with escalating costs, such as healthcare. Some benefits are not funded by employers. For example, an HR department may negotiate discounts for services like gym memberships and arrange for payments to be made by payroll deduction. Some of the most popular additional organization-specific benefits are shown in Figure 8.1 above. Private health insurance tops the list. Some organizations negotiate corporate rates and then fully or partially pay for this benefit. Sometimes, the benefit is extended to the employee's family. Another popular benefit is

**Indirect pay or benefits** – these have a financial value but are rewarded to employees in forms other than cash

sickness days. In some organizations, the number of paid sick days increases with the years of service.

The legal requirements governing employer contributions to occupational pensions vary across Europe. Some employers contribute more than is required by law. A popular method to promote pension savings is for employers to contribute to their employees' pension funds on a matching basis. For example, if the employee pays up to 5 per cent of their income, their employer will match percentage for percentage up to 5 per cent.

Stressful life circumstances can negatively impact on work performance. An employee assistance programme

(EAP) is an important benefit provided to an organization's workers who are experiencing problems in their professional and personal life. The company pays for EAP services, provided in confidence by experts outside the organization. They are most commonly used for depression, stress, anxiety, conflict in the workplace, substance abuse (alcohol or drugs), family and marital problems, and grief and loss.

Finally, subsidized canteens are an important benefit to employees, particularly in manufacturing settings located far from stores and restaurants. Subsidized, on-site crèche facilities are often provided by some large employers.

**Table 8.1** Advantages and disadvantages of different reward components

| Component | Advantages | Disadvantages |
|---|---|---|
| Basic salary/pay | Straightforward to administer<br>Less complex in terms of fairness and equity across employees<br>Costs are known, assisting budgeting | Viewed as an entitlement<br>Limited in terms of motivating employees to higher levels of performance |
| Individual PRP | Focuses employee attention on the performance objectives in the organization's competitive environment<br>Incentivizes those employees motivated by money | Difficult to determine appropriate measures<br>Costs may be higher than predicted<br>Perceived as unfair if inconsistently applied<br>Incentivizing individual behaviour can detract from teamwork and corporate citizenship |
| Team-based PRP | Promotes cooperation and flexibility within teams<br>Provides an incentive for a collective improvement in performance<br>Functions as an effective lever for cultural change, promoting, for example, quality and customer focus | Difficult to determine appropriate measures<br>Risk of 'free-riders' who do little but earn the same as other team members<br>Disliked by some employees who prefer individual incentives |
| Profit-sharing, share options, ESOPs and gainsharing | Promotes corporate citizenship and cooperation at all levels, while also focusing attention on organization-wide performance measures<br>Forms part of a wider employee participation programme, encouraging more open and trusting relations with management and promoting better communication throughout the organization | Line of sight difficult for profit- and share-based schemes, especially in large companies<br>In unfavourable economic circumstances, some companies may not be able to contribute in spite of employee efforts<br>Not suitable for companies in a startup phase, when companies tend not to make profit or have gains to share<br>Share-based schemes are subject to large variations in price, so affecting their value |
| Benefits | Demonstrates employer concern for employee welfare<br>Particularly helpful to employees during periods of stress and illness<br>Differentiates an employer's reward package from others | Additional expense to employers that may not be appreciated or understood by employees<br>Labour intensive for HR departments to explain and administrate |

## Nonfinancial rewards

Some organizations take a 'total rewards' perspective. This means that their reward system includes nonfinancial rewards in addition to direct and indirect pay. These organizations attempt to package all the financial and nonfinancial elements of the employment relationship that are perceived to have value to employees. Employers and HR departments can choose from a wide array of HR policies. The most common choices are shown in Figure 8.1 above. In an increasingly volatile global market, job security is especially prized by some employees. When a job is made 'permanent', an employer recognizes the long-term potential contribution of the employee. It makes it much easier for employees to start families, buy houses and plan for their future in an orderly way.

Career development is another important policy that is added to the reward package. Employees concerned with their employability are always looking for their next job either within or outside their current employment. Career development discussions are normally linked to performance appraisals ▶ Chapter 7 ◀. By planning for training or arranging for different types of work experience within their current role, employees improve their future job prospects and earning power.

Recognition policies and practices can be formal or informal. Both can be promoted through manager training. Informal recognition involves a word of thanks or acknowledgement for work well done. It can be the cheapest and most effective form of reward. Carefully used, it can steer employee behaviour towards achieving organizational goals. Formal recognition programmes vary from individual awards for outstanding behaviour to division events celebrating an important achievement.

Work–life balance policies are particularly valued during parts of employees' lives when they face intense family responsibilities. They complement statutory benefits, allowing employees to remain working when maternity or carers leave entitlements end. A number of different policies fall into this category, including flexible working hours and e-working from home. Employees facilitated with these policies often remain loyal and committed to their organization.

## British Petroleum (BP) and Executive Bonuses after the Gulf Disaster

The Gulf of Mexico oil spill in April 2010 caused immeasurable environmental damage and pollution to southern US states, including Louisiana, Texas, Mississippi, Alabama and Florida. The explosion of BP's Deepwater Horizon oil rig killed 11 people and caused a spill that polluted fishing areas and fouled hundreds of miles of beaches. On 15 July 2010, the leak was stopped by capping the wellhead after it had released about 5 million barrels of crude oil. Recent reports indicate that BP will set aside $14 billion to people who claim the spill affected their business and properties.

In early 2011, BP decided not to pay its chief executive a bonus following the environmental disaster. However, BP's annual report for 2011 showed that two senior directors did receive combined payouts worth nearly £700,000 on top of their regular salaries. Critics view these payments as inappropriate following the environmentally catastrophic oil spill. BP argued that the executives 'met targets in their particular roles and that neither played any part in its offshore exploration division'. The corporate governance consultancy Pirc has urged investors to oppose BP's remuneration report over payouts to outgoing executives, including Tony Hayward, the former chief executive, who got £1 million compensation for loss of office and has share awards yet to vest worth as much as £8 million.

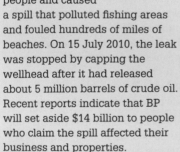

### Questions
1 Do you believe BP has a pay for performance culture?
2 If you could have the final say, what would your decision be on these executive bonuses?

### Sources
Clark, A. (2011) BP investors poised to voice anger at executive bonuses, *The Observer*, 10 April, www.guardian.co.uk/business/2011/apr/10/bp-investors-anger-executive-bonuses.

Davies, R. (2011) Oil giant BP risks investor backlash over pay, *Daily Mail*, 3 March, www.dailymail.co.uk/money/article-1362754/Oil-giant-BP-risks-investor-backlash-pay.html.

Robertson, C. and Krauss, C. (2010) Gulf spill is the largest of its kind, scientists say, *The New York Times*, 2 August, www.nytimes.com/2010/08/03/us/03spill.html?_r=0.

# BUILDING YOUR SKILLS

You are working in a retail store as supervisor. You have noticed that there is poor morale in the shop. Most of the staff are part time and are paid low wages. Given difficult economic conditions, increasing pay rates is not an option. What recommendations can you make to your general manager to improve morale without increasing labour costs?

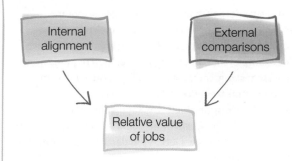

**Figure 8.2** Relative value of jobs within an organization

## DETERMINING THE RELATIVE VALUE OF JOBS

An organization's pay structure is developed using two processes that rely on different bases of information. Using both internal and external sources of information, an organization determines the relative value of jobs within their organization. The two processes are shown in Figure 8.2.

Internal alignment refers to the relative pay relationships between different jobs within an organization. External comparisons are used to determine the amount or range of pay for each job based on an examination of the pay practices of competitors. There are many formal and informal methods used by organizations to gather the required information.

**Job evaluation** – a technique used by organizations to establish the relative worth of jobs

**Felt fair** – acceptance by employees that the difference in pay between jobs is based on the characteristics of the job

## INTERNAL ALIGNMENT

Job evaluation refers to the techniques used by organizations to establish the internal alignment of jobs within their organization. The analysis is carried out on the job itself, as opposed to looking at the person who holds the job.

There are at least three reasons why organizations decide to implement a job evaluation system:

1 To establish an equitable hierarchy or structure of jobs that makes sense to employees. If done properly, the hierarchy should be felt fair. This means that employees should be able to look at other positions within the organization and understand why those jobs are paid more or less than their job. Although the concept of 'felt fair' seems intuitive, it is the final step of the job evaluation process. The process of internal alignment is complete, when the pay structure is felt fair.

2 To ensure that they make consistent decisions on rates of pay that are related to the value added by the position. Although an employee may do excellent work, the amount they are paid must be related to the importance of the job to achieving organizational competitive advantage.

3 A well-conceived and consistently applied job evaluation system provides a strong defence against legal challenges to pay practices.

All forms of job evaluation require job descriptions. For large organizations, the job descriptions are developed using job analysis, a process that examines jobs systematically to identify similarities and differences

## CONSIDER THIS…

In November 2011, Giovanni Trapattoni, the Republic of Ireland's football manager, accepted a cut of about €200,000 to his salary of €1.7 million a year for a fixed term that will end in 2014 after the World Cup campaign.

Why do you think he was willing to accept this pay cut? Was his decision based on internal alignment, external comparisons or something else?

between them ▶ Chapter 2 ◀. Job analysis requires information about job content and the characteristics required of the jobholder. A job analysis would reflect, for example, that an office manager's job requires more diverse tasks, greater responsibility, more conflicting demands, greater education, more years' experience, supervisory responsibilities, greater control over financial resources, and more complex external contacts than the receptionist's job. A job description summarizes this information.

There are different types of job evaluation that range from very simple to very complex. **Non-analytical methods** are relatively simple. Comparisons are made between whole jobs without analysing them into constituent parts or elements. **Analytical methods** are more complex. Important characteristics of jobs that promote organizational competitive advantage are identified and the degrees to which they are present in the job are assessed. Figure 8.3 shows different methods of job evaluation.

An organization can develop its own analytical job evaluation method. In practice, most large organizations adopt systems developed by large consulting firms such as the Hay Group, Mercer and Towers Watson.

**Non-analytical methods** – whole jobs are compared to determine the organization's internal pay structure

**Analytical methods** – they identify characteristics of the job that are valued by the organization and assess the degree to which they are present in the job

| Non-analytical methods | Analytical methods |
| --- | --- |
| Ranking | Point method |
| Paired comparison | Hay System of Compensation |
| | Mercer International Point Evaluation System |
| | Towers Watson Global Grading System |

**Figure 8.3** Non-analytical and analytical methods of job evaluation

## Non-analytical methods of job evaluation

Most organizations are small. Almost 90 per cent of EU businesses are classified as micro-sized, meaning they employ less than 10 employees (European Commission, 2012b). Generally, new positions are added one at a time. The employer compares the new job with existing jobs and decides where it fits by determining the value it adds to the organization. This comparison is the basis of non-analytical job evaluation.

### Ranking and paired comparisons

Ranking is the simplest non-analytical form of job evaluation. Whole jobs are compared to whole jobs and placed in order of importance to the enterprise. Paired comparison is a slightly more complicated variation. It involves a matrix used to compare all possible pairs of jobs before placing them in order of importance.

Consider a self-employed accountant, who hires a bookkeeper to assist them and then a junior accountant. Both jobholders work in the office and neither interact regularly with clients. Later, a senior accountant is hired

to find new clients and manage the junior accountant and bookkeeper. Finally, a receptionist is hired. Figure 8.4 shows an example of a paired comparison for the four employees hired by the business owner.

Start with the bookkeeper (left of matrix) and compare the job with the junior accountant (top of first column). 'Junior accountant' is placed in the box because this job ranks higher than the bookkeeper. The senior accountant's job is compared to the bookkeeper and junior accountant. It ranks higher than both and therefore appears in both boxes. Finally, while the receptionist's job requires interacting with customers and the public, it is an entry-level position that does not require any specific knowledge or experience. The jobs of bookkeeper, junior accountant and senior accountant rank higher than the receptionist and these jobs appear in the boxes in the third column. A score is tallied, counting the number of times a job receives the highest rating. Placing the jobs in order from highest to lowest indicates their importance to the business (shown to the right of the matrix).

When there is a small number of jobs and the decision maker is familiar with all aspects of the jobs, ranking or paired comparisons are quick and easy ways to place the jobs in order. The advantages and disadvantages of ranking and paired comparisons are described in Table 8.3 below.

### Classification systems

Classification systems begin with a set of similar jobs called a 'class' or 'job family' described using a common

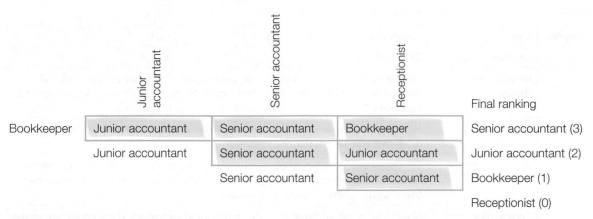

**Figure 8.4** Example of a paired comparison matrix

# BUILDING YOUR SKILLS

Place yourself in the role of the business owner (and senior accountant). Because the business is growing, you decide to hire an office manager. Add this role to the paired comparison matrix illustrated in Figure 8.4. Describe any difficulties you encounter in completing this task.

set of characteristics. The classification should be broad enough to encompass several jobs that are significantly different from jobs in other classifications. Classifications are then divided into grades that are differentiated using characteristics such as impact, knowledge and experience. The characteristics are described rather than quantified as they are for the point method (discussed below).

In the small but growing organization we considered above, there are two classifications. The 'accounting' classification administers, supervises and/or performs professional, technical or related clerical activities related to account preparation for clients. The jobs of senior accountant, junior accountant and bookkeeper would represent separate grades based on differences in impact, knowledge and experience. The 'administrative support' classification administers, supervises or performs all the activities required to support the business. Currently, only the receptionist's job fits into this classification, probably at the lowest grade.

The US government, one of the world's largest employers, uses a classification system to determine the internal alignment of the civil service. There are 23 classifications for the 'white collar occupational group'. The 'trade, craft and labour group' comprises 36 job families that range from painting and paperhanging to ammunition, explosives and toxic materials handling (US Office of Personnel Management, n.d.). The advantages and disadvantages of classification systems are described in Table 8.3 below.

## Analytical methods of job evaluation

### Point methods

The point method is an analytical form of job evaluation based on identifying factors relevant to all jobs within the organization, scaling them and developing an order of jobs based on adding up the points for each job. All point methods, whether tailor-made or purchased from consultants, are based on identifying factors relevant to all jobs within an organization and numerically scaling them to reflect their relative importance to the organization. These methods are more complex to develop and implement than the non-analytical methods. However, they help ensure that equal work receives equal pay. This is important in relation to establishing internal alignment. It is also a strong defence for legal challenges based on claims of unfair pay practices. The process used to develop a point method of job evaluation is shown in Table 8.2.

Rather than creating their own method, many large organizations use 'off-the-shelf' systems developed by large consulting firms. The most frequently used point

**Table 8.2** Steps to develop a point method of job evaluation

| Number | Step | Description |
|--------|------|-------------|
| 1 | Conduct job analysis | Described above |
| 2 | Identify relevant factors | These are based on organizational strategies and values, the nature of the work and acceptability to stakeholders. These may include factors such as impact, knowledge and experience |
| 3 | Scale the factors | Numeric values of increasing value are assigned to each factor to distinguish the degree to which it is present in the job |
| 4 | Weight the factors | Each factor is weighted to reflect its relative importance. For example, an employer may weight the factor 'impact' more highly than 'knowledge', believing it is more important to the organization's competitive advantage |
| 5 | Communicate and train | Manuals are prepared that explain the system for all employees. Those implementing the system are trained. This is important to promote consistent application and acceptance. The appeal system should also be described |
| 6 | Calculate points for each job | Each job within an organization receives a score based on the extent to which each factor is required to adequately perform the job |
| 7 | Place job in order | All jobs are placed in order according to their scores from highest to lowest. Higher scores reflect the relative importance of the job to the organization |
| 8 | Recheck for fairness | The order of jobs is examined to ensure that it is 'felt fair' and that differences between scores reflect the relative importance of the job to the organization |

*Source:* Based on Milkovich et al., 2010

method is the Hay System of Compensation developed in the 1950s. This method gained prominence because it identified a small number of factors that can be compared across a large number of jobs. The factors used for the Hay System include accountability, problem-solving and know-how. Other consulting firms such as Mercer and Towers Watson developed similar systems. There are several reasons why these systems are used:

1 Developing a job evaluation system internally takes months, if not years, so it is more efficient to buy an existing system.
2 Consulting firms train employees and provide computerized systems that make the implementation process easier.
3 Hay, Mercer and Towers Watson conduct salary surveys. Organizations that use their job evaluation system can avail themselves of this additional service and easily compare their jobs with other companies, often those competing in the same sector.

There are advantages and disadvantages to each method of job evaluation. They are summarized in Table 8.3. The choice made by organizations is based on the size of the company, complexity of jobs, availability of resources to buy or develop a system, and the likelihood of legal challenge.

## ENVIRONMENTAL FACTORS

Organizations make decisions about their reward system in a complex external environment where many factors are outside their control. These factors need to be managed for an organization to remain competitive.

Globalization impacts on businesses in the traded sector. These organizations sell goods and services that compete with imports and exports from other countries. This competition places pressure on organizations to keep labour costs as low as possible. If an organization's labour costs are higher than competing businesses in other countries, jobs can be lost. Multinationals operating within a country are 'footloose'. They can easily close in one jurisdiction and open in another to reduce labour costs. All the environmental factors associated with globalization encourage organizations to keep their labour costs low.

**Table 8.3** Advantages and disadvantages of different job evaluation methods

| Method | Advantages | Disadvantages |
|---|---|---|
| Ranking/paired comparison | Easy to understand<br>Quick to implement<br>Inexpensive | Unclear basis of comparison between jobs<br>Unwieldy as the numbers and types of jobs increase<br>Relative difference between jobs is unclear |
| Classification system | Easy to understand and develop<br>Differences between jobs based on characteristics<br>Expands for growing organizations | Unusual jobs not classified<br>Relative position of classification inflexible even if job content changes<br>Relative difference between jobs unclear |
| Point method | Accommodates any number of jobs<br>Establishes order and relative differences between jobs based on systematic analysis<br>Decisions based on factors that are important to organizational competitiveness<br>Defensible against legal challenges | Costly to develop or to buy<br>Off-the-shelf methods use general rather than organization-specific factors<br>Time-consuming to implement<br>Difficult to explain to employees |

Organizations competing in the EU face conflicting pressures. Some promote lower labour costs while others cause them to increase. Labour costs for organizations competing in the eurozone are transparent. It is easy to see if national or organizational wages are out of line with other eurozone countries. This places pressure on organizations to keep labour costs low. However, trade unions place upward pressure on wages. Trade union membership across the EU is difficult to measure, but the numbers appear to be stable between 2003 and 2008 (Carley, 2009). Trade unions are a powerful force, negotiating wage agreements at the national, industry or enterprise level. Also, EU labour market Directives are translated by national governments into legislation. These laws help to protect labour but tend to increase labour costs for organizations operating in the EU.

At the national level, there are also conflicting pressures on labour costs. Periods of recession place downward pressure on wages because the supply of labour is greater than the demand. The opposite is true during periods of expansion. National labour market legislation can also add to labour costs. For example, minimum wage legislation is enacted to help low-paid workers. However, it places a floor under all wages. Countries with a minimum wage that is high relative to other countries will have higher labour costs that can threaten organizational competitiveness. Taxation policy can also impact on labour costs. The tax rates charged to businesses to pay for social insurance, for example, add to labour costs.

Organizations also compete within industries. There are large differences in wages between organizations in the accommodation and food sector when compared

with the information and communications (ICT) sector. A business competing in the ICT sector will have to pay more to attract and retain competent employees. In some industries, like construction, an organization's wage bill is a significant percentage of total costs. Employers in these sectors will be more sensitive to granting a wage increase than employers in high-tech manufacturing, where labour costs comprise a relatively small percentage of total costs.

Finally, there can be competing pressures on pay at the local level. Labour shortages within localities can lead to wage increases across industries especially for unskilled or semi-skilled workers as supermarkets compete with manufacturers for employees. Labour surpluses have the opposite effect. The higher cost of living in urban areas can lead to a premium being paid to urban workers relative to employees doing the same job in towns or rural localities.

These environmental factors are outside an organization's control. While some exert pressure on the organization to reduce labour costs, other factors cause labour costs to increase. They form the context in which pay decisions are made. Some of these factors are reflected in the salary surveys used by employers making external comparisons with competitors.

## EXTERNAL COMPARISONS

All organizations make choices about how much to pay employees and the composition of that pay. There are competing objectives at play here. First, organizations want their reward system to attract and retain competent employees. Second, organizations need to manage their labour costs. Both objectives are achieved by gathering information about the pay packages of competitors.

## Determining competitive markets

The first task is to determine the organization's competitors for employees. For a small corner shop, this is easy. They are competing for employees with other shops in the area. However, a large business with several classes of employees may compete with organizations in several industries or geographic locations for their employees. The different markets for employees are shown in Figure 8.5.

Organizations often hire graduates from degree courses from third-level institutes. However, a graduate may be qualified to enter many different industries. For example, graduate process engineers can find employment in the biotechnology, food, petrochemical, manufacturing or pharmaceutical sectors. If a business in the pharmaceutical industry is hiring process engineer graduates, it will be competing with businesses from several other industries. For senior or specialized positions, organizations often look for candidates with experience in their own product or service market. For example, if Abbott Laboratories Ireland is hiring a senior process engineer, it competes with other companies in the pharmaceutical industry such as Pfizer and GlaxoSmithKline.

Depending on the position within the organization, the relevant geographic market may differ. For example, if Abbott Laboratories Ireland is hiring an administrative assistant and a senior process engineer, they will compete in different geographic markets. For the administrative assistant, the competitors are local, while competitors for the senior process engineer are national. The size of an organization is also important. On average, large organizations pay about 50 per cent more than small companies and 20 per cent more than medium-sized companies (Central Statistics Office, 2011). Abbott Laboratories Ireland will compare itself against businesses of similar size rather than small startups that pay considerably less.

To summarize, before looking for information about competitors' reward systems, the organization must define the relevant markets for competent employees and determine its competitors in those markets. The relevant markets are defined by skills and occupations, products and services, geography and size. A business may compete with different organizations depending on the job.

## Information sources

Organizations can obtain information about competitor's pay policies from many different sources that range from informal to research based, and from free to very expensive. The goal of the organization is to gather information that is sufficiently reliable to make good decisions at the lowest possible cost. There are three basic strategies used by organizations to find relevant pay information – they can access information, buy or collect survey data.

### Access information
They can access free information from internal or external sources. Often, this information is gathered for a different reason but is useful for determining the market value of a job. European countries gather labour market

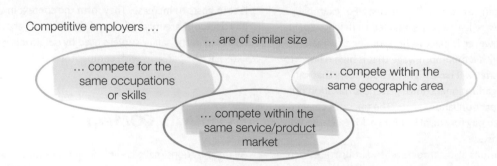

**Figure 8.5** Defining the market for employees

statistics on earnings and labour costs for business sectors on a regular basis to identify competitiveness and inflation trends. Industrial relations (IR) and business periodicals publish occasional surveys and articles on wages and benefits. Sometimes, these relate to jobs across a variety of sectors. Alternatively, they may report on a wage deal made within a particular organization. HR professionals belong to informal and professional networks, and they can often be helpful in providing ad hoc information. Job advertisements in the national press or specialist journals sometimes include information about salaries and benefits. During their exit interviews, departing employees may disclose the terms and conditions offered by their new employer.

The advantage of these sources is that they are free. However, there are disadvantages. Information that is collected on a regular basis by government offices is often out of date by the time it is published. When reported at the sector level, there is often no specific information about jobs within the sector. Articles and surveys in journals and newspapers appear on an irregular basis. Information from colleagues, job advertisements and exit interviews, although specific, are not consistently available. In general, these sources are not reliable because they do not provide consistent information about similar jobs in competitor organizations on a regular basis.

### Buy survey data

Organizations can buy information that is industry specific, occupational specific or related to their job evaluation system. Industry-specific information is gathered by the industry itself, or employers' organizations. Occupational surveys are published by professional associations for groups such as engineers, accountants or HR professionals. The information is often

based on tenure and professional qualifications rather than jobs. Consulting firms like Hay, PricewaterhouseCoopers and Mercer also conduct surveys for large occupational groups, often gathering information from organizations using their job evaluation methods. One advantage of these sources is that consistent information is regularly collected. In relation to disadvantages, these surveys are expensive and may not encompass a wide variety of jobs. Also, the participating organizations may not be competitors within the relevant markets. Finally, the organization may require specific information that is not gathered for these off-the-shelf surveys.

### Collect survey data

Organizations can make their own surveys or pay a consultant to gather information from competitors. Third party bespoke surveys are conducted by consultants who gather information from a number of competitors within the same industry. Although this survey may be repeated regularly, the participants in the survey may change. Pay club surveys are an arrangement between industry competitors to exchange information about pay and benefits on a regular basis. The advantage of these sources is that the same pay information is consistently gathered about similar jobs from comparable organizations. The disadvantage is that they are expensive. The range of information sources is shown in Figure 8.6. At the bottom of the arrow are information sources that are free but not reliable. Moving up the arrow, the information sources are more reliable and expensive.

In practice, large organizations participate in several surveys and use a variety of sources in order to obtain reliable information. This is because they hire employees for a large number of jobs with competitors in many different markets. Although the costs are high, the costs

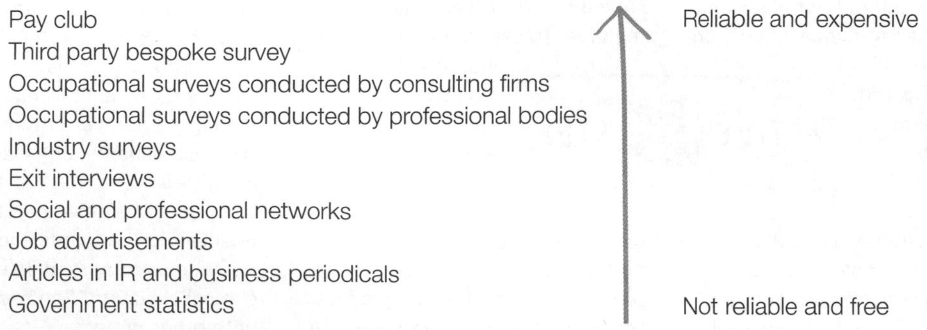

Pay club
Third party bespoke survey
Occupational surveys conducted by consulting firms
Occupational surveys conducted by professional bodies
Industry surveys
Exit interviews
Social and professional networks
Job advertisements
Articles in IR and business periodicals
Government statistics

Reliable and expensive

Not reliable and free

**Figure 8.6 Sources of information about pay and benefits**

of uncompetitive pay practices are higher. If pay and benefits are too low, organizations will not be able to attract and retain productive employees. If pay and benefits are too high, organizations will lose competitiveness within their industries. The order of jobs in an organization is determined using a job evaluation method. The information from competitors is used to determine the salary range for each job within an organization. Combined, the two information sources are used to determine the relative value of jobs within an organization.

## PAY AS A MOTIVATOR

One of the key debates in the HRM field and particularly the reward management area is the link between pay and motivation. The assumption is that the higher the employee motivation levels, the higher their performance. Since Maslow's contribution to the motivation debate, there is much discussion about the impact of pay on motivation levels (Milkovich et al., 2010). Maslow argued that pay is a motivator at the lower levels when employees are addressing physiological needs. However, once satisfied, pay does not motivate higher levels of performance as elements such as self-esteem and self-actualization become important.

Rynes et al. (2004) conducted a meta-analysis (review of many published studies) to explore the importance of pay in determining employee motivation. They found that 'money is not the only motivator and it is not the primary motivator for everyone. However, there is

overwhelming evidence that money is an important motivator for most people' (Rynes et al., 2004: 391). They also found that there is a discrepancy between what people self-report about the impact of pay on their motivation levels and their performance versus their actual choices and behaviours. Rynes et al. report that people tend to say that pay is not important for their motivation, yet their behaviour indicates that, in reality, pay is important in understanding motivation. Studies of actual behaviours in response to motivation initiatives show pay to be the most effective motivator in most cases. The argument made in the study is not that pay is the only motivator – but that it is important.

Rynes et al. (2004) found that pay is an important motivator if:

- there is some form of PRP
- PRP is paid to people on low wages because a small change can make a significant difference
- employees assess that they are being fairly paid in comparison to their colleagues.

### CONSIDER THIS...

Think about a time when you were working (summer job, part-time work and so on). Do you feel you were fairly rewarded? Why? Why not? What change to the reward system would have motivated you to work harder? If your suggestion was implemented, do you think it would motivate other employees to work harder?

### Employee Bonus Schemes

You are the general manager and owner of the Sundance Adventure and Leisure Complex, located in Connemara in Co. Galway, Ireland. It is a private, non-unionized business that employs 125 people in peak season. The enterprise provides activity-based holiday packages for individuals and families. In

November 2011, you asked the HR manager (Mary Lynch) to design a bonus scheme for all staff. She designed the scheme, liaising with you and the other three department heads. In mid-December 2011, she presented it to all the employees through a series of three meetings. The scheme was officially

launched in January 2012. The table below details the elements of the bonus scheme.

This was the first time the HR manager had ever introduced this type of a scheme. She was delighted when the 'roll-out' was complete. She delegated the task of entering the points each week onto a master spreadsheet to her clerical assistant. She became busy with other projects.

In the first week of July 2012, Mary looked at the complex's attendance figures and saw that there hadn't been a significant improvement since the beginning of the scheme. She decided to take a closer look at how the scheme was operating. Mary started by looking at the information her clerical assistant was about to enter into the master table (see Exhibit 1 below). Mary was concerned after looking at the point awards. She decided to conduct a survey to gather feedback from staff about the bonus scheme. She devised a few questions that were added to the employee satisfaction questionnaire conducted semi-annually (see Exhibit 2) and the results of that questionnaire are shown in Exhibit 3. Having reviewed the results of the survey, in September 2012, Mary gave three months' notice that the scheme would terminate in December 2012.

© GETTY

| Elements | Detail |
| --- | --- |
| Participants | Managers, supervisors, staff (125) |
| Method of payment | One4all gift certificates that can be used in multiple shops, retail outlets and department stores throughout Ireland. Chosen in preference to cash so that employees do not have to pay income tax on the bonus; the company pays tax on these awards |
| Frequency of payment | Employees could receive their bonus on a monthly basis. However, the amounts earned per month were small, and the HR director assumed from the outset that employees would collect their certificates after a few months or before Christmas each year |
| Criteria for bonus | Bonus points were awarded per week for each of the following criteria:<br>• *Attendance:* full attendance (10 points)<br>• *Punctuality:* arriving on time each day, returning on time from scheduled breaks and completing entire shift (10 points)<br>• *Appearance:* although the attire is casual throughout the facility, a uniform is provided for staff comprising sweat pants, T-shirt, jacket and name badge. All feature the company logo. (Employees working outside also receive a visor and polo cap.) Points are awarded if the staff member conforms to the procedures for appearance outlined in the employee handbook given during induction training (10 points)<br>• *Teamwork:* outstanding contribution to the employee's work team (30 point maximum)<br>• *Customer comments:* written comments by a customer concerning a staff member, or verbal comments made to another member of staff (20 point maximum) |
| Translating points to payment | Employees received €1 for each 10 points accrued on a weekly basis |
| Points awarded | The employee's immediate supervisor decided the number of points awarded each week, placed the points on a spreadsheet and returned the results to the HR department |
| Notification of points | The points received by each employee were displayed each month on the department bulletin board |
| Termination of scheme | Management reserved the right to discontinue the scheme after three months' notice |

**Exhibit 1** Award points allocation for two departments

| Monthly award for employees in Departments 1 and 2 | | | | | | | |
| --- | --- | --- | --- | --- | --- | --- | --- |
| July 2012: Week 1 | | | | | | | |
| | | Attendance | Punctuality | Appearance | Team | Customer comments | Total |
| **Department: Kitchen** | | | | | | | |
| Barbuto | Tony | 10 | 8 | 10 | 30 | | **58** |
| Conneely | Patrick | 10 | 10 | 9 | 30 | | **59** |
| Donnellan | Nuala | 10 | 9 | 10 | 30 | | **59** |
| Dunne | Tony | 10 | 10 | 10 | 30 | | **60** |
| Evans | Myrtle | 10 | 10 | 9 | 30 | | **59** |
| Fitzgerald | Eithne | 9 | 10 | 10 | 30 | | **59** |
| Green | Rory | 10 | 8 | 10 | 30 | 20 | **78** |
| Jones | John | 10 | 7 | 10 | 30 | | **57** |
| Kreiger | Shirley | 10 | 10 | 10 | 30 | | **60** |
| Lyden | Joe | 6 | 5 | 9 | 30 | | **50** |
| McDonough | Peter | 10 | 8 | 10 | 30 | | **58** |
| McNamara | Maureen | 10 | 9 | 10 | 30 | | **59** |
| Moore | Deirdre | 10 | 10 | 10 | 30 | | **60** |
| O'Carroll | Diarmuid | 10 | 10 | 9 | 30 | | **59** |
| O'Neill | Eamon | 8 | 8 | 10 | 30 | | **56** |
| O'Shea | Jack | 7 | 10 | 10 | 30 | | **57** |
| Quinlivan | Mary | 10 | 8 | 10 | 30 | | **58** |
| Smith | Mary | 10 | 7 | 10 | 30 | | **57** |
| Tormley | Gerry | 10 | 9 | 10 | 30 | | **59** |
| Walsh | John | 10 | 10 | 10 | 30 | 20 | **80** |
| **Department: Service** | | | | | | | |
| Allen | Latisha | 10 | 10 | 10 | 30 | 15 | **75** |
| Burns | Tom | 10 | 10 | 0 | 25 | | **45** |
| Connolly | Ann | 10 | 10 | 10 | 20 | | **50** |
| Conroy | Pam | 10 | 10 | 10 | 10 | 20 | **60** |
| Curley | Michael | 10 | 0 | 10 | 15 | | **35** |
| Cunningham | Eimer | 0 | 0 | 0 | 30 | | **30** |
| Davitt | Patricia | 10 | 10 | 10 | 30 | | **60** |
| Joyce | Mary | 10 | 10 | 10 | 10 | | **40** |
| Joyce | Peggy | 0 | 10 | 10 | 20 | 10 | **50** |
| Long | Mike | 0 | 10 | 0 | 20 | | **30** |
| Lydon | Ellie | 10 | 0 | 10 | 15 | | **35** |
| Maloney | Mike | 10 | 0 | 10 | 25 | | **45** |
| O'Connor | Julia | 10 | 0 | 0 | 30 | | **40** |
| Petrisek | Jean | 10 | 10 | 10 | 15 | 20 | **65** |
| Russell | Jack | 10 | 0 | 0 | 20 | | **30** |

| Monthly award for employees in Departments 1 and 2 | | | | | | |
|---|---|---|---|---|---|---|
| July 2012: Week 1 | | | | | | |
| | | Attendance | Punctuality | Appearance | Team | Customer comments | Total |
| **Department: Service** | | | | | | |
| Scott | Lavinia | 10 | 10 | 10 | 30 | | **60** |
| Smith | Murray | 10 | 10 | 10 | 25 | | **55** |
| Sullivan | James | 10 | 10 | 10 | 15 | | **45** |
| Sullivan | Peggy | 10 | 0 | 10 | 25 | | **45** |
| Ward | Lucy | 10 | 10 | 10 | 30 | 20 | **80** |

**Exhibit 2** Evaluating the award scheme: survey questions

This questionnaire/survey contains a number of questions you are asked to comment on by circling a number that best corresponds to your opinion. Even if you are not sure, try to find the alternative closest to your opinion. If you think it is impossible to form an opinion, just skip the question.

| | | I strongly disagree | I disagree | I neither agree nor disagree | I agree | I strongly agree |
|---|---|---|---|---|---|---|
| 1 | I understand how the incentive scheme operates | 1 | 2 | 3 | 4 | 5 |
| 2 | In order to get more points, I make a special effort to work well with others within my department | 1 | 2 | 3 | 4 | 5 |
| 3 | The way my manager distributes points to each member of staff in my department is fair | 1 | 2 | 3 | 4 | 5 |
| 4 | The managers of other departments distribute points in the same way as my manager | 1 | 2 | 3 | 4 | 5 |
| 5 | I am satisfied with the size of the bonus I received | 1 | 2 | 3 | 4 | 5 |
| 6 | The criteria measured under the incentive scheme are important to my job performance | 1 | 2 | 3 | 4 | 5 |
| 7 | In order to get more points, I am careful to arrive on time every day | 1 | 2 | 3 | 4 | 5 |

**Exhibit 3** Evaluating the award scheme: survey response analysis

The following graphs show the percentage of staff who either strongly disagree, disagree, neither agree nor disagree, agree or strongly agree with the seven statements above.

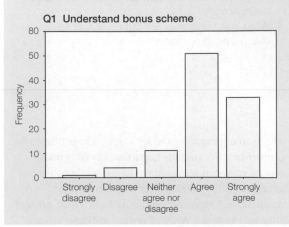

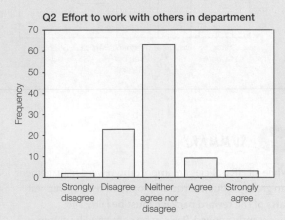

→

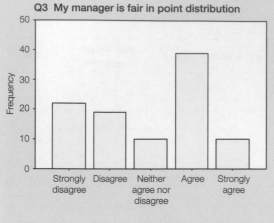

Q3 My manager is fair in point distribution

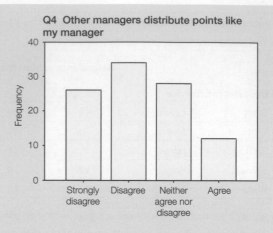

Q4 Other managers distribute points like my manager

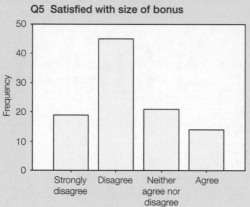

Q5 Satisfied with size of bonus

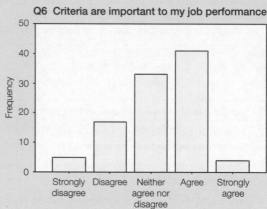

Q6 Criteria are important to my job performance

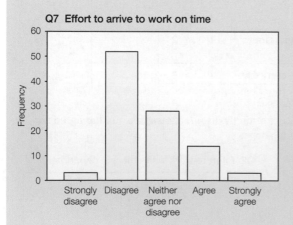

Q7 Effort to arrive to work on time

Evaluate the scheme at the Sundance Adventure and Leisure Complex.

1 What could Mary have done differently in designing and implementing this scheme?
2 What features of the scheme work well and what features are problematic?
3 Did Mary make the right decision in terminating the scheme?
4 What was the cost of the failure of this scheme to Mary? To the company?

## SUMMARY

While all HR policies are important, reward management can greatly influence the employment relationship. All parts of the reward package must be fairly and consistently applied. Pay can be compared by employees within an organization and with the package offered by competitors. So, employers, particularly large ones, expend considerable resources to ensure that their pay structure is internally consistent and externally competitive. Organizations choose from a wide array of financial elements. While all reward packages include base pay and statutory benefits, organizations differentiate their reward package using performance-related pay and benefits. Employers who use a total reward approach also include nonfinancial elements in an effort to capture all the aspects of the employment relationship that are valued by their employees. Recognition, job security, career development and work–life balance policies are presented with financial rewards to capture the total worth of the employment relationship. Labour costs are a significant proportion of total costs for many industries. Reward management must always balance the need to attract, retain and motivate employees with the requirement to control labour costs.

 CHAPTER REVIEW QUESTIONS

1 What is meant by reward management and what are the typical objectives of a reward system?
2 What are the differences between nonfinancial and financial rewards? In your opinion, which are the most important for delivering higher levels of performance?
3 Describe the various PRP options available to organizations.
4 Describe the reasons why organizations conduct job evaluation. Under what circumstances are non-analytical methods effective?
5 Describe the environmental factors that impact on the labour costs of a multinational call centre operating in a rural location.
6 Describe the methods a small retail store owner with five employees may use to determine the relative value of their jobs.
7 Is pay a motivator? Discuss, using examples from your own experience or from friends and family members.

 FURTHER READING

Beardwell, J. and Claydon, T. (2010) *Human Resource Management: A Contemporary Approach*, 6th edn, Harlow: Pearson Education.
Bratton, J. and Gold, J. (2007) *Human Resource Management: Theory and Practice*, 4th edn, Basingstoke: Palgrave Macmillan.
Dillon, K. (2009) The coming battle over executive pay, *Harvard Business Review*, **87**(9): 96–103.

Marchington, M. and Wilkinson, A. (2008) *Human Resource Management: People Management and Development*, London: CIPD.
Pilbeam, S. and Corbridge, M. (2010) *People Resourcing and Talent Planning: HRM in Practice*, 4th edn, Harlow: Pearson Education.
Storey, J. (ed.) (2007) *Human Resource Management: A Critical Text*, 3rd edn, London: Thompson Education.

 USEFUL WEBSITES

http://youtu.be/u6XAPnuFjJc
Highlights from an interview with Dan Pink about motivation.

www.cipd.co.uk/hr-resources/factsheets/reward-pay-overview.aspx
The CIPD provides a broad range of resources on various HR policies and practices. Follow this link to see its pay and reward fact sheets.

www.mercer.com/services/1351270
Read more about Mercer's International Position Evaluation System (IPE) at the link above, which offers organizations an independent method to compare various aspects of a job and rank positions against each other.

www.watsonwyatt.com/tools/globalgradingsystem/tour/index.asp
Towers Watson has developed the Global Grading System (GGS) to help companies level jobs across functions, business units and countries. Follow the link to take a tour of the software that supports the Global Grading System.

www.bbk.ac.uk/jobevaluation/
Follow this link to see how the University of London has used the Hay System for its job evaluation exercise.

www.peoplemanagement.co.uk
*People Management* is the UK's number one HR magazine and official magazine of the CIPD. The website provides news, features and all the latest thinking and advice in HR.

 For extra resources including videos and further skills development guidance go to: www.palgrave.com/business/carbery

# 9 LEARNING AND DEVELOPMENT

**Thomas N. Garavan**

By the end of this chapter you will be able to:

## LEARNING OUTCOMES

- Explain the differences between learning and development (L&D) and other terms used to describe these activities in organizations
- Demonstrate an understanding of the benefits of L&D for individuals and teams, organizations and society
- Assess the different approaches to the development of L&D strategies
- Explain how individuals can learn in organizations and how individual styles and references vary

- Understand how to formulate an L&D strategy
- Evaluate the issues involved in identifying and responding to L&D needs
- Understand the key issues to be considered when designing L&D interventions
- Outline the key steps to be considered when evaluating L&D and measuring return on investment

This chapter discusses ...

© STOCKBYTE/PUNCHSTOCK

# INTRODUCTION

Learning and development (L&D) activities are considered an important component of organizational effectiveness. As organizations seek to compete in the global economy, they increasingly focus on gaining competitive advantage through the knowledge, skill and attitudes of their employees. In the knowledge economy, the capacity of employees to absorb and process new information, acquire new skills and adapt effectively to new realities are important and, some would say, critical to the continued success of an organization.

L&D activities in organizations must be strategic to enhance effectiveness. They must be focused on the most important issues that face an organization in order to maximize the investment in L&D and demonstrate added value. The ultimate objective of L&D activities in organizations should be to generate the greatest value for the investment made. It is well documented that L&D activities have benefits for individuals, teams, organizations and, ultimately, society; however, these benefits are frequently not effectively measured or publicized. In this chapter we will explain the scope of L&D in organizations and outline how it differs from traditional training, and discuss the key decisions that organizations need to make to ensure that L&D activities generate strategic value. We begin by outlining the key differences in terminology that characterize L&D as a subject area and then examine the benefits of those activities. We move on to consider how people learn and explain different learning styles. We consider different approaches to the development of L&D strategies, the key issues to be considered when designing L&D events, and how organizations can demonstrate that L&D activities generate value for an organization.

## L&D AS AN ORGANIZATIONAL PROCESS

Organizations use a variety of terms to describe L&D activities, including 'training and development',

'employee development' and 'strategic human resource development'. Training and development can be considered the traditional way to describe learning activities in organizations. Training is a narrow term that focuses on employees achieving experienced worker standard within the shortest time period possible. The term 'employee development' was in vogue during the 1980s and 90s; however, it fell out of favour with new perspectives on how to describe an employee. Employee development is considered a hierarchical term that does not account for how employers now describe employees. Terms such as 'partner' and 'associate' are now commonplace in organizations. Harrison (2009) suggests that employee development is not sufficiently inclusive and does not reflect the equality and diversity agenda that pervades the world of work today.

The term strategic human resource development (SHRD) is popular among academics to describe the nature of L&D activities in organizations. Harrison (2009) suggests that organizations dislike the term because it equates people with other resources; however, there is no doubt that organizations view skilled employees as a sustainable source of competitive advantage (Garavan, 2007). A key lesson to be derived from the discussion of SHRD is that L&D activities need to be aligned with the strategic goals of the organization and other HRM processes and systems.

The Chartered Institute of Personnel and Development (CIPD) has adopted the term 'learning and development' (L&D), which is sufficiently broad to capture the complexity of such activities in organizations. First, it is a more democratic term that can apply to people irrespective of their contractual position with the organization. This could include contractors, suppliers, volunteers, consultants and customers or anyone who contributes to the success of the organization. Second, it is a term that captures the complexity of L&D processes and incorporates formal, informal, non-formal and incidental L&D processes that are found in organizations. Therefore, the CIPD (2005b: 82) definition suits our purposes, in that it is sufficiently comprehensive and contemporary:

---

**Learning and development (L&D)** – learning refers to activities provided by the organization to enhance employee competencies, develop greater self-awareness and insight, and contribute to individual, team and organizational effectiveness; development refers to activities leading to new knowledge and skills for reasons of personal growth

**Knowledge economy** – where specialist, expert knowledge is perceived to be as critical as other economic resources

**Training** – the process of acquiring the knowledge, skills and attitudes required to perform an organizational role effectively

**Strategic human resource development (SHRD)** – learning activities focused on individuals, teams and organizations aimed at enhancing the alignment of human resources with the strategic objectives of the organization

The organizational process of developing people involves the integration of learning and development processes, operations and relationships. Its most powerful outcomes for the business are to do with enhanced organisational effectiveness and sustainability. For the individual they are to do with enhanced personal competence, adaptability and employability. It is therefore a critical business process, whether in for-profit or not-for-profit organizations.

This definition clearly acknowledges that L&D activities should address the needs of individuals and organizations and that these needs may differ or, at times, conflict with

## SPOTLIGHT ON SKILLS

You have received a request from a line manager that they need you to supply an L&D solution to address a problem within a team. The line manager is not sure what the precise problem is but is convinced that some form of L&D intervention would be of help.

1 How will you initially approach this request?

2 What types of questions will you ask to find out whether it is a problem with an L&D solution?

3 What types of data would you like to obtain concerning the functioning of the team?

4 How will you sell the proposed L&D solution, assuming it is appropriate, to the team?

5 What criteria will you use to assess the effectiveness of any L&D solution you propose?

To help you answer the questions above, visit www.palgrave.com/business/carbery and watch the video of Judi Kinnane talking about learning and development.

each other. It also highlights that L&D activities achieve business objectives but also ethical, corporate social responsibility and sustainability objectives ▶ **Chapter 14** ◀. A number of studies have investigated the link between investment and training and organizational performance. Aguinis and Kraiger (2009) summarized the benefits of training for individuals and organizations as being skill enhancement, competence development and improved organizational performance.

## CONSIDER THIS...

Many organizations invest in L&D activities for the wrong reasons and thus they represent a waste of money. Organizations frequently invest in L&D activities because they are viewed as an easy answer to solve a problem that, in reality, does not have an L&D solution. They may also invest in learning activities in the hope that they will contribute to competitiveness without any systematic evaluation of L&D needs and what L&D activities can contribute to the bottom line. Some organizations view L&D as a luxury, part of employees' benefits, rather than something that will generate value for the organization. So, it is important for organizations to be clear about why they invest in L&D activities. When should organizations invest in L&D activities?

## BENEFITS OF L&D FOR INDIVIDUALS, TEAMS, ORGANIZATIONS AND SOCIETY

There is no doubt that L&D activities can have a positive impact on the performance of individuals, teams, organizations and society as a whole. However, many organizations are prone to consider L&D as a cost rather than an activity that confers significant benefits.

### Benefits for individuals and teams

Investment in L&D activities by individuals should result in the acquisition of new skills, the enhancement of knowledge, and the development of confidence to perform a task or role to experienced worker standard. These benefits should result in improved job performance. The effects of L&D activities on performance may be both direct and subtle. Individuals may perform tasks with greater speed and accuracy and utilize resources more effectively. However, L&D may also lead to greater innovation, confidence to handle a changed job situation, and the development of tacit skills. For example, through continuous performance, an operator can develop new ways of doing things and attain knowledge that is derived from experience. L&D activities may help employees to work more effectively in a different culture and to be more mobile within an organization. Individuals may develop a range of interpersonal and generic skills that will be of value to career opportunities and promotion prospects, both within and outside the organization ▶ Chapter 10 ◀.

**Tacit skills** – intangible skills developed as a result of informal learning processes

There are also documented benefits (see Ardichvili and Manderscheid, 2008) of L&D activities for managers, leaders and teams. These benefits may include the enhanced skill of the manager or leader, and greater self-confidence and flexibility as a leader. The benefits of L&D to teams can also be considerable, including greater team cohesiveness, effectiveness and flexibility. L&D activities can also enhance team communication, the skills to handle team conflicts, team decision-making, enhanced knowledge of teamwork principles, and greater resilience to handle setbacks within the team. In summary, there is a considerable body of evidence (see Wenger et al., 2002) providing support for the many benefits of L&D for individuals and teams. These benefits include individual and team performance as well as interpersonal and self-management skills, cross-cultural skills, leadership skills, expertise and tacit skills, technical skills and a variety of management skills, such as planning, delegating, prioritizing and decision-making.

## Benefits for organizations and society

Research has consistently demonstrated that L&D activities can impact organizational performance (Clardy, 2008; Vidal-Salazar et al., 2012), including profitability, quality, customer service, customer satisfaction, workforce productivity and reduced costs. However, it is clear that the organizational benefits of L&D activities will depend on a number of factors, including the types of L&D activities implemented, the skills or tasks being developed, and the measures used to assess the effectiveness of L&D activities. L&D activities can be used to retain employees, customer and employee engagement levels, organizational social capital and relationship-building with suppliers and customers.

L&D activities can also make an important contribution to economic development and society. L&D activities can enhance the quality of the labour force and the amount of human capital available within an economy. They can be used to ensure social inclusion, enhance community effectiveness, regional development and societal prosperity. L&D activities can be used to gain the involvement of stakeholders, such as trade unions, professional bodies, community groups and employer groups, in enhancing society as a whole. Thus, it is not uncommon for national governments to implement policies to design and deliver L&D activities to achieve objectives such as economic development, training for disadvantaged groups, and social development.

# MODELS OF L&D IN ORGANIZATIONS

Organizations have a number of choices when it comes to how they approach L&D activities. Three models are frequently used by organizations: the systematic model, the strategic HRD model and the learning organization model. Each of these models will be discussed, outlining their key features, advantages and limitations.

## The systematic L&D model

The systematic L&D model remains extremely popular in organizations despite its significant limitations. It essentially involves a planned cyclical process (Figure 9.1). It is used to plan L&D activities at individual, team and organizational level.

Figure 9.1 depicts systematic L&D as a cycle of activities, comprising the identification of L&D needs, the planning and design of L&D interventions to meet the identified needs, the implementation of the planned interventions, and the evaluation of the outcomes of these interventions. The model is extremely simple to understand, which is a significant strength and also its weakness. While it is a useful starting point providing

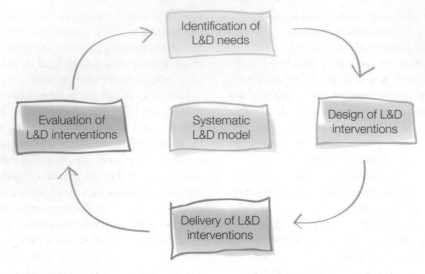

**Figure 9.1** The systematic L&D model

organizations with a basic framework for how L&D activities are formulated, the model's weaknesses include:

- It does not include consideration of organizational strategy, L&D strategy and HRM strategy as key components of the cycle.
- It tells us very little about the complexity of each stage. The identification of L&D needs stage, for example, can be quite simple to undertake if the level of analysis is the individual or job; however, it is much more complex at the organizational level of analysis.
- Kessels and Harrison (1998) have criticized its lack of attention to key stakeholders within and external to the organization. The model is silent on issues of organizational decision-making and the politics of L&D decisions.
- It places too much emphasis on functional knowledge and skills, or what Wright et al. (2004) describe as an 'inside-out mind-set'. This may result in the design and delivery of L&D interventions that are not aligned to the needs of the business, and so the L&D specialist will find it difficult to make a strong link between investment in training and business outcomes.
- Millmore et al. (2007) argue that the design phase of the cycle needs to be informed by learning theory to ensure that the L&D intervention is appropriately designed and matches the learning needs and other characteristics of individual learners.
- It tends to direct L&D specialists to focus on the initial rather than the higher levels of the evaluation process. Frequently, the evaluation process will focus on

measuring participants' reactions to the learning intervention rather than measuring organizational benefits and return on investment (ROI).

In summary, while the systematic model is a useful starting point to organize L&D in organizations, it does not consider issues of alignment with business strategy and other HRM processes directed at enhancing the performance of employees.

## A strategic HRD model

There is an increasing requirement for people to be a source of competitive advantage. Therefore, L&D activities need to be organized to ensure that they make a strategic contribution. The strategic HRD model focuses on articulating the characteristics of L&D activities that are necessary for it to be strategic. A strategic HRD model (Garavan, 1991, 2007) emphasizes three important features:

1 *Strategic integration*: This suggests that SHRD will support the implementation of business goals and shape the formulation of strategic goals. SHRD supports and is supported by other SHRM activities and it will contribute to strategic change.
2 A *multi-stakeholder perspective*: An SHRD model recommends engagement with a variety of stakeholders in order to deliver value to the organization. These stakeholders will include senior

management, line managers, employees and the HRM function. Millmore et al. (2007) argue that engagement with senior management is essential because they reflect the strategic agenda and the desired organizational culture and they are the key decision makers within an organization.

3 *Create a learning culture*: An important component of the SHRD model concerns the creation of a learning culture that promotes L&D for all individuals. A particular dimension of this culture concerns organizational support for development.

In summary, an SHRD model suggests that L&D should be concerned with shaping the strategic agenda rather than simply responding to it. However, it is clear from the available evidence that SHRD experiences difficulties in aligning its activities with strategy and other HRM practices (Wolff, 2007; IBM, 2007). Organizations that implement an SHRD model include Dell, Microsoft, Hewlett-Packard and Kerry Group.

**Organizational support for development** – employees' perceptions that the organization provides opportunities and programmes to enable employees to develop their skills and competencies

**Learning organization** – an organization that enables the learning of all its employees and continually changes itself

learning organization model focuses on learning how to learn, enabling employees' learning to generate outcomes such as creativity, innovation, change and transformation, facilitating learning that focuses on changing organizational behaviour, and viewing learning as an end in itself. Table 9.1 summarizes the characteristic features of the learning organization as a model or approach to L&D in organizations.

The learning organization model is a difficult one to realize in organizations. Important L&D activities that may help in the creation of a learning organization include those that facilitate the emergence of a learning culture, such as recognition and rewards for learning, the allocation of resources to L&D, and role-modelling by senior leaders of openness to learning. A variety of processes can also be implemented, such as structures and routines for knowledge-sharing, the facilitation of communities of practice, and redesigning organizational structures to facilitate collaboration and teamwork. Evaluation is viewed as a vital continuous process to ensure that decisions about L&D are informed by evidence.

In summary, the learning organization model represents an idealized way in which to think about L&D activities in organizations. However, there is doubt concerning its practical application. At best, it represents a progressive process because the conditions necessary for it to flourish are difficult to find in many organizations.

# BUILDING YOUR SKILLS

SHRD is frequently considered to have a major role in shaping the context in which it operates. It suggests that L&D practitioners should become organizational change consultants who possess the skills to influence corporate culture, form strategic partnerships with line managers, participate in top management discussions of strategy and advocate the SHRD agenda. Interview a senior L&D specialist in a large organization. Find out the challenges involved in working at senior levels in the organization and investigate the skills required to perform at such a senior level.

## The learning organization model

The third model that may inform L&D in organizations is the learning organization model. Central to the concept of the learning organization is the idea that learning is a key source of competitive advantage (Sloman, 2010). The

**Table 9.1** Characteristic features of the learning organization

| |
|---|
| Learning is derived from a multiplicity of experiences: planned/unplanned, deliberate/accidental, successes/failures and is used to shape future behaviour |
| Learning has significance of itself and learning how to learn is a critical aspect of the learning organization |
| Organizations learn from the external and internal environment and this occurs at all times within the organization |
| Learning is continuous, habitual and internalized |
| Learning is utilized by an organization to enable organizational transformation |
| Learning occurs because it is facilitated by managers and employees and occurs naturally within an organization |

*Source:* Adapted from Garavan, 1997; Sun and Scott, 2006; Felstead et al., 2007

It visualizes an organization that is continually transforming itself and, in reality, few organizations meet this condition. It is difficult to identify examples of organizations that identify themselves as learning organizations, but those that have features of a learning organization include Apple, Samsung and Merck.

# HOW DO PEOPLE LEARN?

The process of individual learning lies at the heart of the L&D process. We defined learning earlier as a process of acquiring knowledge, skills and developing attitudes. Learning is a process of change that comes about as a result of instruction, experience, self-directed learning activities, reflection, and trial and error. People are motivated to learn by the desire to learn something new, to perform a task or role more effectively, and to avail themselves of incentives or rewards. Motivation is central to the learning process and organizations can do a number of things to enhance this motivation, including encouragement to participate in learning, rewarding learning behaviours, and providing employees with the resources to learn.

## The experiential learning cycle

An important issue concerns how individuals learn from experiences. The experiential learning cycle (Kolb, 1984)

proposes four key stages in the learning cycle (Figure 9.2). Below is a brief overview of each stage.

### Stage 1: having an experience
Learners can seek out experiences in a reactive or proactive way. These learning opportunities may occur in a work and non-work setting. Increasingly, learners are expected to be productive and seek out learning experiences themselves. Learning experiences may involve performing a task for the first time, participating in complex projects or activities, and seeking feedback from a boss, coach or mentor.

### Stage 2: reviewing the learning experience
Reflection is a vital part of the experiential learning process. Thus, in order to maximize the process of reflection, learners should think about what has been learned:

- Think about other ways in which the task or activity could have been undertaken.
- Make comparisons between set targets and realized targets.
- Engage in guided reading and discussion with others.

### Stage 3: reach conclusions about the experiences
Experiential learning requires that learners reach conclusions about what has been learned from the experience. Learners should seek out the lessons learned and reach conclusions. The learner should ask these questions:

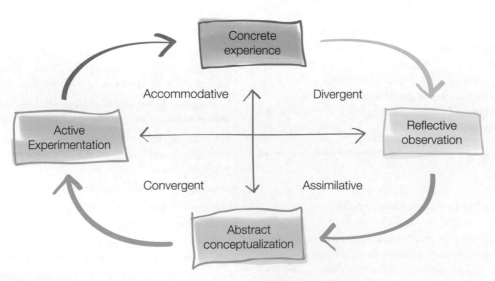

**Figure 9.2** The experiential learning cycle

- What have I learned from the experience?
- How does the experience differ from previous experiences?
- How will I handle similar experiences in the future?
- What could I have done differently?

### Stage 4: planning the next stage

Experiential learning theory argues that having reached a conclusion about what was learned, it is important to plan how to do things better or differently the next time. Learning needs to be translated into subsequent action. To do this effectively, a learner needs to be clear about what will need to be done differently the next time and draw up a plan to create that learning.

## *Learning styles*

It is well established that learners have a preference for different ways of learning. Honey and Mumford (1992) and Kolb (1984) suggest that there are four learning styles that link with the four stages of the learning cycle:

- *Activists:* They like to get fully involved in the action. They continually seek out new experiences and are enthusiastic about new ideas and techniques. Activists are open-minded and may be overenthusiastic about novelty. They have a tendency to act first and reflect on the consequences later.
- *Reflectors:* They like to stand back and observe experiences from different perspectives. They like data collection and analysis and are slow to reach definite conclusions. Reflectors tend to be shy and not necessarily involved in discussions or debate. They will always focus on the big picture when they act and will factor in the observations of others.
- *Theorists:* They continually focus on analysis and the development of theories based on multiple observations. They like to think in a logical, step-by-step way. Theorists have a great capacity to integrate many different facts and observations into coherent explanations.
- *Pragmatists:* They are focused on trying out new ideas, theories and techniques to see how they will work in practice. Pragmatists continually search for new ideas and will avail themselves of every opportunity to try out new applications. They dislike long drawn-out discussions.

It is important that L&D specialists consider learning styles when designing learning activities. Learning styles are important when selecting learning methods. Adult learners have a strong preference to get involved in the learning process. An effective learning experience will provide space for all four learning styles, including opportunities for doing things.

## FORMULATING AN L&D STRATEGY

The process of formulating an organizational L&D strategy is a long-term one. Mayo (2004) argues that it is a rational and staged process and L&D strategy should seek to be both proactive and reactive. Important proactive drivers of L&D strategy include business goals and objectives, organizational change processes, and the organization's HRM philosophy and strategies. Reactive drivers of L&D strategy include operational issues, responding to external changes in customer or supplier expectations, and sudden changes in business strategy. An effective L&D strategy will include a number of important components:

- Articulate a set of beliefs and values about learning in the organization.
- Propose a set of coherent L&D practices that reflect company values and philosophy.
- Select learning strategies that support short-term operational goals as well as medium to long-term objectives.

In formulating the L&D strategy, it is important that an L&D specialist adopts a pragmatic and continuous approach that involves engagement with stakeholders. Anderson (2007) proposes five actions necessary to formulate an L&D strategy:

1 Participate in business planning processes.
2 Engage in dialogue with organizational stakeholders so that they take account of organizational L&D priorities.
3 Develop and communicate a strong business case for investment in learning activities that fall outside the formal business plan.
4 Ensure the cost-effective use of L&D resources and continually focus on organizational priorities.
5 Evaluate the strategy-level contribution that L&D processes make to the organization.

L&D strategies must be sufficiently flexible to account for changes in individual and organizational priorities and be able to cope with emergent opportunities and challenges. Table 9.2 outlines the staged approach to L&D strategy formulation proposed by Mayo (2004) and Harrison (2009). The formulation of an L&D strategy is a collaborative effort involving multiple stakeholders who are committed to its implementation.

## IDENTIFYING AND RESPONDING TO L&D NEEDS

The identification of L&D needs represents a key step in ensuring effective alignment of L&D with organizational goals. Bee and Bee (2003) have suggested that the process of learning needs analysis operates from the assumption that L&D will contribute to organizational performance when learning needs are clearly identified and matched with appropriate learning interventions. Harrison (2009) suggested that the needs identification process consists of three key stages:

1 *Data collection:* This involves finding out the nature of the need and whether it is an individual, team or organizational need. An L&D specialist can consult a variety of information sources to find out about current capability and performance levels. These information sources include:
- self-assessment information such as the opinions of jobholders and personal development plans
- feedback information from appraisal and competency assessments
- the assessments of supervisors and managers
- customer survey data and data derived from benchmark studies and objective measures such as productivity, quality data and exit behaviour data such as absenteeism.

In the case of organizational needs analysis and where the focus is on future capability and performance issues, the L&D specialist will consider information sources such as strategic targets, planned organizational change initiatives, customer and market data, and issues related to the expansion or contraction of the business.

2 *Identification of the capability/performance gap:* L&D interventions are frequently wasted in organizations. They are often not the most appropriate solution or may not be a solution at all. Therefore, the purpose of this stage is to determine the nature and extent of the performance/capability gap and make an assessment as to whether the gap can be addressed using an appropriate L&D intervention. The type of analysis undertaken to determine the performance/capability gap will be decided by the trigger for the needs

**Table 9.2** Staged approach to L&D strategy formulation

| Step | Actions |
|------|---------|
| Take responsibility for L&D strategy development | Create an L&D strategy development group<br>Involve key stakeholders such as line managers, HRM specialists and employees |
| Clarify the organizational mission and strategy | Read formal strategy documents to gain insights on current strategic priorities<br>Gather and interpret information from key individuals in the organization |
| Conduct an internal and external stakeholder analysis | Specify the key performance issues from the perspective of each stakeholder<br>Identify how each stakeholder contributes to L&D and their expectations of L&D<br>Analyse the key barriers and enablers to strategic alignment and the emergence of a learning culture and climate |
| Specify the strategic challenges and opportunities facing the organization | Differentiate strategic from operational effectiveness issues<br>Identify issues that have L&D implications<br>Differentiate between those issues that have L&D implications and those that do not |
| Generate strategic alternatives for L&D and gain commitment from stakeholders | Prioritize L&D goals that add value to the organization's strategic imperatives<br>Focus on issues that can achieve quick wins as well as long-term successes<br>Focus on issues where there are clear L&D applications<br>Identify benefits for individuals as well as the organization |
| Agree a strategic L&D strategy and plan | Specify clear L&D goals to be achieved within a specified time frame<br>Specify the resources required to achieve the goals<br>Allocate accountabilities and responsibilities to achieve L&D goals |

analysis process. In situations where some form of learning intervention is the expected outcome, a trainer-led approach may be appropriate. An organization-wide intervention is appropriate where the needs of all employees are the focus of the analysis.

3 *Recommendations and prioritization of learning needs:* A key outcome of the needs analysis process focuses on making recommendations on training activities that are relevant to the context, feasible within organizational and budgetary constraints, and are capable of being delivered within the capabilities of the L&D function. When recommendations are made concerning prioritizing L&D needs, the following issues should be taken into account:

- the importance and urgency of the learning need
- whether the learning need is related to the strategic objectives of the organization
- whether non-L&D actions are more appropriate to address the problem
- the feelings of jobholders and their managers
- the supporting information is evidence based rather than opinion based
- the business case is supported by a clear indication of the investment involved
- the level at which the need exists in the organization
- whether the learning need requires a buy or design decision.

**Knowledge** – defined as specific information components of a task, job or role that the learner should acquire

**Skill** – dimensions of performance that the learner should be able to demonstrate

**Attitudes** – beliefs and values that the learner should espouse and put into practice and sustain

## DESIGNING AND DELIVERING L&D INTERVENTIONS

The outputs of the learning needs analysis process will inform the design of L&D interventions. A number of important decisions need to be made by the L&D specialist:

- the formulation of learning objectives or outcomes
- the selection of appropriate L&D strategies
- the selection of L&D methods
- the delivery of the learning intervention within the time frame agreed and to the target audience.

### Formulation of learning objectives/outcomes

The formulation of learning objectives/outcomes requires that learning needs are translated into specific objectives/outcomes. Learning objectives/outcomes should be measurable and consist of statements of specific outcomes that will form the basis for the design of the learning intervention. Learning outcomes will focus on knowledge, skill and/or attitudes. Once learning objectives/outcomes have been defined, it is appropriate to consider the selection of L&D strategies.

### The selection of L&D strategies

An L&D specialist will have a wide variety of options when selecting L&D strategies. Pilbeam and Corbridge (2010) suggest that L&D strategies can be categorized on whether they match the dimensions presented in Figure 9.3.

L&D strategies include formal classroom courses, e-learning, coaching, mentoring, job instruction, planned work experience, projects, assignments, bite-sized and blended learning. Detailed discussion of these is beyond the scope of this chapter, but a brief description of each is provided:

**Figure 9.3** Categorizing L&D strategies

- *Classroom courses:* These are structured learning interventions undertaken in a classroom setting. They will vary on whether they are instructional or facilitative, and whether they take place within or outside the organization. They are a frequently used L&D strategy. They have several advantages related to their cost-effectiveness and capacity to deliver common sets of knowledge and skill to a large group of learners. They do, however, encounter transfer of learning problems.

- *E-learning, or technology-delivered instruction:* E-learning, or technology-delivered instruction, has become increasingly popular as an L&D strategy. E-learning can be used as a blended learning strategy and combined with more traditional classroom-based learning. Its major advantage is that it allows learners to choose when, where and what to learn. However, a significant drawback is that it transfers responsibility to the learner to make the decision to participate in L&D activities. E-learning as an L&D strategy has expanded to include online tutoring, chat rooms, discussion groups, social networking sites, audiovisual conferencing and two-way live satellite broadcasts.

- *Coaching and mentoring:* Coaching and mentoring are commonly used L&D strategies to develop managers and leaders. Coaching focuses on helping individuals or groups to perform more effectively, while mentoring involves guiding and suggesting appropriate learning experiences for the mentee. Coaching and mentoring place a strong emphasis on the role of the manager as a facilitator of learning. Both strategies are designed to encourage individuals to learn, and to learn in different ways according to their development needs.

- *Job instruction and planned work experience:* Job instruction focuses on one-to-one or group instruction that is carried out at the workplace and delivered while the learner is engaged in performing work tasks and activities. It is typically conducted between an experienced trainer and a learner. Planned work experience involves the learner performing a variety of roles throughout the organization for specific periods of time in order to sample different tasks, often as part of a graduate development programme. Both strategies take place on the job and therefore maximize the opportunities for the transfer of learning.

- *Projects and assignments:* Projects are a commonly used L&D strategy to develop technical and/or managerial skills. Projects can be undertaken individually or as part of a team. Action learning projects are frequently used to develop teamworking and collaboration skills and skills in the implementation of major change or transformation initiatives. Job assignments are commonly used to prepare managers for promotion and advancement within an organization. The assignment may involve an international component and it may also involve a stretch or hardship component. For example, a manager may be given an assignment to close down a loss-making business unit or to develop cross-cultural awareness and skills. Both strategies can be extremely powerful, provided they are well planned and effectively structured, supported and monitored.

- *Bite-sized and blended learning strategies:* Bite-sized learning strategies have become increasingly popular in organizations. They are typically designed to help employees who have limited time to attend L&D activities to participate in bite-sized training events. They provide employees with an opportunity to dip into learning (Wolff, 2007) and to keep up to date with developments in technical and professional areas. Blended learning is also a popular L&D strategy, because it can be customized to suit the needs of individuals. It typically includes technology-based strategies combined with more individual learning strategies such as coaching, mentoring, guided reading and learning logs. The key challenge is to achieve a blend of approaches appropriate to the learning needs of the individual.

**E-learning** – a broad term that includes computer-based training, technology-based learning and web-based learning activities

**Blended learning** – involves a planned combination of learning strategies such as e-learning, self-managed classroom and coaching activities to suit the needs of the individual

## BUILDING YOUR SKILLS

E-learning is increasingly popular as a learning strategy. However, it is not a strategy that everyone enjoys. Undertake some research on e-learning in an organization and answer the following questions:

1  What do employees think of e-learning?
2  Is it an effective learning strategy?
3  For what types of learning needs is e-learning more and less appropriate?
4  What steps can an organization take to encourage employees to participate in e-learning activities?

## Social Learning: The New Frontier for L&D

Social networking technology is revolutionizing how adults learn how they communicate with each other and their role in the learning process. Bingham and Conner articulate this paradigm shift. They argue that new social learning focuses on the use of networks and technological tools to encourage knowledge transfer and connect learners in a manner consistent with the natural behaviour of people. New social media tools have considerably expanded the opportunities for personal connection. So what does this mean for L&D? L&D has traditionally advocated an 'outside-in' approach to learning, where the trainer provides modules of knowledge and the focus is on the content. However, social learning emphasizes an 'inside-out' approach that is shaped and directed by the learner's desire to participate in shaping the learning process. The distinction between trainer and learner is increasingly becoming blurred. Learners are described as 'prosumers', in that they both produce and consume knowledge. Learners have the ability to create, support and publish their thoughts.

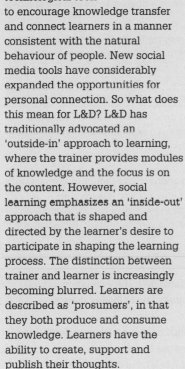

Harrington suggests a number of interesting applications of social technology. Microsharing is a type of social software that provides learners with the potential to update one another with short bursts of text, links and multimedia content through stand-alone applications. Learners will use it as a digest, a check-in and, on occasions, an opportunity to engage. It allows learners to pose questions to the individual who has the right answer. Organizations are also starting YouTube-like channels on their internal intranet to help the mentoring process. For example, Marathon Oil has two dedicated streaming servers and rich media creation software to provide live daily streaming webcasts and a library of archived presentations available on demand. Deloitte, a professional services firm, has also embraced the notion of social learning through the launch of a social platform for all its employees.

These social learning developments open up the possibility of using the training situation as a real-time activity where learning is a continuous process, not an isolated unreal event. L&D specialists need to think about how they can creatively tap into a more collaborative and organic development process, one that combines the roles of learner and trainer. It suggests a vision of L&D as a continuous learning hub.

### Questions

1  How convinced are you by the argument that social media will revolutionize the L&D function and make training approaches redundant?

2  What needs to change in organizations to make social learning happen?

3  How do you think social media learning will enhance trust, transparency and communication within an organization?

### Sources

Bingham, T. and Conner, M. (2010) *The New Social Learning: A Guide to Transforming Organizations through Social Media*, San Francisco, CA: Berrett-Koehler/ASTD.

Harrington, M. (2010) Training: the future of training & development: new social learning, New Directions Consulting Inc., 30 September, http://newdirectionsconsulting. com/4586/blog/the-future-of-training-development-new-social-learning-2/.

## The selection of L&D methods

Within each L&D strategy described above, L&D specialists and others involved in delivering training can select a number of learning methods to achieve specific learning objectives. Table 9.3 summarizes a number of these methods.

## The delivery of L&D

The effective delivery of L&D activities requires that trainers are aware of:

- the different ways in which people learn
- the needs of adult learners, and give them significant control over how and when they learn
- the learning motivations of learners and address those motivations
- the environment in which the learning will take place.

Trainers need to provide:

- opportunities for learners to learn by utilizing practice, trial and error
- feedback to learners during the learning process

**Table 9.3** L&D methods: type, characteristics and suitability

| L&D method | Trainer or learner centred | Suitability |
|---|---|---|
| Lecture: a structured, planned talk usually accompanied by visual aids | Trainer centred | Ideal for large training groups and when large amounts of information need to be communicated. Does not allow for a high degree of participation by learners |
| Group discussion: allows the free exchange of knowledge, ideas and opinions on a particular issue/theme | Learner centred | Appropriate when the learning objective is to share viewpoints or analyse complex organizational issues. Requires the trainer to manage the process and keep the discussion focused |
| Role-play: the enactment of a role in a protected environment. Learner suspends reality and adopts a particular persona | Learner centred | Learners have an opportunity to act as if they were in real-life situations. Learners can practise their responses and receive feedback from a trainer on key learnings. Can provide learners with enhanced self-awareness, self-confidence and the ability to learn from mistakes |
| Case study: the examination of a situation, or events aimed at learning by analysing detailed material and identifying potential solutions | Learner-centred | Provides learners with the opportunity to examine a situation in detail and generate solutions. Allows a group of learners to exchange ideas and discuss complex organizational issues. Key challenge is to select a case study that matches the skills of participants but also stretches their knowledge and skill |
| In-tray exercise: learners are given a series of documents, files, letters and memos and are asked to select appropriate actions | Learner centred | Learners are exposed to a simulation of real life. Provides learners with an opportunity to experience the kinds of issues that will arise in their work |
| Video or film: used to show a real-life situation and different ways of dealing with a particular situation or to provide key information to a large audience | Trainer centred | Suitable to deliver information to large groups of learners and demonstrate examples of effective and less effective behaviours. Demands little in the way of participation by an audience but can be used as a springboard for discussion and questions |

- the opportunity for learners to make sense of what they have learned.

In summary, it is important that the delivery of L&D is sufficiently flexible to account for differences in learning needs, motivations, styles of learning and experience.

## *EVALUATING L&D ACTIVITIES*

Evaluation is a key feature of the systematic model and it is also considered an important part of SHRD. Kirkpatrick's four-level evaluation model (Kirkpatrick and Kirkpatrick, 2006) continues to be the most widely used training evaluation model among practitioners. The four levels are reaction, learning, behaviour and

> Evaluation – establishing the intended and unintended outcomes of L&D activities and assessing whether the benefits justify the investment

results evaluation (Table 9.4). The evaluation of L&D activities seeks to answer the following questions:

- How effectively did the organization undertake the learning needs analysis?
- Were the L&D strategies and methods effective in addressing the identified learning needs?
- Did learners enjoy the learning intervention and did they perceive it as relevant to their current or future roles?
- What did participants learn as a result of participation in the learning intervention?
- What changes in work performance can be attributed to the learning intervention?
- To what extent has the learning intervention contributed to the achievement of organizational objectives?

These questions are asked in order to meet four important purposes:

1 *Prove* that the L&D investment added value to the organization and to understand whether the learning intervention worked and achieved what it was supposed to achieve. Earlier, we highlighted that investment in L&D can lead to performance improvements for individuals and organizations. Therefore, one of the tasks of evaluation is to prove these outcomes.
2 *Control* L&D activities to ensure they are of an appropriate standard, delivered within budget and fit in with organizational priorities.
3 *Improve* the quality of L&D activities.
4 *Reinforce* the learning that took place during the learning intervention.

Table 9.4 summarizes the key evaluation issues to be considered at each level of the Kirkpatrick model.

 **CONSIDER THIS ...**

You have been asked to design a reaction evaluation form to evaluate participants' reactions to a leadership development programme. What questions would you include in the form? How would you sequence them? How many questions would you include? Explain the reasoning behind your decisions.

**Table 9.4** Kirkpatrick's four levels of L&D evaluation: issues and examples

| Evaluation level and type | Evaluation description and characteristics | Examples of evaluation tools and methods | Relevance and practicability |
|---|---|---|---|
| 1  Reaction | Reaction evaluation focuses on the personal reactions of participants to the L&D experience:<br>● Did participants enjoy the training?<br>● Did participants consider the training relevant?<br>● Was the training a good use of participants' time?<br>● Did participants like the administrative arrangements and learning setting? | 'Happy sheets'<br>Feedback forms based on subjective personal reaction to the training experience<br>Verbal feedback at the end of the programme either individually or as part of the group<br>Post-training surveys or questionnaires | Completed immediately after the training ends<br>Easy to obtain reaction feedback<br>Feedback is not expensive to gather to analyse for groups<br>Important to know if participants were not positive about the training |
| 2  Learning | Learning evaluation is concerned with the measurement of learning before and after an L&D event:<br>● Did participants learn what was specified in the learning objectives?<br>● Did participants enhance their skills as a result of the training?<br>● Did the training result in a change in participants' attitudes and values? | Learning is typically assessed using structured assessments or tests that are administered before and after the training<br>Interviews or observation can also be used before and after the training<br>Methods of assessment need to be closely related to the learning objectives specified for the training | Organizations typically undertake post-training assessment; however, pre-training learning assessments are less common and may elicit unfavourable reactions from participants<br>It is important to design valid and reliable learning assessment methods to assess knowledge<br>The assessment of attitude change is complex and the assessment in change in skills can be subjective |

| Evaluation level and type | Evaluation description and characteristics | Examples of evaluation tools and methods | Relevance and practicability |
|---|---|---|---|
| 3 Behaviour | Behaviour evaluation focuses on how the L&D activity impacted on job-related behaviours:<br>• Did participants transfer their learning to the workplace?<br>• Did participants develop the relevant skills and knowledge?<br>• Were there observable and measurable changes in trainees' performance when back in their role?<br>• Did trainees sustain the behaviour and performance changes?<br>• Are trainees aware of changes in their behaviour, knowledge, skill level? | Observation and interviews carried out over time are required to assess changes in behaviour, and the relevance and sustainability of the change<br>One-off assessments are not reliable because people change in different ways, at different paces and at different times<br>Assessments need to be subtle and ongoing, and then transferred to a suitable analysis tool<br>Assessments should be designed to reduce the subjective judgements of the observer or interviewer | Measurement of behaviour change is complex, and more difficult to quantify and interpret than reaction and learning evaluation<br>Surface-level questions and tick box approaches will not generate strong evidence<br>Line managers may not be willing to participate in the evaluation process<br>The analysis of job behaviour evaluation data is complex and there is the problem of being certain that the behaviour change can be directly related to the training |
| 4 Results | Results evaluation focuses on the measurement of ROI and organization performance as a result of investment in training<br>Lag measures will be used because the impact of training and performance may take some time to manifest itself<br>Typical measures include volumes, values, percentages, timescales, ROI, and other quantifiable aspects of organizational performance, for example numbers of complaints, staff turnover, attrition, failures, wastage, noncompliance, quality ratings, achievement of standards and accreditations, growth, retention and so on | Many of these measures will already be in place via normal management systems and reporting<br>The challenge is to identify which measures are relevant and how they relate to the training<br>ROI evaluation requires a clear quantification of the costs and benefits involved in the L&D intervention | ROI evaluations are typically undertaken for single training programmes rather than for a suite of L&D activities<br>ROI evaluations are expensive to conduct as they require a large amount of data collection and sophisticated statistical analysis techniques<br>In the final analysis, it may be difficult to prove that a particular set of benefits can be related to a particular L&D activity |

*Source:* Adapted from Garavan et al., 2003; Kirkpatrick and Kirkpatrick, 2006

## Upskilling your Training Team

You are the L&D specialist in a financial services organization located in Denmark employing 950 people. You joined the organization nearly five years ago as head of L&D. However, during that time, the nature of the role has changed. The core L&D team is relatively small, with two direct trainers delivering standard curriculum-based financial training courses. The third member of the team focuses on L&D processes and performs a range of administrative tasks. You now realize that you need a member of your team who is not just proficient in delivering standardized training courses but can perform a range of duties that correspond to an L&D consultant or business partner role. Increasingly, you receive requests from business unit managers to

ACTIVE CASE STUDY

very comfortable and skilled in performing the direct trainer role. This presents you with a significant dilemma with two possible options: should you select one of your direct trainers and develop that individual into the role, or should you hold off until the recruitment freeze is lifted? You are keen to continue to work in a strategic role within the organization and to provide consultancy and strategic business partner services to three of the most important business units. You would like the two additional business units to come within the remit of one of your existing direct trainers. You are now at a crossroads because the managing director is putting pressure on you to have someone trained up and performing the role within three months.

provide more individualized and customized solutions. They expect the L&D team to deliver tailored learning interventions rather than simply focusing on short courses.

The core skills of an L&D consultant or business partner consist of a combination of systematic training skills, such as learning needs identification, learning design, delivery and evaluation, as well as a variety of business and consultancy competencies, including a broad understanding of the business, an understanding of organizational processes and advanced problem-solving skills. The L&D consultant will also be expected to possess good interpersonal skills and the ability to build strong relationships

with managers and clients at all levels within the organization. It is important that the role is performed with credibility, professionalism and confidence. Stakeholder management is a key requirement of the role and the L&D specialist will be required to demonstrate value and convince business unit managers that L&D interventions add value to their business operations.

You do not have the option to recruit a new member to the team, as a recruitment freeze is in operation and only core business roles will be filled. This freeze will last for at least one more year. As a result, you have to consider your two direct trainers for the role. Both are highly committed but are

1 Write a memorandum to your general manager outlining how you propose to address this situation. What options will you propose?
2 Assuming you decide to select one of your existing direct trainers for the role, set out a development plan to bring that individual up to speed. What particular development strategies do you propose in order to develop their confidence and skill to perform an L&D consultancy or strategic partner role?

## SUMMARY

Learning and development has emerged as a significant strategic issue within organizations, because of the increased recognition that people are an important source of sustained competitive advantage. Skills and competencies enable an organization to be more flexible and meet strategic challenges. Organizations should implement best practice L&D strategies to maximize

business performance. This chapter provides an introduction to L&D in organizations and the emphasis is on the need for a strategic approach where L&D activities contribute to the achievement of strategic organizational objectives. Key L&D activities include the identification of L&D needs, the formulation of learning objectives and outcomes, the selection of appropriate L&D strategies, the delivery of these strategies and the evaluation of the effectiveness of L&D strategies and interventions.

CHAPTER REVIEW QUESTIONS

1 What arguments would you make to persuade a sceptical senior manager of the benefits to be gained from having a strong L&D function?

2 What is strategic HRD? In what ways is SHRD distinct from the systematic L&D model?

3 Interview a senior manager in your organization or an organization you are familiar with about its strategic objectives and priorities. Make an assessment of whether the organization's L&D activities contribute to the achievement of its strategic objectives.

4 Evaluate current L&D practices in your organization or one you are aware of. How effectively are learning needs identified? What aspects of the L&D process receive the most attention and which receive the least? What are the key strengths and weaknesses of L&D in the organization?

5 Compare and contrast the characteristics and effectiveness of the following L&D strategies: e-learning, formal L&D programmes and coaching.

 FURTHER READING

Gibb, S. (2011) *Human Resource Development: Processes, Practices and Perspectives*, 3rd edn, Basingstoke: Palgrave Macmillan.

Gold, J., Holden, R., Iles, P. et al. (2009) *Human Resource Development: Theory and Practice*, Basingstoke: Palgrave Macmillan.

Harrison, R. (2009) *Learning and Development*, 5th edn, London: CIPD.

Stewart, J.C. and Rigg, C. (2011) *Learning and Talent Development*, London: CIPD.

 USEFUL WEBSITES

www.investorsinpeople.co.uk
Investors in People UK is a business improvement tool that provides an accredited framework for organizations wishing to achieve business goals and performance through people.

http://eacea.ec.europa.eu/education/eurydice/
The Eurydice Network provides information on and analyses of European education systems and policies and is coordinated and managed by the EU Education, Audiovisual and Culture Executive Agency in Brussels.

www.ahrd.org
The Academy of Human Resource Development is a global organization comprising a scholarly community of academics and reflective practitioners. It studies HRD theories, processes and practices and disseminates information about HRD through four affiliated peer-reviewed journals.

www.cedefop.europa.eu/EN/
Cedefop is the European Centre for the Development of Vocational Training. It works closely with the European Commission, governments, representatives of employers and trade unions, vocational training researchers and practitioners to strengthen European cooperation.

www.ufhrd.co.uk
The University Forum for Human Resource Development is a not-for-profit partnership that seeks to create, develop and inform leading-edge HRD theories and practices through an international network of universities, individuals and organizations promoting cooperative research initiatives.

 For extra resources including videos and further skills development guidance go to: www.palgrave.com/business/carbery

# 10 CAREER DEVELOPMENT

**Ronan Carbery**

By the end of this chapter you will be able to:

## LEARNING OUTCOMES

- Identify the changing contexts of work and career
- Explain how the traditional notion of a career differs from contemporary career models
- Understand the context of graduate careers
- Identify who is responsible for career development

- Discuss the implications of current career models for individuals and organizations
- Outline the role of the HRM function in facilitating career management

© ADVENTTR/ISTOCKPHOTO

This chapter discusses ...

## INTRODUCTION

In this chapter we look at the concept of contemporary career development. Careers have changed significantly due to economic conditions, market forces and personal interests. As we have seen from Chapter 8, individuals' expectations as to what they want from employment have changed, making it necessary for employers to accommodate more flexible working patterns. A number of new career types have been proposed to describe contemporary careers, such as boundaryless, protean, authentic, portfolio and kaleidoscope careers, which we explore later in the chapter. One commonality shared by these concepts is that of self-directedness. The career is directed by the individual rather than the organization. It is likely to involve a number of shifts in employment, between organizations, industries and, perhaps, cultures. The purpose of this chapter is to look at careers today and understand different career types that people can choose to pursue. We contrast these with a traditional understanding of careers and ask who should be responsible for career development? We also consider the role of the HRM function in managing careers. We begin by first considering what a career is.

## WHAT IS A CAREER?

The term career was initially used to indicate a designation of privilege. Only a small number of individuals, predominately males, had careers in stereotypical professional jobs, for example law, medicine, education. The terms 'occupation' or 'job' were used to describe situations where individuals exchanged their labour or skills for monetary reward. Now, however, the term 'career' has significantly broadened to include the entirety of work experiences that a person engages in, rather than focusing solely on employment in one industry or profession. Arthur et al. (1989: 8) describe a career as 'the evolving sequence of a person's work experiences over time'. The distinguishing characteristics of this definition are:

- its emphasis on the 'evolving sequence', which recognizes that careers are not stationary, but change over time

*Career* – a person's work experiences over the course of their life

## SPOTLIGHT ON SKILLS

You are working as a manager in an organization where you have direct responsibility for a large number of employees. As part of the yearly performance management process, you have to put in place career development plans for your staff.

1  How do you link an individual's specific career development goals with the goals of the business?

2  Is there scope for allowing people to follow some of the career types outlined in this chapter?

3  In the context of graduate development programmes, what specific skills do these programmes concentrate on developing?

To help you answer the questions above, visit www.palgrave.com/business/carbery and watch the video of Anthony Brennan talking about career development and graduate development programmes.

- 'work experiences' includes paid employment, but also denotes homemaking and other productive efforts that provide important career skills
- 'over time' suggests that a career lasts a lifetime.

Perhaps the most important part of this definition is that it indicates that each person has only one career. Even if individuals have worked in three or four different occupations or industries, these experiences form part of the same career. The definition encourages individuals to look at ways in which their different experiences all contribute to one another within the same career.

**Career development** is a lifelong process where individuals look at the occupational options available to them, select an option, and continue to make choices from the vast possibilities available to them. It is a developmental process that occurs over the life of an individual and this series of decisions constitute an integrated career path. The word 'path' in this context is important, as most careers are described in terms that suggest a journey. The use of metaphors is common when talking about careers. Describing careers as a journey, for example 'career path', 'career ladder', 'getting to the top', suggests that a career is characterized by continual movement of the individual. However, the notion of a journey indicates a destination or end point. As we will see, new careers may be more accurately described in more open-ended metaphors, such as 'travelling' rather than 'journeys'.

> **Career development** – how a person manages their life, learning and work to achieve career goals
>
> **Traditional career** – a direct line of career progression where seniority and length of service are rewarded with progression from one specific job to a more senior job

## *TRADITIONAL CAREER PERSPECTIVES*

Traditionally, a person's career was expected to involve employment with one or two organizations over the course of their lives, and, by working hard, they would gradually take on more responsibility when the

organization considered them ready for advancement or promotion (Super, 1957; Levinson, 1978). Success was defined by the organization and measured in subjective terms such as promotions and salary (Hall, 1996). Wilensky (1961: 523) defined a **traditional career** as 'a succession of related jobs arranged in a hierarchy of prestige through which people move in ordered (more or less predictable) sequence'. This type of career can be considered the conventional public sector career path, where employment is characterized by job security and lifelong employment. This way of thinking about careers was standard until the 1990s.

The usual starting point for understanding career development theory is Donald Super's life span theory (1953, 1980), shown in Figure 10.1. The majority of career education programmes have been affected by Super's ideas.

The stages of Super's theory are:

1 *Growth* (birth–14 years): the individual becomes concerned about the future, begins to take control over their lives, demonstrates conviction to work hard in school, and acquires competent work habits and attitudes.

2 *Exploration* (ages 15–24): there is a recognition that an occupation will be an essential part of life and the adolescent begins to express career choices. These can

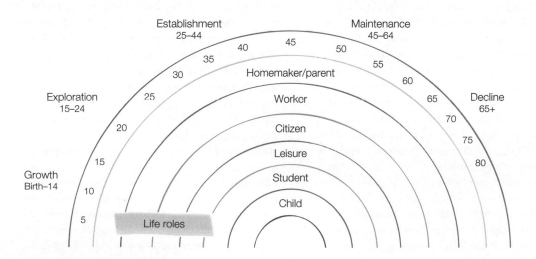

**Figure 10.1 Super's life span model**
*Source:* Super, 1980. Copyright © 1980, Elsevier

be fleeting and often unrealistic and abilities are tried out in fantasy or non-threatening situations such as coursework, role-playing, part-time work, volunteering and shadowing. As the individual begins to gain a better understanding of themselves, they narrow down their choices and make them more realistic. Reality tends to dominate as they enter the job market or further education after school. The individual tentatively tries out different occupations before making an occupational choice.

3 *Establishment* (ages 25–44): here the young adult attempts to make themselves secure in the workplace by performing work satisfactorily and consolidating their position by working to the desired standard. Advancement to new levels of responsibility, for example promotion, is a step taken by a small number of individuals towards the end of this stage.

4 *Maintenance* (ages 45–64): the major task is to continue doing the satisfying parts of work and holding onto employment by updating skills. Little new ground is broken, and the employee continues established work patterns. Super suggested that this is also the stage of the mid-life crisis, when individuals question whether they want to continue doing this job for the next 20 years.

5 *Decline* (over 65): this stage is characterized by a gradual disengagement from the world of work until retirement. Then the employee is challenged to find other sources of satisfaction.

This perspective on careers is very much a product of its time, as it suggests individual careers unfold in a linear manner with a small number of employers. Also, it is generally not applicable to women who may have extended periods of absence from the workforce for family-related reasons.

The work of Arthur and Rousseau (1996) has significantly influenced current career thinking and their definition outlined at the beginning of this chapter highlights that any occupation can be considered the basis for a career. The distinction between traditional and contemporary careers lies in the emphasis that Arthur and Rousseau place on the subjective interpretation of what constitutes a career, which can only be answered by the individual. Contemporary careers are thought to be more flexible and mobile, with goals defined by individuals themselves. Table 10.1 summarizes the differences between traditional and contemporary careers.

**Table 10.1 Comparison between traditional careers and contemporary careers**

| | Traditional career | Contemporary career |
|---|---|---|
| Employment relationship | Job security for loyalty | Employability for performance and flexibility |
| Transitions | Within the firm | Within and between firms, in and out of the labour market |
| Skills | Firm specific | Transferable |
| Determinants of success | Pay, promotion | Psychological |
| Responsible for career management | Organization | Individual |

## RESPONSIBILITY FOR CAREER DEVELOPMENT

Changes in organizations as a result of globalization and advancements in technology have led to a revised notion of the traditional career contract, resulting in a decrease in employers' commitment and willingness to retain individuals (Robinson and Rousseau, 1994). In the knowledge-intensive economies of today, lifetime employment is not guaranteed and individuals need to be resigned to change jobs at least once in their career. This lack of job security places the onus on the individual to take control of their future employability, take responsibility for their own personal development, and view their career in terms of wider employability across industries and sectors. Organizations are now adopting greater flexibility in terms of business risks to employees through the introduction of share ownership, profit-sharing and profit-related pay schemes ▶ **Chapter 8** ◀ and differentiate between core and peripheral employees ▶ **Chapter 2** ◀. Employees are simultaneously seeking individualized opportunities that fit their career and work–family relationships and so expect greater flexibility on the part of their employer to provide opportunities for the achievement of these goals.

In discussing responsibility for career development, we must consider the nature of the psychological contract.

**Psychological contracts** are the individual belief systems held by employees and employers regarding their mutual obligations to each other (Rousseau, 1995). Employment relationships are subjectively interpreted and experienced by each party. How each understands their obligations to and agreements with others constitutes the psychological contract. There are two kinds of psychological contract (Rousseau, 1995):

1  **Transactional psychological contracts**: the focus is on specific monetary exchanges that are short term in focus and include working longer hours and accepting new job roles and responsibilities in exchange for increased pay and training benefits (Herriot and Pemberton, 1997).

2  **Relational psychological contracts**: the focus is on loyalty and discretionary behaviour in exchange for job security, financial rewards and training and development opportunities. Individuals tend to identify with the organization, promoting support for the organization's efforts to improve performance (Rousseau and Tijoriwala, 1999).

It should be noted that transactional and relational psychological contracts are not mutually exclusive; all contracts contain elements of both, but the contract may lean more towards one or the other.

Relational psychological contracts are positively related to employee beliefs that their employer supports them personally. Transactional psychological contracts tend to be related to lower levels of employee flexibility and contribution and are less elastic in times of change (Dabos and Rousseau, 2004). While these arrangements may be characteristic of workers in more peripheral roles in organizations (Dabos and Rousseau, 2004), individuals with high bargaining power, such as managers or highly valued employees, or those pursuing a portfolio or boundaryless career path can also develop transactional contracts.

Transactional psychological contracts have given rise to 'i-deals' (Rousseau, 2005) – idiosyncratic deals that individuals negotiate with their employer regarding terms that mutually benefit both parties. They are voluntary, personalized agreements of a nonstandardized nature that vary in scope from a single feature to the entire employment relationship. For example, an employee studying part time for a degree programme may negotiate fewer travel demands than other employees, but otherwise share the same job duties, pay scales and so on. The market power of individuals and/or the value the employer places on them enables employees to engage in individualized bargaining. When the work offered is neither highly standardized nor easily monitored or where it is scarce, individuals are in a position to exert considerable bargaining power. This level of power allows the individual to decide when, how and for whom to be productive.

Job security is being replaced with security based on the individual's value in the marketplace. While individuals may no longer have a job with a single employer, they may maintain employment with a number of organizations for the duration of their working career. This lack of job security places an onus on individuals to take control of their own employability and adopt independent and assertive career behaviours.

> **Psychological contract** – the unwritten rules and expectations that exist between the employee and employer
>
> **Transactional psychological contract** – a situation where extra money and learning and development opportunities are provided in exchange for commitment and loyalty to the organization
>
> **Relational psychological contract** – a situation where job security is provided in exchange for commitment and loyalty to the organization

**CONSIDER THIS …**

Should organizations finance or part-finance learning and development programmes such as MBAs for their employees? An employee could conceivably obtain their qualification and leave the organization shortly afterwards, so what is the return for the organization?

## CONTEMPORARY CAREERS

A number of career conceptualizations have emerged in the past decade that have influenced career theory and research and become part of the new career vocabulary. These new concepts have emerged as organizations have sought to restructure and downsize to compete on a global scale. In addition, as individuals attempt to develop flexibility in their work arrangements, they frequently depart from traditional careers paths and seek alternative routes for career success.

Current careers tend to be dynamic, less predictable and boundaryless (Lips-Wiersma and Hall, 2007). The essence of careers has changed, and under this revised conceptualization, individuals bear primary responsibility for planning and managing their own careers (Grimland et al., 2012). In particular, two career concepts have dominated the thinking of academics and career practitioners in recent debates. Boundaryless and protean careers have enjoyed considerable recognition as widely accepted descriptions of contemporary career types. Authentic, kaleidoscope and off-ramp careers have also been proposed as being relevant to contemporary careers. The ability to pursue these career types is, however, challenged by the current economic climate. During the period of consistent economic growth from 2002 to 2008, employees had increased job mobility because of a tight labour market. Those with high educational qualifications and enhanced capabilities increased the value of their human capital to organizations, which led to more promotions and higher compensation (Wayne et al., 1999; Stumpf, 2010). This wave of mobility slowed with the beginning of the recession in 2008. An open marketplace where professionals had been experiencing advancement changed to a labour market that threatened their employment and slowed their career progression (Briscoe et al., 2012). While much of the initial research on these contemporary career types was carried out in stable and predictable economic circumstances, recent research looking at their applicability in an economic recession suggests that protean and boundaryless attitudes may help employees develop careers skills and ultimately cope with uncertain career environments (Briscoe et al., 2012). We now look at each of these career concepts in turn.

## Boundaryless careers

The concept of the boundaryless career moves away from the traditional notion of careers sustained within one physical organization. It widens our perspective of careers to incorporate a range of possible careers both within and across organizations, without being determined by the prevailing career system of one employer (Tams and Arthur, 2006). Arthur and Rousseau (1996) describe boundaryless careers as the opposite of organizational careers that play out in a single organizational setting. As

the employment landscape becomes less stable and less structured, normal career boundaries and structures become more permeable, enticing individuals to become more willing to cross them. These careers are not tied to a sole employer, nor represented by an orderly sequence of hierarchical upwards movement, as proposed by Super (1953), and are characterized by less vertical coordination and stability. Boundaryless careers can exist in a variety of forms. The term most often refers to movements across physical boundaries of separate organizations. It can also be used to describe when individuals voluntarily choose or are forced to leave an organization, ending career advancement therein. The emphasis placed on careers that play out beyond a single employer has been interpreted as involving inter-firm, physical mobility (Arthur and Rousseau, 1996). The inclination or preference towards physically crossing organizational boundaries suggests that individuals with a high threshold for employment mobility will be comfortable with a career that unfolds across several employers.

Boundaryless careers are not confined to physical changes of employment, however. The notion also applies to movement across psychological boundaries and includes careers that draw validation and marketability from outside the present employer, for example highly skilled professionals, consultants and academics (Arthur and Rousseau, 1996). The complexity of modern career landscapes, allied with all the factors that influence career decisions, makes it difficult to capture different types of boundaryless career mobility.

A boundaryless career mindset necessitates the navigation of 'the changing work landscape by enacting a career characterized by different levels of physical and psychological movement' (Sullivan and Arthur, 2006: 9). In this context, psychological boundarylessness suggests that individuals will vary in their attitudes towards initiating and pursuing work-related relationships across organizational boundaries. It does not necessarily imply physical or employment mobility and suggests that individuals with a propensity for boundaryless attitudes are comfortable with creating and sustaining relationships beyond organizational boundaries.

Boundaryless careers have particular relevance to organizations operating in unpredictable, opportunistic markets characterized by discontinuous change, such as the IT sector, research and development functions and financial services. Individuals are exposed to a high degree of employment uncertainty because employers seek to pass on this uncertainty from

**Boundaryless career** – sequences of jobs that can cross occupational, organizational and geographic boundaries

external markets with a revised psychological contract, which offers employability in terms of the marketability of skills and competencies in the external market instead of the promise of long-term employment (Arthur and Rousseau, 1996). Individuals continuously evaluate how well their employers are meeting their stated and implied contractual obligations, along with the perceived availability of alternative employment opportunities in the external labour market. Thus, employees may have multiple job movements during their lifetime (Sullivan and Arthur, 2006).

Employees often seek to manage their own careers by taking advantage of opportunities to maximize their success (Judge et al., 1994; Eby et al., 2003). From a boundaryless career perspective, career development requires the strengthening of self-direction and adaptability within a more transactional employment relationship. Self-direction and adaptability are primarily determined through the development of particular competencies and social networks. These skills include an understanding of job-related skills and career-related knowledge, which provide the confidence necessary to master current and future jobs, as well as an understanding of career-relevant networks, in which they can generate knowledge, learn and develop a reputation. An understanding of career competencies allows employees to evaluate which skills, competencies or networks can facilitate mobility in the future and which may become obsolete.

Cheramie et al. (2007) conducted a longitudinal analysis of executive managers from a boundaryless career perspective, using extrinsic rewards such as pay and rewards as determinants of career success. They found that in managing their careers, these individuals sought to maximize their extrinsic rewards ▶ **Chapter 8** ◀. A perceived decline in organizational health also increased the likelihood of physical changes in employment. It is suggested that career movements act as a useful strategy for executive managers to proactively manage their careers by changing employers in order to realize higher levels of salary, bonus and status.

## Protean careers

While the boundaryless career emphasizes the seemingly infinite possibilities that careers afford and how the recognition and use of these opportunities leads to

**Protean career** – a career defined by uniquely individual psychological success and can mean personal accomplishment, feelings of pride, achievement or family happiness

## BUILDING YOUR SKILLS

In a constrained labour market, how easy is it to pursue a boundaryless career? If you were a line manager and an employee came to you seeking to pursue this type of career, what choices do you have to facilitate this? Are there certain industries where people are more likely to be able to pursue a boundaryless career?

success (Arthur et al., 1999), the protean career offers a self-directed approach to careers driven by the values of the individual (Briscoe and Hall, 2002). It focuses on achieving career success through self-directed efforts and centres on the psychological success resulting from individual career management, as opposed to career development by the organization (Hall, 2002). Derived from Proteus, a mythical Greek sea creature who could change shape at will, the literal interpretation of protean indicates something that is versatile, variable and capable of taking many forms.

In an early study of managerial careers, Hall (1976: 201) noted the tendency of organizations to take control of employees' careers for them. He suggested the protean career concept as a contrast, defining it as 'one in which the person, not the organization is managing. It consists of all the person's varied work experiences in education, training, work in several organizations, changes in occupational field, etc.' The protean career is driven by the individual rather than the organization, based on individually defined goals, such as satisfaction, achievement and work–life balance, encompassing the whole life space and being directed by psychological success rather than objective measures of success, such as monetary rewards, power and position within the organization. Briscoe and Hall (2002) posit that a protean career orientation represents a self-directed perspective for an individual to evaluate their career and provide a guide to action. So, it bears similarities to an attitude, in that it has a cognitive component (a set of beliefs about the career), an affective component (beliefs as to what constitutes a 'good' or 'bad' career for the individual), and a behavioural element (a predisposition to react in certain ways). The protean career is therefore a mindset about careers, an attitude towards careers that reflects autonomy, self-direction and making choices based on personal values. A particularly strong form of protean career orientation occurs when the individual's attitude towards their career reflects a sense of calling in their work or an awareness of purpose that gives deep meaning to the career (Hall and Chandler, 2005).

A person pursuing a protean career moves quickly to improvise new ways of working, making the most of the empowerment it provides them. The challenge with an individual practising ongoing self-direction and adaptability in their career is that while they may become skilled at adapting to change, they may also lose a sense of overall direction. The protean career can therefore act as a compass in providing direction (Hall, 2002). The compass comes from the person's sense of identity: understanding who they are and knowing their values, needs, goals and interests. It moves beyond simple adaptability, it also requires self-knowledge and self-identity. One commonly cited example of a protean career is that of Mary Robinson, former president of Ireland (1990–97), and UN High Commissioner for Human Rights (1997–2002). Robinson constantly adapted to new challenges based on her consistent set of values and identity as a lawyer, politician and activist.

Hall (2004) identified two competencies that help individuals become more protean. These are adaptability and/or self-awareness. Self-awareness and understanding are pivotal to the values-driven nature of a protean career, ensuring a secure personal base from which to foster career success and interact with changing external conditions. Adaptability involves the capacity to change career and work behaviours in a way that allows the individual to succeed in a number of contexts with the need for externally driven career development. The capacity for reflection on the part of the individual is central to the ability to drive these two competencies ▶ Chapter 2 ◀. The greater the ability to harness these attributes, the greater the likelihood of promoting protean attitudes and identity.

## Authentic careers

The **authentic career** concept (Baker and Aldrich, 1996; Ibarra, 1999; Svejenova, 2005) defines an authentic individual as one who makes career choices that are consistent with the past or with an imagined future about who they would like to become. The key characteristic is that there is a consistent set of beliefs

guiding the career. Being truthful in authentic terms relates to the notion of consistency between how a person expresses themselves in public and what they feel in private.

Much of the research on authentic careers has been carried out in a creative context by considering the careers of musicians, film directors and actors. For example, an authentic musician is variously considered to be one who doesn't 'sell out' by allowing their music to appear in commercial advertisements, writes their own lyrics, demonstrates social concern, and maintains a sense of consistency between their music and their personality. Claiming authenticity in music has long been a controversial area, with the absence of authenticity igniting heated debate. For example, in 2011, Lana del Ray, a then 25-year-old US singer/songwriter, released her first single 'Video Games' and became an internet sensation, with her apparently home-produced video for the song viewed over 20 million times on YouTube in a matter of weeks. Del Ray was praised for her perceived authenticity and becoming successful on her own terms. It quickly emerged that she was the carefully planned creation of a powerful record label. Indeed, even her name was chosen by her management team. In real life, 'Lana del Ray' was actually Lizzy Grant, who had released an album in 2009 funded by her millionaire father. Attempts were made to remove traces of the album, along with videos and interviews of Grant, from the internet prior to the appearance of del Ray in 2011. Music blogs and other media outlets turned on del Ray in spectacular fashion with sustained attacks on her lack of credibility and authenticity. Interestingly, few of these attacks were based on her perceived talent, suggesting that genuine authenticity in terms of musical ability is difficult to achieve.

In career terms, this perspective suggests that an authentic career-oriented individual is one willing to take the initiative and responsibility for their career and is able to achieve consistency between past and present and private and public expressions of themselves (Svejenova, 2005).

**Authentic career** – a career characterized by consistency between an individual's public and private beliefs

## Kaleidoscope careers

Mainiero and Sullivan (2006) offer another perspective on current careers with the kaleidoscope career concept. Similar to boundaryless and protean careers, a

## CONSIDER THIS...

English footballer Wayne Rooney showed off a T-shirt after he scored a goal for Everton Football Club in 2002 that said: 'Once a blue, always a blue.' Everton wear a blue jersey and Rooney was born and raised in the city of Liverpool where Everton are located. When he joined Manchester United in 2004, Everton fans were quick to remind him of his earlier declaration. How authentic was his original pledge?

**kaleidoscope career** is created and evolved on the individual's own terms, defined by their own values, life choices and parameters, rather than by the organization. As an individual's life changes and evolves, their career path may adjust to these changes rather than surrendering control and allowing an organization to dictate time and energy demands imposed by work. This particular concept has a predominantly female-oriented focus. Individuals amend, adjust and modify this kaleidoscope or career pattern, by rotating the various aspects of their lives to arrange roles and relationships in new ways.

> **Kaleidoscope career** – a career that adjusts to changes in an individual's circumstances and motivation
>
> **Off-ramp career** – a nontraditional career path that recognizes that individuals, usually women, will take some time out from their careers

Like the mechanics of a kaleidoscope, where the movement of one part causes another part to move, changing patterns as new arrangements fall into place, individuals shift the patterns of their careers by changing different aspects of their lives to realign roles and relationships. Mainiero and Sullivan's (2006) longitudinal study of over 3,000 individuals suggests that individuals continually evaluate the choices and options available to them through this kaleidoscopic lens to determine the most beneficial fit between a myriad of relationships, work constraints and opportunities. Making a new decision regarding the career path affects the outcome of the kaleidoscopic career pattern.

Building on Peterson's authentic career concept, Mainiero and Sullivan (2006) suggest that the kaleidoscope career model incorporates a sense of authenticity in terms of being genuine and allowing personal and work behaviours to be closely aligned with personal values. They suggest that individuals also strive for challenging work that facilitates career advancement and increases self-worth, and that a need for balance exists with regard to work, relationships and personal

concerns. Mainiero and Sullivan (2006) found that men and women tend to follow different career patterns. Women tend to focus on challenge in their early career, with balance becoming more important in mid-career, and authenticity becoming the primary focus in late career. Men, on the other hand, focus on challenge in their early career, authenticity in mid-career, and balance in late career.

### Off-ramp careers

A predominantly gender-specific career concept has emerged recently in response to the 'male competitive model' of careers (Hewlett, 2007: 13). Hewlett (2007) presents the idea of the **off-ramp career** that provides an arc of career flexibility, which allows women to 'ramp-down' or take time off from their career and then 'ramp-up' or re-enter the labour market without losing career traction. Women may need to take extended periods of time off from work to have children, raise children, or care for their own parents. Based on the premise that over 60 per cent of women have nonlinear careers (Hewlett, 2007: 29), by taking off-ramps and diverse career paths, it makes it difficult for women to engage in the continuous, cumulative employment that is deemed necessary for success within predominantly male-oriented competitive career models. The end result is that a vast number of talented women either leave their careers or remain on the sidelines.

It is argued that the male competitive model of careers evolved to meet the needs of middle-class white men in the 1950s and 60s when access to well-paid jobs was primarily limited to this demographic group. It developed around a traditional division of labour between men and women, with men acting as primary earners and women playing the role of wife, mother and homemaker (Shelton and John, 1996). This career model is characterized by:

- a strong preference for full-time, continuous, linear employment history
- an emphasis on being physically present in an office for up to ten hours a day
- an assumption that professionals are motivated by money

- a belief that the steepest gradient of a career curve occurs in one's thirties – the individual either achieves objective career success in this period or doesn't at all, there are no second chances.

While broadly suitable for men, this career path presents numerous difficulties for women, to the extent that most women cannot or choose not to attempt to pursue it (Gilligan, 1982: 149). A preference for a continuous employment history penalizes women who need to take time out of their careers for the reasons identified above. Furthermore, the notion that career success is achieved in the thirties occurs at the ages when child-bearing and child-rearing demands are likely to be most pertinent and can be particularly time-consuming. A framework that indicates the need for individuals' careers to take off in their thirties is largely incompatible from a work–life balance perspective for most women. Hewlett (2007: 29) found that 37 per cent of women managers take what she terms an 'off-ramp' at some point in their careers, that is, voluntarily leaving their job for a short period of time, and another 30 per cent take a 'scenic route', for example working reduced hours, working from home, or using flexible working arrangements.

The difficulty women face is when they decide to return to employment, be it for financial, sense of identity or satisfaction reasons. Data suggests that only 40 per cent of professional women return to full-time employment after an off-ramp pause in their career, with a quarter engaging in part-time work, while women at managerial levels find it particularly difficult to return at the same level, citing suspicion that either their skills are outdated or they no longer have the required commitment deemed necessary for the job. Facilitating ease of access in returning to careers has led to organizations introducing a variety of career flexibility and flexible working arrangements, such as reduced hour options, flexible working times, job sharing, telecommuting and seasonal flexibility. This implies a fundamental reimagining of when, where and how work is carried out. Jobs are being delineated and delayered, duties shared and work teams deployed in ways that allow responsibilities to be seamlessly handed over. This allows high-value professionals and managers to carry out work in clearly delineated portions of time. Indeed, rather than label such working initiatives as 'women-specific' accommodations, organizations are beginning to position these arrangements as a key business strategy in the hope of attracting and retaining talented individuals.

**Portfolio career** – a career that involves doing two or more different jobs for different employers

The concept of off-ramping is not, however, the sole preserve of women. Almost a quarter of men in professional careers voluntarily leave their jobs at some stage, although they do so for markedly different reasons from women. Men cite switching careers and undergoing additional training and development as the most important factors in taking a break in their career path, whereas women name childcare and family responsibilities as the determining factors. This suggests that off-ramping from a male managerial perspective is concerned with the strategic repositioning of their career rather than family-related concerns.

Table 10.2 presents a comparison of the five contemporary career concepts we have discussed.

## PORTFOLIO CAREERS

The growth of employment options other than full-time employment with a single employer, for example freelance work, consultancy work, fixed-term work, contract work, project-based work and self-employment, has led to individuals pursuing what Handy (1989) terms **portfolio careers**. Rather than pursuing a single full-time job, the individual balances a portfolio of different and changing employment opportunities. The portfolio career concept envisages that individuals build careers around a collection of skills and interests and places a strong emphasis on self-management. The relatively small amount of literature on this career concept suggests that it is pursued by professionals and managers rather than operative and semi-skilled employees (Mallon, 1998). One consequence of globalization is the emergence of constantly changing organizations offering fixed-term employment opportunities and portfolio careers. In the UK alone, there are over 1 million people who have two or more jobs, and 65 per cent of these work this way out of choice (Clinton et al., 2006).

Portfolio-centred career development is based on a different set of assumptions regarding the nature of careers and the relationship between the organization and the employee. Instead of entering a sequence of hierarchically arranged positions, employees are hired to accomplish specific tasks and become contract employees with portfolio careers. Under portfolio-centred career development, the contract output is identified, the matching portfolio of skills needed to complete the

**Table 10.2** Comparison of contemporary career concepts

| Career concept | Characteristics |
|---|---|
| Boundaryless | Consists of infinite trajectories and possibilities<br>Not tied to a single organization<br>Not an orderly sequence of jobs<br>Focuses on opportunities across organizational boundaries<br>Represents a subjective interpretation by the career actor<br>Transcends physical, psychological and subjective boundaries |
| Protean | Focuses on the subjective perspective of the individual career actor<br>Career actor defines individual goals, which encompass the whole life space<br>Driven by psychological success rather than objective success<br>Has a cognitive and a behavioural component<br>A mindset about a career; an attitude towards a career |
| Authentic | Individuals have ownership of their careers<br>Individuals can enact their careers in different ways<br>Individuals adopt 'true-to-self' strategies in their career roles<br>Individuals search for ways of integrating the present and previous self<br>Individuals seek to be truthful to themselves<br>Individuals adapt and grow and are shaped by context<br>Individuals explore a range of roles and identify which is most satisfactory as an expression of their talents<br>Careers are embedded structurally and historically |
| Kaleidoscope | Created on the individual's own terms<br>Career path adjusts to changes in values, life choices and parameters<br>Individuals modify career pattern by rotating the various aspects of their lives to arrange roles and relationships in new ways<br>Individuals evaluate the choices and options available to them to determine the most beneficial fit |
| Off-ramp | Nonlinear<br>Difficult for women to engage in continuous, cumulative employment<br>Need for career flexibility and flexible working arrangements<br>From a male perspective, off-ramping is concerned with strategic repositioning of the career<br>Women off-ramp for more family-related concerns |

*Sources:* Adapted from Arthur and Rousseau, 1996; Craig et al., 2002; Hall, 2002; Svejenova, 2005; Hewlett, 2007

contract is specified, individuals with those skills are located in the HR information system, the contract is offered and then managed. This shift of focus requires a parallel shift in career development roles and activities. The change in assumptions requires a different emphasis in the traditional roles and responsibilities of HRM in organizations. At the risk of oversimplification, career development professionals will need to recognize some significant differences in the organizational and individual needs of different types of organizations and employees.

Because employees are a long-term investment, success in these areas leads to longer term effectiveness for the organization. Under portfolio-centred HRM, these functions take on some different aspects, as the primary focus of career development is on the definition of core competencies and clarifying which employee groups are considered 'core' (Handy, 1989). Consideration must be given to determining which aspects of the firm's activities could be contracted out or dealt with on a contract basis.

Instead of dealing with the pattern of positions in the organization, portfolio career development concentrates on understanding the skill requirements needed to accomplish the contract. Rather than identifying the best individuals with long-term potential, it focuses on locating individuals with the precise skill sets needed for accomplishing that task or contract. Instead of developing progressive development programmes such as second-level training and management training, career development decreases the focus on learning and development and shifts those resources into identifying individuals with the needed skill sets. Learning and development become the individual's responsibility.

## An Atypical Hollywood Career

James Franco is best known for his Oscar-nominated role in the film *127 Hours* (2010). His other notable film roles include *Rise of the Planet of the Apes*, *Milk*, *Spiderman 3* and *Pineapple Express*. However, he has refused to characterize himself solely as an actor. Unhappy with his career direction, he enrolled at the University of California, Los Angeles as an English major in 2006, graduating in 2008. He then took four master's degrees at once. Once completed, Franco enrolled as a PhD student at Yale University. While managing his film roles with his studies, he has published a short story collection entitled *Palo Alto*, hosted a solo art show installation in Berlin entitled 'The Dangerous Book Four Boys', and directed two music videos for REM in 2011. He has acted on stage and directed theatrical productions in New York's Stella Adler studios, as well as appearing as a recurring guest actor in the daytime soap opera *General Hospital*. In September 2012, Franco's band Daddy released its first single 'Love in the Old Days' and first EP 'MotorCity', along with the accompanying music video.

Franco hosted the Oscars ceremony in 2011 and soon afterwards took on a lecturing role at New York University for a third-year graduate class on adapting poetry into short films. Franco has described these series of activities as being one single career rather than a collection of loosely connected activities. In an interview with *The Guardian* in 2011, he suggested that if it wasn't for his writing and academic activities, he would be unable to enjoy his relative success as an actor: 'Now that I have school, I'm able to enjoy things when they're good. It really is like an anchor; something I can put my energy into and get very solid results.'

### Questions

1 What contemporary career concept most accurately describes James Franco's career?
2 What do you see as the main driver of Franco's career motivation?

### Sources

Anderson, S. (2010) 'The James Franco project', *New York Magazine*, 25 July, http://nymag.com/movies/profiles/67284/.

Brockes, E. (2011) James Franco: 'The King's Speech? It's pretty safe', *The Guardian*, 26 February, www.guardian.co.uk/film/2011/feb/26/james-franco-interview-oscars.

---

Orientation activities change from a socialization focus, providing new long-term employees with an understanding of the organization's culture and expectations, to a specific focus on contract and performance definition. This includes an introduction to specific individuals and policies needed for the accomplishment of the contract. Performance management and career planning activities become short term in orientation.

## GRADUATE CAREERS AND MASS CUSTOMIZATION OF CAREERS

Graduate career paths have changed considerably in recent times. While third-level graduates enjoyed near full employment after graduation in the majority of EU countries, the UK and the USA before 2007, the recent economic climate post-2007 has had a profound impact on graduate careers. High unemployment and increased competition in the wider labour market have led to graduates returning to education. Research from the USA, the EU and the UK indicates that substantial numbers of graduates now re-enter formal education in the years after graduation (Coates and Edwards, 2011). More than half of UK graduates had undertaken some form of additional education or training, within three or four years of graduation, and 40 per cent of US graduates had enrolled in another university-level qualification within ten years of graduation.

In a comparison of graduate and employer perceptions of the skills required to get ahead in the workplace, Rosenberg et al. (2012) highlight that leadership skills, management skills, interpersonal skills, critical thinking skills and a strong work ethic are among the most essential skills for employment. Leadership skills and IT skills have been identified as the strongest predictors of career advancement potential of employees (Heimler et al., 2012). Employers themselves consider leadership skills to be the strongest predictor of career advancement potential when recruiting employees.

Kaplan (2008) indicates that in order to advance their careers, individuals need to take ownership of and responsibility for their careers by:

- assessing their career, skills and performance
- seeking coaches and mentors
- having the modesty to confront personal weaknesses
- having an intrapreneurial attitude – demonstrating entrepreneurial behaviour within their own organization
- seeking opportunities without putting their own self-interests ahead of the organization
- being willing to voice dissenting views.

Initial entry into the labour market is important but the nature of contemporary knowledge work means that the foundations of many careers take years to develop. Research in the UK suggests that graduates' career progression can be relatively slow for three to four years following graduation. For many, the benefits of university study on labour market outcomes only become noticeable a few years after leaving university (Purcell et al., 2005).

In response to evidence of a shrinking pool of skilled labour, rising ratios of female to male employees in the workplace and changing family structures, Benko and Weisberg (2007) proposed an organizational framework they label **mass career customization**. Allied with these factors, younger generations are less motivated by the possibilities of the traditional career model, where career success is measured by prestige, earnings and upward advancement, and are more aware of the trade-offs of pursuing a customized career. In the belief that a one size fits all approach to career development no longer works, organizations such as Deloitte and Google have adopted mass customization with significant success ▸**Chapter 11** ◂.

Customized careers are 'unconventional patterns of workforce engagement by individuals who would ordinarily be expected to adhere to traditional career paths' (Valcour, 2006: 220). They differ from the traditional career on one or more of three dimensions:

1 *work time:* for example working reduced hours rather than full time
2 *timing:* discontinuities in the pattern of work engagement over the span of a career, such as women entering the workforce late or leaving it temporarily to care for children/parents
3 *type of employment relationship:* independent contracting work instead of long-term organizational employment.

The customized career assumes that personal identities are shaped by multiple life roles, including, but not solely limited to, work roles. Individuals who pursue customized careers gain some control over their time and conditions of employment (Valcour, 2006). Individual productivity and job satisfaction tend to be higher among these individuals. They are often generally better able to integrate their work and non-work lives, have less work–family conflict and have higher levels of life satisfaction. A consequence of this is the likelihood that they will suffer in terms of objective determinants of career success, for example earnings or advancement. They tend to receive less support for career development from their employer and have fewer opportunities for promotion. They may also feel that they have made career sacrifices and experience a degree of hesitancy towards the state of their careers, characterized by the normative expectations surrounding the traditional careers they have chosen to forego.

The mass career customization framework proposes a set of employment options along four career dimensions and provides a structure to articulate and manage these options on an ongoing basis rather than one-off accommodations:

> **Mass career customization** a collaborative process that allows an employee and employer to customize a career path along a defined set of options

1 *Pace:* outlines options related to the rate of career progression and addresses how quickly an individual is deemed to progress to increasing levels of responsibility and authority.
2 *Workload:* details choices relating to the quantity of work output and addresses the quantity of work performed, usually measured in days or hours per month, or performance cycle.
3 *Location/schedule:* provides options for when and where work is performed. This examines how work gets done and challenges the 'face-time culture', where employees are either implicitly or explicitly expected to be physically present in the workplace for a set period of time regardless of the quantity of work performed. Technological advancements have facilitated a multitude of choices in this dimension.
4 *Role:* refers to the category of an employee's position, job description and responsibilities. This dimension is likely to be the one that is customized the most based on the nature of each organization's business.

Mass career customization allows organizations to bring career planning to the forefront of HRM processes and facilitate employees who wish to more effectively manage a nontraditional career path. It must be noted that customized careers are closely associated with features of the employment context. The nature of an organization affects its employees' ability to customize. It is more difficult to customize in the context of an economic downturn, where an organization has reduced its workforce and placed additional work on remaining employees than in a situation where there is more flexibility in staffing levels. The success of a mass career customization model from an employee perspective depends primarily on the values and identities of the person who crafts the career, whereas from an organizational perspective, success appears to depend on the existence of social supports such as a flexible organizational culture and the absence of situational constraints to development. Individuals will have little opportunity to customize when they work in organizations with rigid cultures and hierarchical structures and when no alternative career policies have been articulated and implemented. In these cases, individuals are faced with two options: stay on the traditional career path regardless of the personal cost, or quit entirely.

## BUILDING YOUR SKILLS

You are an HR manager recruiting graduate employees from university. What skills and competencies will you look for in these graduates? What responsibility does the organization have for graduate career development?

## CAREER MOTIVATION THEORY

The concept of career motivation applies a motivation theory framework to enable us to understand the decisions people make in respect of their career. Career motivation is the desire to exert effort to achieve career goals and enhance career aspirations. The career motivation model was originally proposed after research findings in the 1970s suggested that young managers were not as motivated to attain

Career motivation – the desire to put in effort to achieve specific career goals

leadership positions as those of a generation earlier (Howard and Bray, 1981). London and Bray (1984) found that an employee's direct boss has control over many of the factors that affect career motivation at a young age.

London (1983) conceptualized career motivation as a multidimensional concept that combines elements of needs, interests and personality characteristics that reflect the stimulus, direction and persistence of career-related behaviours. London (1983) organized the construct into three domains: career resilience, career insight and career identity:

- *Career resilience*: the persistence component, the foundational domain of career motivation. Career resilience is shaped during early childhood and is set by early adulthood. It is the ability to adapt to changing conditions and overcome career barriers even when the circumstances are discouraging or disruptive. It is suggested that career resilience creates the values, attitudes and behaviours recognized as components of career insight and career identity.
- *Career insight*: the stimulus component, and relates to the ability to be realistic about a career and utilize these perceptions to establish career goals and recognize how these goals relate to the organization's goals (Carson and Bedeian, 1994). Strong career insight allows the establishment of 'clear career goals and know(ing) one's strengths and weaknesses' (London and Noe, 1997: 62). As career insight becomes more focused and concise, the individual becomes more able to form their self-perception through career identity. It is conceptually similar to self-concept and openness (London and Mone, 2006).
- *Career identity*: the direction component and is the extent to which people define themselves by their careers. It consists primarily of 'job, organizational, and professional involvement and needs for advancement, recognition, and a leadership role' (London, 1983: 621). Those with high levels of career identity are believed to be highly involved in their jobs, their workplaces and/or their professions (London and Mone, 2006).

London and Noe (1997) suggest that, over time, these three dimensions will affect each other, with career resilience being the least dynamic. They suggest that the other two dimensions are likely to be affected by situations such as training and development, job loss, organizational restructuring and organizational change (Day and Allen, 2004).

The career motivation model suggests that all three dimensions are in a dynamic relationship with the workplace to influence a person's career decisions and behaviours. Lopez (2006) proposes that situational conditions within the workplace are equally important in influencing career decisions and behaviours and so, in order to understand career motivation, the impact of situational constraints and social support in work environments must also be considered.

Gould and Penley (1984) suggest that managers utilize career strategies, such as networking, seek guidance and extended work involvement, and create and invest in more opportunities than operative or professional employees. Managers typically have the greatest potential for extrinsic measures of career success, such as salary progression and career advancement in organizations, so they can be expected to have relatively higher levels of career motivation.

## ROLE OF THE HRM FUNCTION

Organizational career systems are 'the collections of policies, priorities, and actions that organizations use to manage the flow of their members into, through and out of the organizations over time' (Sonnenfeld and Peiperl, 1988: 588). Essentially, they relate to the set of HRM policies and practices and management actions that are used to direct employees during their employment. The majority of research on career systems has focused on the practices contained within organizational career systems (Bowen and Ostroff, 2004). However, changes in the external environment and an organization's strategy often cause employers to change the supposedly objective nature of the employment relationship and the subsequent composition of career systems (Slay and Taylor, 2007).

Cappelli (1999: 1) describes these changes as follows:

What ended the traditional employment relationship is a variety of new management practices, driven by a changing environment, that essentially brings the market – both the market for a company's products and the labour market for its employees – directly inside the firms ... pushing out of its way the behavioural principles of reciprocity and long-term commitment, the internal promotion and

development practices and the concerns about equity that underlie the more traditional employment contract.

Individual-level career perspectives such as boundaryless (Arthur and Rousseau, 1996) or protean (Hall, 1996) careers that transcend organizations (Peiperl and Baruch, 1997) have a strong appeal among academics and individual employees (Baruch, 1999); however, organizations face the practical task of actually managing people in a turbulent business environment. They require guidelines to help them manage individuals, to indicate what practices can be useful, and under which circumstances. A large number of traditional organizational career management systems are based on archaic approaches that assume old-style hierarchical frameworks. The 1990s and 2000s have fostered a new organizational way of thinking, which includes more flexibility, an evolving culture, and the impact of technology and information systems (Baruch and Peirperl, 2003).

The traditional hierarchical management framework, within which long-term career planning was possible, is gradually being abandoned by organizations and individuals. While we have emphasized the role of the individual in career management, it is important to note that organizations should not be excluded from the process. It may not be necessary for organizations to abandon career management, but to adjust the career system to the new patterns of employment (Peiperl et al., 2000). The engagement of employees is important in this respect. Employees who report being engaged at work demonstrate greater workplace performance, and engaged workers possess personal resources, including optimism, self-efficacy, self-esteem, resilience and an active coping style, that help them control and impact on their work environment successfully, and achieve career success (Luthans et al., 2008). Both managers and the HRM function are in a critical position to increase or decrease engagement because they deal with issues such as accountability, work processes, compensation, recognition and career opportunities. From a career development perspective, there is often a mismatch between employees' expectations and the roles offered by the organization. So, processes should be put in place to check that employees' career goals are clearly understood and job roles are defined with as close an alignment to career aspirations as possible.

> **Career systems** – the set of HRM policies and processes that an organization uses to manage employee careers

## Apple Computers

In 1996, the management team at Apple Computers in Cork, Ireland decided that its future in Ireland would not be in traditional manufacturing. According to the senior director of European operations, what was termed 'brawn' (traditional low-value) manufacturing would become impractical, and survival would depend on restructuring the operation to incorporate more 'brain' (high-value) activities. The organization already had a strong history of reviewing its infrastructure and had effective technical resources allied with a workforce dedicated to the organizational philosophy of 'making and meeting commitments'.

A major restructuring took place, which initially resulted in a reduction in the workforce from 1,500 employees to 450. The organization underwent many changes, including:

- re-engineering the manufacturing processes in April 1999 to 100 per cent high-value manufacturing, and outsourcing the existing low-value manufacturing processes to Southeast Asia and Eastern Europe
- opening a European call/technical centre with customer support, online sales, customer relations and back office capabilities in September 2000, which now employs 420 people
- centralizing the European telesales function in the organization in January 2001
- relocating the organization's data centre from Holland to Ireland in February 2002.

The new global environment had implications for the culture of the organization. Employees were now expected to deal with customers and suppliers, and work in a virtual environment that centred around conference calls,

email and travel. The focus was no longer on the physical manufacturing line in the plant; the skills and knowledge used in manufacturing are now being applied globally and across the entire supply chain. For example, at the customer interface in the organization, the engineer had the process knowledge to map a problem with a product into the manufacturing process, resulting in a quicker solution to the problem. The customer service employee may not have had the process skills to do this but may have been stronger in the area of service. The result is the process skills department working directly with the customer skills department to provide the best service to the end customer. The organizational culture change involved an expectation of 'round the clock' commitment, with knowledge of business process skills, engineering skills, IT and supply management expertise. Management highlighted the need to think globally rather than locally, with the customer being the ultimate focus of all members of staff.

The majority of what the organization termed 'professional' employees made the transition to high value-added manufacturing. To cope with the change, individuals had to think globally, which took time to bring about. The new operational focus required the individual to understand the organization as a whole and, in particular, the area of supply chain management (defined as 'getting the product from raw material at the source to a transformed product to the customer'). Most operational staff ('nonprofessionals') failed to make the transition, with approximately 95 per cent leaving the company.

© STOCKBYTE/PUNCHSTOCK

By March 2004, the organization was responsible for operations and service in Europe, employed 1,400 people, with 85 per cent engaged in value-added activities and the remaining 15 per cent engaged in manufacturing, and had $6 billion in revenue in 2003. It is no longer manufacturing centric but customer centric. The operation is involved with all aspects of getting the product to the customer, including manufacturing, operation management, logistics and planning. The transformation presented many challenges and the organization is continually learning lessons on how to survive in this area. According to the senior director of European operations: 'It's one thing to move up the value chain and another to stay up there.'

The need for employees to take responsibility for their own career development and initiate learning and development needs was paramount. The perception of employees in Apple was that only firm-specific skills were provided to facilitate the transition and advanced generic transferable skills had to be sourced by themselves. Many employees took self-financed external learning and development opportunities following the transition period, including night courses and part-time college courses.

1 Explain how the changing business context impacted on careers at Apple.
2 How would you describe the careers of those employees who remained at Apple?
3 What role do you think the HRM department had during the transition period?
4 What are the implications for individuals' responsibility for career development?

 ## SUMMARY

This chapter highlights the importance of individuals taking responsibility for their own careers. This brings with it significant responsibilities. Careers no longer follow a traditional career model. Instead, individuals are expected to be self-directed and pursue careers that are increasingly fragmented, nonlinear and which involve numerous career changes. Employees will find themselves becoming less competitive unless they are open-minded and make career choices that reflect their personal values and career trajectories. They may have to finance some of their development, and participate in more career development activities outside work.

 ## CHAPTER REVIEW QUESTIONS

1 What do you understand by the term 'career'?
2 How do contemporary career development concepts differ from Super's model of career development?
3 Contrast the protean career construct and the boundaryless career construct. In what ways are they similar and different?
4 How has the nature of contemporary careers changed? What are the implications of this for HR practitioners?
5 Should an organization provide career development opportunities?
6 What internal and external factors do you think influence a mass career customization initiative?

 ## FURTHER READING

Arthur, M.B. and Rousseau, D. (1996) *The Boundaryless Career: A New Employment Principle for a New Organizational Era*, Oxford: Oxford University Press.
Baruch, Y. (2004) *Managing Careers*, Harlow: Pearson Education.
Greenhaus, J.H. and Callanan, G.A. (2006) *Encyclopedia of Career Development*, Thousand Oaks, CA: Sage.
Hall, D.T. (2002) *Careers In and Out of Organizations*, Thousand Oaks, CA: Sage.
Inkson, K. (2007) *Understanding Careers: The Metaphors of Working Lives*, Thousand Oaks, CA: Sage.

 ## USEFUL WEBSITES

www.cipd.co.uk/hr-careers
CIPD's HR Careers site provides an excellent overview of the various career options available to those interested in a career in HR, in addition to a 'careers clinic' and various resources that should be of interest to anyone looking for assistance in seeking employment.

 For extra resources including videos and further skills development guidance go to: www.palgrave.com/business/carbery

# 11 HEALTH, SAFETY AND EMPLOYEE WELLBEING

**Ronan Carbery**

By the end of this chapter you will be able to:

## LEARNING OUTCOMES

- Understand the concept of safety culture
- Know why accidents occur and differentiate between theories of accident causation
- Identify how relevant human factors affect health and safety behaviour
- Differentiate between the behaviour-based approach and attitude-based approach to health and safety

- Demonstrate the effect of ergonomics on workplace health and safety
- Examine the relationship between job characteristics and safety
- Understand the implications of stress and bullying in the workplace
- Establish the role of the HRM function in promoting health, safety and wellbeing at work

© ISTOCKPHOTO

NOBODY GETS HURT TODAY !

This chapter discusses ...

176

# INTRODUCTION

In this chapter we look at a number of important aspects of managing health, safety and employee wellbeing in organizations. Developments in the field of health, safety and employee wellbeing indicate an increased concern for the quality of working life. The number of health, safety and wellbeing-related EU Directives highlights the growing concern for safety in the workplace. It is commonly acknowledged that the establishment and maintenance of a safe and healthy working environment is a central feature of good business and modern-day HRM. Over the past 30 years, the subject has become an increasing priority for the HRM function in organizations. Employers are now expected to provide a range of safety, health and wellbeing provisions and proactively manage this important element of the employment relationship. There is a body of research evidence indicating that good safety, health and wellbeing practices contribute to employee morale, lower levels of stress and foster greater commitment to an organization's goals and objectives. The increasing awareness of the need for safe working practices has also been driven by recognition of the considerable costs associated with accidents and unsafe working behaviours. Through an appreciation of these costs and the prospect of further reduced costs through safer and healthier work practices, it is apparent that more proactive safety management practices are now emerging in workplaces.

To understand how organizations manage health, safety and employee wellbeing, we consider key behavioural and psychological concepts and contemporary research. This chapter discusses why accidents occur and theories of accident causation, managing human factors, ergonomics and health and safety, and provides an overview of stress and bullying in the workplace. We first look at the concept of safety culture.

# SAFETY CULTURE

**Safety culture** is a subset of organizational culture, which is thought to affect employee attitudes and behaviour in relation to an organization's ongoing health and safety performance. An analysis of safety culture captures concepts such as overt management commitment to health and safety, employee empowerment for safety,

**Safety culture** – the attitudes, beliefs, perceptions and values that employees share in relation to safety

## SPOTLIGHT ON SKILLS

One of your first tasks as a newly appointed HR manager in a manufacturing company is to organize a training programme to address the large number of accidents. As a result of discussions with the managing director, two priority areas are identified:

1  Manual handling knowledge and skills
2  Investigating and reporting accidents for supervisors.

Describe how you would design this programme. Would you attempt to change behaviours or attitudes?

To help you answer the question above, visit www.palgrave.com/business/carbery and watch the video of Philip Thornton talking about health and safety in the workplace.

reward systems that reinforce health and safety, and efficient reporting mechanisms.

The organization's senior management has a crucial role in promoting a positive organizational safety culture and should demonstrate the extent to which safety is seen as a core value or guiding principle of the organization. A commitment to safety is, therefore, reflected in senior management's ability to demonstrate a long-term, positive attitude towards safety, even in times of economic uncertainty, and to actively promote safety in a consistent manner across the organization. Managerial commitment to safety is also reflected by managers' presence and contribution to safety seminars and training, taking responsibility for safety critical operations, and the extent to which there is regular communication regarding safety issues.

Organizations with a positive safety culture often seek to empower their employees and ensure that they understand their critical role in promoting safety. Empowerment refers to an employee's perceptions or attitudes that arise from being entrusted with authority or responsibility by management. Within the context of health and safety, employee empowerment means that employees have a substantial voice in safety decisions, the power to initiate and achieve safety improvements, hold themselves and others accountable for their actions, and take pride in the safety record of their organization. Cheyne et al. (1998) suggest that employee attitudes are one of the most important measures of safety culture because they are often influenced by other features of the working environment and attitudes towards safety are a basic element of safety culture.

Reward systems are also an important aspect of safety culture as they indicate the manner in which safe and unsafe behaviour is evaluated and the consistency with which rewards or penalties are provided. A transparent evaluation and reward system can promote safe behaviour and discourage or correct unsafe behaviour. Safety culture, therefore, is reflected by the extent to which an organization uses a fair system for reinforcing safe behaviours, for example through monetary incentives or public praise and recognition by management and peers, as well as systems that discourage or punish unnecessary risk-taking and unsafe behaviours.

**Accident** – an unplanned or unforeseen event that could lead to injury to people, damage to plant, machinery or some other loss

Reporting systems are useful in identifying the weakness and vulnerability of safety management before an accident or near miss occurs. The willingness and ability of an organization to proactively learn and adapt its work processes based on incidents and near misses before an accident occurs are fundamental to improving safety. Reporting systems should also encourage the free and uninhibited reporting of safety issues that come to the attention of employees during the course of their work. It is important to ensure that employees do not experience punishments or negative outcomes as a result of using the reporting system, and to have a structured feedback system to inform employees that their suggestions or concerns have been reviewed and what action will be taken to solve the problem.

## WHY ACCIDENTS OCCUR

One of the primary aims of health, safety and wellbeing at work is to reduce accidents and ensure that employees act in a safe manner. Apart from the moral obligation to provide a safe workplace for employees, there is also an economic incentive to minimize the likelihood of accidents occurring. In the UK in 2011, 27 million working days were lost due to work-related illnesses and workplace injuries (Health and Safety Executive, 2012). Workplace injuries and ill health (excluding cancer) cost UK society an estimated £14 billion (Health and Safety Executive, 2012). In the Republic of Ireland, the figure for 2010 was approximately €3 billion (Stack, 2010). According to the International Labour Organization (2003), on a worldwide scale, workplace accidents and work-related illnesses annually result in 2 million fatalities and cost the global economy an estimated $1.25 trillion.

In the UK, 173 people were killed at work in 2012, and 55 people were killed at work in the Republic of Ireland in 2011 (Health and Safety Executive, 2012). According to Eurostat (2012b), on a per capita basis, the UK has the lowest rate of workplace fatalities at 1 fatality per 100,000 workers, which compares well with other large economies, such as France (1.68 per 100,000), Germany (1.87 per 100,000), Italy (2.39 per 100,000), Spain (2.63 per 100,000) and Poland (3.54 per 100,000). Ireland's rate

### CONSIDER THIS...

Management at the Chernobyl nuclear power plant in Russia and the relevant Soviet government officials assumed that a safe culture existed in their nuclear plants because they had never had any accidents. Only after the accident on 26 April 1986 at Chernobyl involving a nuclear reactor, which exposed 20 million people to radiation and resulted in at least 9,000 deaths from cancer as a result of radiation exposure, did it become apparent that the safety culture was completely inadequate. This lack of a safety culture was evident in management's confusion as to how to respond to hazards, but also in the design, engineering, construction, manufacture and regulation of the nuclear plant. Does the absence of a positive safety culture only become apparent after a major accident?

is 2.7 per 100,000 employees. According to the European Commission (2010), small to medium-sized enterprises account for over 80 per cent of all workplace accidents and 90 per cent of all fatal accidents across Europe.

Suchman (1961) suggested that there are three indicators of an accident: a high degree of unexpectedness, a low degree of avoidability, and a low degree of intent. This interpretation defines accidents only as events that result in physical injury to persons or property. Interestingly, many safety practitioners prefer to use the term 'incident' rather than accident, in the belief that the word 'accident' suggests something unavoidable and that whatever happened was simply due to chance or bad luck. Many organizations that adopt a best practice approach to health, safety and wellbeing use the term 'incident' because they want their employees to understand that most accidents can be avoided through safe working practices.

## Accidents and near misses

As performance indicators, accidents are a post-hoc measure; they measure the failure of accident prevention activities. To prevent accidents, the preferred approach is to identify deficiencies before accidents occur. In 1969, a study of industrial accidents was undertaken by Frank Bird of the Insurance Company of North America to investigate the suggestion that for every workplace accident that resulted in 1 major injury, there were 29 minor injuries and 300 near misses. This ratio had first

been discussed by Herbert William Heinrich in his 1931 book *Industrial Accident Prevention*.

Bird's analysis of 1,753,498 accidents reported by 297 companies revealed the following statistics and ratios in the accidents reported (see Roughton and Mercurio, 2002):

- For every reported major injury, resulting in fatality, disability, lost time or medical treatment, there were 9.8 reported minor injuries requiring only first aid.
- 47 per cent of the companies said they investigated all property damage accidents and 84 per cent stated they investigated major property damage accidents, and 30.2 property damage accidents were reported for each major injury.
- Part of the study involved 4,000 hours of confidential interviews by trained supervisors on the occurrence of incidents that, under slightly different circumstances, could have resulted in injury or property damage. Analysis of these interviews indicated a ratio of approximately 300 incidents for every 1 reported major injury.

The data gathered by this survey resulted in what is commonly referred to as the 1:10:30:300 ratio (see Figure 11.1). The 1:10:30:300 ratio indicates how misguided it is for organizations to only concentrate on the relatively few events resulting in serious or disabling injury, when there are so many significant opportunities that provide a much larger basis for more effective control of total accident losses. While the exact ratios have been questioned by Manuele (2002), they demonstrate the

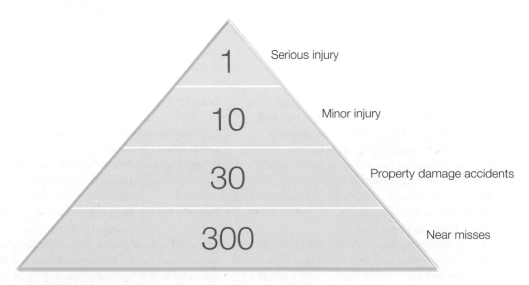

**Figure 11.1 The 1:10:30:300 ratio**

1 — Serious injury
10 — Minor injury
30 — Property damage accidents
300 — Near misses

importance of recording and documenting near misses. A near miss resembles an accident in almost every other respect. It has the same direct cause and similar if not identical contributory factors. If organizations can determine what went wrong and correct the problems, it can minimize the likelihood of accidents occurring.

Incidentally, if we consider the 30 property damage accidents that occur for each serious or disabling injury, these incidents cost hundreds of thousands of euro/pounds/dollars annually and yet they are frequently misnamed and referred to as near misses.

## Costs of accidents

There is often a tendency to underestimate the cost of workplace accidents. It is easy to look at the cost of accidents to an organization in terms of compensation payments for injuries sustained on the job, but relatively few organizations consider the indirect costs of an accident. Direct costs include compensation claims, which cover medical costs and indemnity payments for the injured worker. Other, less well considered indirect costs include:

- safety administration costs that occur as a result of time spent investigating and documenting accidents
- legal costs
- cost of time to other employees assisting the injured employee
- the cost of replacing the injured employee
- training replacement workers
- damage to plant and machinery
- increase in insurance premiums
- low morale among employees
- increased absenteeism.

This has given rise to the iceberg theory of accident costs. This looks at the relationship between direct costs and indirect costs. It suggests that accident and ill health costs can be likened to an iceberg: costs that are recoverable are visible but those that are unrecoverable are hidden below the waterline and are many times greater. It is often assumed that most accident and incident costs are recoverable through insurance. This is a dangerous misconception. In the UK, the Health and Safety Executive estimates that the ratio between insured and uninsured costs lies in the range of £1:8 to £1:36. In other words, for every £1 recovered from insurers, at least

**Human error** – a human decision or behaviour that has undesirable effects

**Figure 11.2** The accident cost iceberg

£8 is lost entirely. Therefore, the real costs of accidents will not be recognized if an organization only considers accidents that result in time off work.

## BUILDING YOUR SKILLS

It is estimated that health and safety programmes in US organizations save \$4–6 for every \$1 invested. Irish organizations invest, on average, approximately €6 per employee on health and safety programmes, yet the average cost of a workplace injury is €30 per employee. If safety is expensive, it is nothing compared to the cost of having an accident.

Prepare a case to present to senior management for investing in health and safety in an organization.

## Accident causation theories

A number of different theories exist that seek to explain why accidents occur. The majority of these theories look at **human error**, in the belief that most accidents can be traced to an erroneous human act. Human error is any deviation from a required standard of human performance that results in an unwanted state of events – delay, malfunction, difficulty, accident and so on. The human decision or behaviour does not necessarily have to cause damage to be classified as an error.

Heinrich (1931) developed a theory of unsafe acts and conditions, which he labelled the 'domino theory'. This influential theory dominated thinking about industrial safety and accidents for decades. Heinrich analysed 75,000 accident reports and concluded that 88 per cent of all accidents are caused by the 'unsafe acts of persons', 10 per cent by unsafe physical conditions and 2 per cent by acts of god. Domino theory states that accidents result from a chain of sequential events, like a line of dominoes falling over. When one domino falls, it triggers the next one and so on, but removing a key factor, such as an unsafe condition or an unsafe act, prevents the start of the chain reaction. Five factors were identified in this chain:

1 *Social environment and ancestry:* This deals with worker personality. Heinrich explains that undesirable personality traits, such as stubbornness or recklessness, can be passed along through inheritance or develop from a person's social environment, and both inheritance and environment contribute to undesirable behaviour or acts.
2 *Fault of person:* This also deals with worker personality traits. Heinrich believed that obtained character flaws such as bad temper, inconsiderateness and ignorance contribute at one remove to accident causation. Natural or environmental flaws in the worker's family or life cause these secondary personal deficiencies, which are themselves contributors to unsafe acts.
3 *Unsafe act and/or unsafe condition:* This addresses the direct cause of incidents. Heinrich (1931) suggested that these factors included acts such as using machinery without warning and the absence of rail guards. Heinrich felt that unsafe acts and unsafe conditions were the central factor in preventing incidents and the easiest of the five factors to correct, a process which he likened to lifting one of the dominoes out of the line. Heinrich (1931) defined four reasons why people commit unsafe acts: improper attitude, lack of knowledge or skill, physical unsuitability, and improper mechanical or physical environment. For example, an employee who commits an unsafe act may do so because they are not convinced that the appropriate preventive measure is necessary, and because of inadequate supervision.
4 *Accident:* Accidents are the occurrence of a preventable injury that is the natural result of a series of events or circumstances, which invariably occur in a fixed and logical order. In other words, accidents result from a combination of steps 1–3.

5 *Injury:* Injury results from accidents, and includes muscle sprains, cuts and broken bones.

Heinrich's theory has two central points: injuries do not occur in isolation and are caused by the action of preceding factors; removal of the central factor (unsafe act/hazardous condition) negates the action of the preceding factors and so prevents accidents and injuries. Most accidents are therefore caused by unsafe acts of people, and a person who gets injured at work is likely to have had many near misses prior to the accident. Heinrich (1931) proposed a set of guidelines to form the basis of any workplace safety programme:

1 Injuries result from a completed series of factors, one of which is the accident itself. Therefore, the accident is directly caused by an unsafe act and/or a physical or mechanical hazard.
2 Most accidents occur as a result of unsafe acts committed by people.
3 An employee, who has had an injury caused by an unsafe act, is likely to have had over 300 narrow escapes from serious injury as a result of committing the very same unsafe act. Likewise, persons are exposed to mechanical hazards hundreds of times before they suffer injury.
4 The severity of an injury is largely fortuitous and the occurrence of the accident that results in the injury is largely preventable.
5 If we can understand the reasons why people do unsafe acts, it can help in taking corrective action.
6 Four basic methods are available for preventing accidents – engineering revision, persuasion and appeal, personnel adjustment, and discipline.
7 Accident prevention techniques are related to best quality and production techniques.
8 Management should assume responsibility for safety as it is in the best position to get results.
9 Supervisors play a key role in accident prevention. A supervisor's control of worker performance is the factor of greatest influence in successful accident prevention.
10 Every accident has direct and indirect costs. The direct cost to the organization of compensation claims and medical treatment for industrial injuries is only one-fifth of the total cost the employer must pay.

While Heinrich's ideas remain popular, most recent theories of accident causation have labelled his ideas too simplistic. They say safety performance measurement must also account for the behaviour of management and supervisors. Barrie and Paulson (1991) suggest that while unsafe acts of workers are the leading cause of accidents and injuries, they are only indicative of other safety management system problems or dysfunctions. They propose that to improve safety in the workplace, the organization must first address the context within which they occur. In other words, an organization-wide approach that includes management and supervisors, and an analysis of all the organizational factors that influence health and safety in addition to human behaviour, is the only way meaningful changes in safety standards can be addressed. This leads us to consider the relationship between human factors and health and safety.

# HUMAN FACTORS AND HEALTH AND SAFETY

Traditional approaches to health and safety in the workplace tended to focus on the engineering design approach, whereby the physical design of the workplace took precedence in making environments, technology and processes safer. This essentially centred on the ergonomics domain, where responsibility for health and safety lay in the hands of engineers and those who were responsible for designing the layout of workplaces and work processes. Organizations also focused on employees' cognitive errors and looked at accidents that occurred as a result of mental lapses or forgetfulness. While these two approaches played an important role in improving organizational health and safety, most organizations tend to hit a glass ceiling in terms of ongoing improvements. The need to take a more proactive role and consider other factors and how they contribute to accidents, and the assessment of the likelihood of accidents occurring, has led to organizations adopting a behavioural science approach to health and safety. This approach suggests that for health and safety programmes to be effective, they must address the agent most responsible for health and safety, the employee. Therefore, organizations need to understand the psychological factors influencing health and safety before they can take steps to improve safety performance. Research suggests that behavioural science allows safety specialists to address:

- the types of hazards people can spot easily and those they are likely to miss
- the time of day and sorts of jobs in which people are likely to create hazards
- the extent to which we can predict the people who will have accidents and in what circumstances
- why certain people ignore safety rules, or fail to use protective equipment
- the role and value of training in fostering safety awareness.

The interaction between individuals and the physical dimensions of the workplace is known as human factors. Human factors focus on human beings and their interaction with products, equipment, facilities, procedures and the surrounding environment. A simple way to look at human factors is to think about three aspects – the employee, the job and the organization – and how they impact on employees' health and safety-related behaviour. Each employee's personal attitudes, skills, habits and personalities can be strengths or weaknesses depending on the task demands. Individual characteristics influence behaviour in significant ways. Their effects on job performance may be negative and may not always be lessened by job design. Characteristics such as personality are fixed and difficult to change. Others, such as motivation and attitude towards risk, can be modified.

From the job perspective, tasks should be designed in accordance with ergonomic principles that take into account the physical and mental characteristics of employees. Matching the job to the person will ensure that they are not overloaded and can make the most effective contribution to organizational performance. Physical fit includes the design of the whole workplace and working environment. Mental fit involves the individual's information and decision-making requirements, as well as their perception of the tasks and risks. Mismatches between job requirements and people's capabilities increase the potential for human error and accidents occurring.

Organizational factors have the biggest influence on individual and group behaviour, yet they are often overlooked during the design of work and during investigation of accidents and incidents. Organizations need to establish their own positive health and safety culture. The culture needs to promote employee

**Ergonomics** – the relationship between employees, physical work equipment and the environment

**Behavioural science approach** – how to describe, explain and predict human behaviour in a work context

**Human factors** – how characteristics of the organization affect employee behaviour

involvement and commitment at all levels, emphasizing that ignoring established health and safety standards is not acceptable. Table 11.1 provides a list of the most relevant human factors for HR practitioners.

**Table 11.1** Categories of human factors

| Personal | Job | Organizational |
|---|---|---|
| Attitude | Equipment design | Size |
| Attributions | Machine systems | Technology |
| Motivation | Working height | Culture |
| Perception | Job tasks | Goals and |
| Memory | | strategies |
| Info processing | | |

Sanders and McCormick (1993) suggest that the human factor perspective is unique, in that it recognizes that:

- Machines, procedures and systems are built to serve employees and must be designed with the end user in mind.
- The design of machines, procedures and systems influences the safety behaviour of employees.
- Employees, machines, procedures and the work environment do not exist independently of each other.
- Objective data should be gathered by organizations on a regular basis to generate information about human behaviour that can allow organizations to minimize the likelihood of accidents occurring.

Two broad approaches to the behavioural science perspective exist: the behaviour-based approach and the attitude-based approach. We will consider both in turn.

## Behaviour-based approach

The behaviour-based approach to safety looks at how people actually behave rather than their attitudes to safety. Many safety campaigns try to change people's attitudes in the hope that this will then change their behaviour, believing that attitudes cause behaviour. Research from the psychology field suggests that this is misguided and that attitudes have a tenuous link to behaviour. Attitudes often express how we would like to see ourselves behave, rather than how we actually behave. Based on the work of H.W. Heinrich in the 1930s that approximately 90 per cent of all accidents are caused by human error, the behavioural

approach advocates that getting people to behave safely reduces accidents. He believed that it was not worth trying to change their attitudes, and that behaviour can potentially influence the formation and change of attitudes. Heinrich (1931) claimed that accidents result from undesirable traits of a person's character that are passed along through inheritance and are the fault of employees who commit unsafe acts.

This approach also emphasizes the encouragement of desirable behaviour, rather than the punishment of undesirable behaviour. For example, employees should be encouraged to wear personal protective equipment when handling dangerous materials or wear hard hats on a construction site. In many organizations, the emphasis on safety is communicated by disciplining employees for noncompliance instead of rewarding them for compliance. Four factors influence behaviour in the presence of potential danger:

1 *Perception*: in order to react to danger and do something about it, it must be perceived by the individual.
2 *Psychological*: once the individual perceives danger, they psychologically evaluate and assess the level of danger, who is responsible for it, the most appropriate action to take, and the practical outcomes of that action.
3 *Action*: the individual takes a specific course of action, which will depend on their reflexes, abilities, experience, dexterity and physical condition.
4 *Outcome*: if the action taken is sufficient, the danger is averted; if the action taken is insufficient, the danger remains or increases.

Thus, behavioural-based safety programmes use a variety of people-focused techniques aimed at modifying employee behaviour via the involvement of employees and management:

**Behaviour-based approach** – focuses on what people do, analyses why they do it, and then applies a research-supported intervention strategy to improve what people do

- setting clear definitions of the desired safety behaviours expected at all levels
- observing existing workplace behaviours
- focusing on specific behaviours identified from safety assessments, incident data, near miss data and observations
- feedback for employees, supervisors, managers and executives on these behaviours in order to improve them

• setting up a process to identify and correct unsafe conditions as well as improving the consistency of safe behaviours.

This approach is popular with many organizations as it shifts responsibility for health and safety to employees and does not require significant change in the work process, engineering design or management system. One frequent criticism of the approach is that it ignores injuries and illnesses that are caused by exposure to hazards. Hazards include any aspect of technology or activity that produces some degree of risk. A best practice HRM approach to behaviour-based safety, however, should never attribute blame to the employee. It should seek to understand the causes of accidents and near misses and correct them through appropriate behaviour. The avoidance of hazards often requires behaviour change from supervisors and managers; and equipment redesign requires behaviour change of engineers (Garavan, 2002).

An important feature of health, safety and wellbeing in any organization is that employees are encouraged to report and document any accidents that occur. The focus should be on rewarding and recognizing improvements in behaviour, not focusing on the lack of accidents. The main purpose of reporting accidents is to find the underlying cause and any factors that might have prompted the accident, in order to prevent it from happening again. In an effort to involve employees in workplace safety, many organizations use incentive schemes that promise employees rewards for a reduction in accident rates or an increase in near miss reporting. The danger with this approach is that such reward schemes can encourage underreporting and allow workplace hazards to go unchecked. While incentive schemes can appear to produce reductions in workplace accidents, employees may essentially be rewarded for not reporting accidents. Effective behavioural-based safety programmes should not include incentives for long periods without an accident precisely because it is understood that this may lead to underreporting. Instead, positive reinforcement is delivered after safe behaviours and improvements in safe behaviours over time.

**Hazards** – any source of potential damage, harm or adverse health effects on something or someone under certain conditions at work

**Attitude-based approach** – focuses on changing a person's feelings and inner thoughts towards safety

**Risk** – a situation involving exposure to danger

## Attitude-based approach

The attitude-based approach adopts the belief that attitudes influence behaviour. While there is a link between attitudes and behaviour, they are not the same thing. Behaviours are everything a person does or says and are usually an outward expression of attitude. Attitudes reflect how we feel about something, either positive or negative. It is not a guarantee that a person will act in the same way every time. Crucially, a person may have a positive attitude towards safety in the workplace, but this does not always translate into safe working behaviours; for example, if a person is under pressure to complete a task, they may avoid wearing the correct protective clothing as it may slow them down.

Cox et al. (1998) suggested that the main influence on employee attitudes to safety was how committed they perceived the management of the organization to be towards safety. This includes the quality of near miss reporting, whether the focus was on accident prevention rather than blame, the encouragement of safety ideas, the effectiveness of safety committees, and how safety is prioritized in relation to other issues. Cheyne et al. (1999) found the factors underlying employee attitudes to safety were dependent on the industry in which they worked. For example, within the manufacturing sector, employee attitudes to safety were linked to how their managers acted. In the transport sector, however, management had no influence on attitudes towards safety, perhaps due to the autonomy in the working practices of transport workers. At the very least, management actions for safety should be the key area for influencing employee attitudes. Central to the creation of a culture where management values health and safety is the perception that safety is a top priority and employee welfare is more important than quotas, deadlines or orders. Lee and Harrison (2000) found that team briefings that included discussion of safety were correlated with positive attitudes towards safety by staff. Training is also important. Employees, especially long-term employees, often take a relaxed approach to health and safety as they become more familiar with their jobs. Training serves as a reminder that no amount of time on the job will keep employees immune from an injury.

The concept of risk is often addressed when examining attitudes towards safety. People tend to be either risk averse or risk takers. The concept of 'risk homeostasis' suggests that individuals have a fixed level of acceptable risk that they are prepared to take. When the level of risk in one part of the individual's life changes, there will be a corresponding rise or fall in risk elsewhere to bring the overall risk back to that individual's equilibrium. For example, research carried out in Germany on taxi drivers looked at cars fitted with an anti-lock braking system (ABS) and compared them with cars fitted with conventional braking systems (Aschenbrenner and Biehl, 1994). The crash rate was the same for both types of cars, indicating that drivers of ABS-equipped cars took more risks in the belief that the ABS system would take care of them, while the non-ABS drivers drove more carefully since the ABS system would not assist them in the event of a dangerous situation. Further research carried out in Sweden on the use of studded and non-studded car tyres looked at driver speed (Rumar et al., 1976). Studded tyres offer greater resistance in icy conditions in order to make driving in these conditions safer. When faced with icy roads, drivers with studded tyres actually drove faster than drivers who did not have studded tyres, believing that the increased safety afforded to them meant they could increase their level of risk.

# BUILDING YOUR SKILLS

Consider any road safety campaigns/advertisements you have seen. Do they tend to focus on changing behaviours or changing attitudes? What techniques are often used in these campaigns to communicate their message?

If you wanted to change employees' attitudes towards health and safety in an organization, what steps would you take?

# EMPLOYEE WELLBEING

**Employee wellbeing** incorporates a number of different dimensions that impact on employees' physical and mental health at work. Physical and mental health can play a huge role in determining safety and satisfaction at work. We look at seven specific factors that influence employee wellbeing: ergonomics, job

**Employee wellbeing** – the overall quality of an employee's experience at work

characteristics, stress, job strain, workplace bullying, sickness absence and workaholism. It is important to note that each of these can be adjusted by the employer.

## Ergonomics

The design of workplaces in most organizations creates conditions that expose employees to numerous hazards, for example poorly designed floor layouts, excessive noise, exposure to chemicals, and improperly designed seats and workstations. Ergonomics is a science concerned with the fit between people and their work. It puts people first, taking account of their physical and mental capabilities and limitations. It aims to ensure that tasks, equipment, information and the environment suit each worker.

To assess the fit between a person and their work, it is important to consider a number of factors:

- the job being done and the demands on the worker
- the type of equipment used
- the information used, for example machine displays and controls
- the physical environment, for example temperature, humidity, lighting, noise, ventilation, vibration
- the social environment, such as teamwork and supportive management.

The physical aspects of an employee that we need to consider include:

- their body size and shape
- fitness and strength levels
- posture
- the senses, particularly vision, hearing and touch
- the stresses and strains on muscles, joints, nerves.

The psychological aspects of employees must also be considered, including their mental abilities, personality, learning, and level of experience. Improper design of the work environment and job activities can cause significant psychological stress and health problems for employees (Smith and Sainfort, 1989). Poor ergonomic characteristics of work can cause visual, muscular and psychological disorders, including visual fatigue, eye strain, sore eyes, headaches, fatigue, muscle soreness, back disorders, tension, anxiety and depression, and repetitive strain injury (RSI). These effects may be temporary and may fade when the employee is removed from the workplace or given an opportunity to rest at work, or when the design of the work environment is improved. When exposure to poor ergonomic conditions is prolonged, the effects can become permanent.

The application of basic ergonomic principles to the workplace not only reduces the likelihood of ill health and the occurrence of accidents, it can also increase productivity and efficiency. For example, if we look at the layout of controls and equipment, these should be located in relation to how they are used by employees. Those used most often should be placed where they are easy to reach without the need for bending or stretching.

Common ergonomic issues in workplaces include:

- *Manual handling:* too much physical demand placed on the employee when lifting heavy or bulky loads; frequent repetitive lifting without sufficient rest periods; lifting loads above shoulder height; lifting on uneven or wet surfaces.
- *Display screens:* poorly positioned screens that are too high/low/close/far from the worker, or offset to one side; too much glare from lights or sunshine that increases the risk of eye strain; staring at a screen for eight hours a day without changes of activity also increases the risk of eye strain.
- *Work-related stress:* if work demands are too high and the employee is under constant pressure to meet targets and deadlines, it can result in work-related stress and increase the likelihood of ill health and reduced performance and productivity.
- *Work design:* chairs that are too high or too low for the employee, desks that are not height adjustable, and telephones that are situated too far away from the employee can all cause muscular fatigue and back strain.

HR practitioners can identify possible ergonomic issues by involving employees in assessing the design of their workplaces, analysing the way work is done in the organization, examining the circumstances surrounding frequent accidents and near misses where mistakes have occurred and people have been injured, and monitoring sickness and absenteeism records. In many instances, a relatively small adjustment is all that is needed to make jobs easier to perform.

Some of the most common ergonomic solutions are:

- provide height-adjustable chairs and desks so individual employees can work at their preferred work height

- ensure that people working on computers take regular breaks from looking at displays
- provide guidance on correct posture to avoid RSI
- remove obstacles from under desks to create sufficient leg room
- arrange items stored on shelving so those used most frequently and those that are the heaviest are between waist and shoulder height
- raise platforms to help operators reach badly located controls
- introduce job rotation between different tasks to reduce physical and mental fatigue.

## Job characteristics

Chapters 2 and 3 looked at the recruitment and selection of employees to fill jobs and roles within organizations. What, however, is a 'good' job? There are two considerations here: individual expectations of what an employee wants from a job; and their perception of work as a central component of their lives. Eklund (1998) developed a set of characteristics of a 'good' job that combines best practice human factors and ergonomic principles:

- *Variation:* employees should be allowed to perform a variety of tasks in their jobs.
- *Overview of process:* if employees are allowed to see an overview of the whole production process, it will make their own job more meaningful.
- *Freedom to move:* employees should have physical freedom to move around.
- *Long cycle time:* employees should have sufficient time between work tasks to allow them enough time to do their jobs correctly.
- *Self-paced work:* employees should be allowed to carry out their job at a pace that best suits them.
- *Influence on choice of working methods:* employees should have some degree of autonomy or freedom to choose how they carry out their job on a daily basis.
- *Influence on production quality:* employees should have a say in ensuring that quality standards are met.
- *Involvement in problem-solving:* employees should feel that their opinion is valued and that they can contribute to solving any problems that arise.
- *Lack of time pressure:* employees should not be put under constant pressure to achieve deadlines.
- *Continuous development of skills:* all employees should be allowed to engage in learning and development to ensure that their skills do not become obsolete.

● *Positive work management climate:* ideally, the organizational culture should advocate a supportive climate where employees interact with colleagues and managers.

There are two particular characteristics of jobs that must be considered when designing jobs: mental workload and work capacity.

The concept of mental workload has recently become important. The use of many modern semi-automated and computerized technologies can impose severe requirements in terms of the burden of mental or information-processing requirements placed on employees. Mental workload looks at the input aspects of tasks, essentially the requirements and demands made by the job on the employee. The mental aspects of workload are conceptualized in terms of information processing and the cognitive and emotional demands placed on employees at work. Air traffic controllers, pilots and anaesthetists are examples of job with high mental workloads. If employees find that the mental requirements of their jobs are too complex or that time pressures and mental requirements are too frequent, they are likely to suffer from mental fatigue and become frustrated and anxious. On the other hand, if the mental requirements are too seldom, or frequent but too simplistic, the employee is likely to suffer from boredom on the job. The challenge with mental workload is not to minimize but optimize it.

Work capacity refers to an employee's capacity to carry out physical work. A number of personal and environmental factors affect work capacity. Personal factors include body weight, age, height, gender, and whether the individual is a smoker or non-smoker. Environmental factors include workplace temperature, level of humidity, noise levels, levels of ventilation and availability of the correct protective equipment.

> **Mental workload** – the mental demands placed on humans at work
>
> **Work capacity** – how much work an individual can do
>
> **Stress** – the demands of the work environment and the ability of the employee to meet these demands

## Stress

The blurring of work and home boundaries as a result of increased connectivity to the workplace has led to increased incidences of work stress. The prevalence of smartphones means that employees cannot 'switch off' from work even outside office hours during the evening or at weekends; they are constantly connected. Stress can contribute to accidents and injuries by causing people to sleep badly, overmedicate themselves and/or drink excessively, feel depressed, nervous or anxious, and feel angry and reckless. Stress is the demand made on the adaptive capacities of the mind and body. There are three important aspects of stress:

1 Stress levels depend on the individual's view of the stressor – the stimulus, condition or event that causes stress – and can be a positive and a negative factor in life.
2 It is the reaction to the events in life, rather than the actual events, that determines whether the outcome is positive or negative.
3 A person's capacities determine the results. When the capacity for handling stress is strong and healthy, the outcome is positive. With a lack of ability to handle the demands, the outcome is negative.

It is important to note that stress can be stimulating and helpful. Life changes and challenges can motivate individuals and provide the drive for accomplishing specific goals in life. The challenge is in finding the right balance. Too little stress leads to boredom and monotony, while too much stress leads to physical and mental breakdown. The Yerkes-Dodson principle (Yerkes and Dodson, 1908) is useful in this respect, suggesting that a specific amount of stress is healthy and even beneficial. For example, consider sporting events, or studying for your exams. As stress levels increase, so too can performance. However, this relationship between increased stress and increased performance does not continue indefinitely. As shown in Figure 11.3, the Yerkes-Dodson principle (or law) illustrates that a lack of stress can cause underperformance. If stress or arousal is increased, it can also increase performance, but only up to a point. Thereafter, when stress exceeds an individual's ability to cope, this overload contributes to diminished

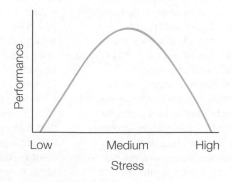

**Figure 11.3 Yerkes-Dodson principle**

## New Approaches to Work Design

For the fourth year in a row, Google topped the list of Fortune's 100 Best Companies to Work For. Google offices are large, open spaces filled with primary colours, couches, large kitchens, massage chairs and hammocks. Google's Zurich office features a gym, pool tables and a slide leading to the canteen, with fireman poles between floors. Google claims a philosophy of work–life integration rather than work–life balance. In conjunction with traditional rewards such as health insurance and competitive pay, Google employees are treated to free breakfast, lunch, dinner, snacks, free on-site massages, on-site gyms, car valeting, and even nap pods. On-site doctors and nurses, convenient medical services, and comprehensive healthcare coverage help keep employees healthy and happy, while new parents get time off and extra spending money to assist with childcare. Google even offers to reimburse up to $5,000 to use towards legal expenses in the adoption of a child. Any classes or degree programmes considered beneficial to an employee's job are also funded by the company.

In an effort to promote employee wellbeing, one of the most well-known efforts to improve the meaningfulness of work at Google is the '20 per cent time' programme. Google allows its employees to use up to 20 per cent of their working week (approximately eight hours a week) at Google to pursue special projects they have a personal interest in. Essentially, for every standard working week, employees can take a full day to work on a project unrelated to their normal workload. These projects do not have to be part of their job descriptions, and most employees who avail themselves of the programme use the time to develop something new, or fix something that is broken. The goal of the programme is to keep employees excited and motivated while at work. Although Google is ostensibly a search engine that makes the majority of its revenue from advertising, additional products such as Gmail, Google Reader, Google Trends and Google Maps have emerged from the '20 per cent time' initiative.

Google News is the product of one Google employee's 20 per cent time. Not long after 9/11, the employee became frustrated by the amount of time he spent attempting to find news stories online. By working out how to extract and collate news stories, Google News was created. Today, millions of people use Google News and had the employee not had that free unpressurized 20 per cent time to explore, it is unlikely he would have had the time to pursue it.

Other organizations such as 3M, a US multinational, and Atlassian, an Australian software company, use similar programmes to make work more meaningful and enhance employee wellbeing. 3M labels its version '15% culture', which encourages employees to spend 15 per cent of their time on projects of their own choosing and initiative. Every quarter, Atlassian gives employees 24 hours, called 'ShipIt Day', to work on anything that relates to the company's products, so long as it is not part of their regular job and they must show their colleagues what they've created when the 24-hour 'hackathon' is over. Atlassian's '20% Time' is 'innovation' time for the engineers. They may use 20 per cent of their time to work on their own innovative ideas and see their work reflected back into the core of the product.

### Questions

1 Are '20 per cent time' projects suitable for all organizations? Are they more likely to work in some industries rather than others?

2 How would you describe the culture of organizations such as Google, 3M and Atlassian?

### Sources

3M, Sustainability at 3M, http://solutions.3m.com/wps/portal/3M/en_US/3M-Sustainability/Global/.

CBS This Morning (2013) Google named best company to work for fourth year, 16 January, www.cbsnews.com/8301-505263_162-57564229/google-named-best-company-to-work-for-for-fourth-year/.

CBS This Morning (2013) Inside Google workplaces, from perks to nap pods, 22 January, www.cbsnews.com/8301-505266_162-57565097/inside-google-workplaces-from-perks-to-nap-pods/.

Chang, J. (2006) Behind the glass curtain, MetropolisMag, July, www.metropolismag.com/story/20060619/behind-the-glass-curtain.

Google Jobs, Benefits, www.google.com/about/jobs/lifeatgoogle/benefits/.

Pink, D.H. (2011) How to deliver innovation overnight, 5 July, www.danpink.com/2011/07/how-to-deliver-innovation-overnight.

Tutton, M. (2009) Boosting employee wellbeing, CNN, 15 October, http://edition.cnn.com/2009/HEALTH/10/14/employee.wellbeing/index.html.

performance, inefficiency and, potentially, health problems caused by excessive pressure and anxiety.

To maximize performance, levels of stress should be neither overly high nor too low. It would be straightforward if this optimal level was the same for everyone, but it is not. Thus, organizational initiatives to aid employees in managing stress should focus on two areas. A stress management programme can help employees and managers identify where this optimal level of stress is, and can also help reduce physical arousal levels, using both coping skills and relaxation techniques so that employees can avoid too much stress.

**Bullying** – inappropriate behaviour at work that undermines an employee's right to dignity at work

## Job strain

Job strain is distinct from job stress, but the two are related. Job strain refers to the negative physical and psychological toll that is placed on employees when jobs involve high demands and workers feel they have little control over decision-making (Kuper and Marmot, 2003). Employees who have both low decision-making ability and high demands cannot manage the stress caused by the high demands through time management or learning new skills, and so become subject to high stress at work. It is the constraints on decision-making, together with high demands, that produce the unhealthy condition of job strain. For example, doctors who have a lot of decision-making ability in their jobs are less likely to have job strain than someone working on a busy factory production line. Job strain has been shown to have a number of adverse health effects, and a recent study looking at over 200,000 employees found that job strain was linked to a 23 per cent increased risk of heart attacks and deaths from coronary heart disease (Kivimäki et al., 2012). The same study also found that job strain was more common among lower skilled employees, due to their reduced autonomy to make decisions on the job.

While experiencing job strain may be unavoidable in some cases, how employees deal with this strain has a significant impact on their likelihood of developing heart disease. Employees who smoke may smoke more when they experience job strain, active employees with job strain tend to become less active, and employees with job strain often eat more. It is important that organizations attempt to minimize the risks of job strain by encouraging employees to eat healthily, take regular exercise, and quit smoking. Also, where possible, jobs should be designed/redesigned to give employees more decision-making control. This has been shown to reduce job strain without changing the level of work completed (Kuper and Marmot, 2003).

## Workplace bullying

Another issue that needs to be considered from a health, safety and wellbeing perspective is bullying at work. It can take many forms, including:

● ignoring or excluding someone
● spreading malicious rumours or gossip
● humiliating someone in public
● giving someone unachievable or meaningless tasks
● constantly undervaluing someone's work performance.

While the UK has no legal definition of workplace bullying, the Irish Health and Safety Authority (2007: 5) defines it as:

repeated inappropriate behaviour, direct or indirect, whether verbal, physical or otherwise, conducted by one or more persons against another or others, at the place of work and/or in the course of employment, which could reasonably be regarded as undermining the individual's right to dignity at work.

An isolated one-off incident of the behaviour described in this definition would be considered an insult to dignity at work but must occur repeatedly to be considered bullying. The cost of bullying in organizations includes direct and indirect costs. There is the cost of sickness absence, staff turnover, reduced productivity for the victims and their colleagues, in addition to the costs of investigation and litigation and industrial unrest. The CIPD (2005c) estimates that bullying costs the UK 80 million lost days each year and that it accounts for half the reported occurrences of work stress.

While bullying can occur in any organization, it is important for HR practitioners to understand what constitutes bullying and what the consequences can be. Bullying can have significant negative effects for employees and organizations. Individual responses to bullying are varied, but include:

● stress, anxiety or sleep disturbance
● panic attacks or impaired ability to make decisions

- loss of self-confidence and self-esteem or reduced output and performance
- depression or a sense of isolation
- physical injury
- reduced quality of home and family life
- suicide.

The costs to the organization include reduced efficiency, an unsafe work environment, increased absenteeism, poor morale, increased compensation claims and legal action. An organization's goal should be to develop a culture in which harassment is known to be unacceptable and where individuals are confident enough to bring complaints without fear of ridicule. Organizations should deal promptly, seriously and discreetly with any issues that are raised.

The first step in minimizing workplace bullying is for organizations to develop an anti-bullying policy. This should summarize the organization's approach to tackling bullying and include:

- a statement from senior management endorsing the policy
- specific definitions of what constitutes unacceptable behaviour
- details as to how employees can raise their concerns about bullying
- any procedures the organization will follow for the complainant and the alleged bully
- information about the potential outcomes and assistance provided.

It is important that this policy is widely publicized and all employees are familiar with it.

## Sickness absence

Employee absence from work is a major cost to organizations. The UK lost approximately 190 million working days to absence in 2010, with each employee taking, on average, 6.5 days off sick. This cost the economy approximately £17 billion, including more than £2.7 billion from 30.4 million days of non-genuine sickness absence (CBI, 2011). In Ireland, eight million work days are lost each year due to absenteeism, with a direct cost of sickness absence of €1.1 billion (Edwards and Greasley, 2010). Sickness absences can be either short or long term. The main causes of employee sickness absence are minor illnesses such as colds and flu, back

pain, stress, musculoskeletal injuries, family issues, recurring medical conditions, and depression. For HR practitioners, effective absence management involves finding a balance between providing support to help employees with health problems stay in and return to work, and taking consistent and firm action against employees who try to take advantage of organizations' sick pay schemes.

Options for managing short-term sickness absence can take the form of return to work interviews, providing sickness absence information to line managers, establishing disciplinary procedures for unacceptable absence levels, establishing formalized leave policies for family circumstances, and offering flexible working. Return to work interviews can help identify short-term absence problems at an early stage. They also provide managers with an opportunity to start a dialogue with staff about any underlying issues that might be causing the absence. Disciplinary procedures for unacceptable absence may be used to make it clear to employees that unjustified absence will not be tolerated and that absence policies will be enforced. Managing long-term sickness absence requires careful consideration of a formal return to work strategy for those returning after a long absence by keeping in touch with sick employees, adjusting workplace design elements if necessary, offering professional guidance and designing a return to work plan. Line managers have a particularly important role to play in the management of sickness absence. It is important that they have good communications skills to encourage employees to discuss any problems they may have at an early stage so that they can be given the necessary support or advice before more serious problems arise.

## Workaholism

The term 'workaholic' is used in everyday language to describe individuals who are addicted to work. Workaholics are defined as task-oriented, compulsive, perfectionist, neurotic, rigid, highly motivated, resourceful, impatient and self-centred individuals (Andreassen et al., 2007). They tend to work overtime on a regular basis, identify themselves with work, and often lack the ability to relax. The main feature is the high investment in work, with those who work more than 50 hours a week often characterized as workaholics, while Machlowitz (1980) defined 'workaholics' as individuals who always devote more time and energy to work than the work situation demands. Griffiths (2011) identifies a number of characteristics that characterize workaholics:

- work is the single most important activity in the workaholic's life
- working gives workaholics positive emotions
- workaholics need to 'up the dose' by increasing the hours they work each day
- when unable to work, workaholics experience withdrawal symptoms such as irritability
- working long hours brings workaholics into conflict with others, including colleagues, partners and friends
- 'reformed' workaholics easily slip back into their old behaviour patterns.

Workaholism is viewed in a different light to other dependencies such as alcohol or drug addiction, in the sense that it is almost a respectable addiction. However, recent research demonstrates the adverse health effects of workaholism. According to Gibb et al. (2011), people who work at least 50 hours a week are up to three times more likely to face alcohol problems. Virtanen et al. (2012) conducted a study of over 22,000 participants showing that overworkers are 40–80 per cent more likely to suffer heart disease than others.

The culture of the organization plays an important role in prompting and reinforcing this sort of addiction. Behaviours become repeated when they are rewarded. Since people tend to abandon behaviours that don't result in some sort of payoff, it is possible that organizations, perhaps unwittingly, reward workaholics as a result of their excessive working. A number of companies have recently created policies instructing employees that they are not to read or answer work emails after normal work hours. However, these policies are the exceptions to the rule, as many companies today are happy to see employees handling work tasks in the evenings, over the weekends and during vacations. Attempts to address workaholism must begin by looking at the culture of the organization to ensure that addictive behaviours are not reinforced by financial or social rewards.

## HEALTH, SAFETY AND WELLBEING AND HRM

It can be argued that health, safety and wellbeing require more involvement from employees, unions, supervisors and management than any other area of HRM. Health, safety and wellbeing issues impact on the majority of HRM activities. Recruitment, training and performance management procedures include aspects such as manual handling, general health status and stress coping mechanisms; job and work design systems incorporate ergonomic considerations; and reward management systems can include incentives for achieving specific safety targets.

With regard to health, safety and wellbeing, HR practitioners have to:

- develop health, safety and wellbeing policies and modify existing policies as necessary, in conjunction with workplace representatives, unions and management
- keep up to date with health and safety issues and the relevant legislation
- communicate these to employees
- analyse accident rates
- promote safe working behaviours
- consider the impact of new technology or work processes on employee health, safety and wellbeing.

A best practice approach to health, safety and wellbeing in an HRM context should be situated within a strategic HRM approach ▶ **Chapter 1** ◀. A strategic HRM approach to health, safety and wellbeing advocates the need for autonomy, individual responsibility, flexibility and adaptability. This is most apparent when we consider the change that has taken place across EU countries in terms of the approach to safety legislation. The focus has shifted from simple compliance with basic, minimum legal requirements to the adoption of a proactive approach to health, safety and wellbeing that advocates the involvement of employees and managers in developing safety management systems, implementing them and evaluating their effectiveness.

Garavan (2002) characterizes the professional HRM approach to health and safety as follows:

- The creation of a culture where health, safety and wellbeing are considered important to the organization. Regularly updated policies and procedures must reflect the importance of a safe and healthy work environment. The safety policy statement contributes to this if it is appropriately constructed, understood, revised and acted upon. The legal requirements must be complied with and risk assessments conducted. Campaigns and publicity materials should be used to promote a culture of health, safety and wellbeing and this should be driven by the HRM function with top management support. This requires the gathering of information about health and safety matters and the conduct of a cost–benefit analysis to determine the contribution that health and safety management practices make to the organization's overall effectiveness.

- Commitment from senior management to the ongoing achievement of increasingly higher standards of health and safety via the implementation of safe working systems and the monitoring of their effectiveness.
- Organization-wide commitment to health, safety and wellbeing. This means that all parties must understand their responsibilities for health and safety, their targets in the area and their contribution to the organization's effectiveness. It is recommended that safety should be considered part of performance management systems ▶ Chapter 7 ◀. If employees themselves are encouraged to take responsibility for health, safety and wellbeing and made accountable for their own actions, this increases the likelihood that they will be committed to fostering a safe working culture.
- Managers should lead by example in demonstrating their commitment to health, safety and wellbeing. This can be done by motivating employees to make a contribution to health and safety improvements and providing feedback or communicating results on health and safety initiatives.
- Policies and procedures should be designed to encourage the prioritization of a safer and healthier working environment. Systems should also be put in place to evaluate the effectiveness of these policies and procedures.
- Sufficient resources should be allocated to health and safety equipment and training and education to reinforce the priority given to health, safety and wellbeing in the workplace. While the provision of these resources can be costly, the absence of investment in this area usually ends up costing more money. Research evidence confirms that those organizations with superior health and safety records allocate greater resources to this area.

A best practice HRM approach to health and safety advocates that all organizations should have safety statements. The safety statement has a central role to play in the management of safety, health and welfare. Ideally, all workplaces should have written safety statements based on the hazards identified and the risk assessment, setting out how the safety, health and wellbeing of employees will be protected and managed.

Safety statements must be specific to the workplace and must set out:

- The hazards identified and the risks assessed.
- The protective and preventive measures taken and the resources allocated to safety, health and welfare.
- The plans and procedures for dealing with emergencies or serious and imminent danger.
- The duties of employees as regards safety, health and welfare at work, and the requirement for them to cooperate with their employer in these matters.
- The names and, where applicable, job titles of persons assigned to perform tasks relevant to the safety statement.
- The arrangements for the appointment of safety representatives. A safety representative is an employee chosen by other workers to represent them in consultations with the employer on matters of safety, health and wellbeing in the workplace.
- A safety representative should have the right to inspect the workplace at a frequency or on a schedule agreed between them and the employer, based on the nature and extent of the hazards in the workplace.

The aims of the safety statement are to:

- Involve management up to the highest level by assigning clear responsibilities in the control of safety, health and welfare at the workplace.
- Ensure that appropriate steps are taken to comply with the relevant statutory provisions and that those measures are monitored and reviewed on a regular basis.
- Identify hazards and prioritize risks.
- Ensure that sufficient resources are allocated to safety management.
- Ensure that every person in the workplace is informed and involved in the control of safety, health and welfare.
- Ensure the systematic follow-up of problems as they arise.

The employer must bring the safety statement to all employees' attention, and in a form, manner and language that is easily understood. This should be done at least annually, or when it is amended. It should be brought to the attention of newly recruited employees at the induction stage ▶ Chapter 4 ◀.

The Health and Safety Authority (HSA) carries out approximately 14,000 workplace inspections each year in the Republic of Ireland. However, there are over 200,000 workplaces in the country, suggesting that each workplace can, on average, expect a visit every 14.5 years (*Irish Times*, 2009). While these visits are supposedly random, the majority of employers have indicated they are usually aware of impending visits. Is the HSA likely to gain a realistic overview of health, safety and wellbeing in these circumstances?

## Health and safety legislative considerations

Common law has a major role to play in health, safety and wellbeing. A third of the world's population live in common law jurisdictions. The UK, the Republic of Ireland, America, Australia and Canada are common law countries. Over the centuries, as judges have heard cases, they have issued judgements. The body of law that has been developed by these judgements is known as 'common law'. Common law develops and expands to meet newly emerging situations.

The significance of common law to health and safety practitioners, and to employers, lies in the fact that most actions for personal injuries, be they employer liability claims or public liability claims, are brought at common law. The plaintiff (injured person) sues their employer or the owner/occupier of the premises where the accident occurred. The plaintiff alleges that the employer or owner/occupier has been negligent and in breach of the duty of care owed to the employee or visitor to the premises. When taking an action, the plaintiff may also allege that the employer is in breach of a statutory duty, so an action may be grounded on the tort (wrong) of negligence and the breach of the provisions of legislative acts.

There is a general obligation under common law requiring employers to take care of employees' safety. This common law duty of care requires that employers:

- provide a reasonably safe workplace
- provide reasonably safe plant and equipment
- operate reasonably safe systems of work
- ensure that staff are competent and safety conscious.

> **Common law** – law developed by judges through decisions made in courts and similar tribunals

An employer may be held negligent by the courts if they failed to take such care, and an employee subsequently suffers an injury and sues. However, the duty is not absolute. Negligence is tried against two tests:

1 Has the employer taken reasonable care to protect its employees?
2 Was it reasonably practicable for the employer to take the measures necessary to protect its employees?

## Health and Safety in a Police Station in the Republic of Ireland

This rural Irish police station was built in 1960 and is over 50 years old. It is open 24 hours a day, 7 days a week and 33 police officers are stationed there. A recent safety audit was carried out, which produced some alarming findings.

The station's safety representative left 6 months ago and has not yet been replaced. Fire drills have been practised in the last 12 months, but usually at night or when only a few people are in the station, due to the perception that they are too much hassle to practise when most people are in the station.

Health and safety training is rarely carried out and is not built into performance reviews. None of the 33 police officers have received first aid training since they left police training college, which, in some cases, was 20 years ago. Police officers are unsure of the location of the safety statement and most cannot recall what it says. There are no names on the safety statement, and no evidence of it ever being read or communicated to officers, even when they first started working at the station. There is no system in place for the maintenance of first aid kits. Police officers do not know where first aid supplies can be found, but most patrol cars have a first aid kit.

Overcrowding is a significant issue in this station. One office, for example, has six people working in a space with three workstations. The majority of chairs and desks

$\rightarrow$

flowing into the room. The state agency responsible for the maintenance of police stations suggested that the room should not be used and sealed the manhole with grease. Few female officers now use this room and most prefer to get changed in their cars. The men's lockers are situated in the basement, which frequently floods when it rains because of poor drainage outside the building.

The canteen is in a particularly poor condition. The floor is dirty and six of the eight fluorescent light strips are not working. Mice traps are also visible. A fire exit in the canteen is blocked by a bin and the exit is locked with a key and has no push bar. On the day of the audit, the key to this door could not be found.

Prisoners have to be brought in through the public entrance. The station has no separate prisoners' showers, so prisoners in need of a shower either have to use the members' private showers or be transferred to a station with shower facilities for prisoners. Staff security is placed at risk by a number of design factors. Members of the public can quite

are in a poor condition, and none are height adjustable. There are a huge number of trailing leads from computers, televisions and radio equipment visible. The station has a doctor's office for use in the event of a prisoner requiring medical treatment, which is currently being used as an immigration office to document immigrants in the town.

When the station was built in 1960, the female locker room was built over a sewage manhole, which burst recently, with sewage

easily secure access to the back office and cell areas, because of the design of the public area and the lack of secure doors. There are no cameras on the exterior of the building, so police officers cannot see who is entering the building. One rear fire exit is being held closed with a cotton belt because it is broken. One fire extinguisher is being used as a coat hanger, and others are used to keep doors open. It is eight years since some of the fire extinguishers have been checked to see if they work.

The station does not have any room for the storage of evidence taken from crime scenes. For ease of access, most police officers store evidence relating to their own cases in their personal locker. At the time of the audit, police-issue bicycles are stored in front of the prisoners' cells.

1 Describe the safety culture in this workplace.
2 Who is currently responsible for safety? Who should be responsible?
3 What steps would you take to change police officers' attitudes towards safety in the workplace?

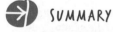 SUMMARY

This chapter demonstrates the often overlooked importance for HR practitioners to understand the significance of ensuring the health, safety and wellbeing of all employees. Developing an organizational culture that truly believes in the value of safe working behaviours is particularly important. If we take the time and effort to understand why accidents occur, and document the causes and factors contributing to accidents, we can lessen the likelihood of future occurrences. By understanding the effect of ergonomic and job design characteristics, we can make work safer and more enjoyable. Organizations have a moral obligation and an economic incentive to provide a safe workplace.

 CHAPTER REVIEW QUESTIONS

1 Outline the concept of safety culture in organizations.
2 In which two ways is the behavioural science approach to health and safety different from the traditional engineering design approach?
3 What is the difference between a behaviour-based approach to health and safety and an attitude-based approach?
4 What is the significance of the accident cost iceberg?
5 Can you give two indirect costs of an accident?
6 Suggest and justify two occupations where mental workload capacity is an important element of safe work behaviour.

7   What are the main features of a person-centred approach to ergonomics?

8   Discuss the role of the HRM function in implementing health, safety and wellbeing initiatives at work.

 **FURTHER READING**

Hughes, P. and Ferrett, E. (2011) *Introduction to Health and Safety at Work*, 5th edn, Oxford: Butterworth-Heinemann.

 **USEFUL WEBSITES**

www.hse.gov.uk
The UK Health and Safety Executive provides a wealth of information on health and safety matters for individuals and organizations.

www.ergonomics.org.uk
The Institute of Ergonomics & Human Factors provides regularly updated news regarding ergonomics in the workplace and has a large library of useful books and journals.

www.hsa.ie
The Irish Health and Safety Authority provides specific guidance for Irish organizations and has a dedicated section for small to medium-sized enterprises.

http://agency.osha.eu.int
The European Agency for Safety and Health at Work looks at risks at work, and how to integrate health and safety into other policy areas, such as education, public health and research at a European level.

http://epp.eurostat.ec.europa.eu/portal/page/portal/health/introduction
Eurostat is the statistical office of the EU and its task is to provide the EU with statistics at European level that enable comparisons between countries and regions, in this case comparisons on health and safety statistics across European countries.

 For extra resources including videos and further skills development guidance go to: www.palgrave.com/business/carbery

# 12 MANAGING THE EMPLOYMENT RELATIONSHIP

Michelle O'Sullivan

By the end of this chapter you will be able to:

## LEARNING OUTCOMES

- Explain the nature of the employment relationship
- Describe the key theoretical perspectives on employment relations
- Outline the role and functions of employee representatives and employer organizations as actors in the employment relationship
- Explain some of the key changes in employment relations since the late twentieth century
- Outline the rationale for employee participation in the workplace and the types of employee voice mechanisms
- Explain the nature of conflict, trends in relation to collective industrial action and conflict resolution procedures
- Describe the role and function of state dispute resolution bodies

© MANKALE/FOTOLIA

This chapter discusses ...

## INTRODUCTION

One of the most difficult parts of the job of a manager, team leader or HR professional is managing the employment relationship. As well as being involved in critical functions such as recruitment and selection and performance management, managers are often placed at the 'intersection' between employees and employers and therefore have key roles in managing the different interests and perspectives of both. To do so effectively, they need to understand what those interests are, how these interests are represented by employee and employer representative bodies, how the employment relationship is regulated, how conflict arises and can be resolved. This chapter will explore these issues in a comparative context, outlining the key national features of employment relations in the USA, the UK and Ireland.

## SPOTLIGHT ON SKILLS

You have started a new job as manager in a call centre with 100 employees. In the middle of the call centre area, an irate and upset employee approaches you. He raises his voice and complains about the behaviour of another colleague.

1   As the manager, how do you think you might handle this situation?

2   What suggestions do you have so that the call centre can improve employment relations?

3   In particular, what mechanisms could the company introduce to deal with problems, preventing a similar shouting match by an employee?

To help you answer the questions above, visit www.palgrave.com/business/carbery and watch the video of Sinead Mullins talking about employment relations.

## THE NATURE OF THE EMPLOYMENT RELATIONSHIP

The manager's role of managing the demands and expectations of their employees and their own senior managers and the employer is a difficult one because of the complexity of the employment relationship. As Brown and Rea (1995: 364) succinctly note: 'the employment contract is rarely in the form of a tidy document. Its content has to be deduced from successive layers of both written and unwritten rules.' In addition to factors such as personalities and human emotions, there are underlying structural reasons why the employment relationship is such a complex one. One reason is that the exchange that takes place between an employer and employee is difficult to define or 'pin down' when the relationship begins. On commencing employment, a new employee will generally be told what salary and benefits they will receive, while employers buy 'employees' capacity to work which requires direction' (Sisson, 2008: 14). Companies have different ways of ensuring that employees do what they want them to do. Some companies try to control employees' behaviour through, for example, strict supervision and penalties for not complying with rules. Other companies offer employees good pay and conditions, and decision-making autonomy to encourage them to be committed to their job. This vagueness in the exchange between an employer and employee can lead to disagreements over what constitutes a 'fair day's pay' (D'Art and Turner, 2006: 524).

A second reason for the complexity of the employment relationship is power. It is argued the differential in power between an employer and an employee is a key feature of the employment relationship (D'Art and Turner, 2006). First, employers' resources are greater than employees. Second, the employment relationship is a hierarchical one, in which managers direct employees to fulfil tasks and enforce employee obligations (Sisson, 2008). Power becomes particularly important when there are specific differences of interests. Employees generally want higher pay, job security, career progression and training, and employers generally want to maximize their human resources to achieve profit. For much of the employment relationship, employers and employees cooperate with each other. However, Sisson (2008: 19) notes that: 'the potential for specific conflicts of interest is ever present and that the expressions of such conflicts … is not just a matter of faulty procedures, "bad" management or wilful employees'. When conflict does arise, both sides may exert power to try to force the other party to give in (Lewis et al., 2003). To reduce the potential for conflict to escalate, many companies use mechanisms such as **grievance procedures** and **disciplinary procedures**, collective bargaining and other forms of employee voice (discussed later) to address differing interests.

Do employers and employees have the same interests and goals or are they different? Is conflict in an organization a good or bad thing?

## THEORETICAL PERSPECTIVES

Theoretical perspectives help us to analyse employment relations in an organization and some of the most influential perspectives were developed by Alan Fox in the 1960s. The first perspective he developed was unitarism. The underlying assumption of unitarism is that employers and employees have the same interests, goals and values and so conflict should not exist in an organization. As employees have the same interests as their employer, there is only one source of authority in the organization (management) and it does not see a need to gain employees' consent to make decisions (Salamon, 2000). As employees should have the same interests as management, there is no need for trade unions – they are seen as troublemakers. If conflict does occur, the unitarist perspective does not view the reasons for this as being related to the nature of employment, such as an imbalance of power. Instead, conflict is believed to occur because of personality clashes and poor communications. While, at first glance, unitarism might seem utopian and unrealistic, Storey (1992) notes that many elements of HRM are unitarist in nature. According to Wallace et al. (2004), unitarist management can manifest itself through two management styles – paternalistic and authoritarian:

**Grievance procedure** – step-by-step process an employee must follow to get their complaint addressed satisfactorily. The formal (written) complaint moves from one level of authority (of the firm and the union) to the next higher level. Grievance procedures are typically included in union (collective bargaining) agreements

**Disciplinary procedure** – written, step-by-step process that a firm commits itself to follow in every case where an employee has to be warned, reprimanded or dismissed. Failure to follow a fair, transparent and uniform disciplinary procedure may result in legal penalties (damages) and/or annulment of the firm's action

**Capitalist system** – an economic system of private enterprise for profit

1 *Paternalistic management:* managers look after employees and use 'soft' HRM practices such as good salaries, benefits to employees, direct communications and teamworking. The purpose of these is to keep employees satisfied, emphasize management as the source of authority, reduce the potential for conflict and prevent unionization.
2 *Authoritarian management:* a more dogmatic management approach, whereby there may be little concern for employees and suppression of any attempts by employees to introduce a trade union into the workplace (Wallace et al., 2004).

Pluralism is a framework with an entirely different perspective of employment relations. Pluralism assumes that the organization is made up of groups with different interests and goals. As there are differing interests, conflict in an organization is inevitable and pluralism accepts the legitimacy of trade unions as representatives of employees. It is management's role to balance the interests of different groups in the organization and it is legitimate to establish mechanisms to address conflict, such as dispute resolution procedures and collective bargaining. These differing interests and any ensuing conflict must not be so great as to be irreparable (Lewis et al., 2003). Those organizations that negotiate with trade unions are based on a pluralist perspective of employment relations. Similarly, governments in many countries have established bodies to help organizations resolve conflict – again reflective of a pluralist perspective.

A more radical perspective on the employment relationship is Marxism, which has been one of the most influential theories in employment relations, sociology, politics and economics over the past 100 years. Karl Marx's ideas have been the subject of extensive analysis in a great many fields, but can only be briefly sketched here. Marx argued that conflict in organizations merely reflected conflict between classes in society – between a minority who are employers (capitalists or bourgeoisie), who own the means of production (companies, assets), and a majority who are workers (proletariat) who only own their labour (Grint, 1991; Salamon, 2000). Marx viewed the **capitalist system** as having negative and alienating effects on workers, because they did not control what they produced, work involved mindless repetition, and workers competed against one another (Grint, 1991). While pluralism views mechanisms for managing conflict, such as dispute resolution procedures, as legitimate and necessary, the Marxist perspective views these mechanisms as advancing the interests of management by not allowing workers' opposing set of interests to be voiced (Salamon, 2000). The value of the Marxist perspective lies in its sophisticated understanding of the employment relationship by relating it to conflict in the wider society – something unitarism and pluralism do not do.

## ACTORS IN THE EMPLOYMENT RELATIONSHIP

The regulation of the employment relationship, in terms of how pay and conditions are set, varies across organizations, industries and countries. In some organizations, pay and conditions are unilaterally set by the employer and in others there is some scope for negotiation between an employer and an individual employee. In other organizations, employees are represented by a trade union and the employer may be a member of an employer organization and both sides negotiate and agree pay and conditions on a collective basis so, for example, all employees would get similar pay increases or similar benefits. Unions remain the dominant employee representative in many countries, particularly Western Europe, but in others, there is more variety, with employees having either no representative or a non-union representative. We now outline the roles and functions of employee representatives and employer organizations.

### Employee representation

Historically, the primary representative of employees has been trade unions. Trade unions are organizations whose aim is to protect and defend the interests of their members, that is, fee-paying individuals usually in a job. They do so by acting collectively because it is argued that acting collectively is the most effective way of challenging employer power (Kelly, 1998). For example, if one employee has a dispute with an employer and decides to take some form of industrial action, it may not have much effect. If a large number of employees take industrial action together, this will interrupt business and be costly to the employer, and so it may persuade the

employer to negotiate with employees or concede to their demands. However, taking industrial action is often a last resort for unions. The most common ways in which they try to protect members' interests are through collective bargaining with employers, lobbying the government for employee-friendly policies, representing members in grievance or disciplinary procedures and providing advice to members. Unions are financed by their members' fees and are staffed by full- or part-time officials. Union officials recruit and organize new members, advise members on their employment rights, and represent members in disputes. Workplaces with a union usually also have workplace representatives or shop stewards. They are employees of the organization who act voluntarily as a union representative in the workplace, effectively acting as the link between the union and the members.

CONSIDER THIS ...

What do you think might be the similarities between student unions and trade unions?

A common feature of employment relations in most countries is the formation of one or more confederation of trade unions. These confederations do not generally represent members in the workplace but act as the voice of the union movement. These include the Trade Union Congress in the UK, the Irish Congress of Trade Unions in the Republic of Ireland, and the American Federation of Labor-Congress of Industrial Organizations and the Change to Win Federation in the USA. These bodies generally devise policies on economic and social issues, organize members, engage in political lobbying, and regulate relations between individual unions (Block, 2006).

There are also forms of non-union employee representation (NER), in which one or more employees act in a representative capacity for other employees 'in dealings with management over issues of mutual concern', such as through committees, forums and works councils (Taras and Kaufman, 2006: 515). Many forms of NER are not involved in bargaining on pay and conditions and, from an employee perspective, may be unsuitable to do so because they are resourced by the employer and are not, therefore, independent (Gollan, 2000). From a management perspective, NER may be introduced to improve communication with employees and enhance employee 'voice' (Taras and Kaufman, 2006) (see below for a discussion of voice).

**CONSIDER THIS...**

From a manager's perspective, what would be the possible advantages and disadvantages of having NER in an organization?

## Employer organizations

Employer organizations represent employer interests nationally and internationally, advise members on HR and industrial relations matters, undertake research and represent members in negotiations with employees and in disputes, although the extent of this varies across organizations. Employer organizations are funded by members' subscription fees. In the UK, many employer associations are affiliated to the Confederation of British Industry, which was formed in 1965, and in Ireland, the largest employer organization is the Irish Business and Employers Confederation, formed in 1993. In Europe, 41 central industrial and employers' federations from 35 countries are affiliated to BusinessEurope, which was founded in 1958 to act as the voice of business and employers in European policy-making. In the USA, there is a much less developed system of employer organizations than in Europe, as the USA has traditionally had lower unionization levels and so there are fewer occurrences of one or multiple employers negotiating collectively with employees. There are some industries where firms organize together to negotiate pay and conditions with trade unions, such as the ports. However, in contrast to the tradition in Europe of employer organizations engaging with trade unions, union avoidance is one of the objectives of some US employer groups (Bamber and Lansbury, 1998; Block, 2006).

## THE CHANGING NATURE OF EMPLOYMENT RELATIONS

### Unionization and collective bargaining

Traditionally, the regulation of the employment relationship in the UK and Ireland was guided by the principal of voluntarism. Voluntarism means minimum intervention by the law; in other words, employers and employees should be free to determine pay and conditions of employment by themselves. As the twentieth century progressed, employers and trade unions in the UK and Ireland voluntarily engaged in collective bargaining. Negotiations often resulted in a voluntary collective agreement, which would stipulate the pay and conditions for all employees in an organization or industry, depending on the situation. Until the late twentieth century, there was very little by way of employment legislation to set standards in the employment relationship, which made collective bargaining all the more important in laying down pay and conditions. If collective bargaining did not result in an agreement but a dispute, there was often no legally right or wrong solution to the dispute but the outcome lay with whichever party exerted the most power.

In the USA, the law has played a more significant role in the union–employer relationship. Under the National Labour Relations Act 1935, a majority of employees in a 'bargaining unit' must either sign authorization cards or vote in an election in favour of a union representing them in collective bargaining and, in this scenario, an employer must negotiate with the union (Block, 2006). A bargaining unit is a group or category of workers represented by a union and covered by a particular agreement. Subsequent to the introduction of the law, unions organized workers in industries such as car manufacturing, steel and coal and the public sector (Bamber and Lansbury, 1998). However, further legislation restricted workers' rights and the process by which unions try to gain collective bargaining rights in the workplace has been cumbersome and hostile. Block (2006: 36) argues that 'the law of organizing has developed in a way that has increased the tools available to employers to resist union organization'. So-called 'union-busting' activities have been reported, whereby employers and their hired consultants use various aggressive tactics to discourage employees from joining a union (Logan, 2002). Historically, then, trade unions in the USA found it more difficult to represent employees in an organization and this affected **union density** rates, which peaked at 35 per cent in 1950 (Taras and Kaufman, 2006).

Trade unions in the USA, the UK and Ireland and many other countries have faced similar challenges, particularly since the early 1980s (see Table 12.1 below). Trade union density in the UK fell by over 22 per cent between 1980 and 2009 and by 20 per cent in Ireland. In

> **Union density** – the proportion of a country's employees who are union members

## 'Bossnappings'

In 2009, two managers of Siemens, the German electrical and engineering group, were released after being held in their offices in France by employees demanding concessions over job cuts. Staff representatives said management had refused to bow to their demands for more generous redundancy terms, but they expected negotiations to continue under the mediation of local government officials. This incident was the latest in a series of so-called 'bossnappings', in which managers in France have been detained by staff to exert pressure in negotiations over wages or layoffs. Other targets included François-Henri Pinault, the boss of luxury retail group PPR, who was blocked in his car outside the company's Paris headquarters for several hours, and the managers of French factories owned by Sony, Caterpillar and 3M, who were held overnight and released unharmed. At a Scapa factory, which makes adhesive tape for the auto industry, those held were the HR manager, the finance director and the European operations director, who are all British, and the French general manager. Ian Bushell, the company's European finance director, described the hostage-taking as a 'nonaggressive action', adding that the unions had brought the four managers dinner. So far none of the bossnappers has been prosecuted and none of the bosses hurt. During his

HRM IN THE NEWS

bossnapping in March, Luc Rousselet, 3M manager, told reporters 'everything's fine', and workers brought him a meal of mussels and French fries for dinner.

Seizing bosses is not a new tactic in France, with examples of bossnapping dating back decades in a country famous for its strikes and known as a place where workers aren't afraid to put up a fight. Reserved for when other, more orthodox forms of protest are going nowhere, bossnapping is the final card played by a workforce at the end of its tether. French President Nicolas Sarkozy promised to put a stop to the fast-spreading practice of bossnapping: 'We are a nation of laws. I won't allow this sort of thing.' Sarkozy, who first gained a national following as France's law and order interior minister, could easily call in police to liberate kidnapped bosses. But should he? It could be a risky political move. In a poll for *Paris Match*, 30% said they 'approved of taking managers hostage', 63% said they 'understood but don't approve', and only 7% said they 'condemned' the practice. It's a situation that more and more French factory managers and HR directors are finding themselves caught up in. With the French economy shrinking at the fastest pace in 30 years, companies are slashing jobs, closing plants and moving production to lower wage sites

abroad. The phenomenon has sparked a growth in providers offering advice for executives worried they could be locked up. One Paris management consultant has begun promoting a 'survival kit' for potential bossnapping victims, including a change of clothes and a mobile phone preprogrammed with the numbers of family, police and a psychologist.

### Questions

1 Company managers who were 'bossnapped' did not prosecute the employees. Why do you think they made that decision?
2 'Bossnappings' are an extreme form of industrial action. What other types of action can be used by employees to achieve their interests?

### Sources

Batty, D. (2009) French workers release 'bossnapped' British bosses, *The Guardian*, 8 April, www. guardian.co.uk/business/2009/ apr/08/bossnapping-france-scapa.

*Huffington Post* (2009) 'Boss-napping' prevention taught by French consultant, 24 May, www. huffingtonpost.com/2009/04/23/boss-napping-prevention-t_n_190554.html.

Lagrange, C., MacKenzie, J. and Balmer, C. (2010) Siemens execs held in latest French 'bossnapping', 2 March, www.reuters.com/ article/2010/03/02/us-siemens-france-hostages-idUSTRE62140J20100302.

Matlack, C. (2009) Sarkozy's 'bossnapping' dilemma, *Business Week*, 8 April.

the USA, union density almost halved between 1980 and 2009, having started at a relatively low level compared with the UK and Ireland. These declines have occurred despite different political systems. In the UK, Conservative-led governments during the 1980s

restricted the power of trade unions. In contrast, in Ireland, successive governments negotiated national wage agreements with trade unions between 1987 and 2009, at which point the agreements collapsed during the economic crisis. In these agreements, trade unions participated in economic and social policy-making but this did not reverse the decline in unionization. The most frequently cited reasons for union density decline in the USA, the UK, Ireland and other countries are:

- globalization and the increasing power of companies to move to different locations
- the growing power of employers to resist unionization
- less union-friendly political environments
- changes in the labour market, with a decline in union-strong industries such as manufacturing and coal and the growth in union-weak industries like services (Roche and Ashmore, 2002; Wallace et al., 2004; Schmitt and Mitukiewicz, 2011).

Union density is generally higher in the public than private sectors, estimated at 57 per cent in the UK and 37 per cent in the USA (www.worker-participation.eu; www.bls.gov). However, this stronghold of unions has come under severe pressure since the onset of the global economic crisis and recession. In the USA, a number of states passed laws in 2011, which weakened or abolished collective bargaining rights of public sector employees (Freeman and Han, 2012).

**Table 12.1** Trade union density in the USA, the UK and Ireland, 1980 and 2009 (%)

|                | 1980 | 2009 |
|----------------|------|------|
| Ireland        | 54.3 | 33.7 |
| United Kingdom | 49.7 | 27.2 |
| United States  | 22.1 | 11.8 |

*Source:* www.oecd-ilibrary.org/statistics

### CONSIDER THIS...

What do you think are the consequences of the decline in unionization for organizations and employees?

## Individual employment law

The growth in employment legislation has been one of the most significant developments in employment relations in many developed countries during the twentieth century. Unlike collective employment relations law, which regulates the trade union–employer

relationship, there are a large number of employment laws, which bestow individuals with certain rights and employers with obligations. In the UK and the Republic of Ireland, the primary impetus for introducing legislation has been the requirement to enforce EU Directives in a wide range of employment matters, including working time, health and safety, parental leave, maternity and adoptive leave, part-time, fixed-term and agency work, and equality ▶ **Chapter 5** ◀. Both countries have also introduced laws on matters not determined by the EU such as the minimum wage. It should be noted that these employment laws lay down minimum standards and employers can choose to give benefits to employees that go beyond minimum legislation. For example, some employees get more holidays than they are legally entitled to. Managers and HR professionals need to be aware of the provisions of employment laws so as to avoid employees taking cases against their organizations, or to be able to provide adequate defences if cases do arise.

In the UK and Ireland, if an individual believes that one of their employment rights has been breached, then the onus is on them to take a claim against their employer to one of the state bodies (discussed later). Most pieces of legislation dictate which state body the claim must be referred to and they also set time limits within which the referral must be made. Each piece of legislation will also set down the forms of redress or remedy that are available, should a state body decide that an employment right has been breached. Redress usually takes the form of financial compensation and is often a proportion, or multiple, of someone's wages. Similar to the UK and Ireland, the USA also introduced a series of national individual employment laws in the 1980s and 90s in the areas of minimum wages, termination of employment, discrimination, and health and safety, and the Wage and Hour Division of the Department of Labor enforces many national employment laws. However, in relation to dismissals and hiring fixed-term workers, Venn (2009) notes that the USA and the UK are among the countries with the least strict employment protection in the Organisation for Economic Co-operation and Development (OECD).

### BUILDING YOUR SKILLS

As a line manager, would you have mechanisms in place to enable employees to express their opinions? If so, what kind?

# EMPLOYEE PARTICIPATION AND VOICE

Some organizations try to encourage their employees to be more committed to their jobs by seeking their views and including them in decision-making. Indeed, the Davignon Group (1997), an EU high-level expert group on workers' participation and involvement, concluded that if companies want skilled, committed, mobile employees, they should be involved in decision-making at all levels in a company and not just follow management instructions. Employee participation occurs when employees have influence over decisions in an organization (Busck et al., 2010). Participation can be direct, through individual employees or teams, or indirect through employee representatives. Busck et al. (2010) argue that direct participation often involves employees having an influence over operational issues such as job performance, whereas indirect participation suggests more strategic-level influence. In Germany, for example, employee representatives on works councils have significant influence on company decisions and employee representatives have a legal right to sit on the supervisory board of large companies. In order for employee participation to take place, employee voice mechanisms must be in place (Wilkinson and Fay, 2011). Employee voice has been defined as 'an opportunity to have "a say" but this does not necessarily mean that employees will have influence or participation' (Wilkinson and Fay, 2011: 66). Voice is important for employees, enabling them to express their opinions and grievances and act as 'industrial citizens' (Dundon et al., 2005). Employers have introduced voice mechanisms for a range of reasons, such as wanting to improve the employment relations environment, improve productivity and quality, and prevent employees from joining a union (Dundon et al., 2004).

Organizations' choice of voice mechanism can be influenced by the country of origin of the company, the size of organization and the industry (Lavelle et al., 2010). Laws can also influence voice. A number of EU Directives have favoured indirect forms of voice. The 1994 Works Council Directive (94/45/EC) requires large multinational companies to have a works council, in which management consults with employee representatives across countries. Similarly, under the 2006 Information and Consultation of Employee Directive (202/14/EC), all organizations, except small firms, must inform and consult employee representatives about certain company decisions such as restructuring.

Studies show the growing incidence of direct voice, where individual employees are involved in decisions affecting their jobs and immediate work environment (Lavelle et al., 2010: 396). In the UK, the incidence of union-only voice dropped from 18 per cent of workplaces to 4 per cent between 1984 and 2004, while 'direct voice rose dramatically'; for example, the number of team briefings doubled (Bryson et al., 2009: 6). A large-scale study of multinational companies in Ireland found that many preferred to use direct voice mechanisms to distribute information, for example through team briefings, newsletters or emails, a company intranet, meetings, problem-solving groups and attitude surveys (Lavelle et al., 2010).

## BUILDING YOUR SKILLS

From a manager or employer position, on what kinds of decisions would you seek the input of employees?

# THE NATURE OF CONFLICT AND ITS RESOLUTION

A pattern evident across developed and developing countries since the early 1980s has been a fall in the number of **strikes** and **working days lost** (Wallace and O'Sullivan, 2006). Table 12.2 shows that there have been significant reductions in working days lost in the USA, the UK and Ireland. While some might suggest that the fall in strikes is reflective of a 'better' employment relations environment, Wallace and O'Sullivan (2006) argue that other factors explain the decline, pointing to globalization and a more neoliberal political environment, which favours minimal state intervention in the employment relationship and is opposed to unions. In addition, counter to the 'better

**Strike** – a work stoppage caused by the refusal of employees to work, in order to persuade an employer to concede to their demands

**Working days lost** – a measure of strike activity, calculated by multiplying the number of persons involved by the number of normal working days during which they were involved in the dispute

relations' argument, evidence from the UK and Ireland shows that there has been a significant rise in the number of employment law cases taken by employees against their employer (Colling, 2006; Teague and Thomas, 2008).

**Table 12.2** Working days lost in Ireland, the UK and the USA, 1979 and 2009

|  | 1979 | 2009 |
| --- | --- | --- |
| Ireland | 1.4 million | 329,000 |
| United Kingdom | 29 million | 435,000 |
| United States | 20 million | 124,000 |

*Note:* Each country has different definitions of working days lost.

*Sources:* von Prondzynski, 1998; European Industrial Relations Observatory, 2010a; Bureau of Labor Statistics, 2012

Many organizations recognize that mechanisms are needed to be able to address and resolve conflict in the workplace. Conflict can take many guises. Individual employees could express conflict by raising a grievance with their manager, being frequently absent from work, leaving the organization, or taking a legal case against an employer. Collective forms of conflict, involving groups of employees or trade unions, include strikes, sabotage, refusal to work overtime, sit-ins and work-to-rules, where employees work strictly to the letter of their contract. Employers can also engage in conflict through, for example, lockouts, where they prevent employees from entering a workplace (Wallace et al., 2004).

It is generally good employment relations practice for companies to introduce policies and procedures. In addition, particularly in the UK and Ireland, companies may be required by law to have, for example, procedures governing dismissals and equality ▶ **Chapter 5** ◀. This is to ensure that due process and natural justice are followed. In a disciplinary/dismissals situation, this means that:

● employees would be informed of company rules and what would happen if they're breached
● employees must be allowed to defend themselves
● employees must be allowed representation
● there must be an appeals mechanism if an employee is dissatisfied with a management decision.

Similarly, if employees believe they have a grievance about a workplace issue, the procedures should inform them what steps they can take to have their grievance brought to management's attention. Managers should ensure that they familiarize themselves with company

procedures to help them deal with employment problems. If a company does not have procedures, managers can refer to state-provided guidelines from the Advisory, Conciliation and Arbitration Service (Acas) in the UK and the Labour Relations Commission in Ireland. US employers do not have the same level of obligations as in the UK and Ireland in relation to dismissals procedures. The legal situation differs in the USA, where the principle of 'employment-at-will' exists, whereby employers can dismiss an employee without reason except in certain situations such as discrimination. In the equality area, the US Equal Employment Opportunity Commission offers guidance to employers. Unlike the UK and Ireland, in the USA, if a company does include grievance and disciplinary procedures in a collective agreement, the outcome of the procedure is enforceable in court (Block, 2006).

## State agencies for conflict resolution

Over half of OECD countries have special courts or tribunals to hear employment disputes (Venn, 2009). Some provide conciliation and mediation services, in which an independent third party seeks to encourage a settlement between employers and employees, and others provide arbitration services in which a third party will hear the arguments of an employer and employee in dispute and make a decision (European Industrial Relations Observatory, 2010b). In the UK, Acas aims to promote better employment relations by providing advice on workplace problems and offering conciliation, mediation and arbitration services. If Acas services do not result in resolution, employment tribunals are available, which are judicial bodies with legally qualified and lay members that investigate claims made under employment legislation. Decisions can generally be appealed on a point of law to the Employment Appeal Tribunal, whose decisions are binding unless appealed to the Court of Appeal.

In the Republic of Ireland, five state bodies assist employers and employees to resolve disputes. Two generally help resolve collective disputes between employers and trade unions: the Labour Court, which makes recommendations, and the Labour Relations Commission, which provides conciliation, mediation and advisory services. Two bodies are responsible for making decisions in individual employment law cases: the Rights Commissioner Service and the Employment Appeals Tribunal. Lastly, the Equality Tribunal investigates claims made under employment equality law. With this multiplicity of bodies, the state dispute resolution system has become complex and, in 2012, the government produced proposals to merge the functions of the five bodies into two.

In the USA, the National Labor Relations Board is a quasi-judicial body that enforces the National Labor Relations Act 1935. It supervises employee elections on union representation and investigates claims by employers or employees of unfair labour practices. The Federal Mediation and Conciliation Service provides mediation, conciliation and voluntary arbitration to assist in employment disputes and help employers and unionized employees negotiate a contract and advise organizations in developing dispute resolution systems. There also state bodies that assist employment relations in specific sectors, such as public sector employment (the Federal Labor Relations Authority) and railway and airline industries (the National Mediation Board).

## Firefighting on the Job

You have been in a new job for two months as an operations and HR manager in a fast-growing apps development and software company started by a college friend, the CEO. The company is only two years old but already has 20 employees. There is no HR department as your friend has been doing all the HR-related tasks. However, she has no HR qualification or experience and there are no written procedures in the company.

Since you started the job, you've been concerned about employment relations because you've heard rumours that some employees are not happy about some of their working conditions and their treatment by the CEO. While the employees love working in an exciting, fast-paced industry, they work long hours with no overtime pay and they are often required to cut short their annual leave to travel, at short notice, long distances to trade fairs. In addition, four employees left the company recently. Three resigned and one was dismissed over an issue about claiming expenses. An employee has said to you that nobody is clear what expenses to claim, because while one employee was dismissed, another was kept in the job even though they didn't claim correctly either. You've asked the CEO about why three people resigned and she said that they wanted compensation for their holidays being shortened, but the CEO told them they were lucky to have jobs. Now the CEO shows you a letter from a state tribunal saying that the employee is taking a case against the company for unfair dismissal. As the new HR professional, you realize that much work needs to be done to improve employment relations.

1 You decide that grievance and disciplinary procedures are needed in the company and you need to research how to write them. Using the code of practice guidelines issued by the British Acas or Irish Labour Relations Commission, identify the key principles of such procedures and what rights should be afforded to an employee.

2 Identify other workplace issues in the company that procedures could be written for.

3 If the CEO is reluctant to introduce procedures, what benefits of having procedures might you highlight to her?

4 You are concerned that a state body could become involved in a workplace issue involving a current or former employee. To prepare for any potential action, you should research what would be involved in a UK employment tribunal hearing, an Irish Employment Appeals Tribunal hearing or a US Wage and Hour Division investigation.

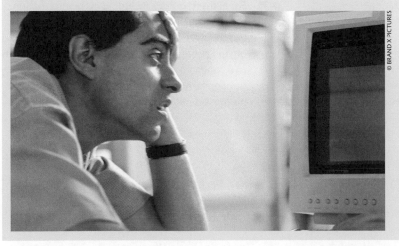

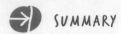 SUMMARY

This chapter has outlined that the employment relationship is a complex one and consequently a range of institutions have developed around it. There is no one dominant or best type of employment relations system or set of practices. Instead, a range of employment relations practices have emerged. Given the complexity of the employment relationship, conflict is inevitable and can take various forms. Many organizations have procedures to prevent conflict from escalating, but if problems cannot be addressed within the workplace, a variety of state bodies have been created in each country to offer independent assistance, as an alternative to cases being processed through civil courts. Many companies have instituted direct forms of communication and employee voice to share information, deal with conflict and include employees in decision-making, although the extent of this varies hugely. Some companies negotiate with trade unions, others have NER, while others have both or none. The choices companies make may depend on internal factors, such as employer attitudes to employment relations, the size and type of organization and external factors like the law.

 CHAPTER REVIEW QUESTIONS

1  How do the unitarism, pluralism and Marxist perspectives view the employment relationship?
2  What are the different services generally offered by state dispute resolution bodies?
3  What is the difference between the functions of employee representatives and employer organizations?
4  What are the common reasons for increasing employee participation in an organization?

 FURTHER READING

Creaton, S. (2004) *Ryanair: How a Small Irish Airline Conquered Europe*, London: Aurum Press.

Eurofound (2010) *Individual Disputes at the Workplace: Alternative Dispute Resolution*, Dublin: Eurofound.
Hiltrop, J.M. and Udall, S. (1995) *The Essence of Negotiation*, London: Prentice Hall.
Kaufman, B.E. (2004) *The Global Evolution of Industrial Relations: Events, Ideas and the IIRA*, Geneva: ILO.
Social Science & Parliamentary Affairs Team (2011) *Trade Unions, Collective Bargaining and the Economic Crisis: Where Now?*, Spotlight, no. 4, Dublin: Oireachtas Library & Research Service.

 USEFUL WEBSITES

www.acas.org.uk
The Advisory, Conciliation and Arbitration Service (Acas) website offers information and advice on common HR practices and issues and handling conflict in the workplace.

www.eurofound.europa.eu/eiro
The European Industrial Relations Observatory (EIRO) website contains news and comparative studies on employment relations in Europe.

www.dol.gov
The US Department of Labor website has information and guidance on labour laws.

www.workplacerelations.ie
Workplace Relations is an Irish government website with information on state dispute resolution mechanisms and employee and employer rights and obligations under employment law.

 For extra resources, including more information on managing the employment relationship in an Irish context (including trade unions, employer organizations, the nature of employment relations and conflict and its resolution), videos and skills development guidance go to: www.palgrave.com/business/carbery

# 13 INTERNATIONAL HUMAN RESOURCE MANAGEMENT

Jonathan Lavelle

By the end of this chapter you will be able to:

## *LEARNING OUTCOMES*

- Outline the differences between domestic and international human resource management
- Discuss the impact of globalization on international human resource management (IHRM)
- Examine the influences on the transfer of HRM practices within multinational companies
- Identify the key issues in the recruitment, selection and preparation of employees undertaking international assignments
- Describe the complexities in compensating and managing the performance of employees on international assignments
- Explain the importance of the repatriation stage in the management of employees on international assignments

© PHOTOALTO

This chapter discusses ...

## INTRODUCTION

Up to this point, this book has largely focused on managing HR in companies that operate in only one country. However, as we know, a company may have operations across a number of different countries and managing HR is just as, if not more, important in companies that operate in an international context. This chapter will examine the issue of managing HR in companies that operate across a number of different countries, namely the field of international human resource management (IHRM). There has been a growing interest in IHRM, with Scullion (2005: 9–10) providing a summary of the reasons that have contributed to this interest:

- The growth in and significance of multinational companies (MNCs) and small and medium-sized enterprises operating at an international level has meant that IHRM is of interest to a increasing number of companies.
- There are many problems associated with internationalizing the HRM function and effectively managing IHRM is seen as a key determinant of success or failure in international business (Black et al., 1999; Brewster et al., 2007).
- There is a need for a better understanding of how to manage employees on international assignments, particularly with a shortage of international managers (Scullion, 1994).
- HRM plays an important role in companies moving to a more networked type of organizational structure – multiple organizations work together to produce goods and services – in the implementation and control in MNCs (Scullion and Starkey, 2000), in the process of organizational learning in international companies, and greatly facilitates the transfer of knowledge across borders (Gooderham and Nordhaug, 2003; Minbaeva, 2005).

This chapter addresses many of these issues identified by Scullion (2005), particularly understanding what IHRM is about, the challenges of internationalizing the HRM function, and exploring the issues involved in the management of employees on international assignments. First, we define what IHRM is and how we might understand it, and discuss how IHRM differs to what we refer to as 'domestic HRM'. We then focus on the impact of globalization on HRM before considering the transfer of HRM practices within MNCs. We go on to explore a

key function in IHRM, namely the management of employees on international assignments. Finally, we look at expatriate failure and some alternative arrangements.

## SPOTLIGHT ON SKILLS

The corporate headquarters of a US MNC has developed a new induction policy and is keen to transfer this new policy to its foreign operation in Brazil. Identify the advantages and disadvantages of sending an expatriate to manage this process.

An important issue for an expatriate going on an international assignment is the quality of life at the foreign location. Evaluate quality of life issues for an American expatriate travelling to Germany for a long-term international assignment. What issues are likely to be of concern?

To help you consider the issues above, visit www.palgrave.com/business/carbery and watch the video of Claire Campion talking about expatriate issues.

## INTERNATIONAL HUMAN RESOURCE MANAGEMENT

IHRM is a relatively new field, emerging largely due to the pressures of globalization and growth of companies operating internationally. For the purposes of this chapter, the focus is on HRM within MNCs. While there are many ways of defining what an MNC is, it generally refers to a company that has operations across different countries, often called 'foreign subsidiaries', but is managed centrally by a corporate headquarters (HQ) or parent company located in the country from which the company originated. Some of the largest and most well-known MNCs include IBM, Google, Samsung Electronics, Toyota, Axa, Facebook and General Electric. Traditionally, the field of study of IHRM largely focused on the issue of expatriation, concentrating on the management of expatriates on international assignments. The field of study has developed, however, and now encompasses a greater variety of HR issues. A commonly used definition identifies IHRM as 'the HRM issues and problems arising from the internationalisation of business and the HRM strategies, policies and practices which firms pursue in response to the internationalisation process' (Scullion, 1995: 352).

Morgan (1986) provides a useful model to gain a broader understanding of IHRM. According to Morgan (1986), IHRM involves the interaction of the following three dimensions:

> **Expatriation** – the process of transferring an employee to other international operations of the MNC to carry out a particular assignment
>
> **Expatriates** – also known as 'international assignees', are employees who undertake international assignments

1  The three broad HR activities of procurement, allocation and utilization. These include:
   - employee resourcing: HR planning, recruitment and selection, induction, retention ▶ **Chapters 2, 3 and 4** ◀
   - performance management: performance management systems, performance appraisal ▶ **Chapter 7** ◀
   - reward management: reward packages, performance based pay ▶ **Chapter 8** ◀
   - training and development: learning and development for employees and the organization, learning styles ▶ **Chapters 9 and 10** ◀
   - employment relations: the employment relationship, key employment relations actors, employment legislation ▶ **Chapter 12** ◀.
2  The three national or country categories involved in HRM tasks:
   - *host country:* where a foreign subsidiary of the MNC is located
   - *home country (or country of origin):* where the MNC originated from or is headquartered
   - *third countries:* may be a source of labour, finance and other inputs.
3  The three categories of employees that exist in MNCs:
   - host country nationals – HCNs
   - parent country nationals – PCNs
   - third country nationals – TCNs.

Below, Table 13.1 provides a description of each of these types of employees.

A key question at this point is how does IHRM differ from domestic HRM? The broad answer is that the functions are quite similar but the issues are more complex. Dowling et al. (2008: 5–8) identify a number of examples as to how IHRM differs from domestic HRM (see Dowling et al. 2008 for a more comprehensive discussion):

1  *More HR activities:* IHRM deals with HR issues that have a strong international aspect, which domestic HRM generally does not have to deal with, for example international relocation.
2  *A need for a broader perspective:* Generally, domestic HR involves developing and implementing HR policies and practices for a single national group of employees, although this is changing as workforces become more diverse. IHRM involves developing and implementing HR policies and practices for more than one national group of employees, for example PCNs, HCNs and TCNs.
3  *Greater involvement in employees' lives:* In IHRM, there is a greater need for involvement in employees' lives. For example, in supporting expatriates on international assignments, it is often necessary to deal with issues around housing, visas, taxation, healthcare, cost of living and the expatriate's family circumstances.
4  *Managing different employees:* The need to manage different categories of employees and how this changes as the mix of these categories – PCNs, TCNs and HCNs – varies.
5  *Risk exposure:* The human and financial consequences of failure in the international arena are more severe than in domestic business.
6  *Broader external influences:* Major external factors that can influence IHRM are the type of government, the state of the economy, and the generally accepted practices of doing business in all the host countries in which the MNC operates. Again, these external issues are confined to one country when looking at domestic HRM.

Having understood what IHRM is, we now explore some of the HRM issues and problems that MNCs face within international business – the impact of globalization on IHRM and the transfer of HRM practices within MNCs.

**Table 13.1** Types of employees

| | |
|---|---|
| **Host country nationals (HCNs)** | HCNs are employees from the country the foreign subsidiary is located in; for example, an Irish national working in a US-owned MNC in Ireland<br>HCNs are most likely to fill mid-level and lower level jobs, but may fill more senior positions<br>Advantages of filling more senior positions with HCNs include their in-depth knowledge of the local business environment, provides career opportunities for local employees, and is cheaper than using PCNs or TCNs<br>Disadvantages include difficulties for the MNC HQ to coordinate, control and communicate with subsidiaries as HCNs may be unfamiliar with HQ, and HCNs may lack the required technical and managerial competence for the job |
| **Parent country nationals (PCNs)** | PCNs are employees from the country where the MNC originated from or is headquartered; for example, a US national working in a US-owned MNC<br>PCNs are generally used to fill upper level and technical positions<br>Advantages of using PCNs include their ability to help control the MNC's foreign subsidiaries and transfer corporate philosophy/culture and expertise<br>Disadvantages include the high cost of sending PCNs to international assignments and issues around inequality, such as restricting career opportunities for local employees, and pay, as PCNs are often paid more than local employees |
| **Third country nationals (TCNs)** | TCNs are employees that come from neither the host nor the parent country, that is, they come from third countries; for example, a German national working in a US-owned MNC in Ireland<br>TCNs are often used for upper level and technical positions<br>Advantages include that they may have a better understanding of the local environment due to geographical proximity and they may possess important technical and managerial competencies<br>Disadvantages include difficulties in returning TCNs back to their country as there may not be an appropriate position for them, they often may be viewed as substitutes for PCNs, and the country from which they originate may not have a good relationship with the host country, for example India and Pakistan |

*Source:* Based on Collings and Scullion, 2006

# GLOBALIZATION AND IHRM

'Globalization' is an often used term but, as Sparrow et al. (2004) noted, a phenomenon that is not easily or well defined. Briscoe et al. (2012: 15) state that globalization generally refers 'to the ever-increasing interaction, interconnectedness, and integration of people, companies and cultures and countries'. MNCs are seen as the key drivers of globalization (Ferner and Hyman, 1998), with FDI dramatically increasing in the past ten years (United Nations Conference on Trade and Development, 2008). A glance at the statistics illustrates the role of MNCs in the internationalization of business. For example, in 2007, FDI inflows reached a record $1,833 billion, surpassing the previous peak in 2000. Also in 2007, MNCs' FDI stock exceeded $15 trillion, their sales amounted to $31 trillion and the value-added activity (gross product) of foreign subsidiaries globally accounted for 11 per cent

> **Globalization** – the opening up of national markets and the creation of a global economy through the deregulation of trade, growth in foreign direct investment (FDI), movement of people and capital, and advances in information technology

of GDP (United Nations Conference on Trade and Development, 2008).

Globalization has had a significant impact on HRM, most notably on the development of IHRM as a field of study. One particular area where globalization impacts on HRM is in relation to the debate about the convergence or divergence of management practice. Scholars have debated whether HRM is becoming similar across all countries, the convergence thesis, or whether it will continue to differ across countries, the divergence thesis. Proponents of the convergence thesis (Harbison and Myers, 1959; Kerr et al., 1960) point to the increasing pressures of globalization on companies, particularly those that operate in an international context. These common pressures, it is claimed, will lead to companies adopting similar responses, leading to similarity in management practice across companies. According to this school of thought, we are likely to see a set of dominant or 'best practice' set of HRM policies emerge to deal with these pressures. It is suggested that these best practices are likely to reflect a US model of HRM, given the significance of the US way of doing business. Proponents of the divergence thesis (Hofstede, 1980; DiMaggio and Powell, 1991; Scott, 1995; Whitley, 2000; Hall and Soskice, 2001) disagree with the notion of convergence and argue that, far from converging, HRM policies and practices are likely to become more different across countries because of institutional and cultural reasons. For example, each country has its own unique mix of institutions – such as educational and training institutions, financial institutions, industrial relations actors, government agencies – and culture – people's values, beliefs, attitudes and behaviours – so they will continue to have HRM policies and practices consistent with their cultural and institutional values. The evidence to date regarding this debate is largely inconclusive in terms of support for either side (Katz and Darbishire, 2000; Brewster et al., 2004, 2008; Pudelko and Harzing, 2007).

**Country of origin effects** – the influence the country from which the MNC originates has on HRM in its foreign subsidiaries

## CONSIDER THIS...

Many scholars have suggested that HRM policies and practices are likely to converge globally. This largely means that the practice of HRM will be the same, regardless of the country context. How likely do you think it is that this convergence of HRM policies and practices will happen?

## The transfer of HRM practices in MNCs

A major debate within IHRM is the extent to which MNCs transfer their HRM practices across their operations. MNCs have the ability to transfer practices to all or some of their operations globally, meaning that HRM practices developed in operations in one country (usually at the corporate HQ) may be transferred to operations in other countries. Not all MNCs look to transfer their HRM practices, however, and even where they do, this transfer of practices can be contested or disrupted by foreign operations (Edwards, 2011). Edwards and Ferner (2002) and Edwards (2011) identify four factors that influence the transfer of HRM practices across national borders within MNCs – country of origin effects, dominance effects, international integration, and host country effects (Figure 13.1), which we now briefly discuss.

### Country of origin effects

The country from which the MNC originates exerts a distinct effect on the way labour is managed (Ferner, 1997), giving rise to **country of origin effects**. A range of sources indicate that even the largest MNCs retain strong roots in their home country. For example, the majority of sales, assets, employment, financial resources and research and development activity are likely to be located within the country of origin. Furthermore, individuals from the country of origin are likely to hold the most senior managerial positions within the

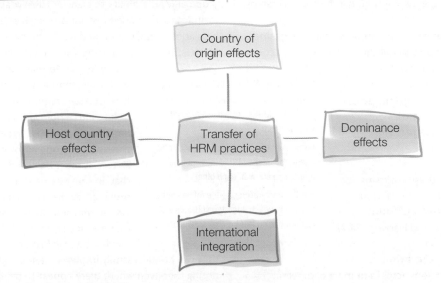

**Figure 13.1** Factors that influence the transfer of HRM practices

company. These strong roots in the home country mean that senior managers at the company HQ may seek to transfer HRM practices to their foreign subsidiaries (Ferner, 1997). In other words, many foreign subsidiaries' HRM practices resemble those of the parent company back in the country of origin. For example, in Ireland, a large-scale survey of MNCs found evidence of strong country of origin effects, particularly among US MNCs (Lavelle et al., 2009). As time goes on and the MNC evolves and becomes more international, the country of origin effect may weaken. For example, it may be the case that there is no apparent benefit to transferring home country practices and it is more beneficial to look outside the country of origin for best practices.

## Dominance effects

Dominance effects relate to the dominance of the economy where the practices originate. This notion of dominance effects largely originates from the work of Smith and Meiskins (1995), who argue that there is a clear hierarchy of economies within the international system, with economies at the top of this hierarchy enjoying an influential position. Traditionally, the US economy was seen as the dominant player and thus many countries looked to it as the source of best practices. Managers within MNCs, both at the parent company and in foreign subsidiaries, may look to implement HRM practices from these dominant economies. Edwards (2011) identifies a number of problems with the dominance idea. These include:

- its reliance on the assumption that there is a hierarchy of economies
- that differences between economies can be explained by superior organizational and management practices
- the assumption that a homogeneous set of structures and practices exist that operate across firms, and that countries can identify and emulate them (Edwards, 2011).

Notwithstanding these criticisms, the dominance effect retains value in explaining the transfer of HRM practices (Pudelko and Harzing, 2007).

## International integration

MNCs have operations across a number of different countries, and it is the international integration of these operations that is of interest when considering the transfer of HRM practices. MNCs that are internationally integrated are defined as those that generate inter-unit linkages between their operations across countries (Edwards, 2011). This integration may take many forms (Edwards, 2011):

- *Outsourcing*: operations in one country provide components or services to those in another country.
- *Segmentation*: the roles of operations in different countries are quite distinct from one another. For example, research and development is located in the home country, with production performed in another country.
- *Standardization*: operations in different countries perform similar activities.

Edwards (2011) postulates that the scope for the transfer of HRM practices is limited in MNCs that outsource or segment their international operations as there is no benefit to having standardized practices. However, operations that are standardized are much more likely to benefit from standardized practices and therefore more likely to transfer HRM practices.

## Host country effects

The host country, the country in which the foreign subsidiary operates, can have a significant influence on the transfer of HRM practices, so-called host country effects. There are a number of aspects of the host country's national business system that can limit the scope of MNCs' ability to transfer HRM practices. These include labour market institutions, such as employment legislation, trade unions and works councils, cultural barriers, and lack of specific skills or aptitudes. For example, the German national business system is noted for its high level of coordination between trade unions and employers, emphasis on long-term interests, high levels of trust, and a strong vocational training system. It must be noted, however, that, in some cases, the limitations provided by the national business system may only be partial; for example, it may that HRM practices need to be tweaked or adapted so that they can be successfully implemented. It is also worth noting that even where there appear to be institutional and/or cultural constraints to the transfer of HRM

**Dominance effects** – the influence that dominant economies, like the USA, have on HRM in MNCs, regardless of where they are from or located

**International integration** – how strongly integrated all the MNC's international operations are with each other

**Host country effects** – the influence the country in which a foreign subsidiary is located has on HRM in that subsidiary

practices, these constraints may often be malleable to the influence of large MNCs, particularly MNCs from dominant economies. Collings et al. (2008), for example, note the ability of US MNCs in Ireland to implement HRM practices that are at odds with the host country's institutional environment. MNCs can also pressurize governments to relax regulations and pressurize unions; again Ireland is a case in point here, with MNCs particularly vocal and influential in the drafting of employment legislation implementing EU Directives (*Industrial Relations News*, 2005).

## BUILDING YOUR SKILLS

You are a HR manager working for a subsidiary of a large US MNC in Ireland. The corporate HQ is looking to roll out a new performance appraisal scheme and has requested that you fully implement the new scheme in your subsidiary. However, the local trade union objects to the introduction of such a scheme and is threatening strike action if it is implemented. Identify a number of ways in which to resolve this problem.

## MANAGING EMPLOYEES ON INTERNATIONAL ASSIGNMENTS

Having explored some of the HRM issues, problems and challenges that MNCs face, we now move to the HRM strategies, policies and practices that MNCs employ. Specifically, we focus on a major function within IHRM – the management of people undertaking international assignments, often referred to as 'expatriation'. Indeed, much of the interest in IHRM focuses on this particular aspect. This process of expatriation involves relocating an employee – referred to as an 'expatriate' – from the MNC's operations in one country to another operation in another country to perform a particular assignment. Generally, much of the focus on international assignments has been on the movement of employees to and from the MNC's company HQ; that is, employees from the company HQ relocating to a foreign subsidiary or employees from a foreign subsidiary relocating to the company HQ, but it also includes employees who move between different foreign subsidiaries.

Edstrom and Galbraith (1977) identify three primary reasons for relocating employees across operations:

1 *To fill a position:* A particular job may require specific skills, competencies or experiences, which are not available locally, and therefore an MNC will send an expatriate to carry out the job.
2 *To develop individual employees and organizational development:* The use of expatriates is seen as having a positive impact on the development of an employee and the MNC. Employees can gain valuable international experience, which can assist them in career progression, while the MNC can accumulate a stock of knowledge, skills and abilities on which it can draw.
3 *To facilitate knowledge transfer, and the control and coordination of foreign subsidiaries:* Expatriates are a useful means of achieving this.

Managing the expatriation process is complex and there are many issues that need to be considered. These include how to recruit and select people to undertake an international assignment, how to prepare people for, and help them adjust to, the assignment, how to reward and manage their performance, and finally how to bring these people back when their assignment is finished. We now discuss each of these issues.

### Recruitment and selection

The first step in managing expatriates is to recruit and select the individual ▶ **Chapters 2 and 3** ◀. There are many issues that are important when recruiting and selecting a candidate to undertake an international assignment (Brewster et al., 2007; Dowling et al., 2008; Briscoe et al., 2012). These include:

● *Job suitability:* This is about matching the requirements of the job with the person. It is important to identify the required professional and technical skills and abilities the person will need in order to successfully perform the assignment. Other useful characteristics when undertaking international assignments include motivation, leadership, communication, problem-solving and relational abilities.
● *Language skills:* Where the assignment is in a country with a different language, it may be important for the person to be proficient, or at least conversational, in this language. However, language skills are not always

necessary to be successful in the role, particularly where the assignment involves a strong technical aspect.

- *Ability to adapt to the foreign culture:* There may be strong cultural differences between the home and host country, so an ability to adapt to the new culture will be important.
- *An awareness of issues in international management:* Individuals who are more aware of international management issues may be better prepared to deal with the many challenges they may encounter when on an international assignment.
- *Previous international experience:* Past performances in international assignments can be a useful predictor of a person's ability to carry out another assignment successfully.
- *The family situation:* While being mindful of legislation covering family status ▶ Chapter 5 ◀, a candidate's family situation can have a strong influence in determining whether they are suitable for undertaking an international assignment. One important point is the dual career issue, whereby the trailing spouse may have to give up their career or put it on hold. Furthermore, having a spouse and children may also make adjusting to the foreign location more difficult.
- *Desire for international assignment:* Undertaking an international assignment can be a difficult and daunting task, and the decision to undertake such an assignment should not be taken lightly. It helps if the individual has a strong desire for such a task.

There are a number of different selection methods that may be used when choosing a person to go on an international assignment (Briscoe et al., 2012: 232–3). These include:

- *Interviews:* often carried out by a mix of representatives from the home and host country.
- *Formal assessment:* instruments designed by psychologists to evaluate a candidate's personal traits and competencies.
- *Committee decision:* many MNCs have committees made up of HR representatives at the company HQ and managers from the home and host countries who select individuals to carry out international assignments.
- *Career planning:* many assignments undertaken by expatriates form part of a larger career or succession plan.

- *Self-selection:* individuals themselves assess whether they are ready and prepared to undertake an international assignment.
- *Internal job posting:* usually combined with other methods such as interviews.
- *Recommendations:* candidates are selected on the back of recommendations by people in the MNC, often senior executives.
- *Assessment centres:* some MNCs use assessment centres but usually in conjunction with other selection methods.

One particularly popular selection method noted in the literature is that which Harris and Brewster (1999) refer to as the 'coffee machine' system of selection. This method involves discussions over coffee about an international assignment, which then leads to selection.

## Preparation

Once the individual has been selected, the next stage in the process is preparing them to undertake the assignment. This is seen as a critical step in ensuring the international assignment is a success from both the individual and the MNC's point of view.

In preparing an individual to undertake the international assignment, a number of methods can be used. As well as cross-cultural awareness training, these include preliminary visits, language training and assistance with practical matters (Brewster et al., 2007; Dowling et al., 2008):

- *Cross-cultural awareness training:* involves providing individuals with an understanding of and appreciation for the prevailing culture in the foreign location. Ideally, such training should be provided to trailing spouses/partners and families.
- *Preliminary visits:* the advantages of preliminary visits to the foreign location are that they allow the individual, and families where applicable, to get a feel for the foreign location, including the local culture and business environment, and assess their suitability and interest in the location.
- *Language training:* often viewed as a lower priority in pre-departure training, because MNCs from English-speaking countries do not feel the need to provide training in other languages, as English is seen as the business language. This can, however, restrict an individual on international assignment, as they may

not be able to fully understand and monitor what is happening in the local environment and so will have to rely on locals to provide them with the necessary information. Being able to speak the language will not only help the individual in work situations, such as negotiations, but also in adjusting to the local environment.

- *Practical matters:* involves providing assistance with matters such as schooling, housing, language training, social clubs and security, which are all important to travelling individuals, and families.

CONSIDER THIS...

You work for a large MNC and have been chosen to carry out a long-term international assignment at its foreign subsidiary in China. The assignment is to aid the transfer of a new reward system. Which issues would you consider important in your preparation for this assignment?

## Adjustment

A key concern for all involved in the process is the successful adjustment of the employee, and their family if applicable, to the local environment. Adjustment is often broken down into three dimensions (Black and Stephens, 1989):

1 *Work adjustment:* how the employee adjusts to the new work environment.
2 *Interaction adjustment:* how the employee adjusts to interacting with people from the host country.
3 *General adjustment:* how the employee adjusts, in general, to the new environment, including housing, food, shopping, schooling and so on.

According to Brewster et al. (2007: 250–1), a number of factors can influence adjustment:

- *individual factors:* interpersonal skills and self-confidence, cultural empathy, emotional stability, language ability and previous international experience
- *non-work factors:* family situation and cultural distance
- *organizational factors:* organizational culture novelty, social support and logistical help

- *job factors:* role novelty, role clarity, role discretion, role conflict and role overload.

An adjustment cycle or curve is helpful in understanding the typical stages that expatriates may encounter when getting used to their new surroundings (Black and Mendenhall, 1991) (see Figure 13.2). Black and Mendenhall (1991) identify four stages that an expatriate may encounter when they go on international assignments:

1 *Honeymoon stage:* when the expatriate first arrives, they may be full of excitement about the novelty of their surroundings and role.
2 *Culture shock:* this can be a critical time, as this is when the expatriate may feel disillusioned and frustrated and may decide to return home.
3 *Adjustment:* the expatriate gradually begins to adapt to their new environment.
4 *Mastery:* the expatriate is now at a healthy level of adjustment.

## Compensation

Another issue in managing employees on international assignments is how to compensate them. What do you pay an employee on an international assignment? Do they receive the same payment as they receive at home? If they do, you are not providing any incentives for the

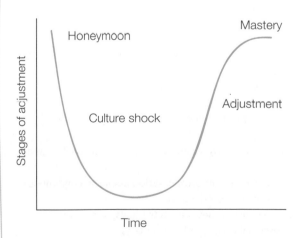

**Figure 13.2 U-shaped curve of cross-cultural adjustment**

*Source:* Black and Mendenhall, 1991. *Journal of International Business Studies*, published in 1991 by Palgrave Macmillan. Reproduced with permission of Palgrave Macmillan

employee to take up the international assignment, apart from gaining useful international experience. On the other hand, if the expatriate receives higher pay than local employees but is doing a similar job, this may cause problems at the foreign subsidiary. Do you pay the employee the local rate? But what if the local rate is lower than that in their home country, which means they may actually earn less money? Add in issues around different laws and regulations in relation to compensation, different currencies, different taxation systems, different inflation rates, cost of living adjustments and lifestyle issues and it soon becomes clear that compensating expatriates is a complex and costly process.

International compensation packages may include all or some of the following elements – a base salary, a foreign service inducement/hardship premium, allowances, and other benefits (Dowling et al., 2008). There are many approaches to international compensation that companies can take, with the two most well known being the going rate approach and the balance sheet approach.

The going rate approach favours a compensation package based on local market rates. Local market rates are usually determined by survey comparisons with local countries, expatriates of the same nationality or expatriates of all nationalities. Once a suitable comparison is found, compensation is based on that. Generally, base pay and benefits are supplemented by additional payments, particularly for expatriates operating in low-pay countries. The benefits of the going rate approach are:

- it is simple to administer
- it encourages the individual to identify with the host location
- it ensures equality in terms of pay with local employees and employees of other nationalities (Dowling et al., 2008).

The negatives associated with such an approach include:

- the variation in compensation between assignments for the same individual
- the variation between individuals of the same nationality in different countries
- the potential for re-entry problems (Dowling et al., 2008).

The balanced sheet approach, which tends to be the most popular approach to compensating expatriates, is designed to maintain expatriates' living standards irrespective of their assignment location. The objective is to maintain the expatriates' home country living standard, and to provide some additional financial incentives for undertaking the assignment. Thus, expatriates are kept on their home pay, while allowances and differentials are used to maintain home equity for items such as goods and services, housing and income tax. The idea is that the expatriate should neither gain nor lose, thus encouraging mobility. The benefits associated with the balanced sheet approach are that:

- it provides equity between assignments
- it provides equity between expatriates of the same nationality
- it can facilitate expatriate re-entry
- it can easily be communicated to employees (Dowling et al., 2008).

The negatives associated with such an approach are that:

- it is difficult to administer
- it can result in great disparities between expatriates of different nationalities and between expatriates and local nationals
- it can be quite intrusive in employees' lives (Dowling et al., 2008).

## Performance management

Performance management is another issue of concern when managing an employee on an international assignment. Managing and effectively conducting performance management for expatriates is a complex task.

When it comes to evaluating performance, issues such as what should be evaluated, who should do the evaluation and how to carry out the evaluation are important (Briscoe et al., 2012). What should be evaluated relates to the criterion used to evaluate performance. Identifying these criterion is problematic as there may be differences between expectations held at the parent company compared to those at the local level. Briscoe et al. (2012: 356), drawing on a range of sources, identify the following performance criterion in Table 13.2.

**Table 13.2** Performance criterion for evaluating expatriate performance

| Qualifications | Training, experience, technical skills, social and language skills, education |
|---|---|
| Targets | Derived from the parent company's objectives, the subsidiary objectives, local objectives and targets individually dictated |
| Attitudes | Flexibility, interpersonal understanding and communication skills, dealing with stress, openness to change |
| Job performance | Results, development of locals, communication and decision-making, individual growth and development, application of new expertise |

Another issue is who should carry out the performance evaluation. Generally, they are carried out by superiors; but, in relation to expatriates, this is complicated by the fact that their superiors are located in the home country and may not be in the best position to evaluate their performance. On the other hand, host country superiors may be in a better position to evaluate their performance but this will generally only relate to goals and objectives at the local level and they may not be in a position to evaluate the expatriate's broader goals and objectives. Many MNCs use multiple raters, for example 360-degree evaluations, which include superiors, peers, subordinates, customers and clients. However, trying to involve so many raters across different countries makes 360-degree evaluations difficult when evaluating an expatriate's performance.

How the evaluation should be carried out relates to the form the evaluation will take, the frequency of evaluation, and feedback. The dilemma facing MNCs is whether to use a standardized evaluation form or a customized form, specific to the expatriate. Most companies develop standardized evaluation forms, and while they work fine in domestic settings, when you move to the international level it becomes more problematic; for example, some questions may not be appropriate or effective in another country. The frequency of evaluations can differ enormously – they can be monthly, quarterly, biannual or annual, and even more ad hoc, such as at the end of the assignment or whenever the opportunity arises. Generally, most companies aim to carry out evaluations once a year,

which usually extends to expatriates. Providing feedback is an important part of evaluations but is more complex when it comes to expatriates. For example, issues like time and distance hamper effective feedback to the expatriate on performance.

A key practice of a performance management system is performance appraisal ▶ **Chapter 7** ◀. But for expatriates on assignment, what type of appraisal system do you use? Is it the local appraisal system that exists in the foreign subsidiary? This might not capture the expatriates' work accurately. Do you develop a global appraisal system? But how do you do this? What criteria do you use to evaluate their performance? Is it related to the success of the foreign subsidiary? This may not always be accurate, as the expatriate may be performing very well but the foreign subsidiary, for reasons outside the control of the expatriate, is not. MNCs tend to use a variety of methods to appraise performance. They may combine formal performance appraisal with visits from HQ, visits back to HQ, an assessment of results in the area under the expatriate's command, reports, emails, generally adopting an approach of gathering as much information as possible. Evidence suggest that a majority of companies prefer to use host country performance reviews to evaluate expatriate performance, with a surprisingly significant number of companies not knowing how their expatriates' performances are evaluated (Brookfield Global Relocation Services, 2011).

## Repatriation

The final concern in managing employees on international assignments is to successfully bring them back to their original location – the process of repatriation. This is an important activity as a major problem for MNCs is employees leaving the company on their return. A number of reasons for this have been identified (Brewster et al., 2007; Dowling et al., 2008; Briscoe et al., 2012), including:

**Repatriation** – the process that involves bringing the expatriate back to their home country after completing their international assignment

- *No position available in the company:* when the expatriate returns, the least they will expect is their previous job back, but they will more than likely expect a newer role, reflecting their new level of international experience.
- *Loss of status:* when on assignment, the expatriate often enjoys a high(er) level of status. But when they

## Female Expatriates

HRM IN THE NEWS

A key issue within international HRM is the use of female expatriates. Indeed, there are many websites specifically dedicated to the issue of female expatriates. The expatriate population has traditionally been dominated by men. For example, in the 1980s, it was estimated that only 3 per cent of the expatriate population were women. Pressures for equality and from globalization through the 1990s and 2000s have helped boost the female expatriate population, but according to the *2011 Global Relocation Trends Survey*, only 18 per cent of expatriates were women in 2011. There have been many reasons offered to explain this, including:

- Women are not interested in undertaking international assignments. They are seen as being less mobile than their male counterparts.
- Many foreign countries do not want female expatriates. It is suggested that in certain locations, locals would prefer to do business with men.
- Companies are reluctant to send woman on expatriation, fearing that they will suffer prejudice.
- Women lack the skills/competencies to succeed.
- Women are underrepresented in positions from which many expatriates are chosen.
- Where the selection of expatriates is based on informal networks, women can be discriminated against as they often do not form part of these networks.
- There are a relatively small number of female expatriates

and so there are few female role models.
- The global recession has accentuated the dual career issue, as women's careers are not seen as the primary career.

While some of these reasons may have merit, many are best regarded as myths when it comes to female expatriation. For example, research has shown that women desire international assignments as much as men and are just as successful as men in completing them. Perry Yeatman outlines that woman are 20 per cent more likely to succeed in international assignments as compared to men. Yeatman points to cultural sensitivity and communication skills possessed by females as important factors in achieving higher success scores. Rosalie Tung's research on female expatriates suggests that women may, in fact, be the 'model' global manager. Furthermore, it has been suggested that women have much better relational skills, which we know are important in successfully completing international assignments. Yet, despite the growth in female expatriates, numbers have largely stagnated around the 20 per cent mark.

Some companies are actively looking to tap into this pool of candidates for international assignments. For example, Jared Shelly identifies the large consultancy firm Deloitte as making a concerted effort to attract women in this regard – Deloitte runs many different programmes under its Initiative for the Retention and Advancement of Women. In a seminar held at Macquarie University in Australia,

and reported on numerous dedicated expatriation websites, Rosalie Tung has called for companies to do more in relation to the issue of female expatriation. She suggests that clear and articulated information sessions, decisions by female managers, establishment of female networks and mentors are all key corporate support strategies to boost female expatriates. It is also clear that support for the trailing male spouse is important in assisting female expatriates. Often, males find it difficult to adapt to the foreign location as the support networks are often geared towards females and not males.

The topic of female expatriates remains an area in IHRM that requires further exploration. Why, given the demand for expatriates and the success of women in international assignments, has the percentage of female expatriates not risen to a comparable level with men?

### Questions

1  Critically analyse the reasons given for the relatively small number of female expatriates.
2  What can companies do to attract female candidates for international assignments?

### Sources

Brookfield Global Relocation Services (2011) *2011 Global Relocation Trends Survey*, www.brookfieldgrs.com/knowledge/grts_research/.

Human Capital Online (2011) 'Send women on international assignments: Expert', www.hcamag.com/article/send-women-on-international-assignments-expert-117863.aspx.

Shelly, J. (2011) Where are all the expat women?, Human Resource Executive Online, 7 February, www.hreonline.com/HRE/story.jsp?storyId=533329676.

Shortland, S. (2006/7) The rise and rise of female expatriates, *Re:locate Magazine*, www.relocatemagazine.com/international-assignments/international-assignment-

articles/364-the-rise-and-rise-of-female-expatriates-.

Yeatman, P. (2008) 'Get ahead by going abroad', www.ceoforum.com.au/article-detail.cfm?cid=9144&t=/Perry-Yeatman--Kraft-Foods/Get-ahead-by-going-abroad/.

Zillman, S. (2011) 'Send more women on international assignments' say experts, *Human Capital Magazine*, 25 November, www.expatica.co.uk/hr/story/Send-more-women-on-international-assignments-say-experts.html.

return, they often simply fit back in again to their old role and do not maintain the level of status they enjoyed when on assignment.

- *Loss of autonomy:* similar to status, expatriates often enjoy quite a significant level of autonomy when on assignment. However, when they return home, this autonomy is often no longer available and returning expatriates can feel aggrieved.
- *Loss of career direction:* employees who undertake an international assignment often do so as part of a structured career path. However, where the assignment is not part of a career path, the returning expatriate may often feel a loss of direction. Having completed an international assignment, the returning expatriate often expects that this experience will lead to some kind of career progression.
- *A feeling of being undervalued:* expatriates often report that they feel their work is undervalued. It is often a case of 'out of sight, out of mind'. The good work and skills developed by the expatriate are not acknowledged and this can leave the employee feeling aggrieved.
- *Loss of income:* depending on the type of compensation package the expatriate enjoys while on assignment, they can suffer a loss of income when they return to their original location.
- *Lifestyle:* the expatriate may have become accustomed to a particular standard of lifestyle and if this lifestyle is not matched when they return, this can have a negative impact on the returning expatriate.
- *Family readjustment:* the family's readjustment to their home location is not always straightforward. This is particularly the case when the family has been away from their home country for a long period of time. The home country may have changed and the family may simply not be able to readjust to their original location.

Many MNCs do not provide post-assignment guarantees – that is, promotion or the return of the expatriate's previous job – but a majority do hold repatriation discussions (Brookfield Global Relocation Services, 2011). Briscoe et al. (2012) note that MNCs can provide support for repatriation at different stages:

- *Before the assignment:* the MNC may provide expatriates with career planning prior to the assignment, so that expatriates have an idea of what to expect when they return home. Also, an MNC may appoint a mentor in the home country to act as a point of contact and look after expatriates' interests when they are away.
- *During the assignment:* MNCs should look to provide clear, constant and regular communication with expatriates, regular travel trips home, a mentor in the home country, and any intra-office communication should include expatriates (Briscoe et al., 2012).
- *After the assignment:* managers in the home country must be aware that expatriates and their families may experience readjustment problems and may therefore need to put in place plans to reintegrate them back into the home country.

## BUILDING YOUR SKILLS

John has just completed a two-year international assignment and, by all accounts, he performed the role to a high standard and the assignment was a huge success. You have heard from a colleague that, on the back of his successful international assignment, John is expecting to be promoted to senior manager when he returns. However, there is no senior management position available. As HR manager, you are scheduled to meet John next week to talk about his return. John is a valued employee and you do not want him to leave. What steps would you take to deal with this situation?

## EXPATRIATE FAILURE

Having outlined the issues in managing expatriates on international assignments, it is clear that it is complex and there are significant opportunities for something to go wrong. Hence, IHRM also focuses on expatriate failure. Expatriate failure is generally referred to as the early return of an expatriate to their home country. As noted earlier, the cost of a failed international assignment is extremely high. Failure rates are estimated to run between 16 and 50 per cent (Harzing, 1995). However, the real cost is much higher; for example, one needs to factor in not only the cost of recruitment and selection, training, preparation and moving, but also the consequences of poor performance in lower revenues, lost business opportunities, and damage to the company's reputation, which may undermine future ventures in the host country. There are a number of reasons as to why expatriate failure might occur. Briscoe et al. (2012: 236), in a review of the existing literature, list some of the main reasons for failure:

- inability of the expatriate and/or the expatriate's family to adjust
- mistake in selecting the expatriate to undertake the assignment
- the international assignment did not live up to expectations
- personality traits of the expatriate
- expatriate not able to match expectations of the assignment
- expatriate's lack of technical competence
- expatriate's lack of motivation for the assignment
- expatriate's dissatisfaction with the quality of life in the foreign location
- expatriate's dissatisfaction with compensation and benefits
- inadequate pre-departure training
- inadequate support for the expatriate and family while on the assignment.

### Alternative international assignments

Given the complexity, failure rates and high costs involved in long-term expatriate assignments, there are now questions over the utility and viability of such assignments. Collings et al. (2007) identify a number of reasons for this debate:

- *Supply side issues:* The shortage of international managers to undertake long-term international assignments.
- *Cost issues:* It is estimated that it costs, on average, three to five times more to employ an expatriate compared to employing a host country national (Selmer, 2001).
- *Demand side issues:* The demand for such managers has increased due to the rapid growth of emerging markets in places such as Asia and Eastern Europe and a greater number of organizations looking to use expatriates, for example small and medium-sized enterprises and international joint ventures.
- *Failure issues:* Problems of expatriate failure in terms of direct costs, that is, salary, training costs, travel and relocation expenses, and indirect costs – damaged relations with foreign subsidiaries and potential loss of market share.
- *Management issues:* Complexities around the management of expatriate performance.
- *Career issues:* Collings et al. (2007) note two trends here:
  - employees are focusing more on career mobility and becoming less committed to organizations. Thus, companies may invest in an employee through an expatriation programme but lose them when they return.
  - the growth in self-initiated international assignments or assignments initiated by employees without company support or assistance. This means that companies may look to use these people to fill positions at a lower cost than a traditional expatriate.

Despite these problems, there is little evidence of a significant decline in the use of long-term assignments. However, alternative forms of international assignments are beginning to emerge, including short-term international assignments, frequent flyer assignments, commuter and rotational assignments, and global virtual teams. Table 13.3 provides a brief review of each of these assignments (cf. Collings et al., 2007). While the traditional expatriate assignment is likely to continue, we are also likely to see a continuation in the strong growth of these alternative forms of international assignments (Collings et al., 2007: 204–7).

**Table 13.3** Alternative international assignments

| | |
|---|---|
| **Short-term international assignments** | 'A temporary internal transfer to a foreign subsidiary of between one and twelve months duration' (Collings et al., 2007: 205)<br>Family generally remains at home<br>Useful for the transfer of problem-solving skills, as a means of control, managerial development, training of local workforce and to work on specific project-based tasks (Tahvanainen et al., 2005) |
| **Frequent flyer assignments** | Involve short international business trips; employees who undertake such assignments are often referred to as 'international business travellers'<br>Family remains at home<br>Suitable for irregular specialized tasks, such as annual budget meetings, production scheduling, networking and to maintain personal contact with subsidiary without locating physically (Collings et al., 2007). Particularly useful in developing markets or volatile countries where people may be reluctant to relocate (Welch and Worm, 2006) |
| **Commuter and rotational assignments** | Commuter assignments: employees commute from their home base to their post in another country<br>Rotational assignments: employees commute from their home base to their post in another country for a short period followed by a period of time off in their home country<br>Family generally remains at home<br>Rotational assignments are commonly used on oil rigs<br>Seen as viable alternatives to expatriate transfers, particular in places like Europe where travel is shorter and easier (Mayrhofer and Brewster, 1996) |
| **Global virtual teams** | Employees remain geographically dispersed but coordinate their work through electronic information and communication technologies<br>Family and employee remain at home<br>Particularly useful for relatively routine activities (Collings et al., 2007). Evidence suggests that companies have not quite maximized the potential of global virtual teams (Collings et al., 2007) |

## IrishCo Acquires French Company

You are an HR manager at a large Irish-owned company called IrishCo. It is a manufacturing company employing over 1,000 workers across two different sites in Ireland. IrishCo also has a small sales office employing 5 employees in London. To date, your work has largely focused on managing the HR issues at the two sites in Ireland, with little time spent dealing with the UK employees. IrishCo has won many awards for its sophisticated HR policies and practices in Ireland and prides itself on having a direct relationship with employees, without the interference of a trade union. In the past 12 months, senior directors in the company have identified opportunities to expand the business, particularly in mainland Europe, and recently launched an internationalization strategy. A key part of this new internationalization strategy was the acquisition last month of a company in Toulon, in the southeast of France. IrishCo viewed the acquired company as the ideal opportunity to expand its operations in Europe. The acquired company operates in largely the same sector as IrishCo and manufactures a similar product for the French market. However, on closer inspection, it was revealed that it employs outdated manufacturing processes. The acquired company's employees are all unionized and it has an active works council in operation. From your brief understanding of the French business system, you are aware that the industrial relations system is extremely fragmented and complex and characterized by extensive legal regulations.

The next stage of the internationalization process is to integrate the newly acquired company into IrishCo. Among other things, this would include transferring the manufacturing processes employed in the company in Ireland to the newly acquired company in France. Senior directors are also keen to

transfer many of the successful management practices they have developed in the Irish operations to the acquired company, particularly the award-winning HR policies and practices. It was decided that the best way to achieve the integration of the newly acquired company was to send a number of its Irish employees to carry out this work. The plan is to send one general manager, two senior manufacturing technicians, one financial manager and one HR generalist from the Irish operations to the newly acquired company in France. As the HR manager, you have been tasked with the management of these international assignments.

1 What issues are likely to be important in recruiting the different types of employees to carry out these assignments?
2 Outline a pre-departure training programme for the different types of employees.
3 What issues need to be considered when designing a repatriation programme for each of the different types of employees?
4 Identify any potential barriers to the transfer of management practice to the newly acquired operations in France.

 ## SUMMARY

This chapter has provided a brief introduction to the field of international human resource management (IHRM). We addressed issues such as defining IHRM and how IHRM differs to domestic HRM. We then looked at some of the main debates within the field of IHRM. We discussed the impact of globalization on HRM and focused on the convergence versus divergence debate within the IHRM literature. We examined the transfer of HRM practices within MNCs, addressing the key debate of whether MNCs employ standardized practices across their foreign subsidiaries or whether foreign subsidiaries adopt practices similar to those in local companies. Lastly, we explored one of the main features of IHRM – the management of employees on international assignments. We outlined the various aspects of managing employees on international assignments from the initial stages of recruitment and selection, preparation and adjustment, to compensation and performance management, and then finally to repatriation. We also dealt with issues around expatriation failure and the growth in alternative forms of international assignments.

 ## CHAPTER REVIEW QUESTIONS

1 Identify the ways in which international human resource management differs from domestic human resource management.
2 There are a number of factors that influence the transfer of HR practices across the multinational company. Explain these factors.
3 Selecting the right person to undertake an international assignment is important from the company and the individual's point of view. With this in mind, evaluate the 'coffee machine' selection method.
4 Describe a number of methods that may be used to prepare an employee to undertake an international assignment.
5 The utility and viability of long-term international assignments is a key issue in IHRM. Describe the emerging alternative forms of international assignments.

 ## FURTHER READING

Brewster, C., Sparrow, P. and Vernon, G. (2007) *International Human Resource Management*, London: CIPD.
Briscoe, D., Schuler, R. and Tarique, I. (2012) *International Human Resource Management: Policies and Practices for Multinational Enterprises*, New York: Routledge.

Dowling, P.J., Festing, M. and Engle Sr, A.D. (2008) *International Human Resource Management*, London: Cengage Learning.

Edwards, T. and Rees, T. (2011) *International Human Resource Management: Globalization, National Systems and Multinational Companies*, 2nd edn, Harlow: Pearson.

Harzing, A.W. and Pinnington, A.H. (2011) *International Human Resource Management*, London: Sage.

Hollinshead, G. (2010) *International and Comparative Human Resource Management*, Maidenhead: McGraw-Hill.

 USEFUL WEBSITES

www.brookfieldgrs.com
Brookfield Global Relocation Services produces the Global Relocation Trends Surveys, a huge source of data for issues to do with expatriation.

www.harzing.com
Harzing.com is Anne-Wil Harzing's website. She is a professor in international management and provides information, online papers and resources about IHRM.

www.shrm.org
SHRM is the Society for Human Resource Management's website, the world's largest association devoted to HRM.

www.expatfocus.com
Expat Focus provides comprehensive information and support resources for expatriates. Has impartial information on countries and provides opinions and advice from experienced expatriates.

 For extra resources including videos and further skills development guidance go to: www.palgrave.com/business/carbery

# 14 CORPORATE SOCIAL RESPONSIBILITY AND HUMAN RESOURCE MANAGEMENT

**Colm McLaughlin**

By the end of this chapter you will be able to:

## LEARNING OUTCOMES

- Explain the concept of corporate social responsibility (CSR) and its connection to HRM

- Outline some of the arguments for business adopting a CSR philosophy, including the 'business case'

- Discuss some of the arguments made by critics of CSR

- Contrast a CSR approach to a regulatory approach to addressing issues at work

- Demonstrate an understanding of some contemporary CSR labour issues

© IQONCEPT/ISTOCKPHOTO

This chapter discusses ...

# INTRODUCTION

Society expects business to adhere to certain social and ethical standards, that is, to meet its corporate social responsibility (CSR). While a business needs to make a profit in order to survive and grow, profit maximization is not the only concern of business. Increasingly, business leaders are recognizing that companies must make a positive contribution to addressing some of the social and environmental challenges society faces. This is reflected in the growth of CSR as a mainstream business issue. In relation to HRM, how a company treats its own staff and how workers are treated in supplier firms are elements of the CSR agenda. In other words, the HR practices of a company matter not only to those within the firm, but increasingly to the outside world as well. We can best illustrate the connection between CSR and HRM by looking in detail at a recent example of redundancy in Ireland.

TalkTalk Telecom Group is listed on the London Stock Exchange and is part of the FTSE 250 Index. It has over 4.8 million customers in the UK and is now the third largest communications network operator there. In the year ended March 2011, it reported a pre-tax annual profit of £57 million, up from £11 million the previous year, and its annual report predicted a profitable future (TalkTalk, 2011). The company celebrated its recent financial success with a staff party held on 11 September 2011 at the exclusive Capesthorne Hall estate in Cheshire, UK. The celebration was headlined by the indie band Noisettes and rapper Tinchy Stryder, and attendees could enjoy clay pigeon shooting, Ferris wheel rides, massages and a range of other entertainment. The company covered all costs including flights and hotels; the total cost of the event was reported in the media to be around £0.5 million (Gibney and Murphy, 2011).

TalkTalk's CSR approach is set out in its Brighter Basics corporate statement: 'five core values that define what kind of team we aspire to be … and [which] guide us in implementing our plans to make TalkTalk a brighter place for everyone'. Part of its philosophy is 'keeping our people informed of developments and the Company's progress, while enabling them to engage in two way communication', both directly and through the (non-union) employee forum system. It also sponsors family concerts, encourages its employees to volunteer in local schools and supports its long-term charity partner, Ambitious About Autism (TalkTalk, 2011).

> **Corporate social responsibility (CSR)** –
> the duty of a business to go beyond profit
> maximization and act responsibly and
> contribute positively to society

TalkTalk's CSR commitment to communities and its employees has been rewarded through its inclusion in the FTSE4Good Index, an index of companies that meet global corporate responsibility standards. The index is designed to help socially responsible investors make their investment decisions.

In September 2011, TalkTalk gave 30 days' notice that it was closing its call centre in Waterford, Ireland, with the loss of all 585 jobs. Waterford has had a number of high-profile company closures in recent years and is in the region with the highest unemployment rate in the country. The company announced that some of the jobs will move to the UK, while much of the work will be taken up by outsourced call centres in South Africa and India. It justified the decision on the basis that call volumes had fallen by 40 per cent year on year as more customers had opted to deal with support issues online (Clancy, 2011). The news was broken to staff in Waterford at a meeting, although employees who were not rostered to work that day heard the news via the radio and social networking sites. The announcement came as a shock to the staff as they had received an email from management only the previous day telling them that the Waterford call centre had achieved a record performance during the month of August (Murphy, 2011). It also came as a shock to those Irish employees who had been sent to the UK to train staff there in recent months, as it now dawned on them that they had been training other people to do their own jobs: 'We were told that it was in case we got busy, that they would be a backup. But all along we were training them to take our jobs', said one employee (Clancy, 2011). Another noted that he was under the impression he was climbing the corporate ladder when asked to help the company expand by training staff in the UK. He said he now felt 'corporately violated' and added: 'It's all about the profit margin and pleasing the shareholders' (Gibney and Murphy, 2011).

Under Irish redundancy law, companies must enter into a period of consultation with employees in a collective redundancy situation of at least 30 days, so TalkTalk was acting legally. However, Richard Bruton, minister for jobs, enterprise and innovation, stated that the 'decision to close within 30 days was too abrupt and unfair to people … [and that] businesses have a responsibility to their employees' (RTE, 2011a). Barry O'Leary, the head of the IDA Ireland (the agency responsible for attracting foreign investment into Ireland), said the corporate behaviour of TalkTalk was 'as bad as it gets in terms of company behaviour' (RTE, 2011b) and not what you would expect in business today. He claimed its actions indicated a lack of respect for the workforce and he could not recall any case involving so many job losses and such short notice (RTE, 2011a). Fintan O'Toole (2011), a columnist in the *Irish Times*, described TalkTalk's CSR strategy as 'nauseating bilge'. He said that the company was the 'epitome of irresponsibility'.

As a result of TalkTalk's actions, it was suggested to the Irish government that the law be changed to extend the minimum 30-day consultation period for future company closures. Senator David Cullinane went so far as to table an amendment in Seanad Éireann (the upper house of the Irish Parliament) to increase the period to 90 days, the same as the consultation period under UK law in the case of 20 or more employees. He also tabled an amendment that the government introduce legislation for collective bargaining and trade union recognition, so as to increase the bargaining power of workers in such situations. Both Cullinane's amendments were defeated (Sinn Fein, 2011), and Bruton said that the government did not want to start creating regulatory requirements when what was needed was a proper approach by business (RTE, 2011c).

The negative publicity surrounding TalkTalk's sudden announcement to close its Waterford call centre illustrates that society expects firms to be socially responsible. It also highlights that there is often a gap between the rhetoric of CSR and the reality of the practices firms engage in. For this reason, some argue that CSR is ineffective and regulation would be a better way of getting firms to meet the standards that society expects of them. Cullinane was of this view in suggesting that regulation was needed to prevent this happening again. In contrast, Bruton advocated for CSR in stating that firms should do the right thing.

These different attitudes towards CSR will be explored in this chapter. First, we set out what CSR is, look at some of the HRM issues that come within a firm's CSR ambit, and examine some of the ethical and financial reasons why firms engage in CSR. Next, we examine some of the controversies surrounding CSR. In particular, we assess its effectiveness in addressing employment-related CSR issues vis-à-vis a greater role for government regulation.

**CONSIDER THIS ...**

Do you think TalkTalk lived up to its stated CSR philosophy? Are the redundant employees and the Irish politicians justified in being disappointed with TalkTalk? What reasons can you think of for and against the government adopting Cullinane's suggestion?

## CORPORATE SOCIAL RESPONSIBILITY

CSR is a mainstream business issue. A study by KPMG (2008) found that 80 per cent of Global Fortune 250 companies and over 90 per cent of the UK's FTSE 100 firms report CSR-related information in their annual reports. Companies are hiring CSR managers, participating in CSR performance indices such as the FTSE4Good, and joining CSR membership organizations such as Business in the Community, Opportunity Now and Race for Opportunity (Grosser and Moon, 2008). The importance of CSR is also reflected in the fact that responsibility for it increasingly lies with a member of the board of directors and that a weblink to corporate responsibility is generally found on the home page of most large publicly listed companies. There are numerous international agreements relating to CSR drawn up by organizations such as the United Nations and the Organisation for Economic Co-operation and Development, which many multinational companies and investment funds have signed up to. There has been an explosion in 'codes of conduct' used by international brands to govern the working conditions in the factories that supply their products. This interest in CSR by corporations is partly reactive, driven by the fear of reputational damage to brand images from negative publicity. Trade unions, community groups and **nongovernmental organizations (NGOs)** can use the internet to quickly and widely circulate information about the practices used in the manufacture of a company's products, and to call for product boycotts. But part of the motivation is also proactive, with firms realizing that the public is increasingly conscious of social

**Nongovernmental organizations (NGOs)** – organizations that are independent of government and generally run on a not-for-profit basis. Examples include Greenpeace, Friends of the Earth, Oxfam, the Fair Labor Association, and the Institute for Global Labour and Human Rights

and environmental issues and there are significant business opportunities to be developed in response. *The Economist* (2008), which admits that it has not always been a supporter of CSR, now argues that few businesses can afford to ignore it.

## What is corporate social responsibility?

So what exactly is CSR and what does society expect of business? CSR is a broad umbrella and there is no one clear definition of exactly what it entails. While there is a shared acceptance in the literature that businesses have a responsibility to a wider societal good, different definitions stress different dimensions. The Confederation of Business Industry (CBI, 2001) describes CSR as: 'the acknowledgement by companies that they should be accountable not only for their financial performance, but for the impact of their activities on society and/or the environment'. This definition suggests that business is responsible for its *own* impact on society. The European Commission (2001) defines CSR as: 'a concept whereby companies decide voluntarily to contribute to a better society and a cleaner environment'. This goes further than the CBI by implying that businesses need, more generally, to have a positive impact on societal progress. Stuart Rose, former CEO of Marks & Spencer (2008), a leading UK retailer, describes the company's social responsibility as offering 'exceptional products, service and store experiences in a way that reflects our customers' and stakeholders' expectations that Marks and Spencer is amongst the leaders in managing environmental and social issues'. His comments suggest that CSR is about responding to market demands for responsible behaviour. In other words, this is what customers and other stakeholders expect and therefore businesses must respond to these expectations in order to ensure their own long-term survival. He uses the word **stakeholders**, a key phrase in the CSR field.

Interestingly, none of these definitions of CSR mention obeying the law. This is because while the legal framework sets minimum standards, CSR is about a higher standard. TalkTalk broke no laws in Ireland, but critics of its behaviour believe it should adhere to higher standards. The phrase often used by CSR managers is going 'beyond compliance'. So CSR is about voluntary action and self-regulation by firms to go beyond what the law requires of them.

Many writers in the field of CSR and firms who engage with CSR no longer use the word 'social', preferring instead to use 'corporate responsibility', 'responsible business', 'corporate citizenship' or some other broad title. This is because the CSR agenda has widened beyond social issues, to include the environmental and sustainability issues of our time. When CSR initially gathered momentum in the 1970s and 80s, social issues in business were its prime focus. High-profile cases of that period included the unethical marketing of infant milk formula in Africa by Nestlé, the gas leak in 1984 at the Union Carbide factory in Bhopal, India, where thousands were killed and many suffered horrendous injuries, and the Ford Pinto car that could explode in a fireball if another vehicle crashed into it from behind. In recent decades, environmental degradation, global warming, sustainable production and other 'green' topics have become major issues of concern.

## Which CSR issues should firms address?

If you were to draw up a list of social, ethical and environmental issues, you would need a fairly large canvas. The range of potential CSR issues is endless and includes: protection of the environment, sustainability, fair trade, poverty, human rights, labour standards, equality and diversity, employee engagement, health and safety, animal welfare, safe products, ethical marketing and supporting charities, to name but a few. The suggestion is not that all firms should address all these issues, but that firms should address those that are of relevance to the nature of their business and in proportion to their size and locality. A small local business, for example, might sponsor a local charity or sports team, purchase materials from other local businesses in order to support the community, and treat its employees fairly and with respect.

The expectations of society of a large multinational business such as Tesco would be far greater. As a result, Tesco considers a broad range of CSR issues, such as the sustainability of fish stocks, animal welfare, global warming, fair trade, and promoting healthy eating. Given its significant presence in many communities, it supports local communities in a range of ways. As the largest private sector employer in the UK, its employment policies are an important area of CSR, such as its approach to promoting diversity and equality and treating its staff fairly. For example, it invests significant

> **Stakeholders** – any individuals, groups or organizations who are affected by or can affect the actions of a company

resources in apprenticeships, training and development, and succession planning. Its website claims that more than 80 per cent of management positions are filled by internal candidates. It has long built a positive relationship with the trade union Usdaw (Union of Shop, Distributive and Allied Workers) through the negotiation of a partnership agreement. In 2007, Tesco and Usdaw reached an agreement that staff would be entitled to five paid leave days for training if they wished to become foster carers.

Tesco also has some responsibility for the working conditions of workers in its many supply chains. It was a founding member of the Ethical Trading Initiative (ETI), an alliance formed between companies, trade unions and NGOs who work together to improve working conditions for vulnerable workers across the globe in a range of industries that grow or manufacture consumer goods. Member companies agree to adopt the ETI Base Code in full (Table 14.1). Thus, Tesco expects all its suppliers worldwide to comply with the ETI Base Code on labour standards, which is founded on International Labour Organization (ILO) conventions. It also provides training for its suppliers on its ethical trading policy. Another consideration that might influence which issues a firm chooses to address is any negative publicity it has received. As the largest supermarket chain in the UK, Tesco has come in for criticism on a number of issues and undoubtedly this has had some effect on its CSR policy.

Issues to do with employees and labour rights are central to CSR. Stories of child labour and other forms of exploitation of workers revealed by trade unions and labour NGOs travel quickly around the globe, damaging the reputation of leading brands and high-street chains. In recent years, the supply chains of many leading high-street brands have been associated with underage workers. Poor working conditions have been highlighted in factories manufacturing IT products for household names such as IBM, Hewlett-Packard, Microsoft, Lenovo and Dell (Thompson, 2009), and in leading apparel companies such as Nike (Ballinger, 2008). In the case of Nike, its own audits of factories manufacturing Nike footwear and clothing showed physical and verbal abuse of workers, restricted access to drinking water and toilets, widespread use of excessive working hours and overtime, and workers being paid below the local legal minimum wage (Teather, 2005). In the manufacture of toys for McDonald's, accusations have been made of 'appalling working conditions, slave wages and instances of child labour' (Royle, 2005: 50). In early 2009, allegations emerged in an undercover investigation by the BBC and

**Table 14.1** ETI Base Code

Employment is freely chosen
Freedom of association to join a trade union and the right to collective bargaining are respected
Working conditions are safe and hygienic
Child labour shall not be used
Living wages are paid
Working hours are not excessive
No discrimination is practised
Regular employment is provided
No harsh or inhumane treatment is allowed

As part of the ETI Principles of Implementation, members also agree to:

engage in ethical trade
continually improve working conditions
support their suppliers through training and advice to improve working conditions
report annually on their progress, setting out how much they spend on improving working conditions, the training they have undertaken, how they monitor their suppliers/ working conditions, and how they then ensure that any shortcomings identified are rectified. All reporting must be honest and transparent

*Source:* www.ethicaltrade.org/eti-base-code; www.ethicaltrade. org/about-eti/what-companies-sign-up-to

*The Observer* that two suppliers of knitwear to Primark (Penneys in Ireland) were employing illegal immigrants in the UK on half the minimum wage and for 12-hour shifts over seven days per week. The ETI, of which Primark was a member, '[was] horrified at allegations of abuses exposed by this investigation' (McDougall, 2009) and instructed Primark to remove all the ETI branding from its stores and website until the ETI had conducted a full investigation into Primark's adherence to its Base Code.

While these companies do not directly engage in these practices themselves, they are perceived to profit from them. Thus, society holds them responsible for rectifying such abuses and instigating fair employment practices in the companies that supply their products. In response to such accusations, many of these companies have drawn up codes of conduct setting out the labour standards their supply firms must adhere to. Internal and external auditors are then used to ensure that these standards are met, and where breaches are found, the factories are required to improve working conditions or risk losing the supply contract. Nike, for example, employs a compliance team of more than 90 staff in 21 countries, who monitor adherence by its suppliers with the Nike code of conduct. Additionally, Nike allows the Fair Labor Association to conduct independent and unannounced inspections (Locke et al., 2006). While HRM departments are not responsible directly for HR issues in supply chain factories, they are often involved in drawing up codes of conduct and have input into CSR issues (Sachdev, 2006).

### CONSIDER THIS ...

Log on to the home page of Tesco (www.tescoplc. com). What HRM-related issues of corporate responsibility does it address? Why do you think Tesco publicly makes these commitments?

Log on to www.tescopoly.org.uk, a website run by an alliance of various community groups critical of the power of all the leading UK supermarkets, not just Tesco. Click on 'Impacts' and then on the various workers links: Workers worldwide, Garment Workers, UK Workers, Homeworkers. What HRM-related criticisms of UK supermarkets do they identify?

How effective do you think NGOs and civil society organizations like Tescopoly are at making large companies act more responsibly?

## THE CONTROVERSY OF CSR

While CSR has only become a mainstream business issue over the past decade, some companies have sought to act responsibly for as long as business has existed. The Quaker-owned companies, such as the chocolate manufacturers Cadbury, Rowntree and Fry, were well known for their enlightened employee welfare and housing schemes introduced in Victorian England in the 1800s, when working and living conditions were generally appalling. Such practices in a small number of large British companies gave birth to what became known as the 'welfare tradition', which is viewed as the early foundations of modern HRM (Gunnigle et al., 2011). The Cadbury family were also involved in wider social reforms, such as providing education to working-class adults and leading the campaign against children working as chimney sweeps (Cadbury, 2010). John D. Rockefeller, who founded the Standard Oil company in the USA, was a shining example of philanthropy and gave

**Philanthropy** – the practice of making charitable donations to good causes

away US$550 million during his lifetime to education, science, health and the arts (Steiner and Steiner, 2012).

There are also contemporary examples of companies driven by a motive beyond just profit. Scientists at Merck came up with what they thought would be a cure for onchocerciasis, or river blindness, a parasite that affects more than 18 million people, mostly in poor African countries. The company could develop the drug at great expense, but this would not be a profitable venture because neither the sufferers nor their governments would be able to afford the drug. The company decided to produce the drug anyway and to provide it free. To date, it has given away more than 1.4 billion tablets in 37 countries at a cost to the company of over US$2 billion. In doing so, it has prevented an estimated 40,000 cases of blindness. Merck's motivation was that it can afford to do so and, having discovered a cure for a debilitating disease, it was the humanitarian thing to do (Steiner and Steiner, 2012). The Body Shop, founded in 1976 by Anita Roddick in the UK, became a global brand based on its environmental, animal welfare and ethical trade philosophy. It has supported a range of environmental, human rights and animal welfare charities, and has led awareness-raising campaigns on a number of social issues, such as domestic violence, human trafficking, women's rights and the prevention of HIV/AIDS (Purkayastha and Fernando, 2007). The Body Shop was widely seen as being a model example of socially responsible business and has had a significant impact on embedding CSR in contemporary corporate culture (Hausman, 2007).

However, some of these exemplars of social responsibility have not been immune from criticism. Cadbury was accused in 1909 of gaining financially from slavery on cocoa plantations (Blowfield and Murray, 2011), even though the campaign against slavery had been Quaker led (Sachdev, 2006). Rockefeller was criticized for crushing his competitors through predatory pricing, underselling and other anti-competitive practices. So successful was he that Standard Oil refined more than 90 per cent of US oil by the late 1800s. The *New York World* described Standard Oil as the 'most cruel, impudent, pitiless, and grasping monopoly that ever fastened upon a country' (Visser, 2011). The Body Shop's social responsibility has also been called into question. In an article in *Business Ethics*, Entine (1994) accused the company of hypocrisy in trading on an ethical image when much of this image was no more than public relations spin. He pointed out that the company had a reputation for supporting numerous charities and yet official data showed that the company had made no charitable donations during its first 11 years, and over the subsequent decade, company donations were about average for large corporations. He detailed how the concept for The Body Shop, and many of the branding and product ideas, had been copied from a small retailer in California called 'The Body Shop'. Later, he even challenged its claims of selling natural products, citing evidence of synthetic materials and petrochemicals used in production (Entine, 2002; Purkayastha and Fernando, 2007). The Body Shop was also accused by London Greenpeace (an independent activist group, not to be confused with Greenpeace International) of anti-union practices, low pay, exploiting indigenous peoples, fuelling consumerism and misleading the public. The company was sold to L'Oréal in 2006, a company known to test products on animals and one which Roddick had previously criticized for its sexualization of women (Purkayastha and Fernando, 2007).

These examples raise a number of important questions about CSR that we will explore in more depth below. Can firms actually be socially responsible or will the pressure for profits trump ethical behaviour when the two come into conflict? Is CSR on the part of corporations a real attempt to grapple with important social, ethical and environmental issues, or is it just window dressing to appeal to consumer idealism and pre-empt governments from introducing regulations? If society expects business to meet higher standards of behaviour, is it not the job of the government to set these standards through legislation?

While CSR has become a mainstream corporate concern in recent years, it is not without its critics. For some, CSR is a distraction from the core concern of business, which is making a profit; this is known as the **shareholder view of the firm**. We briefly explain this view, but it is no longer the mainstream view of business, having been largely replaced by the **stakeholder view of the firm**. In this view, while firms still exist to maximize profits, they need to balance this objective against the legitimate needs of other stakeholders.

Arguments in support of this position are both ethical (the 'social contract') and self-interested (the 'business case'), as set out below.

The real debate over CSR, however, occurs between those who think that business should *voluntarily* make a

> **Shareholder view of the firm** – the primary objective of management should be to maximize profit for shareholders
>
> **Stakeholder view of the firm** – management should take the interests of all stakeholders into account when making decisions

contribution to the public good and those who think that government *regulation* is the best way to ensure that corporations adhere to the standards society expects of them. Thus, in this debate, it is not the aims of CSR that are called into question, it is the effectiveness of CSR as a method to bring about widespread change in corporate behaviour. Should working conditions be left to corporations to address voluntarily in conjunction with concerned stakeholders, such as labour rights organizations, or should governments take stronger action through regulation to set out the minimum standards that firms must adhere to? This debate is often characterized as one between the 'carrot' of the business case that incentivizes firms to do the right thing and the 'stick' of government regulation that forces firms to act in a certain way. Which is more effective at aligning corporate behaviour with the interests of society, the 'carrot' or the 'stick'?

## The shareholder view of the firm

At the heart of the shareholder view of the firm is the belief that the sole aim of business is profit maximization. This was the dominant view of business for much of the twentieth century. It finds support in the theory of Adam Smith, who, in his book *The Wealth of Nations* ([1776]2009), put forward that when individuals pursue their own interest, the invisible hand of the market delivers benefits for everyone. Through competition, resources such as capital and labour are allocated efficiently and prices are driven down. As Smith stated: 'it is not from the benevolence of the butcher, the brewer or the baker that we expect our dinner, but from their regard to their own self-interest' (p. 13). Moreover, the individual, 'by pursuing his own interest … frequently promotes that of the society more effectually than when he really intends to promote it' (p. 264). Thus, business makes a significant contribution to society by creating jobs, contributing to taxation revenues, delivering economic growth, and providing new products and services that society wants and needs. Getting involved in solving complex social and environmental issues is a distraction best left to government, while business gets on with what it does best, which is providing goods and services in order to make profit. This view can be summed up by the economist Milton Friedman, who is widely credited with using the expression: 'the business of business is business'. As Friedman (1970) argued in an article in the *New York Times Magazine*: 'there is one and only one social responsibility of business – to use its resources and engage in activities designed to increase its profits so long as it stays within the rules of the game'. He points out that senior executives of corporations are in the service of shareholders to maximize profits. Engaging in CSR raises costs and is thus 'spending someone else's money for a general social interest'. If it results in lower profits, shareholders suffer; if it leads to higher prices, consumers suffer; and if it results in lower wages, employees suffer. Hence, managers of corporations have what is known as a 'fiduciary duty' in law to act in the best interests of the shareholders by maximizing shareholder value.

## The stakeholder view of the firm: the 'social contract' arguments

From an ethical perspective, businesses exist in a society and although society benefits from the wealth creation, taxation revenue and job creation of successful companies, firms also benefit from the communities they operate within. For example, publicly funded universities provide educated graduates, the state provides a legal system, and the community allows a company to build plants and use local resources. A symbiotic relationship exists between business and society, resulting in the social contract (Steiner and Steiner, 2012). Society expects business to be guided by certain values. Even Adam Smith ([1759]2007: 239) was a strong advocate of values underpinning the operation of business. While he advocated individuals pursue their self-interest, he also stressed the need for the values of 'humanity, justice, generosity and public spirit'. Additionally, some social problems can only be solved with the help of business, such as unemployment or discrimination in the workplace, and therefore society needs business to assist in finding solutions. Indeed, some of the problems society faces have, at least in part, been caused by business, such as environmental degradation and pollution. Finally, businesses are powerful actors in society. This power has increased since the 1980s, as Western governments have increasingly liberalized and deregulated markets and

> **Social contract** – an implicit agreement between business and society that sets out the broad standards that business should adhere to and duties they should fulfil in order to maintain the support and legitimacy of society. These standards are partly reflected in law but are mostly contained in social norms, values and expectations

undermined collective bargaining structures and trade union influence. Modern capitalism has seen a concentration of ownership in certain sectors, resulting in a small number of powerful corporations. For example:

- In the UK grocery trade, four companies account for 75% of all sales, with Tesco controlling one-third of the UK market.
- In the global pesticide industry, six companies control 75–80% of the market.
- Two firms, Du Pont and Monsanto, dominate the world seed market, while Monsanto controls 91% of genetically modified seeds.
- Five companies account for 80% of the international trade in bananas (Boyle and Simms, 2009). Similar statistics apply in coffee, textiles and the media (Sachdev, 2006).

As Steiner and Steiner (2012: 58) note, 'business has tremendous power to change society', to change its ideas, values and institutions. Similarly, James Gross (1998: 63), professor at Cornell University, argues that corporations have:

> the power to affect people's lives, to harm or benefit them, to violate or protect their rights, to favour some over others for various reasons, to make or break their communities, and to decree many of the rules that govern who gets what in the economy and what they have to do to get it.

With great power comes great responsibility. However, the public have become increasingly disenchanted with business and its exercise of this power. From the late 1960s onwards, public opinion surveys in the USA showed a dramatic drop in the public's confidence in business to strike a fair deal between profit and public good, with little recovery in public trust in business since (Steiner and Steiner, 2012). Some of the issues that have undermined trust in business include:

- a raft of corporate scandals, such as the collapse of Enron in the USA, which engaged in fraudulent practices, including hiding significant debts and falsifying profits, resulting in the largest corporate bankruptcy case at the time and the subsequent demise of its accounting firm Arthur Andersen

- the constant flow of media stories about the use of child labour and exploitation of workers in developing countries by suppliers to brand name corporations
- astronomical bonuses for bankers and an exponentially increasing gap in pay between executives and blue-collar workers.

On the issue of pay, the influential management writer Peter Drucker stated that the pay of the CEO should be no more than 20 times greater than the pay of the average employee in the company. In an interview with *Wired*, Drucker said it was 'morally and socially unforgiveable' for senior executives to be rewarded exorbitantly, while making thousands of their workers redundant (Schwartz and Kelly, 1996). In the USA, the ratio of CEO pay to that of the average blue-collar worker has risen from 42 in 1980 to 343 in 2010 (AFL-CIO, 2011).

This low level of confidence in business has plummeted further in the wake of the recent financial meltdown, the state bailout of privately owned banks, the ensuing deep recession, soaring unemployment levels, and ongoing austerity budgets. It is no surprise that the Occupy movement, which calls for capitalism to be regulated or even replaced, gained some sympathy from the public. The Occupy movement is an international protest movement against social and economic inequality, which held large-scale protests in London, New York and elsewhere, beginning in September 2011. Dominic Barton, the global managing director of McKinsey, went so far as to suggest that if there isn't a fundamental reform of the way business is done, 'the social contract between the capitalist system and the citizenry may truly rupture, with unpredictable but severely damaging results' for the system of capitalism itself (Barton, 2011: 86). Business has lost some of its legitimacy and CSR is one method in which it seeks to regain the trust of the public.

## The stakeholder view of the firm: the 'business case' arguments

From a self-interest perspective, the argument for CSR is that it can improve a firm's financial performance. This is the 'business case' for CSR. It is sometimes described as 'doing well by doing good'. By acting in the best interests of society, society will, in turn, reward business for their efforts. For example, if firms support local charities, this can improve their public image and increase their customer base. By developing a new product that

responds to a social or environmental need, they can increase profits. By ensuring good employment standards, they can avoid negative publicity that can lead to reputational damage to their brand. The actions of firms can thus generate positive benefits and reduce reputational risk. In this sense, CSR is, in fact, 'enlightened self-interest'. The benefits of such actions may not be immediate, however, and so CSR is seen as adding value to the firm in the long run. A long-term approach to adding value is not incompatible with the fiduciary duty of managers to act in the owners' best interests. In fact, pension funds and other institutional investors in the UK are required to disclose their social, ethical and environmental investment principles and have been encouraged to adopt a long-term view of their investments. Following changes to UK company law in 2006, boards of directors must now take account of employee interests alongside other stakeholders when pursuing their duty to maximize financial returns. Such a longer run view is referred to as 'enlightened shareholder value' (McLaughlin and Deakin, 2012).

According to advocates of CSR, three groups in particular will reward businesses for acting responsibly: employees, customers and investors. These are now addressed in turn.

### Employees

The ethical practices and reputation of a company are important issues for the recruitment and retention of staff, as various studies show that employees want to work for companies that are ethical and make a positive contribution to social and environmental issues. In a study of MBA graduates in five business schools in the USA and Europe, over 90 per cent reported that they would be willing to forgo some financial remuneration in order to work for a company that cared about its employees, its stakeholders and sustainability (Montgomery and Ramus, 2003). Nike is reputed to have improved the employment standards in its supply chains partly because of staff embarrassment at being associated with sweatshops. Maria Eitel, vice-president for corporate responsibility, said that staff 'were going to barbecues and people would say: "How can you work for Nike?" I don't know if we were losing employees but it sure as hell didn't help in attracting them' (Vogel, 2006: 59).

CSR is not restricted to issues external to the firm. How a firm looks after its own employees is also a key CSR issue. People want to work for companies that treat their own employees well and other stakeholders want companies to treat their employees well. Thus, a reputation for good HRM practices is important for attracting the best and brightest talent and improving the reputation of the firm among various stakeholders. As a result, many employers want to be the 'employer of choice'. A range of league tables now exist to rank companies in terms of their attractiveness to work: Sunday Times 100 Best Companies, Fortune 100 Best Companies to Work For, Where Women Want to Work Top 50 and The Times Top 100 Graduate Employers are just a few of the many league tables that have proliferated in recent years. HRM policies such as flexible working, training and development, equality and diversity, fairness at work, whistleblowing, health and safety, employee engagement and so on are seen as increasingly important for HRM and CSR.

The benefits of such policies for a firm's financial performance are many. Better HRM increases competitive advantage by attracting top talent, raising employee morale, and reducing costs associated with high turnover, such as recruitment and training. Policies that promote equality and diversity lead to a diverse workforce. This, in turn, reflects a diverse customer base, providing insights into customer needs and attracting new customers to the business. It can also reduce any potential litigation risk and reputational damage associated with discrimination claims (McLaughlin and Deakin, 2012). An example of reputational damage occurred during 2010 at the Dublin office of PricewaterhouseCoopers (PwC). Photos of the 'top 10' new female graduate recruits based on their physical appearance were collated by a few male members of PwC and circulated in an email to selected colleagues (Hickey, 2010). As is often the case with such emails, it was circulated more widely within the firm and quickly went viral around the globe to the humiliation of the women concerned and the embarrassment of the company. As a high-profile promoter of equality and diversity at work, a member of Opportunity Now (a membership organization that promotes gender equality at work), and a company that goes to great lengths to recruit, develop and promote female employees, PwC will be well aware of the potential reputational damage of this action. Not only might such behaviour affect recruitment and existing employee morale, it might also undermine its reputation with clients. Were PwC a publicly listed company looking for external investment, this negative publicity might also put off potential investors. Thus, employee issues not only come under the HRM umbrella but they are also central to CSR.

## Customers

In relation to customers, it is argued that CSR can build brand loyalty. Customers are increasingly aware of the social and environmental issues surrounding the goods they purchase, and the internet and social media provide them with easy access to information about the behaviour of corporations. Socially responsible firms will be rewarded with customer loyalty, while socially irresponsible firms will be punished through loss of sales and consumer boycotts. Evidence of socially responsible shopping is seen in the rise of ethical labelling schemes, which companies are increasingly eager to sign up to. A range of labelling schemes now exist covering an array of products and sectors, such as the ETI, Fairtrade, GoodWeave (carpets), Marine Stewardship Council (fish sustainability), LEAF (sustainable farming) and Freedom Food (animal welfare), to name but a few. The United Nations set up the UN Global Compact for MNCs. This sets out 10 principles relating to human rights, labour standards, the environment and corruption that signatories must adhere to. The importance that firms place on these labels can be seen in the example given earlier of Primark and the removal of the ETI label following reports in the British media. This represented significant reputational damage for the company and, in response, Primark went to great lengths to restore its reputation for CSR. For example, it has increased its auditing of suppliers and stepped up its levels of investment in community projects in the developing countries in which its products are produced. Primark has now regained the ETI label, which it clearly sees as important for its brand image and the long-term financial performance of the firm.

CONSIDER THIS ...

When you graduate, what sort of company do you wish to work for? Will their social, ethical and environmental record affect your decision? Are there any companies that you do not wish to work for based on their CSR reputation?

As a customer, has the behaviour of a company influenced your purchasing behaviour? Ask some of your friends the same question. How much influence do you think customer buying power has over corporate behaviour?

## Investors

Investors are also interested in the social responsibility of business, and engagement by shareholders with issues of social responsibility has grown significantly over the past decade. While shareholders are interested in a financial return on their investment, many do not want that return to come at any cost. Thus, they can influence the behaviour of firms through their share ownership, either individually by buying shares or institutionally through an investment or pension fund. This is known as **socially responsible investment (SRI)** and it is now a large part of the investment market. It is estimated that as much as $1 in every $8 in the US is SRI, whereas in the UK, the SRI fund market is worth around £330 billion (Waring and Edwards, 2008). Internationally, the UN launched the United Nations Principles for Responsible Investment (UNPRI) in 2006, whereby signatory investment funds agree to integrate social, environmental and good governance principles and practices into their investment decisions and to implement them in the companies in which they invest. It is a labelling scheme for investors, similar to the labelling schemes for consumers. The aim is to provide individual investors with some certainty that their funds will be invested responsibly. By 2008, the UNPRI had over 360 institutional signatories representing US$14 trillion in assets (UNPRI, 2008). The FTSE4Good is another example of a labelling scheme for investors.

> **Socially responsible investment (SRI)** – investments made directly, or via a managed fund, in companies that are considered to be socially responsible

There are three ways that SRI influences firm behaviour:

- *Negative screening*: involves eliminating certain products or behaviours from funds. If someone invests in an SRI fund, they might, for example, want to know that their money isn't being invested in tobacco or armaments.
- *Positive screening*: involves a fund actively investing in industries or sectors that will make a positive contribution to society, such as green energy or sustainability.
- *Engagement*: SRI funds invest in a range of firms that have not been screened in or out, and work with them to improve their CSR where issues emerge. SRI firms are likely to try and work with a company first, but failing this might engage in what is termed 'investor activism', where they either table a motion at the company AGM or publicly embarrass the firm into changing its behaviour. An example of this is where four investment firms from the USA and the UK wrote a joint open letter to the chairman of Walmart's audit committee, stating that it needed to improve its employment practices as they were damaging the share price. This followed a number of embarrassing stories in the media relating to illegal immigrant workers, a class action sex discrimination suit and cuts to employee healthcare benefits (BBC, 2005).

## THE CASE AGAINST CSR

One of the key arguments of advocates of CSR is that firms can improve their financial performance by improving their social behaviour and so it just makes good business sense to do the right thing. However, critics of CSR, such as Aneel Karnani (2010) and Robert Reich (2008), argue that this is not always the case. Yes, sometimes what is good for the firm and what is good for society will coincide, and in such cases firms can make profits by acting in the public interest. But when these two coincide,

BUILDING YOUR SKILLS

© CROSS DESIGN/FOTOLIA

You have been appointed to the CSR department of a large MNC clothing company. The department is new and the firm currently has no CSR code of conduct for its supply chain, but there have been several stories in the media about poor working conditions in the factories that manufacture clothes your company sells. You have been asked to review the CSR approach of any four competitors and to come up with a list of principles and practices you think your firm should adopt so as to improve working conditions in your supply chain.

why call it corporate social responsibility? If a firm can reduce its electricity bill by investing in energy-saving technology, it makes sense to do it for financial reasons. In other words, managers should do it because it reduces costs and enhances the bottom line. If a firm can develop a new socially beneficial product that consumers want, it should do so to improve long-term value. Reducing costs, improving the bottom line, increasing long-term value and so on are what managers are paid to do. As Karnani (2010) points out, fast-food chains have not introduced healthy salads into their menus because of public health concerns, but because they realized it could increase sales. Similarly, car manufacturers are investing in fuel-efficient cars because consumers are concerned about rising energy costs and want to purchase such vehicles. Reich (2008) argues that Walmart switched to using environmentally friendly packaging because it was cheaper, while Starbucks introduced health insurance for its part-time employees to reduce staff turnover. However, 'to credit these corporations with being "socially responsible" is to stretch the term to mean anything a company might do to increase profits if, in doing so, it also happens to have some beneficent impact on the rest of society' (Reich, 2008: 171). As Karnani (2007) posits, when what is good for the firm and what is good for society coincide, then CSR is irrelevant, because firms will do it anyway. Friedman (1970) went so far as to suggest that it was 'approaching fraud' for firms to cloak self-interest in social responsibility.

Of more concern to critics is when profits and the public good do not coincide. In such cases CSR is ineffective. In many cases, doing the right thing does not lead to enhanced profit. For example, poverty wages and poor working conditions in the supply chains of leading brands could easily be resolved, but it would lead to lower profits and higher prices. Firms often respond to criticism of working conditions in their supply chains by developing codes of conduct or announcing audits by independent organizations. But critics would argue this is simply public relations spin, or corporate gloss, aimed at deflecting negative media attention, and it will not improve working conditions. In the case of green issues, this is often referred to as 'greenwashing'. Even *The Economist* (2008) acknowledges that, for many firms, 'the real motive [of CSR] is public relations, and the telltale sign is that the person responsible for CSR sits in the corporate-communications department'. Thus, CSR is too often about communication and public relations, not action. As Klein (2000: 430) notes, codes of conduct are often written by corporate public relations departments in response to negative publicity. Their aim is to 'muzzle the offshore watchdog' of NGOs and labour rights groups, not to bring about changes in working conditions. Few supplier contracts are ever terminated due to breaches of codes of conduct, and where conditions do improve following an inspection, they soon return to where they were previously. Others question the 'independence' of NGOs like the Fair Labor Association that audit big brand companies. Much of its funding comes from these same companies, and thus it is unlikely to be overly critical (Ballinger, 2008).

Nike is a company that is sometimes held up as an example of how CSR can be effective. It came under intense public scrutiny by labour rights NGOs and trade unions throughout the 1990s for manufacturing its shoes in 'sweatshops'. Its initial response to the criticism was a public relations campaign. However, when the negative publicity did not abate and consumers began boycotting the company, it finally began to seriously address the issues. Indeed, it is now widely acknowledged as one of the CSR leaders in the apparel industry. Vogel (2006) argues that the Nike code of conduct provides working conditions in countries like Vietnam that are well above the statutory minimum. This, he argues, is evidence that pressure from NGOs and the media is an effective mechanism for raising corporate standards. However, critics would respond that this change only came about after more than a decade of negative publicity and campaigning by NGOs. Moreover, despite significant resources being spent on auditing its supply chain companies, instances of labour rights abuses and poor working conditions continue to emerge (Locke and Romis, 2009). An analysis of more than 800 Nike audits in 51 countries found that the monitoring process has had minimal impact. As the authors of this report noted, voluntary codes of conduct are an ineffective strategy for improving working conditions (Locke et al., 2007). Ballinger (2012) cites a recent example where an Indonesian union won a $950,000 settlement in court for 4,500 workers who were forced to work seven-day weeks without overtime pay. This was in a factory supplying Nike that had allegedly been monitored by the Fair Labor Association for over 10 years. As Ballinger sardonically notes: 'it's easy to miss 570,000+ unpaid overtime hours, right?'

Reich (2008) suggests that people should not be surprised that firms say one thing to divert attention while continuing to engage in practices that drive profits. He describes the past 30 years of global capitalism as a period of 'supercapitalism', in which firms are facing relentless pressure to lower costs. This pressure comes from institutional investment funds that want increased profits and consumers who want lower prices. While there has been some growth in socially responsible investment, this is still not a large enough proportion of the investment market to make a significant impact. As for consumers, while they say they care, this is not reflected in their buying behaviour. In a 2004 EU survey, 75 per cent of respondents said they would change their shopping behaviour in response to the social and environmental performance of firms, but in the same survey, only 3 per cent reported ever having done so (Sachdev, 2006). And the way employees are treated will have more to do with the competitive strategy of the firm than any potential reputational risk. A high-tech company like Google will view its employees as strategic assets, but for firms competing on the basis of low price, employees may be seen as a cost to be minimized and as easily replaceable. Thus, the 'business case' pressures for CSR from employees, investors and consumers are simply not strong enough against the short-term pressure for profits. As Ballinger (2008: 95–6) points out in relation to Nike:

My research shows that about 75 cents per pair of shoes to the worker would be needed to fix problems that workers have been complaining about since the 1980s. That is roughly 80 per cent more to workers, or $1.80 on a $70 pair of shoes at Foot Locker. If Nike, instead, paid workers that 75 cents more per pair of shoes, the cost to Nike would be $210 million a year compared to the much lower CSR cost of less than $20 million.

Voluntary codes of conduct and audits are cheaper than addressing the real issues, which are a business model predicated on cheap labour, a lack of regulation, and weak collective bargaining power to counteract the greater power of global brands. Tight deadlines, production quotas, price targets and other aspects of the business model set by the brand actually incentivize manufacturers to breach aspects of the code of conduct, such as long working hours or forced overtime (Steiner and Steiner, 2012).

## Apple and CSR

HRM IN THE NEWS

Apple is the world's most valuable company. In mid-2012, it was worth over US$600 billion and its shares peaked at just over US$700 per share.

Its products – the iPhone, the iPad, the iPod – are ubiquitous symbols of coolness and chic. Many of its customers see these products as not just electronic gadgets, but as extensions of their personalities. When new models of the iPhone and iPad are released, there are queues outside Apple stores in cities worldwide. And yet, despite this remarkable success, Apple has been in the news lately for all the wrong reasons, its brand tarnished by growing criticisms over inhumane working conditions in the factories in China that make these products. Among the accusations levelled at Apple's supply chain factories are long hours and excessive overtime, low pay, discrimination, humiliating treatment of workers by management, crowded living conditions, use of child labour, and poor health and safety standards. Some workers complain of standing for such long hours that their legs swell. In 2011, two explosions at separate factories making iPads resulted in four fatalities and injury to 77 employees, and in 2010, reports emerged about employee exposure to toxic chemicals in the manufacture of iPhone screens. Much of the criticism has been focused on Foxconn (the Taiwanese MNC, otherwise known as Hon Hai Precision Industry Co. Ltd, the world's largest electronics contract manufacturer), a company that employs more than one million workers in its Chinese factories, manufacturing products for Apple and other leading electronic brands, including Microsoft, Dell, Hewlett-Packard, Lenovo, Motorola, Nokia and Sony.

In 2010, 14 Foxconn employees committed suicide by jumping off the factory buildings, and 150 workers threatened mass suicide in early 2012 in protest at the working conditions. While Foxconn manufactures for a range of leading MNCs, Apple has been the focus of critics' attention because it is the largest player and so is best placed to bring about an improvement in working conditions in factories run by Foxconn and other large supply chain manufacturers. Apple has a 'code of conduct' covering employment conditions that all suppliers are meant to adhere to, and since 2007 it has been conducting audits of its suppliers. Where breaches of the code are found, Apple requires the supplier to rectify the problem, or risk having the contract terminated. Apple argues that its own audits show that progress is being made to improve adherence levels with the code of conduct. However, following continued negative publicity and an online petition signed by more than 250,000 people in 2012 requesting that Apple ensures 'ethical, fair and safe' working conditions, the company agreed to allow the Fair Labor Association to conduct independent audits of its supply chain factories in China.

Critics say audits do not address the real issues and that if Apple wanted to improve working conditions it could do so fairly easily, but at a cost to its profits and the speed of delivery of new products. This is evidenced by the fact that supplier contracts are rarely cancelled for breaches of the code of conduct. Former Apple executives quoted in a *New York Times* article agree. One said: 'We've known about labor issues in some factories for four years, and they're still going on. Why? Because the system works for us. Suppliers would change

everything tomorrow if Apple told them they didn't have another choice.' Another noted that 'noncompliance is tolerated, as long as the suppliers promise to try harder next time. If we meant business, core violations would disappear.' According to the critics, part of the reason companies like Foxconn push their workers so hard and ignore elements of the code of conduct is that the profit margins Apple allows them to make are very tight. The only way they can increase their margins is to cut corners. As one former Apple executive pointed out: 'You can set all the rules you want, but they're meaningless if you don't give suppliers enough profit to treat workers well. If you squeeze margins, you're forcing them to cut safety.' Despite the negative publicity, consumers keep buying new Apple products. As a current Apple executive pointed out: 'Right now, customers care more about a new iPhone than working conditions in China.'

## Questions

1  To what extent do you think Apple has responsibility for the working conditions in other companies that make and supply its products?

2  In light of the Apple case, how effective do you think the business case for CSR is at improving working conditions in factories like Foxconn?

## Sources

Apple (2012) *Supplier Responsibility Progress Report*, www.apple.com/supplierresponsibility/reports.html.

Arthur, C. (2012) Apple supplier audit begins with Foxconn plant, *The Guardian*, 13 February, www.guardian.co.uk/technology/2012/feb/13/apple-supplier-audit-foxconn.

Duhigg, C. and Barboza, D. (2012) In China, human costs are built into an iPad, *New York Times*, 25 January, www.nytimes.com/2012/01/26/business/ieconomy-apples-ipad-and-the-human-costs-for-workers-in-china.html?pagewanted=all.

Foley, S. (2012) Apple admits it has a human rights problem, *The Independent*, 14 February, www.independent.co.uk/news/world/asia/apple-admits-it-has-a-human-rights-problem-6090617.html.

Moore, M. (2012) 'Mass suicide' protest at Apple manufacturer Foxconn factory, *The Telegraph*, 11 January, www.telegraph.co.uk/news/worldnews/asia/china/9006988/Mass-suicide-protest-at-Apple-manufacturer-Foxconn-factory.html.

## *A ROLE FOR REGULATION?*

If, as critics argue, CSR is an ineffective way of bringing about real reform in working conditions, then CSR could actually be dangerous. It lulls the public into a false sense of security that the issues are being addressed and thus reduces the clamour for government regulation (Reich, 2008; Karnani, 2010). Reich (2008) goes further in arguing that CSR undermines the democratic process. In a CSR model of governance, firms decide what the minimum labour standards are in the factories in which their products are manufactured. He would argue, however,

that it is the job of governments in a democratic society to decide what the appropriate standards should be and then for companies to adhere to them. As Reich stated in a debate on CSR with Vogel: 'Without regulation, CSR is whatever you want it to be. Democratic capitalism is meant to put some limits on capitalist organizations in order to deal with the social costs, externalities [a cost or benefit for a third party that is not reflected in the price of a product or service, such as pollution], and side effects of profit accumulation' (Vogel and Reich, 2008).

Given that the legal standards in many of the countries in which leading global brands operate are very low, one way of addressing the concerns of Western consumers would be for Western governments to pass extraterritorial legislation. An extraterritorial law passed in the USA, for example, would govern US firms in whichever countries they operated. Such a law would not be based on US minimum wage and labour laws, but would be based on the sorts of standards included in current codes of conduct, such as those in the ETI Base Code. The difference is that the standards would apply to all companies, and breaches of the standards would result in prosecution and penalties for the company concerned, a strong incentive for them to ensure that their supply chain manufacturers adhere to them. Currently, firms decide what standards they wish to apply and the only penalty for breaching these standards is negative publicity.

In an age of liberalization and free markets, the business community is generally opposed to regulation. They see it as being inflexible, bureaucratic and introducing compliance costs. Compliance costs relate to the expenditure of time or money in conforming to regulatory standards, for example keeping detailed records of employee working hours. They also argue it brings about a 'tick box' response, where firms do the minimum to meet the legal standard, whereas what is required for addressing many CSR issues is real engagement and a change of behaviour. Thus, they see the current CSR approach of voluntary 'self-regulation' and working in cooperation with NGOs and other stakeholders to develop and monitor codes of conducts as the best way forward.

Trade union organizing at the factory level could play an important role in driving up labour standards in supply chains as an alternative to regulation. However, there have been many reports of instances where workers joined or formed trade unions to bargain for higher wages, with the end result being that the supplier contract was cancelled and a cheaper alternative was found (Ballinger, 2008). While the ETI Base Code (see Table 14.1 above) includes freedom of association to join a trade union and engage in collective bargaining, research suggests that only 15 per cent of codes include such provisions and many Western MNCs are accused of being anti-union (Sachdev, 2006).

While the critics of CSR make some valid points about its ineffectiveness, governments are averse to introducing too much regulation. They have accepted the business community line that regulation distorts the market and voluntarism is a better way of bringing about change. Where regulation is introduced, it is often aimed at disclosure of information in order to facilitate pressure

for corporate reform from stakeholders such as consumers, investors, employees and NGOs. For example, many members of the public are shareholders in companies through their pension funds, although they don't actually realize it. Recent developments in UK pension company law requiring disclosure of CSR information have been aimed at enabling pension fund members and investors more generally to make ethical investment decisions. Rather than regulate the behaviour of companies directly, it is trying to encourage 'ethical market forces' to drive corporate behaviour in the right direction. However, as we have seen, the evidence suggests that consumers and investors are unlikely to make a significant impact. More effective is the role of NGOs and the media in embarrassing corporations about ethical, social and environmental issues and it is unlikely that this will stop.

 ## SUMMARY

This chapter explored some of the HRM issues that come under the CSR umbrella. We also looked at why CSR has become such an important business issue and examined some of the ethical and financial reasons why firms choose to engage in CSR. However, as we saw, CSR is not universally acclaimed. While many critics of CSR share the social and environmental aims of its advocates, they have significant doubts that these aims can be achieved through a purely voluntarist approach. Relying on consumers, employees, investors and civil society organizations to change corporate behaviour is not an effective way of addressing the social and environmental issues of our time. In particular, they highlight the inevitable tension between making profits and addressing social and environmental issues, and their argument is that profits will trump CSR. For critics, it is the job of government to set the standards society expects, not corporations. Given the reluctance of governments to increase regulation, CSR will continue to be a mainstream business issue that most large businesses need to integrate into their corporate strategy.

 ## CHAPTER REVIEW QUESTIONS

1 Explain the various definitions of CSR and find some examples on the internet of companies that illustrate

the various approaches. Which approach to CSR do you think is best and why?

2  Explain the difference between the shareholder and stakeholder views of the firm. Which do you think is the most appropriate in the current economic climate? Justify your decision.

3  Outline the 'business case' arguments for CSR and evaluate how effective this approach is.

4  Outline the arguments of the critics of CSR and evaluate how convincing their arguments are.

5  To what extent do you think CSR is a real attempt on the part of companies to grapple with important social, ethical and environmental issues as opposed to window dressing to appeal to consumer idealism and pre-empt government regulation?

6  Which do you think will be more effective at aligning corporate behaviour with the interests of society, the 'carrot' of the business case or the 'stick' of regulation?

7  Search the internet for examples of MNCs that have been criticized by NGOs or other pressure groups about the employment practices in their supply chains. Now look at the CSR pages of the websites of these companies. Contrast what the companies say they are doing with some of the criticisms raised.

 **FURTHER READING**

Blowfield, M. and Murray, A. (2011) *Corporate Responsibility*, 2nd edn, Oxford: Oxford University Press.

Reich, R. (2008) *Supercapitalism: The Battle for Democracy in an Age of Big Business*, Cambridge: Icon Books.

Steiner, J. and Steiner, G. (2012) *Business, Government, and Society: A Managerial Perspective, Text and Cases*, 13th edn, New York: McGraw-Hill.

 **USEFUL WEBSITES**

www.fairlabor.org/
The Fair Labor Association is one of the leading international organizations working with MNCs to monitor and improve working conditions in supply chain factories. It is an affiliation of NGOs, universities and CSR-minded companies. The website provides information on the companies it works with and the Fair Labor Association code of conduct.

makeitfair.org/en
The Make It Fair website is a source of information on working conditions and environmental issues in the electronics industry.

www.globallabourrights.org/
The Institute for Global Labour and Human Rights conducts research on working conditions and public campaigns to promote workers' rights. The website has a wide range of information about working conditions in the global economy.

www.bitc.org.uk/
Business in the Community is a business membership organization that promotes CSR. The website contains reports and information on a range of CSR issues. It also has case studies of best practice CSR. The Irish website is www.bitc.ie/. Affiliated organizations addressing gender and diversity issues are Opportunity Now and Race for Opportunity, which share a website www.bitcdiversity.org.uk/.

 For extra resources including videos and further skills development guidance go to: www.palgrave.com/business/carbery

# GLOSSARY

**Accident** An unplanned or unforeseen event that could lead to injury to people, damage to plant, machinery or some other loss

**Analytical methods** They identify characteristics of the job that are valued by the organization and assess the degree to which they are present in the job

**Attitude-based approach** Focuses on changing a person's feelings and inner thoughts towards safety

**Attitudes** Beliefs and values that the learner should espouse and put into practice and sustain

**Authentic career** A career characterized by consistency between an individual's public and private beliefs

**Behaviour-based approach** Focuses on what people do, analyses why they do it, and then applies a research-supported intervention strategy to improve what people do

**Behavioural science approach** How to describe, explain and predict human behaviour in a work context

**Blended learning** Involves a planned combination of learning strategies such as e-learning, self-managed classroom and coaching activities to suit the needs of the individual

**Boundaryless career** Sequences of jobs that can cross occupational, organizational and geographic boundaries

**Buddy approach** An informal approach to assisting a new employee learn about the organization and how things work around or within the organization

**Bullying** Inappropriate behaviour at work that undermines an employee's right to dignity at work

**Business case** The business case for equality holds that fostering, promoting and practising equality in business is good for business and contributes to profits; and on this basis, organizations should engage with principles of equality

**Capitalist system** An economic system of private enterprise for profit

**Career** A person's work experiences over the course of their life

**Career development** How a person manages their life, learning and work to achieve career goals

**Career motivation** The desire to put in effort to achieve specific career goals

**Career systems** The set of HRM policies and processes that an organization uses to manage employee careers

**Coaching** The practice of supporting an individual through the process of achieving a specific personal, professional or work-related result

**Common law** Law developed by judges through decisions made in courts and similar tribunals

**Comparator** A person or group that someone making a claim of discrimination will compare themselves to, with the purpose of demonstrating that they have been treated differently/unfairly using that comparator as a standard

**Competency-based interviews** These interviews are structured around job-specific competencies, with candidates asked questions based on critical incidents in the role

**Compliance-driven diversity management** Diversity is managed because governments and/or regulatory bodies develop legislation and regulations with which organizations are encouraged/forced to comply

**Core workers** Workers whose skills and competencies are considered 'core' to the effective operation of the organization, whom the organization will seek to recruit and employ on a full-time permanent basis. They are typically paid a regular salary, benefits, receive training and development, have defined career paths with promotion opportunities and are involved in a performance management system

**Corporate social responsibility (CSR)** The duty of a business to go beyond profit maximization and act responsibly and contribute positively to society

**Country of origin effects** The influence the country from which the MNC originates has on HRM in its foreign subsidiaries

**Devolved** The process of moving decision-making downwards, from HR to line managers

**Dignity at work policies** Policies that specifically address behaviour in the workplace that would serve to undermine a person's dignity. They are usually associated with bullying and harassment and should clearly set out the company's position on bullying and harassment, responsibilities, roles, training, procedures, rules and penalties with respect to this issue

Direct discrimination  Discrimination that is obviously contrary to the terms of equality legislation, such as explicitly excluding people over 50 from applying for a job

Direct pay  The part of pay received by the employee in the form of cash, cheque or direct deposit

Disciplinary procedure  Written, step-by-step process that a firm commits itself to follow in every case where an employee has to be warned, reprimanded or dismissed. Failure to follow a fair, transparent and uniform disciplinary procedure may result in legal penalties (damages) and/or annulment of the firm's action

Discrimination  Treating a person or group differently and unfairly on the basis of certain traits or characteristics, such as sexuality, gender, race, religion or disability

Diversity management  The systematic and planned commitment by organizations to recruit, select, retain, reward and promote a heterogeneous mix of employees

Dominance effects  The influence that dominant economies, like the USA, have on HRM in MNCs, regardless of where they are from or located

E-learning  a broad term that includes computer-based training, technology-based learning and web-based learning activities

Employee attitude surveys  Research carried out to assess the feelings of a target group of employees towards various aspects of their work, their team and their organization

Employee turnover  The number of people who leave an organization and need to be replaced in order to maintain production or service

Employee wellbeing  The overall quality of an employee's experience at work

Employer brand  An organization is recognized in its own right as a desirable place to work – positive employer brand – by the internal and external labour market

Equality  The state of being equal, especially in status, rights or opportunities

Equality policies  A written policy that comprehensively sets out the philosophy of the company with respect to equality and clearly indicates all responsibilities, procedures, processes, training, rules and penalties in this area

E-recruitment  A vacancy is advertised to potential candidates via the internet. It can target internal and/or external recruits

Ergonomics  The relationship between employees, physical work equipment and the environment

Evaluation  Establishing the intended and unintended outcomes of L&D activities and assessing whether the benefits justify the investment

Expatriates  Also known as 'international assignees', are employees who undertake international assignments

Expatriation  The process of transferring an employee to other international operations of the MNC to carry out a particular assignment

External recruitment  A vacancy is advertised to potential candidates outside the existing employee base in the organization

Felt fair  Acceptance by employees that the difference in pay between jobs is based on the characteristics of the job

Financial flexibility  The ability for organizations to adapt their wage costs depending on the ratio of core and peripheral workers employed

Flexible benefits  From a defined set of available benefits, employees select the benefits that best meet their needs

Flexible workforce  A workforce that an organization can quickly and easily adjust in order to meet its changing labour needs

Flexible working practices  A range of initiatives where the organization provides more flexible work schedules to employees, to adequately staff positions when, where and how required

Functional flexibility  The ability to develop skills in line with demand

Globalization  The opening up of national markets and the creation of a global economy through the deregulation of trade, growth in foreign direct investment (FDI), movement of people and capital, and advances in information technology

Grievance procedure  Step-by-step process an employee must follow to get their complaint addressed satisfactorily. The formal (written) complaint moves from one level of authority (of the firm and the union) to the next higher level. Grievance procedures are typically included in union (collective bargaining) agreements

Hazards  Any source of potential damage, harm or adverse health effects on something or someone under certain conditions at work

**Host country effects** The influence the country in which a foreign subsidiary is located has on HRM in that subsidiary

**Human capital pool** The collection of employee skill that exists within a firm at any given time

**Human error** A human decision or behaviour that has undesirable effects

**Human factors** How characteristics of the organization affect employee behaviour

**Human resource management** The strategic and integrated approach taken by an organization to the management of its most valued assets, namely its people

**Human resource planning (HRP)** The ongoing consideration of staffing requirements – now and in the future – with regards to the specific jobs and skills that are and will be required in the organization. It results in the development of specific HR strategies to achieve organization-specific staffing requirements

**Indirect discrimination** This occurs when a seemingly neutral provision attached to a job acts to exclude a person or group protected under equality legislation; for example, a requirement for people to be over 2m tall for a job in a shop would effectively exclude more women than men

**Indirect pay or benefits** These have a financial value but are rewarded to employees in forms other than cash

**Induction** The whole process whereby new employees in an organization adjust to their new roles and responsibilities within a new working environment

**Industrial relations** Areas of the employment relationship where employers deal with employee representatives rather than individual employees

**Informational approach** This approach to induction focuses on supplying new starters with basic information regarding the working of procedures within the organization

**Institutional barriers** Those barriers to employment or progression within employment posed by existing structures, systems and rules, which act to exclude certain groups of people, for example a lack of childcare facilities

**Internal recruitment** A vacancy is advertised to potential candidates from within the existing employee base in the organization

**International integration** How strongly integrated all the MNC's international operations are with each other

**International recruitment** A vacancy is advertised to potential candidates who are currently residing overseas

**Interpersonal skills** Skills used by a person to interact in an appropriate manner with others. In the business domain, generally refers to a manager's or employee's ability to get along with others while getting the job done. They are also described as 'people' or 'communication skills', involving techniques such as active listening, appropriate questioning, using empathy and the right tone of voice, body language and attitude fitting to the circumstances. In essence, it is about how well one communicates and behaves or carries oneself

**Job analysis** The process used to gather detailed information about the various tasks and responsibilities involved in a position. Through this process, the knowledge, skills, abilities, attitudes and behaviours associated with successful performance in the role are also identified

**Job description** The detailed breakdown of the purpose and various tasks and responsibilities involved in a particular job

**Job evaluation** A technique used by organizations to establish the relative worth of jobs

**Kaleidoscope career** A career that adjusts to changes in an individual's circumstances and motivation

**Knowledge** Defined as specific information components of a task, job or role that the learner should acquire

**Knowledge economy** Where specialist, expert knowledge is perceived to be as critical as other economic resources

**Learning and development (L&D)** Learning refers to activities provided by the organization to enhance employee competencies, develop greater self-awareness and insight, and contribute to individual, team and organizational effectiveness; development refers to activities leading to new knowledge and skills for reasons of personal growth

**Learning organization** An organization that enables the learning of all its employees and continually changes itself

**Line managers** Managers who have employees directly reporting to them and who have a higher level of responsibility than those employees

**Management by objectives (MBO)** A management system in which the objectives of the organization are explicitly stated, so that management and employees understand their overall or ultimate purpose and the specific implications for their role in the organization

**Mass career customization** A collaborative process that allows an employee and employer to customize a career path along a defined set of options

Mental workload  The mental demands placed on humans at work

Mentor  The person charged with developing and assisting an employee to advance their career

Mentoree  The individual who is being mentored by a more senior individual within the organization

Mentoring process  A developmental process focused on formal career development and advancement

New starter  An employee who is relatively new to or has just joined the organization

Non-analytical methods  Whole jobs are compared to determine the organization's internal pay structure

Nongovernmental organizations (NGOs)  Organizations that are independent of government and generally run on a not-for-profit basis. Examples include Greenpeace, Friends of the Earth, Oxfam, the Fair Labor Association, and the Institute for Global Labour and Human Rights

Numerical flexibility  The ability to increase or decrease the number of people working in the organization

Off-ramp career  A nontraditional career path that recognizes that individuals, usually women, will take some time out from their careers

Onboarding  The mechanism through which new employees acquire the necessary knowledge, skills and behaviours to become effective organizational members and insiders

Organizational citizenship behaviours  The behaviour of individual employees that is not directly or explicitly required by an organization as part of the role but which promotes the effective functioning of the organization

Organizational fit  The 'fit' or alignment of the personal values/work ethic of the employee with those of the organization's culture and values

Organizational support for development  Employees' perceptions that the organization provides opportunities and programmes to enable employees to develop their skills and competencies

Performance management  An ongoing activity relating to all scenarios where people meet for the purpose of attaining objectives

Performance management review meeting  An assessment of an employee's work and/or development, undertaken at a fixed point in time, often used to determine the degree to which stated objectives and expectations have been reached, to set down objectives for the future, and frequently bearing some relationship to promotion and/or pay rise/bonus prospects

Performance-related pay (PRP)  A form of direct pay linked to the performance of an individual, team or all employees when predefined objectives are achieved

Peripheral workers  Workers whose skills and competencies are considered 'peripheral' or nonessential to the effective operation of the organization, and so the organization will seek to recruit and employ them on a part-time, fixed-term contract or outsourced basis

Person–job fit  The enthusiasm, knowledge, skills, abilities and motivations of the individual match those required by the job

Person–organization fit  The values, interests and behaviours of the individual match the organizational culture

Person specification  Specifies the type of person needed to do a particular job. It essentially translates the job description into human terms

Peter Principle  The belief that, in an organization where promotion is based on performance and achievement, an organization's members will eventually be promoted beyond their level of ability

Philanthropy  The practice of making charitable donations to good causes

Portfolio career  A career that involves doing two or more different jobs for different employers

Positive action  Measures undertaken with the aim of achieving full and effective equality for members of groups that are socially or economically disadvantaged

Positive discrimination  Preferential discriminatory treatment of a minority group over a majority group to try and counter disadvantage in the labour market

Productive diversity management  Diversity is managed because of the positive effect it can have on the bottom line (profitability) of the organization

Protean career  A career defined by uniquely individual psychological success and can mean personal accomplishment, feelings of pride, achievement or family happiness

Protected grounds  Those identified by national institutions as relating to areas where discrimination has or is likely to occur, such as race, sex, sexual orientation, religion, age and disability, and which are subsequently covered by equality legislation

Psychological contract  The unwritten rules and expectations that exist between the employee and employer

Pull factors  Those factors beyond the control of the organization that may cause an employee to leave the organization such as moving to a new location/country, the arrival of children, retirement and so on

Push factors  Those factors that negatively impact on an employee and may be the trigger to start them thinking about leaving an organization, such as dissatisfaction with their work, their boss or their promotional opportunities, a lack of developmental opportunities and so on

Ranking matrix  A document that lists those candidates who scored highest in the shortlisting, from highest to lowest

Recruitment  A process whereby the organization sources or attracts people to apply for a position in the organization

Relational approach  This approach to induction focuses on helping new starters rapidly establish a broad network of relationships with co-workers from whom they can access the information they need to be productive members of the team

Relational psychological contract  A situation where job security is provided in exchange for commitment and loyalty to the organization

Reliability  A method is identified as reliable if it consistently measures what it sets out to measure

Repatriation  The process that involves bringing the expatriate back to their home country after completing their international assignment

Resourcing  A process where people are identified and deployed to undertake work within an organization

Retention  A strategic approach adopted by organizations to keep productive employees from seeking alternative employment

Reward package  The financial and nonfinancial elements offered to employees in return for their labour

Reward system  The combination of financial and nonfinancial elements used by an organization to compensate employees for their time, effort and commitment at work

Risk  A situation involving exposure to danger

Safety culture  The attitudes, beliefs, perceptions and values that employees share in relation to safety

Selection  A process used to find the candidate who most closely matches the specific requirements of a vacant position

Shareholder view of the firm  The primary objective of management should be to maximize profit for shareholders

Shortlisting  A sifting process where those candidates who most closely match the predetermined job-specific requirements are separated out from all other applicants

Shortlisting matrix  A scoring mechanism for placing the candidates who have applied for the position in a ranking order, based on their suitability for the role

Skill  Dimensions of performance that the learner should be able to demonstrate

Social contract  An implicit agreement between business and society that sets out the broad standards that business should adhere to and duties they should fulfil in order to maintain the support and legitimacy of society. These standards are partly reflected in law but are mostly contained in social norms, values and expectations

Social inclusion  A measure of the extent to which a person or groups can participate in aspects of society to the same level as (or relative to) the average population. Key measures of social inclusion are access to work, adequate housing, education levels and access to education, healthcare and so on

Social justice approach  The social justice case for equality holds that organizations have a moral obligation, regardless of profit, to promote, foster and practise equality in all facets of the business

Socially responsible investment (SRI)  Investments made directly, or via a managed fund, in companies that are considered to be socially responsible

Stakeholders  Any individuals, groups or organizations who are affected by or can affect the actions of a company

Stakeholder view of the firm  Management should take the interests of all stakeholders into account when making decisions

Strategic human resource development (SHRD)  Learning activities focused on individuals, teams and organizations aimed at enhancing the alignment of human resources with the strategic objectives of the organization

Strategic human resource management  The linkage between HRM policies and practices and the strategic objectives of the organization in creating organizational competitive advantage

Stress  The demands of the work environment and the ability of the employee to meet these demands

Strike  A work stoppage caused by the refusal of employees to work, in order to persuade an employer to concede to their demands

Survival curve  A model stating that new starters in an organization are more at risk of leaving in the first six weeks of commencing a new job. The likelihood of leaving decreases as the length of employment increases

Tacit skills  Intangible skills developed as a result of informal learning processes

Tangible benefits  Benefits that can be measured and reported on

Temporal flexibility  The ability to adjust the hours/times people work in an organization

Trade unions  An organized group of employees who represent employees' interest in maintaining or improving the conditions of their employment

Traditional career  A direct line of career progression where seniority and length of service are rewarded with progression from one specific job to a more senior job

Training  The process of acquiring the knowledge, skills and attitudes required to perform an organizational role effectively

Transactional psychological contract  A situation where extra money and learning and development opportunities are provided in exchange for commitment and loyalty to the organization

Union density  The proportion of a country's employees who are union members

Validity  The extent to which a selection method measures what it purports to measure and how well it does this

Values-driven diversity management  Diversity is managed because organizations believe it is 'the right thing to do'

Victimizing  An act that treats someone unfairly

Work capacity  How much work an individual can do

Working days lost  A measure of strike activity, calculated by multiplying the number of persons involved by the number of normal working days during which they were involved in the dispute

Workplace diversity  When there are increasing numbers of people with different characteristics at work together

# BIBLIOGRAPHY

AFL-CIO (2011) *Why CEO Pay Matters*. Available at: www.aflcio.org/apps/paywatch/paywatch_infographic.html (Accessed: 14 March 2012).

Aguinis, H. and Kraiger, K. (2009) Benefits of training and development for individuals and teams, organisations, and society, *Annual Review of Psychology*, **60**: 451–74.

Anderson, V. (2007) *The Value of Learning: From Return on Investment to Return on Expectation*, London: CIPD.

Andreassen, C.S., Ursin, H. and Eriksen, H.R. (2007) The relationship between strong motivation to work, 'workaholism', and health, *Psychology and Health*, **22**(5): 615–29.

Anker, R. (2001) Theories of occupational segregation by sex, in M.F. Loutfi (ed.) *Women, Gender and Work: What is Equality and How Do We Get There?*, Geneva: ILO.

Appelbaum, E., Bailey, T., Berg, P. and Kalleberg, A. (2000) *Manufacturing Advantage: Why High-performance Work Systems Pay Off*, Ithaca, NY: ILR Press.

Ardichvili, A. and Manderscheid, S. (2008) Emerging practices in leadership development: an introduction, *Advances in Developing Human Resources*, **10**(5): 619–31.

Armstrong, C., Flood, P., Guthrie, J. et al. (2010) The impact of diversity and equality management on firm performance: beyond high performance work systems, *Human Resource Management*, **49**(6): 977–98.

Armstrong, M. (2009a) *Armstrong's Handbook of Performance Management: An Evidence-based Guide to Delivering High Performance*, 4th edn, London: Kogan Page.

Armstrong, M. (2009b) *Armstrong's Handbook of Human Resource Management Practice*, 11th edn, London: Kogan Page.

Armstrong, M. and Baron, A. (1998) *Performance Management: The New Realities*, London: IPD.

Armstrong, M. and Baron, A. (2004) *Managing Performance: Performance Management: Action and Impact*, London: CIPD.

Armstrong, M. and Baron, A. (2005) *Managing Performance: Performance Management in Action*, London: CIPD.

Arnold, J., Randall, R., Patterson, F. et al. (2010) *Work Psychology: Understanding Human Behaviour in the Workplace*, 5th edn, Harlow: Financial Times/Prentice Hall.

Arthur, J.B. (1994) Effects of human resource systems on manufacturing performance and turnover, *Academy of Management Journal*, **37**(3): 670–88.

Arthur, M.B. and Rousseau, D. (1996) *The Boundaryless Career: A New Employment Principle for a New Organizational Era*, Oxford: Oxford University Press.

Arthur, M.B., Hall, D.T. and Lawrence, B.S. (1989) *Handbook of Career Theory*, Cambridge: Cambridge University Press.

Arthur, M.B., Inkson, K. and Pringle, J.K. (1999) *The New Careers: Individual Action and Economic Change*, Thousand Oaks, CA: Sage.

Arvey, R.D. (1979) Unfair discrimination in the employment interview: legal and psychological aspects, *Psychological Bulletin*, **86**: 736–65.

Aschenbrenner, M. and Biehl, B. (1994) Improved safety through improved technical measures? Empirical studies regarding risk compensation processes in relation to anti-lock braking systems, in R.M. Trimpop and G.J. Wilde (eds) *Challenges to Accident Prevention: The Issue of Risk Compensation Behaviour*, Groningen: Styx.

Atkinson, J. (1984) Manpower strategies for flexible organizations, *Personnel Management*, August, 28–31.

Baker, T. and Aldrich, H.E. (1996) Prometheus stretches: building identity and cumulative knowledge in multiemployer careers, in M.B. Arthur and D.M. Rousseau (eds) *The Boundaryless Career: A New Employment Principle for a New Organizational Era*, Oxford: Oxford University Press.

Bakke, E.W. (1958) *The Human Resources Function*, New Haven, CT: Yale University.

Ballinger, J. (2008) No sweat? Corporate social responsibility and the dilemma of anti-sweatshop activism, *New Labor Forum*, **17**(2): 91–8.

Ballinger, J. (2012) State of the Apple (rotten), *Counterpunch*, 26 January.

Bamber, G.J. and Lansbury, R.D. (1998) *International and Comparative Employment Relations*, London: Sage.

Bamberger, P. and Meshoulam, I. (2000) *Human Resource Management Strategy*, Thousand Oak, CA: Sage.

Barber, A.E. (1998) *Recruiting Employees: Individual and Organizational Perspectives*, Thousand Oaks, CA: Sage.

Barlow, G. (1989) Deficiencies and the perpetuation of power: latent functions in management appraisal, *Journal of Management Studies*, **26**(5): 499–517.

Barney, J. (1991) Firm resources and sustained competitive advantage, *Journal of Management*, **17**: 99–120.

Baron, J.D. and Cobb-Clark, D.A. (2010) Occupational segregation and the gender wage gap in private- and public-sector employment: a distributional analysis, *Economic Record*, **86**(273): 227–46.

Barrie, D.S. and Paulson, B.C. (1991) *Professional Construction Management*, New York: McGraw-Hill.

Bartlett, C. and Ghoshal, S. (2002) Building competitive advantage through people, *MIT Sloan Management Review*, **43**(2): 34–41.

Barton, D. (2011) Capitalism for the long term, *Harvard Business Review*, **89**(3): 84–91.

Bartz, D., Hillman, L., Lehrer, S. and Mayhugh, G. (1990) A model for managing workplace diversity, *Management Education and Development*, **21**(5): 321–6.

Baruch, Y. (1999) Integrated career systems for the 2000s, *International Journal of Manpower*, **20**(7): 432–57.

Baruch, Y. and Peiperl, M.A. (2003) An empirical assessment of Sonnenfeld's career systems typology, *International Journal of Human Resource Management*, **14**(7): 1267–83.

Barzantny, C. and Festing, M. (2008) Performance management in France and Germany, in A. Varma, P. Budwhar and A. DeNisi (eds) *Performance Management Systems: A Global Perspective*, New York: Routledge.

Bauer, T.N. and Erdogan, B. (2011) Organizational socialization: the effective onboarding of new employees, in S. Sedeck (ed.) *APA Handbook of Industrial and Organizational Psychology*, vol 3: *Maintaining, Explanding and Contracting the Organization*, Washington, DC: American Psychological Association.

BBC (2005) Wal-Mart urged to 'clean up act', 3 June. Available at: http://news.bbc.co.uk/2/hi/business/4605733.stm (Accessed: 14 March 2012).

Beaumont, C. (1999) Gender, citizenship and the state 1922–1990, in S. Brewster, V. Crossman, F. Becket and D. Alderson (eds) *Ireland in Proximity: History, Gender, Space*, London: Routledge.

Becker, B. and Gerhart, B. (1996) The impact of human resource management on organisational performance: progress and prospects, *Academy of Management Journal*, **39**: 779–801.

Bee, R. and Bee, F. (2003) *Learning Needs Analysis and Evaluation*, London: CIPD.

Beer, M., Spector, B., Lawrence, P.R. et al. (1984) *Managing Human Assets*, New York: Free Press.

Benko, C. and Weisberg, A. (2007) *Mass Career Customization: Aligning the Workplace with Today's Non-traditional Workforce*, Boston, MA: Harvard Business Press.

Bernthal, P., Rogers, R. and Smith, A. (2003) *Managing Performance: Building Accountability for Organisational Success*, Pittsburgh, PA: Development Dimensions International.

Bevan, S. and Thompson, M. (1991) Performance management at the crossroads, *Journal of the Chartered Institute of Personnel and Development*, November, 36–9.

Black, J.S. and Mendenhall, M.E. (1991) The U-curve adjustment hypothesis revisited: a review and theoretical framework, *Journal of International Business Studies*, **22**(2). 225–47.

Black, J.S. and Stephens, G.K. (1989) The influence of the spouse on American expatriate adjustment and intent to stay in Pacific Rim overseas assignments, *Journal of Management*, **15**(4): 529–44.

Black, J.S., Gregerson, H.B., Mendenhall, M.E. and Stroh, L.K. (1999) *Globalizing People through International Assignments*, Reading, MA: Addison-Wesley.

Blau, F.D. and Kahn, L.M. (2006) The U.S. gender pay gap in the 1990s: slowing convergence, *Industrial and Labor Relations Review*, **60**(1): 45–66.

Block, R. (2006) Industrial relations in the United States and Canada, in M.J. Morley, P. Gunnigle and D.G. Collings (eds) *Global Industrial Relations*, New York: Routledge.

Blowfield, M. and Murray, A. (2011) *Corporate Responsibility*, 2nd edn, Oxford: Oxford University Press.

Bowen, D.E. and Ostroff, C. (2004) Understanding HRM-firm performance linkages: the role of the 'strength' of the HRM system, *Academy of Management Review*, **29**(2): 203–21.

Bowles, M. and Coates, G. (1993) Image and substance: the management of performance as rhetoric or reality, *Personnel Review*, **22**(3): 3–21.

Boxall, P. and Purcell, J. (2003) *Strategy and Human Resource Management*, Basingstoke: Palgrave Macmillan.

Boyatzis, R. (1982) *The Competent Manager: A Model for Effective Performance*, New York: Wiley Interscience.

Boyle, D. and Simms, A. (2009) *The New Economics: A Bigger Picture*, London: Earthscan.

Bratton, J. and Gold, J. (2012) *Human Resource Management: Theory and Practice*, 5th edn, Basingstoke: Palgrave Macmillan.

Bresser, F. and Wilson, C. (2006) What is coaching?, in J. Passmore (ed.) *Excellence in Coaching: The Industry Guide*, London: Kogan Page.

Brewster, C. (2007) A European perspective on HRM, *European Journal International Management*, **1**(3): 239–59.

Brewster, C., Mayrhofer, W. and Morley, M. (2004) *Human Resource Management in Europe: Evidence of Convergence?*, Oxford: Butterworth-Heinemann.

Brewster, C., Sparrow, P. and Vernon, G. (2007) *International Human Resource Management*, London: CIPD.

Brewster, C., Wood, G. and Brookes, M. (2008) Similarity, isomorphism or duality? Recent survey evidence on the human resource management policies of multinational corporations, *British Journal of Management*, **19**(4): 320–42.

Briscoe, D., Schuler, R. and Tarique, I. (2012) *International Human Resource Management: Policies and Practices for Multinational Enterprises*, New York: Routledge.

Briscoe, J.P. and Hall, D.T. (2002) The protean orientation: creating the adaptable workforce necessary for flexibility and speed, paper presented at the annual meeting of the Academy of Management, Denver.

Briscoe, J.P., Henagan, S.C., Burton, J.P. and Murphy, W.M. (2012) Coping with an insecure employment environment: the differing roles of protean and boundaryless career orientations, *Journal of Vocational Behavior*, **80**(2): 308–16.

Brookfield Global Relocation Services (2011) *2011 Global Relocation Trends Survey*. Available at: www.brookfieldgrs.com/knowledge/grts_research/ (Accessed: 10 December 2011).

Brown, W. and Rea, D. (1995) The changing nature of the employment contract, *Scottish Journal of Political Economy*, **42**(3): 363–77.

Bryson, A., Gomez, R., Kretschmer, T. and Willman, P. (2009) *Employee Voice and Private Sector Workplace Outcomes in Britain, 1980–2004*, NIESR Discussion Paper 329, London: NIESR.

Bureau of Labor Statistics (2012) *Economic News Release: Major Work Stoppages in 2011*. Available at: www.bls.gov/news.release/archives/wkstp_02082012.htm (Accessed: 10 December 2012).

Burgess, J., French, E. and Strachan, G. (2009) The diversity management approach to equal employment opportunity in Australian organisations, *Economic and Labour Relations Review*, **20**(1): 77–92.

Busck, O., Knudsen, H. and Lind, J. (2010) The transformation of employee participation: consequences for the work environment, *Economic and Industrial Democracy*, **31**(3): 285–305.

Cadbury, D. (2010) *Chocolate Wars: From Cadbury to Kraft: 200 Years of Sweet Success and Bitter Rivalry*, London: HarperPress.

Caldwell, D.F. and O'Reilly, C.A. (1990) Measuring person-job fit within a profile comparison process, *Journal of Applied Psychology*, **75**(6): 648–57.

Campbell, R.B. and Garfinkel, L.M. (1996) Performance management strategies for success, *HRMagazine*, **41**(6): 98–102.

Cappelli, P. (1999) *The New Deal at Work: Managing the Market-driven Workforce*, Boston: Harvard Business School Press.

Carley, M. (2009) *Trade Union Membership 2003–2008*. Available at: www.eurofound.europa.eu/eiro/studies/tn0904019s/tn0904019s.htm#hd2 (Accessed: 6 June 2012).

Carroll, S.J. and Schneier, C.E. (1982) *Performance Appraisal and Review Systems: The Identification, Measurement and Development of Performance in Organizations*, Glenview, IL: Scott, Foresman.

Carson, K.D. and Bedeian, A.G. (1994) Career commitment: construction of a measure and examination of its psychometric properties, *Journal of Vocational Behavior*, **44**: 237–62.

CBI (2011) *Healthy Returns?: Absence and Workplace Health Survey 2011*. Available at: www.cbi.org.uk/media/955604/2011.05-healthy_returns_-_absence_and_workplace_health_survey_2011.pdf (Accessed: 27 February 2013).

Central Statistics Office (2007) *Women and Men in Ireland*, Cork: CSO.

Central Statistics Office (2011) *Statistical Yearbook of Ireland 2011*, Cork: CSO.

Central Statistics Office (2012) *Women and Men in Ireland*, Cork: CSO.

Cheramie, R.A., Sturman, M.C. and Walsh, K. (2007) Executive career management: switching organizations and the boundaryless career, *Journal of Vocational Behavior*, **71**(3): 359–74.

Cheyne, A., Cox, S., Oliver, A. and Tomas, J.M. (1998) Modelling safety climate in the prediction of levels of safety activity, *Work and Stress*, **12**(3): 255–71.

Cheyne, A., Tomas, J.M., Cox, S. and Oliver, A. (1999) Modelling employee attitudes to safety: a comparison across sectors, *European Psychologist*, **4**(1): 1–10.

Chiswick, B.R. and Miller, P.W. (2009) The international transferability of immigrants' human capital, *Economics of Education Review*, **28**(2): 162–9.

CIPD (Chartered Institute of Personnel and Development) (2005a) *Performance Management Survey Report*, London: CIPD.

CIPD (2005b) The learning and development generalist standard, in *CIPD Practitioner-Level Professional Standards*, London: CIPD

CIPD (2005c) *Bullying at Work: Beyond Policies to a Culture of Respect*, London: CIPD.

CIPD (2006) *Achieving Best Practice in Your Business: High Performance Work Practices – Linking Strategy and Skills to Performance Outcomes*, London: CIPD.

CIPD (2010a) *Next Generation HR: Time for Change – Towards a Next Generation for HR*. Available at: www.cipd.co.uk/binaries/5126Nextgenthoughtpiece.pdf (Accessed: 20 February 2013).

CIPD (2010b) *Resourcing and Talent Planning: Annual Survey Report 2010*, London: CIPD.

CIPD (2011) *Resourcing and Talent Planning: Annual Survey Report 2011*, London: CIPD.

CIPD (2012a) *History of HR and the CIPD*. Available at: www.cipd.co.uk/hr-resources/factsheets/history-hr-cipd.aspx (Accessed: 10 February 2012).

CIPD (2012b) *Competence and Competency Frameworks*. Available at: www.cipd.co.uk/hr-resources/factsheets/competence-competency-frameworks.aspx (Accessed: 22 September 2012).

CIPD (2012c) *Selection Methods*. Available at www.cipd.co.uk/hr-resources/factsheets/selection-methods.aspx (Accessed: 22 February 2012).

Clancy, P. (2011) Possible huge job loss for Waterford as TalkTalk exit, *IrishCentral*, 15 September. Available at: www.irishcentral.com/news/Possible-huge-job-loss-for-Waterford-as-Talk-Talk-exit-129834208.html (Accessed: 14 March 2012).

Clardy, A. (2008) The strategic role of human resource development in managing core competencies, *Human Resource Development International*, **11**(2): 183–97.

Clegg, H. (1979) *The System of Industrial Relations in Great Britain*, Oxford: Blackwell.

Clinton, M., Totterdell, P. and Wood, S. (2006) A ground theory of the portfolio working: experiencing the smallest of small businesses, *International Small Business Journal*, **24**(2): 179–203.

Coates, H. and Edwards, D. (2011) The graduate pathways survey: new insights on education and employment outcomes five years after bachelor degree completion, *Higher Education Quarterly*, **65**(1): 74–93.

Cohen B. (2007) Positive action, institutional discrimination and mainstreaming equality: a framework for discussion, keynote address, Equality & Diversity/One World Week 2007, seminar: Equality, Human Rights and Community Cohesion, University of Northampton.

Colling, T. (2006) What space for unions on the floor of rights? Trade unions and the enforcement of statutory individual employment rights, *Industrial Law Journal*, **34**(2): 140–60.

Collings, D.G. and Scullion, H. (2006) *Global Staffing*, London: Routledge.

Collings, D.G., Gunnigle, P. and Morley, M.J. (2008) Between Boston and Berlin: American MNCs and the shifting contours of industrial relations in Ireland, *International Journal of Human Resource Management*, **19**(2): 242–63.

Collings, D.G., Scullion, H. and Morley, M.J. (2007) Changing patterns of global staffing in the multinational enterprise: challenges to the conventional expatriate assignment and emerging alternative, *Journal of World Business*, **42**(2): 198–213.

Collinson, D. and Hearn, J. (1994) Naming men as men: implications for work organization and management, *Gender, Work & Organization*, **1**(1): 2–22.

Combs, J., Liu, Y., Hall, A. and Ketchen, D. (2006) How much do high-performance work practices matter? A meta-analysis of their effects on organizational performance, *Personnel Psychology*, **59**(3): 501–28.

Compton, R., Morrissey, W. and Nankervis, A. (2009) *Effective Recruitment and Selection Practices*, 5th edn, Sydney: CCH Australia.

Cooper-Thomas, H.D. and Anderson, N. (2006) Organizational socialization: a new theoretical model and recommendations for future research and HRM practices in organizations, *Journal of Managerial Psychology*, **21**(5): 492–516.

Cox, S., Tomas, J.M., Cheyne, A. and Oliver, A. (1998) Safety culture: the prediction of commitment to safety in the manufacturing industry, *British Journal of Management*, **9**, S3–11.

Craig, E., Kimberly, J. and Bouchikhi, H. (2002) Can loyalty be leased?, *Harvard Business Review*, **80**(9): 24.

Cunneen, P. (2008) Executive coaching, *People Focus*, **6**(3): 38.

Dabos, G.E. and Rousseau, D.M. (2004) Mutuality and reciprocity in the psychological contracts of employee and employer, *Journal of Applied Psychology*, **89**(1): 52–72.

D'Art, D. and Turner, T. (2006) New working arrangements: Changing the nature of the employment relationship?, *International Journal of Human Resource Management*, **17**(3): 523–38.

Datta, D.K., Guthrie, J.P. and Wright, P.M. (2005) HRM and labour productivity: Does industry matter?, *Academy of Management Journal*, **48**(1): 135–45.

Davignon Group (1997) *Report of the High Level Group of Experts on 'European Systems of Worker's Involvement'*, Brussels: European Commission.

Davila, A. and Elvira, M. (2008) Performance management in Mexico, in A. Varma, P. Budwhar and A. DeNisi (eds) *Performance Management Systems: A Global Perspective*, New York: Routledge.

Day, R. and Allen, T.D. (2004) The relationship between career motivation and self-efficacy with protégé career success, *Journal of Vocational Behavior*, **64**(1): 72–91.

De Geus, A. and Senge, P.M. (1997) *The Living Company*, Boston, MA: Harvard Business School Press.

Delery, J. and Doty, D.H. (1996) Modes of theorising in strategic human resource management: tests of universalistic, contingency and configurational performance predictors, *Academy of Management Journal*, **39**(4): 802–35.

Deming, W.E. (1986) *Out of the Crisis*, Cambridge, MA: Cambridge Press.

DeNisi, A., Varma, A. and Budhwar, P. (2008) Performance management: What have we learned?, in A. Varma, P. Budhwar and A. DeNisi (eds) *Performance Management Systems: A Global Perspective*, New York: Routledge.

DiMaggio, P.J. and Powell, W.W. (1991) Introduction, in W.W. Powell and P.J. DiMaggio (eds) *The New Institutionalism in Organizational Analysis*, Chicago: University of Chicago Press.

Dipboye, R.L. (2005) The selection/recruitment interview: core processes and contexts, in A. Evers, N. Anderson and O. Voskuijl (eds) *The Blackwell Handbook of Personnel Selection*, Malden, MA: Blackwell.

Dowling, P.J., Festing, M. and Engle, A.D. Sr (2008) *International Human Resource Management*, London: Cengage Learning.

Dundon, T., Wilkinson, A., Marchington, M. and Ackers, P. (2004) The meanings and purpose of employee voice, *The International Journal of Human Resource Management*, **15**(6): 1149–70.

Dundon, T., Wilkinson, A., Marchington, M. and Ackers, P. (2005) The management of voice in non-union organisations: managers' perspectives, *Employee Relations*, **27**(3): 307–19.

Eby, L.T., Butts, M. and Lockwood, A. (2003) Predictors of success in the era of the boundaryless career, *Journal of Organizational Behavior*, **24**(6): 689–708.

Edenborough, R. (1999) *Using Psychometrics: A Practical Guide to Testing and Assessment*, 2nd edn, London: Kogan Page.

Edstrom, A. and Galbraith, J. (1977) Alternative policies for international transfers of managers, *Management International Review*, **17**(2): 11–22.

Edwards, J.R. (1991) Person-job fit: a conceptual integration, literature review and methodological critique, *International Review of Industrial and Organizational Psychology*, **6**, 283–357.

Edwards, P. and Greasley, K. (2010) *Absence from Work*, Dublin: Eurofound.

Edwards, T. (2011) The transfer of employment practices across borders in multinational companies, in A.W. Harzing and A.H. Pinnington (eds) *International Human Resource Management*, London: Sage.

Edwards, T. and Ferner, A. (2002) The renewed 'American Challenge': a review of employment practices in US multinationals, *Industrial Relations Journal*, **33**(2): 94–111.

Eklund, J.A. (1998) Organisation of assembly work: recent Swedish examples, in E.D. Megaw (ed.) *Contemporary Ergonomics*, London: Taylor & Francis.

Elson, D. (1999) Labour markets as gendered institutions: equality, efficiency and empowerment issues, *World Development*, **27**(3): 611–27.

England, P. (2005) Gender inequality in labor markets: the role of motherhood and segregation, *Social Politics*, **12**(2): 264–88.

Entine, J. (1994) 'Shattered image: Is the Body Shop too good to be true?', *Business Ethics*, **8**(5): 23–8.

Entine, J. (2002) Body flop, *Globe and Mail*, 31 May. Available at: www.theglobeandmail.com/report-on-business/rob-magazine/body-flop/article465059/ (Accessed: 14 March 2012).

Eurofound (2007) *Parental Leave in European Companies: Establishment Survey on Working Time 2004–2005*, Dublin: Eurofound.

European Commission (2001) *Promoting a European Framework for Corporate Social Responsibility*, Green Paper 366, Brussels: European Commission.

European Commission (2005a) *Joint Report on Social Protection and Social Inclusion*, SEC69, Brussels: European Commission.

European Commission (2005b) *The Business Case for Diversity: Good Practices in the Workplace*, Luxembourg: Publications Office.

European Commission (2008) *Diversity Management in 2008: Research with the European Business Test Panel*, Luxembourg: Publications Office.

European Commission (2009) *Employment in Europe 2009*, Luxembourg: Publications Office.

European Commission (2010) *Health and Safety at Work in Europe (1997-2007): A Statistical Portrait*, Luxembourg: Publications Office.

European Commission (2012a) *Conference Report: Reducing Early School Leaving: Efficient and Effective Policies in Europe*, Brussels: Directorate-General for Education and Culture.

European Commission (2012b) *Small and Medium-sized Enterprises (SMEs)*, DG Enterprise and Industry. Available at: http://ec.europa.eu/enterprise/policies/sme/facts-figures-analysis/index_en.htm (Accessed: 6 June 2012).

European Federation of Employee Share Ownership (2011) *Economic Survey of Employee Ownership in European Countries in 2010*. Available at: www.efesonline.org/annual%20economic%20survey/2010/Survey%202010%20-%20Main%20numbers.pdf (Accessed: 6 June 2012).

European Industrial Relations Observatory (2010a) *Developments in Industrial Action 2005–2009*. Available at: www.eurofound.europa.eu/eiro/studies/tn1004049s/tn1004049s.htm (Accessed: 6 June 2012).

European Industrial Relations Observatory (2010b) *Individual Disputes at the Workplace: Alternative Disputes Resolution*. Available at: www.eurofound.europa.eu/eiro/studies/tn0910039s/tn0910039s.htm (Accessed: 6 June 2012).

European Union Agency for Fundamental Rights (2011) *Handbook on European Non-Discrimination Law*, Luxembourg: Publications Office.

Eurostat (2005) *Euro Indicators News Release*, Luxembourg: Eurostat Press Office.

Eurostat (2006) *A Statistical View of Women and Men in the EU 25*, Luxembourg: Eurostat.

Eurostat (2012a) *Gender Pay Gap in Unadjusted Form, Population and Social Conditions*, Luxembourg: Eurostat.

Eurostat (2012b) *Health and Safety at Work Statistics*, Luxembourg: Eurostat.

Felstead, A., Gallie, D., Green, F. and Zhou, Y. (2007) *Skills at Work 1986–2006*, Oxford: ESRC Centre on Skills, Knowledge and Organisational Performance.

Ferner, A. (1997) Country of origin effects and HRM in multinational companies, *Human Resource Management*, **7**(1): 19–37.

Ferner, A. and Hyman, R. (1998) Introduction, in A. Ferner and R. Hyman (eds) *Changing Industrial Relations in Europe*, Oxford: Blackwell.

Fletcher, C. (1993) Appraisal: An idea whose time has gone?, *Personnel Management*, September, 34–7.

Fletcher, C. (2004) *Appraisal and Feedback: Making Performance Review Work*, 3rd edn, London, CIPD.

Foley, S. (2012) Apple admits it has a human rights problem, *The Independent*, 14 February. Available at: www.independent.co.uk/news/world/asia/apple-admits-it-has-a-human-rights-problem-6898617.html (Accessed: 14 March 2012).

Fombrun, C.J., Tichy, N.M. and Devanna, M.A. (1984) *Strategic Human Resource Management*, New York: Wiley.

Freeman, R.B. and Han, E. (2012) The war against public sector collective bargaining in the US, *Journal of Industrial Relations*, **54**(3): 386–408.

Friedman, M. (1970) The social responsibility of business is to increase its profits, *The New York Times Magazine*, 13 September.

Gaines Robinson, D. and Robinson, J.C. (2005) *Strategic Business Partner: Aligning People Strategies with Business Goals*, San Francisco, CA: Berrett-Koehler.

Garavan, T.N. (1991) Strategic human resource development, *Journal of European Industrial Training*, **15**(1): 17–30.

Garavan, T.N. (1997) The learning organisation: a review and evaluation, *The Learning Organisation*, **4**(1): 18–29.

Garavan, T.N. (2002) *The Irish Health and Safety Handbook*, 2nd edn, Dublin: Oak Tree Press.

Garavan, T.N. (2007) A strategic perspective on human resource development, *Advances in Developing Human Resources*, **9**(1): 11–30.

Garavan, T.N., Hogan, C. and Cahir-O'Donnell, A. (2003) *Making Training and Development Work: Best Practice Guide*, Dublin: Oaktree Press.

Gardiner, J. (1998) Beyond human capital: households in the macroeconomy, *New Political Economy*, **3**(2): 209–21.

Garger, E.M. (1999) Holding on to high performers: a strategic approach to retention, *Compensation and Benefits Management*, **15**(4): 10–17.

Gatewood, R.D., Field, H.S. and Barrick, M. (2011) *Human Resource Selection*, 7th edn, Mason, OH: South-Western/Cengage Learning.

Gibb, S.J., Fergusson, D.M. and Horwood, L.J. (2012) Working hours and alcohol problems in early adulthood, *Addiction*, **107**(1): 81–8.

Gibney, E. and Murphy, C. (2011) TalkTalk lay off 575 Irish workers … then bosses hold giant party with free beer, clay pigeon shooting, food and music, *MailOnline*, 11 September. Available at: www.dailymail.co.uk/news/article-2036093/TalkTalk-lay-575-Irish-workers--bosses-hold-giant-party-free-beer-clay-pigeon-shooting-food-music.html (Accessed: 14 March 2012).

Gilligan, C. (1982) *In a Different Voice: Psychological Theory and Women's Development*, Cambridge, MA: Harvard University Press.

Gollan, P.J. (2000) Non-union forms of employee representation in the United Kingdom and Australia, in B.E. Kaufman and D.G. Taras (eds) *Non-union Employee Representation*, Armonk, NY: M.E. Sharpe.

Gooderham, P.N. and Nordhaug, O. (2003) *International Management: Cross-boundary Challenges*, Oxford: Blackwell.

Gould, S. and Penley, L.E. (1984) Career strategies and salary progression: a study of their relationships in a municipal bureaucracy, *Organization Behaviour and Human Performance*, **34**, 244–65.

Grant, A. (2006) Prepare for take-off, *People Management*, 6 April, 46–7.

Gratton, L. (2000) *Living Strategy: Putting People at the Heart of Corporate Purpose*, London: Pearson.

Griffiths, M. (2011) Workaholism: a 21st-century addiction, *The Psychologist*, **24**(10): 740–4.

Grimland, S., Vigoda-Gadot, E. and Baruch, Y. (2012) Career attitudes and success of managers: the impact of chance event, protean, and traditional careers, *The International Journal of Human Resource Management*, **23**(6): 1074–94.

Grint, K. (1991) *The Sociology of Work*, Cambridge: Polity Press.

Gross, J. (1998) The common law employment contract and collective bargaining: values and views of rights and justice, *New Zealand Journal of Industrial Relations*, **23**(2): 63–76.

Grosser, K. and Moon, J. (2008) Developments in company reporting on workplace gender equality? A corporate social responsibility perspective, *Accounting Forum*, **32**(3): 179–98.

Grund, C. and Sliwa, D. (2007) *Individual and Job-based Determinants of Performance Appraisal: Evidence from Germany*, Discussion Paper 3017, Bonn: Institute for the Study of Labor.

Guest, D.E. (1987) Human resource management and industrial relations, *Journal of Management Studies*, **14**(5): 503–21.

Guest, D. (1989) Personnel and HRM: Can you tell the difference?, *Personnel Management*, **21**(1): 48–51.

Guest, D. (1997) Human resource management and performance: a review and research agenda, *International Journal of Human Resource Management*, **8**(3): 263–76.

Guest, D.E. (2011) Human resource management and performance: still searching for some answers, *Human Resource Management Journal*, **21**(1): 3–13.

Gunnigle, P. and Flood, P. (1990) *Personnel Management in Ireland: Practice, Trends and Developments*, Dublin: Gill & Macmillan.

Gunnigle, P., Heraty, N. and Morley, M. (2011) *Human Resource Management in Ireland*, 4th edn, Dublin: Gill & Macmillan.

Guthrie, J.P. (2001) High involvement work practices, turnover and productivity: evidence from New Zealand, *Academy of Management Journal*, **44**(1): 180–90.

Guthrie, J.P., Flood, P.C., Liu, W. et al. (2011) Big hat, no cattle? High performance work systems and executives perceptions of HR capability, *International Journal of Human Resource Management*, **22**(8): 1470–4684.

Hall, D.T. (1976) *Careers in Organizations*, Glenview, IL: Scott, Foresman.

Hall, D.T. (1996) Protean careers of the 21st century, *Academy of Management Executive*, **10**(4): 8–16.

Hall, D.T. (2002) *Careers In and Out of Organizations*. Thousand Oaks, CA: Sage.

Hall, D.T. (2004) The protean career: a quarter-century journey, *Journal of Vocational Behavior*, **65**(1): 1–13.

Hall, D.T. and Chandler, D. (2005) Psychological success: when the career is a calling, *Journal of Organizational Behavior*, 26, 155–76.

Hall, L. (2009) Coaching: the highlights, *People Management*, 1 January.

Hall, P.A. and Soskice, D. (2001) An introduction to varieties of capitalism, in P.A. Hall and D. Soskice (eds) *Varieties of Capitalism: The Institutional Foundations of Comparative Advantage*, Oxford: Oxford University Press.

Hamel, M.B., Julie R., Ingelfinger, J.R. et al. (2006) Women in academic medicine: progress and challenges, *New England Journal of Medicine*, **355**(3): 310–12.

Handy, C. (1989) *The Age of Unreason*, London: Random House.

Harbison, F. and Myers, C. (1959) *Management in the Industrialized World*, New York: McGraw-Hill.

Harrington, D., Linehan, M. and Cross, C. (2008) Flexible working in an Irish public sector organisation: still a gender issue, *International Journal of Business and Management*, **3**(9): 166–78.

Harris, H. and Brewster, C. (1999) The coffee-machine system: how international selection really works, *The International Journal of Human Resource Management*, **10**(3): 488–500.

Harrison, R. (2009) *Learning & Development*, 5th edn, London: CIPD.

Harzing, A.W. (1995) The persistent myth of high expatriate failure rates, *Human Resource Management*, **6**(2): 457–75.

Hausman, C. (2007) Who was Anita Roddick?, *Ethics Newsline*, 17 September. Available at: www.globalethics.org/newsline/2007/09/17/who-was-anita-roddick/ (Accessed: 14 March 2012).

Health and Safety Authority (2007) *Code of Practice for Employers and Employees on the Prevention and Resolution of Bullying at Work*, Dublin: HSA.

Health and Safety Executive (2012) *The Health and Safety Executive Statistics 2011/12*, London: HSE.

Heimler, R., Rosenberg, S. and Morote, E.S. (2012) Predicting career advancement with structural equation modelling, *Education + Training*, **54**(2): 85–94.

Heinrich, H.W. (1931) *Industrial Accident Prevention: A Scientific Approach*, New York: McGraw-Hill.

Herring, C. (2009) Does diversity pay? Race, gender, and the business case for diversity, *American Sociological Review*, **74**(2): 208–24.

Herriot, P. and Pemberton, C. (1997) Facilitating new deals, *Human Resource Management Journal*, **7**(1): 45–56.

Hewlett, S.A. (2007) *Off-ramps and On-ramps: Keeping Talented Women on the Road to Success*, Boston, MA: Harvard Business School Press.

Hickey, S. (2010) Women caught up in 'sexist email' inquiry, *Irish Independent*, 11 November. Available at: www.independent.ie/national-news/women-caught-up-in-sexist-email-inquiry-2415801.html (Accessed: 14 March 2012).

Hill, J. and Trist, E. (1955) Changes in accidents and other absences with length of service, *Human Relations*, **8**(2): 121–52.

Hofstede, G. (1980) *Culture's Consequences: International Differences in Work-related Values*, London: Sage.

Holbeche, L. (1999) *Aligning Human Resources and Business Strategy*, Oxford: Butterworth-Heinemann.

Honey, P. and Mumford, A. (1992) *A Manual of Learning Styles*, 3rd edn, Maidenhead: Peter Honey.

Houldsworth, E. (2003) Managing individual performance, paper presented to the CIPD National Conference, Harrogate, 22–4 November.

Houldsworth, E. (2007) In the same boat, *People Management*, 25 January, 35–6.

Houldsworth, E. and Jirasinghe, D. (2006) *Managing and Measuring Employee Performance*, London: Kogan Page.

Howard, A. and Bray, D.W. (1981) Today's young managers: They can do it, but will they?, *Wharton Magazine*, **5**(4): 23–8.

Howe, M. (2008) Putting down routes, *People Management*, 20 March, 34–5.

*HR Focus* (2005) Getting to the most productive results, *HR Focus*, 1 January, http://business.highbeam.com/4710/article-1G1-131599244/getting-most-productive-results (Accessed: 14 February 2013).

Huselid, M.A. (1995) The impact of human resource management practices on turnover, productivity, and corporate financial performance, *Academy of Management Journal*, **38**(3): 635–72.

Huselid, M.A. and Becker, B.E. (1995) High performance work systems and organizational performance, paper presented at the annual meeting of the Academy of Management, Vancouver.

Ibarra, H. (1999) Provisional selves: experimenting with image and identity in professional adaptation, *Administrative Science Quarterly*, **44**(4): 764–91.

IBM (2007) *Unlocking the DNA of the Adaptable Workforce: The Global Human Capital Study 2008*, London: IBM.

Immervoll, H. and Barber, D. (2005) *Can Parents Afford to Work? Childcare Costs, Tax-Benefit Policies and Work Incentives*, OECD Social, Employment and Migration working papers No.31, Geneva: OECD.

Income Data Services (2007) *Performance Management*, HR Studies, London: IDS.

*Industrial Relations News* (2005) US Chamber leaves indelible stamp on Employee Consultation Bill, *Industrial Relations News*, **30**: 2–3.

Industrial Relations Services (2001) Performance appraisal must try harder, *IRS Employment Trends*, London: IRS.

Industrial Relations Services (2005) Appraisals (2): learning from practice and experience, *IRS Employment Review*, London: IRS.

Institute of Personnel Management (1992) *Performance Management in the UK: An Analysis of the Issues*, London: IPM.

Institute for Public Policy Research (2010) *Youth Unemployment and the Recession*, London: IPPR.

International Labour Organization (2003) *Safety Culture at Work: Safety in Numbers – Pointers for a Global Safety Culture at Work*, Geneva: ILO.

International Labour Organization (2012) *Maternity Protection in the Context of Work Life Reconciliation for Men and Women*, Geneva: ILO.

Irish Business and Employers Confederation (2009) *The Essential Guide to Diversity: How to Harness Diversity and Create an Integrated Workplace*. Dublin: IBEC.

*Irish Times* (2009) Work related deaths are under-reported – SIPTU, 27 April.

Jackson, S.E., Joshi, A. and Erhardt, N.L. (2003) Recent research on teams and organizational diversity: SWOT analysis and implications, *Journal of Management*, **29**(6): 801–30.

Jawahar, I.M. and Williams, C. (1997) Where all the children are above average: the performance appraisal purpose effect, *Personnel Psychology*, **50**(4): 921.

Johnston, W. and Packer, A. (1987) *Workforce 2000: Work and Workers for the 21st Century*, Washington: Hudson Institute.

Judge, T.A., Boudreau, J.W. and Bretz, R.D. (1994) Job and life attitudes of male executives, *Journal of Applied Psychology*, **79**(5): 767–82.

Kaplan, R.S. (2008) Reaching your potential, *Harvard Business Review*, **86**(7/8): 45–9.

Karnani, A. (2010) The case against corporate social responsibility, *MIT Sloan Management Review*, 22 August.

Katou, A. and Budhwar, P. (2007) The effect of human resource management policies on organizational performance in Greek manufacturing firms, *Thunderbird International Business Review*, **49**(1): 1–36.

Katz, H. and Darbishire, O. (2000) *Converging Divergences: Worldwide Changes in Employment Systems*, Ithaca, NY: ILR/Cornell University Press.

Kay, E., Meyer, H.H. and French, J.R. (1965) Effects of threat in a performance appraisals interview, *Journal of Applied Psychology*, **49**: 311–17.

Kelly, J. (1998) *Rethinking Industrial Relations: Mobilisation, Collectivism and Long Waves*, London: Routledge.

Kepes, S. and Delery, J.E. (2007) HRM systems and the problem of internal fit, in P. Boxall, J. Purcell and P. Wright (eds) *The Oxford University Press Handbook of Human Resource Management*, Oxford: Oxford University Press.

Kerr, C., Dunlop, J.T., Harbison, F.H. and Myers, C.A. (1960) *Industrialism and Industrial Man*, Cambridge, MA: Harvard University Press.

Kessels, J. and Harrison, R. (1998) External consistency: The key to success in management development programmes?, *Management Learning*, **29**(1): 39–68.

Kirkpatrick, D.L. and Kirkpatrick, J.D. (2006) *Evaluating Training Programs*, 3rd edn, San Francisco, CA: Berrett-Koehler.

Kirton, G. and Greene, A.M. (2005) *The Dynamics of Managing Diversity: A Critical Approach*, 2nd edn, Oxford: Butterworth-Heinemann.

Kivimäki, M., Nyberg, S.T., Batty, G.D. et al. (2012) Job strain as a risk factor for coronary heart disease: a collaborative meta-analysis of individual participant data, *The Lancet*, **380**(9852): 1491–7.

Klein, N. (2000) *No Logo*, London: HarperCollins.

Kline, R.B. (1998) *Principles and Practice of Structural Equation Modeling*, New York: Guilford Press.

Knox, S. and Freeman, C. (2006) Measuring and managing employer brand image in the service industry, *Journal of Marketing Management*, **22**(7/8): 695–716.

Kolb, D.A. (1984) *Experiential Learning: Experience as the Source of Learning and Development*, Englewood Cliffs, NJ: Prentice Hall.

KPMG (2008) *KPMG International Survey of Corporate Responsibility Reporting 2008*, Amstelveen: KPMG.

Kristof, A.L. (1996) Person-organisation fit: an integrative review of its conceptualizations, measurement, and implications, *Personnel Psychology*, **49**(1): 1–49.

Kuper, H. and Marmot, M. (2003) Job strain, job demands, decision latitude, and risk of coronary heart disease within the Whitehall II study, *Journal of Epidemiology & Community Health*, **57**(2): 147–53.

Lambert, S.J. (2000) Added benefits: the link between work–life benefits and organizational citizenship behaviour, *Academy of Management Journal*, **43**(5): 801–15.

Landy, F. and Farr, J. (1983) *The Measurement of Work Performance: Methods, Theory and Applications*, New York: Academic Press.

Latham, G. and Latham, S. (2000) Overlooking theory and research in performance appraisal at one's peril: much done, more to do, in C. Cooper and E. Locke (eds) *Industrial and Organizational Psychology: Linking Theory with Practice*, Oxford: Blackwell.

Latham, G. and Locke, R. (1979) Goal setting: a motivational technique that works, *Organizational Dynamics*, **8**(2): 68–80.

Lavelle, J., Gunnigle, P. and McDonnell, A. (2010) Patterning employee voice in multinational companies, *Human Relations*, **63**(3): 395–418.

Lavelle, J., McDonnell, A. and Gunnigle, P. (2009) *Human Resource Practices in Multinational Companies in Ireland: A Contemporary Analysis*. Dublin: TSO.

Lawler, E.E. (1994) Performance management: the next generation, *Compensation and Benefits Review*, **26**(3): 16–19.

Lawton, A. and Rose, A. (1994) *Organisation and Management in the Public Sector*, London: Pitman.

Lee, T. and Harrison, K. (2000) Assessing safety culture in nuclear power stations, *Safety Science*, **30**: 61–97.

Legge, K. (1995) HRM: rhetoric, reality and hidden agendas, in J. Storey (ed.) *Human Resource Management: A Critical Text*, London: Routledge.

Le Grand, J. (2003) *Individual Choice and Social Exclusion*, CASE paper 75, London: LSE.

Lengnick-Hall, C.A. and Lengnick-Hall, M.L. (1988) Strategic human resources management: a review of the literature and a proposed typology, *Academy of Management Review*, **13**: 454–70.

Levinson, D. (1978) *The Seasons of a Man's Life*, New York: Knopf.

Lewis, P., Thornhill, A. and Saunders, M. (2003) *Employee Relations: Understanding the Employment Relationship*, Harlow: Pearson Education.

Lips-Wiersma, M. and Hall, D.T. (2007) Organizational career development is not dead: a case study on managing the new career during organizational change, *Journal of Organizational Behavior*, **28**(6): 771–92.

Locke, E., Shaw, K., Saari, L. and Latham, G. (1981) Goal setting and task performance: 1969–1980, *Psychological Bulletin*, **90**: 125–52.

Locke, R. and Romis, M. (2009) The promise and perils of private voluntary regulation: labor standards and work organization in two Mexican garment factories, *MIT Sloan Research Paper No. 4734-09*.

Locke, R., Qin, F. and Brause, A. (2006) Does monitoring improve labour standards: lessons from Nike, *Industrial and Labour Relations Review*, **61**(1): 3–31.

Logan, J. (2002) Consultants, lawyers, and the 'union free' movement in the USA since the 1970s, *Industrial Relations Journal*, **33**(3): 197–214.

London, M. (1983) Toward a theory of career motivation, *Academy of Management Review*, **8**(4): 620–30.

London, M. and Bray, D.W. (1984) Measuring and developing young managers' career motivation, *Journal of Management Development*, **3**: 3–25.

London, M. and Mone, E.M. (2006) Career motivation, in J.H. Greenhaus and G.A. Callanan (eds) *Encyclopedia of Career Development*, Thousand Oaks, CA: Sage.

London, M. and Noe, R.A. (1997) London's career motivation theory: an update on measurement and research, *Journal of Career Assessment*, **5**(1): 61–80.

Longenecker, C. (1997) Why managerial performance appraisals are ineffective: causes and lessons, *Career and Development International*, **2**(5): 212–18.

Lopez, T.P. (2006) Career development of foreign-born workers: Where is the career motivation research?, *Human Resource Development Review*, **5**(4): 478–93.

Lovelace, K. and Rosen, B. (1996) Differences in achieving person-organization fit among diverse groups of managers, *Journal of Management*, **22**(5): 703–22.

Luthans, F., Norman, S.M., Avolio, B.J. and Avey, J.B. (2008) The mediating role of psychological capital in the supportive organizational climate: employee performance relationship, *Journal of Organizational Behavior*, **29**: 19–38.

McDougall, D. (2009) Primark in storm over conditions at UK supplier: fashion giant acts after investigation, *The Observer*, 11 January. Available at: www.guardian.co.uk/business/2009/jan/11/primark-ethical-business-living (Accessed: 14 March 2012).

MacDuffie, J.P. (1995) Human resource bundles and manufacturing performance: flexible production systems in the world auto industry, *Industrial Relations and Labor Review*, **48**(2): 197–221.

McGregor, D. (1957) An uneasy look at performance appraisal, *Harvard Business Review*, **35**(3): 89–94.

McGregor, D. (1960) *The Human Side of Enterprise*, New York: McGraw-Hill.

McKinsey & Company (2011) *Women Matter 2010: Women at the Top of Corporations: Making it Happen*, McKinsey & Company.

McLaughlin, C. and Deakin, S. (2012) Equality law and the limits of the 'business case' for addressing gender inequalities, in J. Scott, S. Dex and A. Plagnol (eds) *Gendered Lives: Gender Inequalities in Production and Reproduction*, Cheltenham: Edward Elgar.

McLoughlin, I. and Gourlay, S. (1994) *Enterprise without Unions*, Buckingham: Open University Press.

McMahon, G. (2009) *Successful Performance Management: Effective Strategy, Best Practice and Key Skills*, Dublin: Liffey Press.

McMahon, G. (2012) P.M.D.S.: People, process and problems?, *Aontas*, **76**(8): 7.

McMahon, G. and Gunnigle, P. (1994) *Performance Appraisal: How to Get It Right*, Dublin: Productive Personnel Ltd/Institute of Personnel Management.

Machlowitz, M. (1980) *Workaholics: Living with Them, Working with Them*, Reading, MA: Addison-Wesley.

Maier, N. (1958) Three types of appraisal interview, *Personnel*, March/April, 27–40.

Mainiero, L.A. and Sullivan, S.E. (2006) *The Opt-out Revolt: Why People are Leaving Companies to Create Kaleidoscope Careers*, Mountain View, CA: Davies-Black.

Mallon, M. (1998) The portfolio career: pushed or pulled to it, *Personnel Review*, **27**(5): 361–77.

Manuele, F.A. (2002) *Heinrich Revisited: Truisms or Myths*, Itasca, NY: National Safety Council Press.

Marchington, M. and Wilkinson, A. (2005) *Human Resource Management at Work: People Management and Development*, London: CIPD.

Marks & Spencer (2008) *Your M&S: How We Do Business Report 2008*. Available at: http://corporate. marksandspencer.com/documents/publications/ 2008/2008_hwdb_report.pdf (Accessed: 14 March 2012).

Marlowe, C.M., Schneider, S.L. and Nelson, C.E. (1996) Gender and attractiveness biases in hiring decisions: Are more experienced managers less biased? *Journal of Applied Psychology*, **81**(1): 11–21.

Mayo, A. (2004) *Creating a Learning and Development Strategy: The HR Partners Guide to Developing People*, London: CIPD.

Mayrhofer, W. and Brewster, C. (1996) In praise of ethnocentricity: expatriate policies in European multinationals, *International Executive*, **38**(6): 749–78.

Miles, R.E. and Snow, C.C. (1978) *Organizational Strategy, Structure and Process*, New York: McGraw-Hill.

Milkovich, G. and Wigdor, A. (eds) (1991) *Pay for Performance: Evaluating Performance Appraisal and Merit Pay*, Washington DC: National Academy Press.

Milkovich, G., Newman, G. and Gerhart, B. (2010) *Compensation*, 10th edn, Boston: McGraw-Hill Irwin.

Millar, J. and Evans, M. (2003) *Lone Parents and Employment: International Comparisons of What Works*, Bath: University of Bath.

Millmore, M., Lewis, P., Saunders, M. et al. (2007) *Strategic Human Resource Management: Contemporary Issues*, Harlow: Financial Times/Prentice Hall.

Minbaeva, D. (2005) HRM practices and MNC knowledge transfer, *Personnel Review*, **34**(1): 125–44.

Mone, E. and London, M. (2009) *Employee Engagement through Effective Performance Management: A Practical Guide for Managers*, Oxford: Routledge/ Taylor & Francis.

Monks, K. (2007) *The Business Impact of Equality and Diversity: The International Evidence*, Dublin: Employment Equality Authority/National Centre for Partnership and Performance.

Montgomery, D. and Ramus, C. (2003) *Corporate Social Responsibility Reputation Effects on MBA Job Choice*, Research Paper No. 1805, Stanford: Graduate School of Business.

Morgan, P. (1986) International human resource management: Fact or fiction?, *Personnel Administrator*, **31**(9): 43–7.

Mosley, R.W. (2007) Customer experience, organisational culture and the employer brand, *Journal of Brand Management*, **15**(2): 123–34.

Murphy, C. (2011) We've worked like dogs for them for the last six years. We were like robots, *Irish Times*, 8 September. Available at: www.irishtimes.com/ newspaper/ireland/2011/0908/1224303700277.html (Accessed: 14 March 2012).

Murphy, N. (2010) HR Roles and Responsibilities: The 2010 IRS Survey, *IRS Employment Review*, London: IRS.

Noon, M. (2004) Managing equality and diversity, in I. Beardwell, L. Holden and T. Claydon (eds) *Human Resource Management: A Contemporary Approach*, 4th edn, London: Prentice Hall/Financial Times.

OECD (2010) *Usual Working Hours per Week by Gender*, LMF2.1, OECD Family Database, Paris: OECD.

OECD (2011) *Key Characteristics of Parental Leave Systems*, PF2.1, OECD Family Database, Paris: OECD.

Osterman, R. (2005) Repeat performance: a growing number of companies think they can improve worker evaluations by doing more of them, *Sacramento Bee*, California, 21 February.

O'Toole, F. (2011) Reckless, feckless and feral employer is all talk, talk, *Irish Times*, 13 September. Available at: www.irishtimes.com/newspaper/opinion/ 2011/0913/ 1224304020095.html (Accessed: 14 March 2012).

Özbilgin, M., Mulholland, G., Tatli, A. and Worman, D. (2008) *Managing Diversity and the Business Case*, London: CIPD.

Peiperl, M.A. and Baruch, Y. (1997) Back to square zero: the post-corporate career, *Organizational Dynamics*, **25**(4): 7–22.

Peiperl, M.A., Arthur, M., Goffee, R. and Morris, T. (2000) *Career Frontiers*, Oxford: Oxford University Press.

*Personnel Today* (1990) Do you play the rating game?', October, 28–31.

Petrongolo, B. (2004) Gender segregation in employment contracts, *Journal of the European Economic Association*, **2**(2/3): 331–45.

Pfeffer, J. (1994) *Competitive Advantage through People: Unleashing the Power of the Work Force*, Boston, MA: Harvard Business School Press.

Pfeffer, J. (1995) Producing sustainable competitive advantage through the effective management of people, *The Academy of Management Executive*, **9**(1): 55–69.

Pfeffer, J. (1998) *The Human Equation: Building Profits by Putting People First*, Boston, MA: Harvard Business School Press.

Philp, T. (1990) *Appraising Performance for Results*, 2nd edn, London: McGraw-Hill.

Pilbeam, S. and Corbridge, M. (2006) *People Resourcing; Contemporary HRM in Practice*, 3rd edn, Harlow: Pearson Education.

Pilbeam, S. and Corbridge, M. (2010) *People Resourcing and Talent Planning: HRM in Practice*, 4th edn, Harlow: Pearson.

Pollitt, D. (2010) Golden jobs under the McDonald's arches, *Human Resource Management International Digest*, **15**(1): 23–6.

Porter, M.E. (1985) *Competitive Advantage: Creating and Sustaining Superior Performance*, New York: Free Press.

Presser, H.B., Gornick, J.C. and Parashar, S. (2008) Gender and nonstandard work hours in 12 European countries, *Monthly Labor Review*, February, 83–103.

Price, A. (2004) *Human Resource Management in a Business Context*, 2nd edn, London: Thomson Learning.

Procter, S. and Ackroyd, S. (2009) Flexibility, in D. Torrington, L. Hall, S. Taylor and C. Atkinson (eds) *Fundamentals of Human Resource Management: Managing People at Work*, Harlow: Pearson.

Pudelko, M. and Harzing, A.W. (2007) Country-of-origin, localization, or dominance effect? An empirical investigation of HRM practices in foreign subsidiaries, *Human Resource Management*, **46**(4): 535–59.

Purcell, J., Kinnie, N., Hutchinson, S. et al. (2003) *Understanding the People and Performance Link: Unlocking the Black Box*, London: CIPD.

Purcell, K., Elias, P., Davies, R. and Wilton, N. (2005) *The Class of '99: A Study of the Early Labour Market Experiences of Recent Graduates*, Warwick: University of Warwick.

Purkayastha, D. and Fernando, R. (2007) *The Body Shop: Social Responsibility or Sustained Greenwashing?* Oikos Sustainability Case Collection.

Raia, A.P. (1974) *Managing by Objectives*, Glenview, IL: Scott, Foresman.

Redman, T. and Wilkinson, A. (2009) *Contemporary Human Resource Management: Text and Cases*, 3rd edn, Harlow: Prentice Hall/Financial Times.

Reich, R. (2008) *Supercapitalism: The Battle for Democracy in an Age of Big Business*, Cambridge: Icon Books.

Renwick, D. (2003) HR managers: Guardians of employee wellbeing?, *Personnel Review*, **132**(3): 341–59.

Richard, O.C. (2000) Racial diversity, business strategy and firm performance: a resource based view, *Academy of Management Journal*, **43**(2): 164–77.

Riordan, C.M. (2000) Relational demography within groups: past developments, contradictions, and new directions, in G. Ferris (ed.) *Research in Personnel and Human Resource Management*, Greenwich, CT: JAI Press.

Robinson, S.L. and Rousseau, D.M. (1994) Violating the psychological contract: not the exception but the norm, *Journal of Organizational Behaviour*, **15**(3): 245–59.

Roche, W.K. and Ashmore, J.S. (2002) Irish unions in the 1990s: testing the limits of social partnership, in P. Fairbrother and G. Griffin (eds) *Changing Prospects for Trade Unionism: Comparisons between Six Countries*, London: Continuum.

Rodgers, R. and Hunter, J. (1991) Impact of management by objectives on organisational productivity, *Journal of Applied Psychology Monograph*, **76**(2): 322–35.

Rollag, K., Parise, S. and Cross, R. (2005) Getting new hires up to speed quickly, *MIT Sloan Management Review*, **46**(2): 35–41.

Rosenberg, S., Heimler, R. and Morote, E.S. (2012) Basic employability skills: a triangular design approach, *Education + Training*, **54**(1): 7–20.

Roughton, J. and Mercurio, J. (2002) *Developing an Effective Safety Culture: A Leadership Approach*, Woburn, MA: Butterworth-Heinemann.

Rousseau, D.M. (1995) *Psychological Contracts in Organizations: Understanding Written and Unwritten Agreements*, Newbury Park, CA: Sage.

Rousseau, D.M. (2005) *I-deals: Idiosyncratic Deal Employees Bargain for Themselves*, Armonk, NY: M.E. Sharpe.

Rousseau, D.M. and Tijoriwala, S. (1999) What's a good reason to change? Motivated reasoning and social accounts in promoting organizational change, *Journal of Applied Psychology*, **84**(4): 514–28.

Royle, T. (2005) Realism or idealism? Corporate social responsibility and the employee stakeholder in the global fast-food industry, *Business Ethics: A European Review*, **14**(1): 42–55.

RTE (2011a) TalkTalk decision 'devastating' – Kenny, RTE News, 8 September. Available at: www.rte.ie/news/2011/0908/talktalk.html (Accessed: 14 March 2012).

RTE (2011b) IDA anger at TalkTalk exit from Waterford, RTE News, 8 September. Available at: www.rte.ie/news/2011/0908/talktalk-business.html. (Accessed: 14 March 2012).

RTE (2011c) Bruton fails to get TalkTalk notice extended, RTE News, 12 September. Available at: www.rte.ie/news/2011/0912/talktalk.html (Accessed: 14 March 2012).

Rumar, K., Berggrund, U., Jernberg, P. and Ytterbom, U. (1976) Driver reaction to a technical safety measure: studded tires, Human Factors, 18(5): 443–54.

Russell, H., Smyth, E. and O'Connell, P.J. (2005) Degrees of Equality: Gender Pay Differentials among Recent Graduates, Dublin: ESRI.

Rynes, S., Gerhart, B. and Minette, K.A. (2004) The importance of pay in employee motivation: discrepancies between what people say and what they do, Human Resource Management, 43(4): 381–94.

Sachdev, S. (2006) International corporate social responsibility and employment relations, in T. Edwards and C. Rees (eds) International Human Resource Management: Globalization, National Systems and Multinational Companies, Harlow: Pearson Education.

Salaman, J.G., Storey, J. and Billsberry, J. (eds) (2005) Strategic Human Resource Management: Theory and Practice, London: Sage.

Salamon, M. (2000) Industrial Relations: Theory and Practice, Harlow: Pearson Education.

Sanders, M.G. and McCormick, E.J. (1993) Research to Determine the Contributions of System Factors in the Occurrence of Underground Injury Accidents, Pittsburgh, PA: Bureau of Mines.

Saville and Holdsworth (1997) UK Survey of Views of Performance Appraisal, Thames Ditton: Saville and Holdsworth.

Schmitt, J. and Mitukiewicz, A. (2011) Politics Matter Changes in Unionization Rates in Rich Countries, 1960–2010, Washington: Center for Economic and Policy Research.

Schuler, R.S. and Jackson, S.E. (1987) Organisational strategy and organisational level as determinants of human resource management practices, Human Resource Planning, 10(3): 125–41.

Schuler, R.S. and Jackson S.E. (eds) (2007) Strategic Human Resource Management: A Reader, London: Blackwell.

Schwartz, P. and Kelly, K. (1996) The relentless contrarian, Wired, 4 August. Available at: www.wired.com/wired/archive/4.08/drucker.html?topic=&topic_set= (Accessed: 14 March 2012).

Scott, R. (1995) Institutions and Organizations, Thousand Oaks, CA: Sage.

Scullion, H. (1994) Staffing policies and strategic control in British multinationals, International Studies of Management and Organization, 24(3): 18–35.

Scullion, H. (1995) International human resource management, in J. Storey (ed.) Human Resource Management: A Critical Text, London: Routledge.

Scullion, H. (2005) International HRM: an introduction, in H. Scullion and M. Linehan (eds) International Human Resource Management: A Critical Text, Basingstoke: Palgrave Macmillan.

Scullion, H. and Starkey, K. (2000) The changing role of the corporate human resource function in the international firm, International Journal of Human Resource Management, 11(6): 1061–81.

Seager, A. (2007) One third of employees think bosses are unfair, The Guardian, 5 November. Available at: www.guardian.co.uk/business/2007/nov/05/workandcareers.money (Accessed: 14 March 2013).

Selmer, J. (2001) Expatriate selection: Back to basics?, The International Journal of Human Resource Management, 12(8): 1219–33.

Shelton, B.A., and John, D. (1996) The division of household labor, Annual Review of Sociology, August, 299–322.

Sinn Fein (2011) Sad day for Waterford as TalkTalk closes – Cullinane, 7 October. Available at: www.sinnfein.ie/contents/21667 (Accessed: 14 March 2012).

Sisson, K. (2008) Putting the Record Straight: Industrial Relations and the Employment Relationship, Coventry: University of Warwick.

Sisson, K. and Storey, J. (2000) The Realities of Human Resource Management, Buckingham: Open University Press.

Slay, H.S. and Taylor, M.S. (2006) Career systems and psychological contracts, in H. Gunz and M. Peiperl (eds) Handbook of Career Studies, Thousand Oaks, CA: Sage.

Sloman, M. (2010) L&D 2020: A Guide for the Next Decade, Littleport: Fenman.

Smith, A. ([1759]2007) The Theory of Moral Sentiments, Minneapolis, MN: Filiquarian.

Smith, A. ([1776]2009) An Inquiry into the Nature and Causes of the Wealth of Nations, Digireads.com Publishing.

Smith, C. and Meiskins, P. (1995) System, society, and dominance effects in cross-national organisational analysis, Work, Employment and Society, 9(2): 241–67.

Smith, M. (2010) The Gender Pay Gap in the EU: What Policy Responses?, Grenoble: Grenoble Ecole de Management.

Smith, M. and Smith, P. (2005) *Testing People at Work: Competencies in Psychometric Testing*, Oxford: BPS Blackwell.

Smith, M.J. and Sainfort, P.C. (1989) A balance theory of job design for stress reduction, *International Journal of Industrial Ergonomics*, **4**: 67–79.

Smyth, E. and McCoy, S. (2009) *Investing in Education: Combating Educational Disadvantage*, Dublin: ESRI.

Snyder, M. and Swann, W.B. (1978) Hypothesis-testing processes in social interaction, *Journal of Personality and Social Psychology*, **36**(11): 1202–12.

Sonnenfeld, J.A. and Peiperl, M.A. (1988) Staffing policy as a strategic response: a typology of career systems, *Academy of Management Review*, **13**(4): 568–600.

Sparrow, P., Brewster, C. and Harris, H. (2004) *Globalizing Human Resource Management*, London: Routledge.

Stack, S. (2010) Work accidents cost €3bn a year, *Irish Examiner*, 24 March. Available at: www.irishexaminer.com/archives/2010/0324/business/work-accidents-cost-3bn-a-year-115325.html (Accessed: 14 March 2012).

Steiner, J. and Steiner, G. (2012) *Business, Government, and Society: A Managerial Perspective, Text and Cases*, 13th edn, New York: McGraw-Hill.

Stewart, R. (1965) Reactions to appraisal interviews, *Journal of Management Studies*, **2**(1): 83–99.

Storey, J. (1989) Human resource management in the public sector, *Public Money and Management*, **9**(3): 19–24.

Storey, J. (1992) *Developments in the Management of Human Resources*. Oxford: Blackwell.

Storey, J. (1995) *Human Resource Management: A Critical Text*, London: Routledge.

Stumpf, S.A. (2010) Stakeholder competency assessments as predictors of career success, *Career Development International*, **15**(5): 459–78.

Suchman, E. (1961) On accident behavior, in E. Suchman (ed.) *Behavioural Approaches to Accident Research*, Washington DC: Association for the Aid of Crippled Children.

Suk, J.C. (2012) From antidiscrimination to equality: stereotypes and the lifecycle in the United states and Europe, *American Journal of Comparative Law*, **60**(1): 75–98.

Sullivan, S.E. and Arthur, M.B. (2006) The evolution of the boundaryless career concept: examining physical and psychological mobility, *Journal of Vocational Behavior*, **69**(1): 19–29.

Sun, P.Y. and Scott, J.L. (2006) Process level integration of organisational learning, learning organisation and knowledge management, *International Journal of Knowledge and Learning*, **2**(3/4): 308–19.

Super, D. (1953) A theory of vocational development, *American Psychologist*, **8**(5): 185–90.

Super, D. (1957) *Psychology of Careers*, New York: Harper and Brothers.

Super, D. (1980) A life-span, life-space approach to career development, *Journal of Vocational Behaviour*, **16**: 282–98.

Svejenova, S. (2005) 'The path with the heart': creating the authentic career, *Journal of Management Studies*, **42**(5): 947–74.

Swinburne, P. (2001) How to use feedback to improve performance, *People Management*, **7**(11): 46–7.

Tahvanainen, M., Welch, D. and Worm, V. (2005) Implications of short-term international assignments, *European Management Journal*, **23**(6): 663–73.

TalkTalk (2011) *TalkTalk Telecom Group PLC Annual Report 2011*, Available at: www.talktalkgroup.com/investors/reports/2011.aspx (Accessed: 14 March 2012).

Tams, S. and Arthur, M.B. (2006) Boundaryless career, in J.H. Greenhaus and G.A. Callanan (eds) *Encyclopedia of Career Development*, Thousand Oaks, CA: Sage.

Taras, D.G. and Kaufman, B.E. (2006) Non-union employee representation in North America: diversity, controversy and uncertain future, *Industrial Relations Journal*, **37**(5). 513–42.

Taylor, S. (2005) *People Resourcing*, 3rd edn, London: CIPD.

Teague, P. and Thomas, D. (2008) *Employment Dispute Resolution and Standard-setting in the Republic of Ireland*, Dublin: Oak Tree Press.

Teather, D. (2005) Nike lists abuses at Asian factories, *The Guardian*, 14 April. Available at: www.guardian.co.uk/business/2005/apr/14/ethicalbusiness.money (Accessed: 14 March 2012).

*The Economist* (2008) Do it right: corporate responsibility is largely a matter of enlightened self-interest, 17 January. Available at: www.economist.com/node/10491124 (Accessed: 14 March 2012).

Thompson, R. (2009) 'Prison-like' conditions for workers making IBM, Dell, HP, Microsoft and Lenovo products, *Computerweekly.com*, 17 February. Available at: www.computerweekly.com/news/2240088431/Prison-like-conditions-for-workers-making-IBM-Dell-HP-Microsoft-and-Lenovo-products (Accessed: 14 March 2012).

Toegel, G. and Conger, J. (2003) 360-degree feedback: time for reinvention, *Academy of Management Learning and Education*, **2**(3): 297–311.

Tomlinson, J., Olsen, W. and Purdam, K. (2009) Women returners and potential returners: employment profiles and labour market opportunities – a case study of the United Kingdom, *European Sociological Review*, **25**(3): 349–63.

Torrington, D., Hall, L. and Taylor, R. (2008) *Human Resource Management*, Harlow: Prentice Hall/Financial Times.

Tregaskis, O., Daniels, K., Glover, L. et al. (2012) High performance work practices and firm performance: a longitudinal case study, *British Journal of Management*, doi: 10.1111/j.1467-8551.2011.00800.x.

Turner, T. and McMahon, J. (2011) Women's occupational trends in the Irish economy: Moving towards high-skilled occupations or evidence of deskilling?, *Gender, Work & Organization*, **18**: 222–40.

Ulrich, D. (1998) *Human Resource Champions*, Boston: Harvard Business School Press.

Ulrich, D. and Brockbank, W. (2005) Role call, *People Management*, **11**(12): 24–8.

United Nations Conference on Trade and Development (2008) *World Investment Report: Transnational Corporations and the Infrastructure Challenge*, New York: UN.

UNPRI (UN Principles for Responsible Investment) (2008) *Principles for Responsible Investment: PRI Report on Progress 2008*, New York: UNPRI Secretariat.

*USA Today* (2010) BMW to pay German workers bonus for 'stamina' during recession, 16 July. Available at: www.usatoday.com/money/autos/2010-07-16-bmw-worker-bonus_N.htm (Accessed: 6 June 2012).

US Office of Personnel Management (n.d.) *Federal Classification and Job Grading Systems*. Available at: www.opm.gov/fedclass/html/gsclass.asp (Accessed: 6 June 2012).

Valcour, P.M. (2006) Customized careers, in J.H. Greenhaus and G.A. Callanan (eds) *Encyclopedia of Career Development*, Thousand Oaks, CA: Sage.

Varma, A., Budwhar, P. and DeNisi, A. (eds) (2008) *Performance Management Systems: A Global Perspective*, London: Routledge.

Venn, D. (2009) *Legislation, Collective Bargaining and Enforcement: Updating the OECD Employment Protection Indicators*, OECD: Paris

Vidal-Salazar, M.D., Hurtado-Torres, N.E. and Matías-Reche, F. (2012) Training as a generator of employee capabilities, *International Journal of Human Resource Management*, **23**(13): 2680–97.

Virtanen, M., Heikkilä, K., Jokela, M. et al. (2012) Long working hours and coronary heart disease: a systematic review and meta-analysis, *American Journal of Epidemiology*, **176**(7): 586–96.

Visser, W. (2011) *The Age of Responsibility: CSR 2.0 and the New DNA of Business*, Chichester: John Wiley & Sons.

Vogel, D. (2006) *The Market for Virtue: The Potential and Limits of Corporate Social Responsibility*, Washington DC: The Brookings Institute.

Vogel, D. and Reich, R. (2008) Corporate social responsibility: Is it responsible?, 2 September, www.youtube.com/watch?v=OreAJnDuVzk.

Von Prondzynski, F. (1998) Ireland: corporation revived, in A. Ferner and R. Hyman (eds) *Changing Industrial Relations in Europe*, Oxford: Wiley.

Wallace, J. and O'Sullivan, M. (2006) Contemporary strike trends since 1980: peering through the wrong end of a telescope, in M.J. Morley, P. Gunnigle and D.G. Collings (eds) *Global Industrial Relations*, London: Routledge.

Wallace, J., Gunnigle, P. and McMahon, G. (2004) *Industrial Relations in Ireland: Theory and Practice*, Dublin: Gill & Macmillan.

Walton, R. (1985) From control to commitment in the workplace, *Harvard Business Review*, **63**: 77–84.

Wanous, J.P. and Colella, A. (1989) Organizational entry research: current status and future directions, in G.R. Ferris and K.M. Rowlands (eds) *Research in Personnel and Human Resource Management*, Greenwich, CT: JAI Press.

Waring, P. and Edwards, T. (2008) Socially responsible investment: explaining its uneven development and human resource management consequences, *Corporate Governance*, **16**(3): 135–45.

Wayne S.J., Liden, R.C., Kraimer, M.L. and Graf, I.K. (1999) The role of human capital, motivation, and supervisor sponsorship in predicting career success, *Journal of Occupational Behavior*, **20**: 577–95.

Welch, D.E. and Worm, V. (2006) International business travellers: a challenge for IHRM, in G.K. Stahl and I. Björkman (eds) *Handbook of Research in International Human Resource Management*, Cheltenham: Edward Elgar.

Wenger, E.C., McDermott, R. and Snyder, W.M. (2002) *Cultivating Communities of Practice*, Boston: Harvard Business School Press.

Wernimont, P.F. and Campbell, J.P. (1968) Signs, samples and criteria, *Journal of Applied Psychology*, **52**: 372–6.

Whitley, R. (2000) *Divergent Capitalism: The Social Structuring and Change of Business Systems*, Oxford: Oxford University Press.

Whittaker, S. and Marchington, M. (2003) Devolving HR responsibility to the line: Threat, opportunity or partnership?, *Employee Relations*, **25**(3): 245–61.

Wilensky, H. (1961) Work, careers and social integration, *International Social Science Journal*, **12**(4): 543–74.

Wilkinson, A. and Fay, C. (2011) Guest editors' note: New times for employee voice?, *Human Resource Management*, **50**(1): 65–74.

Wingrove, C. (2003) Developing an effective blend of process and technology in the new era of performance management, *Compensation and Benefits Review*, January/February, 25–30.

Wolff, C. (2007) Workplace training: budgets and challenges, *IRS Employment Review*, London: IRS.

Wright, P.M., Snell, S.A. and Jacobsen, P.H. (2004) Current approaches to HR strategies: inside out versus outside in, *Human Resource Planning*, **27**(4): 36–46.

Yerkes, R.M. and Dodson, J.D. (1908) The relation of strength of stimulus to rapidity of habit-formation, *Journal of Comparative Neurology and Psychology*, **18**: 459–82.

Zibarras, L.D. and Woods, S.A. (2010) A survey of UK selection practices across different organization sizes and industry sectors, *Journal of Occupational and Organizational Psychology*, **83**(2): 499–511.

# INDEX